WAR OVER THE TRENCHES

WAR OVER
THE
TRENCHES
AIR POWER AND WESTERN FRONT
CAMPAIGNS 1916-1918

E.R. HOOTON

MIDLAND
An imprint of
Ian Allan Publishing

War Over The Trenches
E. R. Hooton

First published 2010

ISBN 978 0 7110 3415 0

Published by Midland Publishing

an imprint of Ian Allan Publishing Ltd, Hersham, Surrey KT12 4RG.
Printed in England by Ian Allan Printing Ltd, Hersham, Surrey KT12 4RG.

Visit the Ian Allan Publishing website at www.ianallanpublishing.com

Project Editor: Robert Forsyth / Chevron Publishing

The editor would like to thank Mr G. Stuart Leslie, the Fleet Air Arm Museum at RNAS Yeovilton, Mr Paul Leaman and Mr Greg VanWyngarden for their kind co-operation in regard to the provision of photographs in this book.

Contents

Preface

The First World War, or Great War, was a historical watershed of which almost every aspect has been studied and revised. Yet there is one which has remained an enigma that this book hopes to help resolve.

We know less about the air war, especially over the Western Front, than Roman Army campaigns. The paradox is that whole forests have been felled to supply the insatiable demand for information on the subject and there is a galaxy of talented historians feeding that demand. Without the researches of men such as Frank W. Bailey, J. M. ('Jack') Bruce, Christophe Cony, Dr James J. Davilla, Rick Duiven, Norman L. R. Franks, Peter Gray, Peter M. Grosz, Russell Guest, Arthur M. Soltan, Trevor Henshaw, Alex Imrie, Wing Commander C.G.Jefford, Peter Kilduff, W. M. Lamberton, Christopher Shores, James J. Sloan, Jr, Greg Van Wyngarden and others we would know virtually nothing about the subject. I would certainly have been left floundering and, from the start, I wish to acknowledge whole-heartedly my debt to them and to absolve them for any blame in errors through my interpretation of their work.

While valuable collections of data have been published over the past decade, for the most part publications tend to focus upon man and machine with the result that the study of air operations in the Great War is becoming ossified. Certainly, the lives of individual airmen, especially fighter pilots, descriptions of the development and operational use of aircraft and the works which are virtually photo-albums, breath life into documents from dusty archives. But they are a 'view from the cockpit' while the wider picture is largely ignored.

There has been little attempt to analyse the operations, to examine the issues or even to look beyond national boundaries and consequently the history of air warfare on the Western Front is littered with self-perpetuating myths and half-truths. Documents have largely been used in a 'cut and paste' way for contemporary views of air combat or aircraft and little attempt has been made to exploit them to provide the 'eagle's eye view'.

There has been a noticeable shortage of proper histories of the air war between 1914 and 1918; accounts based upon documentary evidence which describe the course of operations and the events which shaped them. The first was the gallant attempt by Texas lawyer John R. Cuneo with his perceptive *Winged Mars* series, based entirely upon published sources but still a ground-breaking work which was tragically curtailed by the publishers. The lack of documents did not prevent Raymond H. Fredette and Douglas Robinson producing fine histories of the German air campaign against Great Britain and as documents were officially released in the past few decades another American, John H. Morrow, wrote *The Great War in the Air* which shows a breadth of vision and a willingness to research foreign material which some of his fellow countrymen might follow.

Astonishingly, this book is the first history of air operations over the Western Front, a subject which the printed and electronic media often treats like 'Snoopy versus the Red Baron', and it seeks to analyse the operations of all the main combatants and to examine the issues. The absence of any comparable history is due partly to an accident of fate and partly due to deliberate choice. After the war, the armies and navies of most combatants produced multi-volume histories based upon official documents and unit accounts, the most noticeable exceptions being the United States and the Soviet Union. The status of air forces in the post-war period meant that it was not until the late 1930s that France and Germany began to address the need for an air official history and these had barely begun to run down the runway when a new war engulfed the world and saw the destruction of even more documents.

Only three complete official accounts have emerged about air operations during the First World War; Wise's *Canadian Airmen and the First World War*, Raleigh/Jones' *War in the Air* and Vrancken's *De Geschiedenis van de Belgische Militaire Vliegerij*. The first is damned because, at Trenchard's behest, it was produced as an uneasy mixture of history and chronicle which deliberately avoided analysis. What might have been achieved for the Royal Air Force is shown by the handful of RAF Air Historical Branch accounts in the United Kingdom National Archives. The Belgian and Canadian works are extremely useful but inevitably are more restricted, although Wise is less so.

Useful accounts of the development of German military aviation which exploited documents now lost were produced by Bülow, Hoeppner and Neumann. Büdinggen's account of the *Flakwaffe* is extremely useful while I found Loewenstern, although largely focused on the lesser-known fronts, to be especially valuable. But, like so much writing on air operations over the Western front, they lack perspective and this criticism is sadly true of accounts of the US contribution which have been published in the past 40 years. Works notably by James Sloan (*Wings of Honor*), James.J.Cooke, James J.Hudson, Herbert A. Johnson and Terry C. Treadwell are very well researched but tend to focus too narrowly upon their own countrymen unlike William Edward Fischer's extremely valuable account on night operations. The French contribution is shamefully neglected by English writers but, to be fair, the French have made little attempt to fill the gap. Général Charles Christienne's book appears to be one of the few modern attempts and there have been some valuable studies, clearly based upon documentary evidence, by René Martel on bombers and Général André Voisin on fighters although the recent work of Davilla and Soltan provides much valuable information.

Sadly, there have been few biographies or autobiographies of the air leaders. Lionel Charlton provides some fascinating and racy personal insights but nothing of significance on his leadership, indeed he deliberately dismissed his experience with V Brigade, while that of William 'Billy' Mitchell has the reliability of a chocolate coffee-pot. Biographies of Trenchard and Salmond provide some information but appeared before the release of most official documents and suffer accordingly although the recent biography of Barès does provide a great insight.

In preparing this history and shooting down myths and half-truths I have exploited two long neglected sources which have been hidden in plain sight, some for up to 85 years! The first, and most obvious, are national archives which are treasure chests of information on a wide range of subjects and, while the staffs are always most helpful most writers have merely pilfered a few coins of information and ignored the gems and bullion. The most complete collections are those of Belgian, the United Kingdom and the United States but I was pleasantly surprised at the scale of material available at the Chateau de Vincennes in Paris, France especially as much was apparently destroyed during the Second World War. The archives are divided between the Service Historique de l'Armée de l'Air and the Service Historique de l'Armée de Terre but they are neighbours on the same easily accessible site (where

England's Henry V died) and the staff are extremely helpful and courteous even to one who speaks French 'comme la vache espagnol.'

I was especially astonished that the *Reichsarchiv* responses to British Air Historical branch questions in the British National Archives have been totally neglected (apart from the one on the German order-of-battle at the Third Ypres which has disappeared) despite the insights they offer into German operations. The neglect of archive sources is also shown in accounts of US air operations, none of which uses details of sorties available in the US National Archives in Maryland. Time restricted research and I was unable to exploit the valuable collections of German material at the University of Texas in Dallas or to use Germany's regional or local museums and archives such as Bremen and Munich where, I suspect, there is more buried treasure. Hopefully these will be augmented by the transfer of documents from the former East Germany to the *Bundesarchiv*.

The second source, which is the most obvious and the most neglected, is official army histories. Poring through dozens of books, many of them weighty tomes, takes time rather like panning for gold, but the French and German histories in particular repay this with large amounts of 'pay dirt'. The French official history not only has much material within the pages but also within the numerous annexes, often including the texts of key documents. The German account is especially valuable providing much information based upon long lost documents, notably about German air operations in 1916 and the use of massed aircraft in ground operations during the First Somme, a point underlined by Reichsarchiv documents in the British National Archives. Even the British official histories prove valuable by providing information on the impact of German attacks upon their infrastructure. It is also worth noting the German semi-official accounts of individual battles are sometimes very valuable, that of the Cambrai campaign, for example, providing a complete order-of-battle of the *Luftstreitkräfte*.

From these sources not only have I tried to provide a balanced account of the development of air power from 1916 onward but also statistics with more than 60 tables. I make no apology for this, although I recognise the truth of nineteenth century politician George Canning's observation: 'Statistics can tell you everything you wish to know…except the truth' while, of course, Benjamin Disraeli famously railed against 'Lies, damned lies and statistics.'

Yet statistics are the foundation for operational analysis and can highlight changes and trends. Table 3-2 shows how the British used fighters over the Somme in 1916, Tables 4-2 and 4-4 help provide the first explanation for the heavy British losses over Arras in Bloody April beyond the hoary old cliché of technical obsolescence while other tables help analyse each campaign. Statistical analysis provides a means of assessing success or failure in the air by studying loss rates, the percentage of aircraft despatched on a mission which failed to return to friendly lines.

The foundation of such statistics is the sortie, a flight by an individual aircraft, but a researcher into Great War air operations is handicapped by the idiosyncratic nature of records which, in the case of the British and French, frequently combine references to sorties, missions, patrols and 'cruises.' The British statistics are usually based upon each brigade's daily record of activities. However, these run from 18:00 hours of the previous day to 18:00 hours of the day in question (e.g Monday's records include Sunday evenings) and sometimes they can be somewhat vague. While fighter, reconnaissance and night bomber sorties are usually available, although one or two brigades occasionally referred to 'missions', corps squadron activities have to be worked out from the relevant section while day bomber activities are shown only in terms of bomb-loads despatched and delivered. However, some British war diaries confine themselves to a general statement of hours flown while some reports, especially for April 1918, are missing.

Careful study makes it possible to calculate approximately the sorties, allowing for missions outside the time period, and to cross-check against hours flown. The figures were then compiled, rounded to the nearest five to allow for variables and assembled into weekly tables, beginning on a Monday and when compared to the occasional detailed statistical data they appear to be quite accurate. French statistics come from a variety of sources including overall daily summaries of air operations on the Western Front, divided into army group sections (also rounded out), reports on specific operations and the activities of the Division Aérienne. Belgian and US statistics are usually available in their archives. Losses have been taken from books whose authors have researched the subject in great depth and to whose expertise I bow.

Many readers may find it disconcerting that I use metric terms for distances, bomb totals and height. But all the world's armed forces have gone metric and it is easier to calculate tonnage in metric terms e.g. 1,000 kilogrammes is 1 tonne. I have left untranslated French and German terminology in terms of ranks, formations and terminology. For rapid understanding all German words are in italic while references to French armies follow the contemporary fashion e.g. Ier Armée, IIeme Armée.

My study starts in 1916 because until then air operations were largely experimental. From Verdun onwards the emergence of air power as a growing influence upon the battlefield becomes clearer. I have tried to produce a balanced account giving the appropriate weight to the air forces of the five major powers – with what success I will leave the reader to judge. The easier access to archives may mean the reader finds over-emphasis upon American and British activity but I have tried hard to produce a detailed picture of the development and activities of French air power, a subject long neglected even by Gallic historians.

With the exception of Chapter 2, which deals with background issues, each chapter runs in a particular sequence. The outline of the land campaign is sketched, then the background to the air campaign with information on leaders and overall strength. The campaigns are then split into Operational and Tactical elements; the former sub-divided into fighter and bomber operations and the latter with the activities of corps squadrons (a British term which describes air units supporting the army corps) and fighter-bombers. A daily description would not only take too many pages but would leave the reader hopping around like a flea on a hot stone and so I have confined myself to a broad-brush description of the general events in the air which I hope the reader will find easy to follow.

It is the conceit of historical writers that they have found the Holy Grail and will be praised for prising out the secrets of the past, but all too often the plaudits become brickbats. My views may be controversial and many will criticise my failure to cover this, or that, aspect but the subject of First World War aviation (even the narrow field of the Western Front) is so large that an individual author can hope only to provide an outline. I would have wished to cover the French and Germans in greater detail but must live with my inadequacies. To use a Second World War Bomber Command comparison, I am no more than a Pathfinder who has marked the target for the Main Force.

There is certainly a very great deal to do even on the Western Front and I hope this work will encourage other historians both 'professional' and 'amateur' to expand our knowledge. There is a need for new biographies of air force leaders including their relationships with the army commanders and politicians while biographies are also needed for air leaders at army level. This is relatively easier for British and American leaders for a similar study of their French and German contemporaries is hindered by the absence of even a list of their names but I am confident that specialised studies will identify them.

The domestic and foreign relationships between the various air services has been ignored while more detailed studies of air campaigns supporting each major battle are long over-due. Another neglected area is the effect of bombing, especially upon railways which could be studied through surviving rail operators records in Belgium, France and Germany, contacts with railway enthusiasts as well as the detailed bombing data in Allied archives.

For those wishing to pursue more limited goals, the development of national fighter and bomber doctrines and equipment requires study together with an examination of operations at squadron level. Army co-operation is another important but neglected field (although there are signs this is changing) and subjects worth investigation include co-operation between corps squadrons and ground forces, air-artillery fire direction (including balloons) and the roles of observers for which Wing Commander Jefford's study on observers and navigators provides a fine template. The true impact of aviation on army operations is another subject which requires more detailed study. Also requiring investigation are the subjects of production, the development of training both pilots and observers and its influence upon accident rates. It would be especially interesting to see the impact of Smith-Barry's new training methods upon the RFC and how it was rolled out through the training organisation.

Beyond the Western Front there is a need to study the private air war along the Channel coast between the Allied air forces and the Germany Navy on the other (most German naval records have survived). Air operations along the Italian front, which helped influence strategic bombing as well as tactical air development, are worth studying. I have reason to believe that considerable information is available in both Rome and Vienna making possible an even more detailed account than might be possible elsewhere, and similar potential may be possible with operations in the Balkans, where air power was born.

Acknowledgements

While a book may have a single author that person depends upon others for assistance and here I have the delightful task of thanking the many institutions and their helpful staffs who provided me access to archive material. In Belgium the Library and Centre de Documentation et Archives of Belgium's Musée Royal de l'Armée et d'Histoire Militaire in Brussels, in France the Service Historique de l'Armée de Terre and the Service Historique de l'Armée de l'Air at the Chateau de Vincennes in Paris. Within the United Kingdom the National Archives, the National Army Museum, the Royal Air Force Museum, Hendon, the Royal United Services Institute and the Imperial War Museum Reference Library all in London, the National Library of Scotland in Edinburgh and Langley Library, Slough which acquired so many rare books through the Inter-Library loan service. In the United States the National Archives in College Park, Maryland provided key data while the National Air and Space Museum (especially Ms Melissa Keiser) also proved extremely helpful.

I also owe much to the kindness of strangers whom I would like to thank. Général M.Berlaud, Chef du Service Historique de l'Armée de Terre provided access to the French Army archives at a time when the service was deep in the throes of re-organization. The staff of the Centre de Documentation et Archives of Belgium's Musée Royal de l'Armée et d'Histoire Militaire under Dr Richard Boijen proved extremely kind and helpful when I wandered into their premises by accident on the way to a neighboring site. Also in Belgium Major Bernard Cambrelin, Head of the Divisie Veiligheid, of the Defensie Stafdepartement Intlichtingen en Veiligheid was kind enough to provide me with copies of the personal files and supporting information about senior Belgian air leaders.

Mr John Greenwood of the Office of the Surgeon General of the US Army provided a detailed answer about the first US Army casualty in World War One within moments of picking up the telephone. Mr John Montgomery, the Librarian of the Royal United Services Institute, London received a volume of the French Official History from Mr Patrick Ryan, Chief Librarian of the British Ministry of Defence Information & Library Service which was not available anywhere else and allowed me to complete research on French activity.

With regard to research on the French I would like to thank Mr Mike Pearce of Cross & Cockade International and Ms Laura Soyer, who was kind enough to examine in her own time the personal file of Paul du Peuty in the Service Historique de l'Armée de Terre and produce a report which would shame many professional researchers. Above all my French research would have been impossible but for the great kindness, enthusiasm and expertise of Mrs Alison Macdonald who provided key translations, and Mr Will Fowler who arranged an introduction.

Old friends also helped. My research into German air power would have got nowhere without the assistance of Herr Hans-Eberhard Krüger who provided me both with rare books and a complete copy of the *Lufstreitkräfte Nachrichtenblätter*. Alex Vanags-Baginskis was especially helpful in translating extracts from these and other works with a diligence for which I thank him from the bottom of my heart. I would also like to thank my former colleague Martin Streetly, Editor of Jane's Radar and Electronic Warfare Systems and to my friend John Wise for advice and material on electronic warfare. Martin also drew my attention to aspects of aerial navigation which I would not otherwise have considered.

The former Smithsonian Institution Press Aviation, Space and Military History Editor Mr Mark Gatlin planted the seed for this work and provided much-needed support and timely advice. But it grew and has been published through the untiring efforts and enthusiasm of Mr Robert Forsyth of Chevron Publishing to whom I owe the very greatest debt and without whose efforts this work would never have seen the light of day.

Finally, to paraphrase a well-known saying 'Behind every man stands a great woman…' In my case it is three women; my wife Linda, who has had to put up with so much and with such understanding, and my daughters Caroline and Jennifer who have provided valuable editorial services.

E. R. Hooton
March 2009

Glossary –

A list of Abbreviations and Acronyms

A	German designation for unarmed monoplane
AEF	American Expeditionary Force
AFA	Artillerie Feldfliegerabteilungen (German artillery co-operation squadron to October 1916)
AR	Dorand AR (French squadron abbreviation)
B	German designation for unarmed biplane
BEF	British Expeditionary Force
Bogohl	Bombengeschwader der OHL (OHL bomber wing from late 1917)
Bosta	Bombenstaffel (German bomber squadron from late 1917)
BRE	Bréguet (French squadron abbreviation)
C	Caudron (French squadron abbreviation)
C	German designation for single-engined, two-seat, armed biplane.
CAP/CEP	Caproni (French squadron abbreviation)
CFS	Central Flying School (British)
CIB	Central Information Bureau
CL	German designation for lightweight (250–260 kg lighter than C-type) single-engine, two-seat, armed biplane.
COMINT	Communications intelligence (interception of radio signals)
Daé	Division Aérienne
DAN	Détachment d'Armées du Nord
D	Doppeldecker (German designation for single-engined, single-seat, armed biplane)
Dr	Dreidecker (German designation for triplane fighter)
DP	Defensive Patrol
E	Eindecker (German designation for monoplane fighter)

Eingreifdivision Reaction Division (Special counter-attack unit).

F	Farman (French squadron abbreviation)
FA	Fliegerabteilung (German army co-operation squadron post 1916)
FA (A	Fliegerabteilung (Artillerie) (German artillery co-operation squadron post 1916)
FA (Lb)	Fliegerabteilung (Lichtbild) (German photographic reconnaissance squadron post-1916)
FEBA	Forward-Edge-of-Battle Area
Feldflugchef	Chef des Feldflugwesens (German Chief of Field Aviation)
FFA	Feld Fliegerabteilung (German army cooperation squadron to 1916)
Flak	Fliegerabwehrkanone (German for anti-aircraft gun)
G	German designation for twin-engined aircraft
GAC	Groupe des Armées de Centre (French Army Group Centre)
GAE	Groupe des Armées de l'Est (French Army Group East)
GAF	Groupe d'Armées des Flandres (Franco-Belgian Army Group Flanders)
GAN	Groupe des Armées du Nord (French Army Group North
GAR	Groupe des Armées de Reserve (French Reserve Army Group)
GB	Groupe de Bombardement (French bomber group)
GC	Groupe de Chasse (French fighter group)
GHQ	General Headquarters
GQG	Grand Quartier Général (French Army GHQ)
Grufl	Gruppenführer der Flieger ('Group Aviation Leader' German officer responsible for coordinating air operations at army corps level)
Jasta	Jagdstaffel (German fighter squadron)
JGr	Jagdgruppe (German fighter group)
Kagohl	Kampfgeschwader der OHL (OHL 'Combat' or Bomber Wing to 1918)
Kasta	Kampfstaffel ('Combat' or bomber squadron to 1918)
KEK	Kampfeinsitzer-Kommandos (Ad hoc German fighter command of squadron strength)
Kofl	Kommandeur der Flieger ('Aviation Commander'. German officer responsible for directing air operations at army headquarters)

Kogenluft	Kommandierender General der Luftstreitkräfte (German Army Commander of the Air Service)
MF	Maurice Farman (French squadron abbreviation)
MRAHM	Musée Royal de l'Armée et d'Histoire Militaire (Belgium)
MS	Morane Saulnier (French squadron abbreviation)
N	Nieuport (French squadron abbreviation)
OHL	Oberste Heeresleitung (German Army GHQ)
OP	Offensive Patrol
R	German designation for large aircraft with three or more engines
RAF	Royal Air Force
RFC	Royal Flying Corps
RFV	Région Fortifée Verdun (Verdun Fortified Region)
RNAS	Royal Naval Air Service
Sal	Salmond (French squadron abbreviation)
Schlasta	Schlachtstaffel (German ground attack squadron)
Schlagru	Schlachtgruppe (German ground attack groups)
Schusta	Schutzstaffel (German escort, later ground attack, squadron)
SHAA	Service Historique de l'Armée de l'Air (French Air Force Historical Service)
SHAT	Service Historique de l'Armée de Terre (French Army Historical Service)
Sop	Sopwith (French squadron abbreviation)
SPA	Spad (French squadron abbreviation for single-seat Spad squadrons)
SPA-Bi	Spad two-seater (French squadron abbreviation for two-seat Spad squadrons)
SRA	Service de Renseignements Aériens (Aerial reconnaissance Service)
Stofl	Stabsoffizier der Flieger (Staff Officer for Aviation at a German Army headquarters)
UKNA	UK National Archives
USNA	US National Archives
USAS	United States Air Service
V	Voisin (French squadron abbreviation)

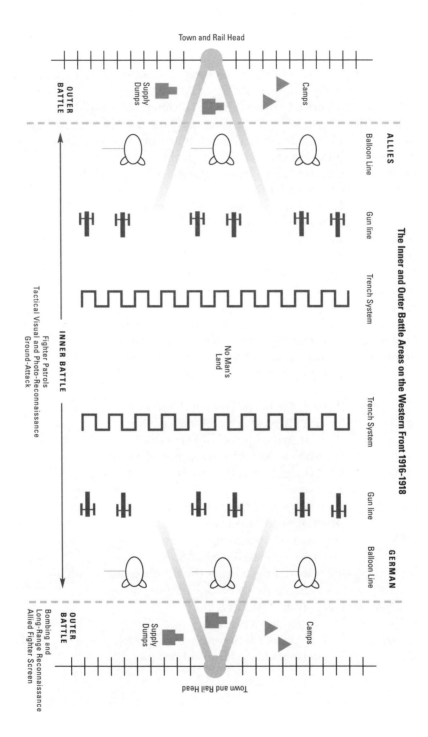

The Inner and Outer Battle Areas on the Western Front 1916-1918

Town and Rail Head

OUTER BATTLE

Supply Dumps

Camps

ALLIES

Balloon Line

Gun line

Trench System

No Man's Land

INNER BATTLE

Fighter Patrols
Tactical Visual and Photo-Reconnaissance
Ground-Attack

Trench System

Gun line

GERMAN

Balloon Line

OUTER BATTLE

Supply Dumps

Camps

Town and Rail Head

Bombing and
Long-Range Reconnaissance
Allied Fighter Screen

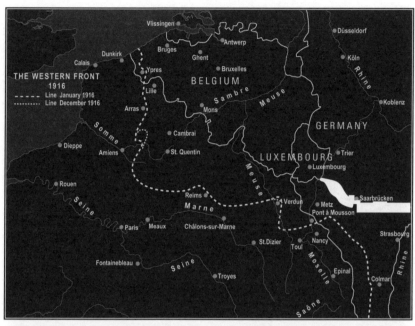

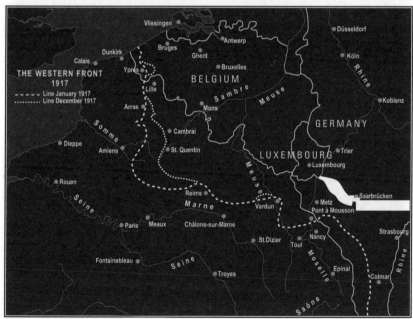

THE WESTERN FRONT
January to June 1918
- - - - Line January 1918
.... Line June 1918

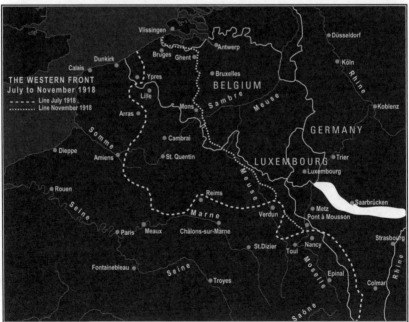

THE WESTERN FRONT
July to November 1918
- - - - Line July 1918
.... Line November 1918

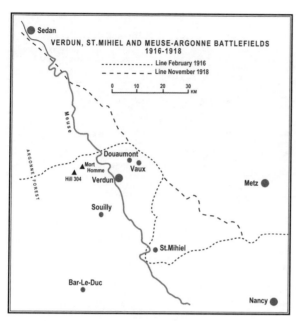

VERDUN, ST.MIHIEL AND MEUSE-ARGONNE BATTLEFIELDS
1916-1918

.... Line February 1916
— — — — — Line November 1918

0   10   20   30
|___|___|___|___| KM

Sedan

Meuse

ARGONNE FOREST

Douaumont

Mort
Homme   Vaux
▲
Hill 304   Verdun

Metz

Souilly

St.Mihiel

Bar-Le-Duc

Nancy

THE FIRST BATTLE OF THE SOMME

.... Line July 1916
— — — — — Line November 1916

0   5   10
|_____|_____| KM

Bapaume

Martinpuich
Pozieres   Flers

Sailly Saillisel

Guillemont

Albert

Bouchavesnes

Ancre

Peronne

Somme

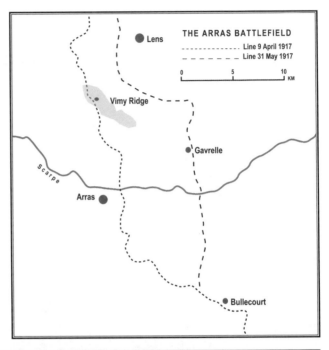

THE ARRAS BATTLEFIELD

------------- Line 9 April 1917
- - - - - - - Line 31 May 1917

0 .... 5 .... 10 KM

Lens

Vimy Ridge

Gavrelle

Scarpe

Arras

Bullecourt

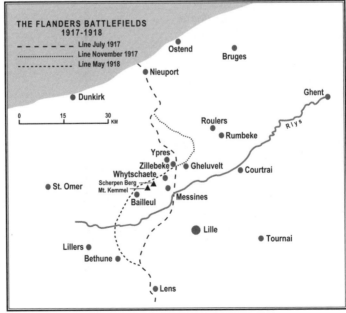

THE FLANDERS BATTLEFIELDS
1917-1918

- - - - - - Line July 1917
.... Line November 1917
- - - - - - Line May 1918

Ostend

Bruges

Nieuport

Dunkirk

Ghent

0 .... 15 .... 30 KM

Roulers

Rys

Rumbeke

Ypres

Zillebeke

Gheluvelt

Whytschaete

Courtrai

Scherpen Berg
Mt. Kemmel

St. Omer

Messines

Bailleul

Lille

Tournai

Lillers

Bethune

Lens

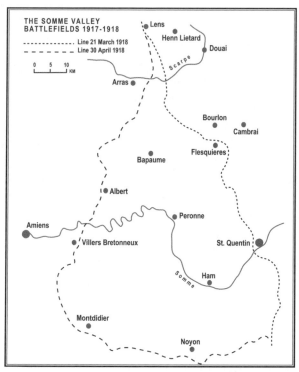

THE SOMME VALLEY
BATTLEFIELDS 1917-1918

.... Line 21 March 1918
– – – – – – Line 30 April 1918

0   5   10
|___|___|___| KM

Lens
Henn Lietard
Douai
Scarpe
Arras
Bourlon
Cambrai
Flesquieres
Bapaume
Albert
Peronne
Amiens
Villers Bretonneux
St. Quentin
Somme
Ham
Montdidier
Noyon

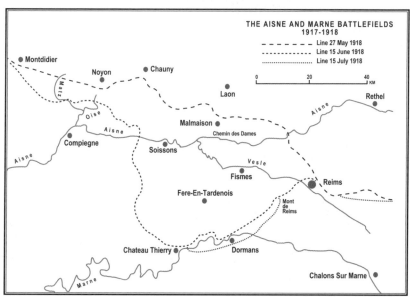

THE AISNE AND MARNE BATTLEFIELDS
1917-1918

– – – – – Line 27 May 1918
.... Line 15 June 1918
.... Line 15 July 1918

0   20   40
|___|___|___|___| KM

Montdidier
Noyon
Chauny
Matz
Laon
Rethel
Oise
Aisne
Malmaison
Chemin des Dames
Aisne
Aisne
Compiegne
Soissons
Vesle
Fismes
Reims
Fere-En-Tardenois
Mont de Reims
Chateau Thierry
Dormans
Chalons Sur Marne
Marne

French Organisation 1916-1918

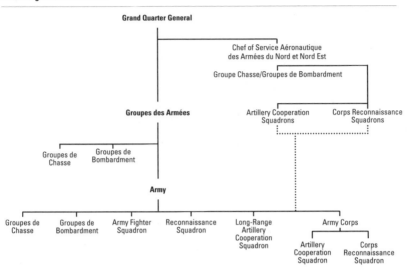

Grand Quarter General

Chef of Service Aéronautique
des Armées du Nord et Nord Est

Groupe Chasse/Groupes de Bombardment

Groupes des Armées — Artillery Cooperation Squadrons — Corps Reconnaissance Squadrons

Groupes de Chasse — Groupes de Bombardment

Army

Groupes de Chasse — Groupes de Bombardment — Army Fighter Squadron — Reconnaissance Squadron — Long-Range Artillery Cooperation Squadron — Army Corps

Artillery Cooperation Squadron — Corps Reconnaissance Squadron

German Organisation 1916-1918

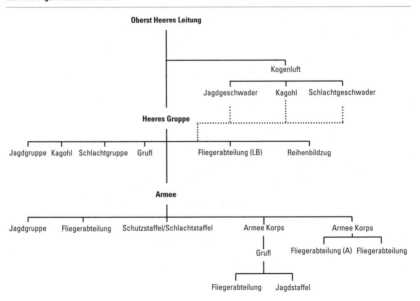

Oberst Heeres Leitung

Kogenluft

Jagdgeschwader — Kagohl — Schlachtgeschwader

Heeres Gruppe

Jagdgruppe — Kagohl — Schlachtgruppe — Grufl — Fliegerabteilung (LB) — Reihenbildzug

Armee

Jagdgruppe — Fliegerabteilung — Schutzstaffel/Schlachtstaffel — Armee Korps — Armee Korps

Grufl — Fliegerabteilung (A) — Fliegerabteilung

Fliegerabteilung — Jagdstaffel

British Air Organisation 1916-1918

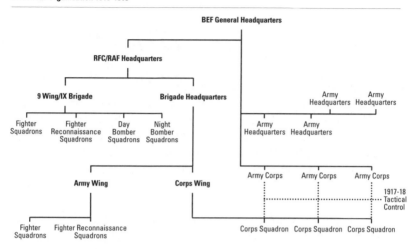

BEF General Headquarters

RFC/RAF Headquarters

9 Wing/IX Brigade — Brigade Headquarters

Fighter Squadrons — Fighter Reconnaissance Squadrons — Day Bomber Squadrons — Night Bomber Squadrons

Army Headquarters — Army Headquarters

Army Headquarters — Army Headquarters

Army Wing — Corps Wing — Army Corps — Army Corps — Army Corps

1917-18 Tactical Control

Fighter Squadrons — Fighter Reconnaissance Squadrons

Corps Squadron — Corps Squadron — Corps Squadron

Prologue

With tanks harassing their rearguards the columns of troops trudged their weary way along Belgian roads. The smell of defeat hung in the air. While they no longer heard the incessant rumble of gunfire, their journey was marked by the milestones of wrecked vehicles and bodies – victims of the air attacks that lashed them mercilessly.

The ominous drone of the bomber was a familiar and feared noise both day and night. But the days also brought the hornet-like whine of the fighters which swept across fields to spray machine gun fire. Even more demoralising were the dive bombers that screeched down and departed as their bombs exploded, leaving only screams for stretcher - bearers. The Germans' ordeal would end only with the Armistice on the eleventh hour, of the eleventh month of 1918[1].

It was small comfort to the unfortunate German soldiers in 1918 that shortly after the Great War broke out the aeroplane was regarded as a failure. Although the first successful aeroplane had flown along an obscure American beach on 17 December 1903 the impact was not felt for nearly six years when the Wright brothers demonstrated the superiority of their aeroplane at the Reims Air Week in August 1909. The ensuing popular fervour forced every European army and navy to invest in the new technology initially with reluctance but then with greater enthusiasm as the aeroplane proved a valuable reconnaissance tool during exercises[2].

Unfortunately, these exercises proved unrealistic because in peacetime the aeroplanes could fly with impunity over the opposing forces at only a couple of hundred metres. The reality of combat was very different as 2nd Lieutenant M.W. Noel and his observer, Sergeant-Major D.S. Jillings, discovered when they flew over a German cavalry regiment in Belgium on 22 August 1914 and the cavalrymen promptly discharged a volley skywards hitting the unfortunate NCO in the leg. French observer Capitaine Tiersonnier had been wounded on 6 August while six days later *Oberleutnant* Reinhold Jahnow was killed and his observer *Oberleutnant* Heinrich Koch was mortally wounded near Malmedy, a similar fate befalling a crew from No 5 Squadron RFC even as Jilling's wounds were being treated[3]. Ground fire forced the airmen to fly higher, often above the clouds, making it difficult to detect movements on the ground and with cavalry unable to fulfil their traditional reconnaissance role the initial operations in France became a colossal game of blind man's buff.

However, air reconnaissance did have some successes and proved the key factor in the Allied riposte at the Battle of the Marne. This forced the Germans to withdraw to commanding heights where they promptly dug trenches to create a pool of reserves for use in vain attempts to outflank the Allies. Even as they did so the generals on both sides reluctantly realised the trench systems stopped cavalry movement, leaving aviation (aeroplanes and balloons) as the sole means of reliable reconnaissance as well as providing the only means of artillery fire direction which was key to the new warfare. During the autumn of 1914 the commanders of the three main armies on the Western Front demanded expansion of their aeronautical arm both in size and capability.

By 1915 aeroplanes were used like packhorses burdened with radios and cameras to help the generals' attempts to break the trench war deadlock and the generals expected their warplanes to perform a variety of tasks[4]. French corps squadrons not only carried out reconnaissance and artillery fire direction but also bombing, escort and fighter patrol duties while even bombers were used to patrol the skies above the trenches. Multiple roles were also a feature of British air operations with the RFC's No 27 Squadron, using single-seat Martinsyde G.100, flying an offensive Operational Patrol (OP) on 9 August 1916, a bombing mission on 12 August and a long-range visual reconnaissance of the Cambrai rail marshalling yards the following day [5].

The generals continued to believe in the multi-task warplane into 1918 as if a cavalry charger could be a draft horse. The British and French aircraft were hamstrung by inadequate engines (usually rotaries which rotated with the propeller) and their achievements into 1917 were more due to the courage of their crews than the adequacy of their aircraft.

The Germans exploited their position as Europe's premier automotive nation to up-engine their B-type single-engine, two-seat work-horses with powerful 150hp and 160hp in-line engines (which rotated the propeller through a crankshaft) to produce the C-type aircraft. They were powerful enough to carry not only radios and cameras but also a machine gun as clashes between airmen became more frequent during 1915[6].

At first airmen used rifles, whose slow rate of fire made them almost useless for air warfare where targets stayed in the sights for seconds. Only automatic weapons could inflict significant damage or neutralise the enemy aircrew in so short a time, but the dilemma was to select the right weapon; the heavy machine gun or the lighter automatic rifle.

The machine gun is a sustained fire weapon and during the First World War, was usually fed by a canvas belt containing 250 rounds. Successful operation depended upon robust mechanical design and keeping the barrel cool, usually by encasing it in a water-filled container (jacket), which created a heavy, cumbersome weapon. The Maxim (upon which the Vickers was based) weighed 18 kilogrammes with full water jacket, although German aircraft weapons were soon adapted for air cooling, unlike the Allies' Vickers gun.

The air-cooled automatic rifle was a less reliable alternative designed to fire short bursts with ammunition provided either by a spring-operated box or drum magazine. The most famous automatic rifle, used by most Allied aircraft, was the Lewis gun which was designed with a water jacket but whose air-cooled Mark 1 aircraft version weighed 9.66 kilogrammes. It featured a 47 -round (later 97 -round) drum which was difficult and time-consuming to replace[7].

Initially only observers used automatic weapons which covered an arc on the opposite side to the propeller for fear of shooting it off. Then the French dare-devil, Sous-Lieutenant Roland Garros, installed a forward-firing, air-cooled, Hotchkiss machine gun in a Morane monoplane. Steel wedges on the propeller blades deflected the bullets as the blades crossed the machine gun barrel and with this crude device Garros claimed three victories in April[8].

A clogged fuel line during a bombing mission on 18 April 1915 forced Garros to land behind enemy lines where he and his aeroplane were captured, but German attempts to reproduce his deflector failed because their Maxim had a higher muzzle velocity than his Hotchkiss. Testing of the deflector was conducted by the Dutchman, Anthony Fokker, whose factory was the only one still supplying monoplanes to the Royal Prussian Army. By happy coincidence before the war one of Fokker's technicians had designed a mechanism which momentarily interrupted the machinegun's fire when the propeller swept in front of the barrel.

This interrupter gear was quickly developed and tested and installed in a Fokker issued to *FFA6*.On 1 July *Leutnant* Kurt Wintgens claimed his first victory, although the potential victim (probably from MS 48) returned with a wounded crew[9]

This began the period of 'The Fokker Scourge', although the impact was psychological rather than physical for at the end of 1915 there were only 86 Fokker monoplane fighters (and some Pfalz in Bavarian units) along the whole Western Front, scattered in ones and twos among the *Feld Fliegerabteilungen* which usually controlled the KEK fighter units and assigned them pilots on a rota basis[10]. Most air combat was between two-seaters, often initiated by the Allies whose records frequently note the presence of single-seat biplanes in these actions.

From July 1915 to January 1916, 90 RFC aircraft failed to return to friendly airfields (shot down or forced to land) and 109 aircrew were killed, interred or became prisoners of war. Operations by the RFC's 1 Wing on the Lille front suggest that traceable Fokker victories accounted for about only half the wing's 19 losses with two-seaters, anti-aircraft fire or even mechanical failure claiming the remainder (see Table 1-1 Yet the wing flew more than 4,400 sorties to give an overall loss rate on combat missions of less than 0.5%. Less comprehensive French statistics suggest 66 aircraft were lost or forced down in the same period but it is uncertain how many fell to 'Fokkers'[11].

Table 1–1:
Wing operations July 1915–January 1916

Date	Sorties	Combats (Fokkers)	Losses	To Fokkers	Total RFC losses
July	498	12 (3)	2 (4)		13 (18)
August	496	10 (5)	3 (3)	1 (1)	7 (10)
September	1,150	17 (3)	1 (2)	1 (2)	11 (16)
October	749	38 (8)	5 (5)	2 (4)	11 (14)
November	544	33 (7)	4 (6)	2 (2)	13 (12)
December	459	49 (9)	4 (5)	1 (2)	17 (19)
January	534	22 (5)	5 (4)	2 (2)	18 (20)
Total	**4,430**	**181 (40)**	**19 (23)**	**9 (13)**	**90 (109)**

Sources: Henshaw: 41–70. UKNA Air 1/2166/209/11/9–12;Air1/2167/209/11/17 (Air 1/2166/209/11/12 is incomplete); Air 1/2174/209/14/1. Note: Figure in parenthesis in 'Losses' is dead and missing aircrew.

While the Fokkers claimed the lives of relatively few Allied airmen, hundreds of them fell victim to German propaganda as the German Army publicity machine lionised the exploits of successful pilots such as *Leutnants* Erwin Boelcke and Max Immelmann (who faced 1 Wing) as their scores steadily increased. Yet the Fokkers provided a catalyst in air warfare as the nimble single-seater fighters grew in importance seeking and destroying enemy aircraft and providing an imperative for specialised warplane roles in the face of the threat.

While the notion of multi-tasking aircraft did not disappear it did become more focused; bombers were given more powerful engines to provide higher speed and greater range which could be exploited for long-range reconnaissance missions while the higher speed of fighters meant they could swiftly attack ground targets. The corps aircraft continued to multi-task but at Tactical (army corps) level, although even in 1918 they were occasionally used for bombing and defensive patrols.

Against the background of a technical kaleidoscope, air warfare on the Western Front would follow a pattern of two distinct but overlapping struggles. The outer air battle was at the Operational Level (supporting army and army group operations) and complemented the inner air battle which was at the Tactical Level (supporting division and army corps operations). The boundary between the outer and inner battles was loosely marked by the parallel lines of kite balloons up to 15 kilometres behind each front line. The outer battle was fought beyond the balloon line, although much air combat was around it, with the focus upon reconnaissance, bombing of rail and logistics targets. For the French and Germans it also included counter-battery work against very long-range guns while espionage missions also featured (see Chapter Two).

The inner battle was vital to the Western Front's lethal routine and was fought within the balloon line. It consisted mainly of visual and photographic reconnaissance as well as the direction of artillery fire, although each army had its own system[12]. It would also later include ground-attack missions, tactical re-supply and what would later be called electronic warfare specifically the interception (COMINT) and jamming (ECM) of radio signals and sometimes the spreading of disinformation (see Chapter Three).

For both sides 1915 was a year of technical and tactical experiment and by the time 1916 dawned it was clear that air power would, for the first time, be an important factor for success on the ground leading to more intense air combat.

Chapter One

Verdun:
The First Clashes: – 1916–1917

The new age of air warfare dawned over the 35-kilometre-long inferno north of Verdun which became synonymous with the nightmare of trench warfare. Verdun was both a triumph of the human spirit in the machine age and also a cynical exercise which cost hundreds of thousands of men their lives or health.

The architect was German Chief of the General Staff, *General* Erich von Falkenhayn who contemplated a year's tenure by the end of 1915 with quiet satisfaction. Germany, and her Central Power ally Austria, augmented by Bulgaria and Turkey, had repulsed most of the assaults upon them including those of their one-time ally Italy. Yet victories are not won purely by remaining on the defensive and on 8 December Falkenhayn recognised that to win the war he must wreck France's army and, hopefully, repeat the political collapse of the French Second Empire in 1870. On the eve of the 'season of peace and good will' he concluded there were places which the French would feel compelled to defend to the last man. 'If they do so the forces of France will bleed to death … whether or not we reach our goal.'

He intended enticing the French into a killing ground where he would exploit his superior heavy artillery. He selected historic Verdun as the bait for a trap using 5. *Armee* supported by more than 1,300 guns (500 heavy) with 2.5 million shells in an offensive ominously designated *Unternehmen 'Gericht'* (Operation 'Judgement'). Falkenhayn would subtly hamstring 5. *Armee's* attempts to take the town, informing only a select few of the real objective with even the army commander, Crown Prince Wilhelm of Prussia, excluded from the magic circle as the Army took the first steps to betraying its lord and master, the *Kaiser* [1].

Tactical surprise was achieved by abandoning the usual trappings of offensives, such as expanding the trench system, although there was a nine-day delay as the region upheld its reputation for rain. The attackers faced a formidable task, for Verdun lay on the River Meuse within a hollow surrounded by wooded hills and ridges, the latter arranged almost like the teeth of a zipper exposing any advance to enfilade fire from the opposite bank. Many ridges were topped by modern, concrete fortresses stripped of garrisons and shielded by weak defences. The Machiavellian Falkenhayn refused to sanction an advance down both banks of the Meuse, which would have led to a speedy conclusion, and 'Gericht' began only on the eastern side during 21 February. Initially there was steady progress against the military backwater that was Région Fortifée Verdun (RFV) which had received some last-minute reinforcements[2].

These failed to prevent the fall on 25 February of Fort Douaumont, which dominated the eastern bank, bringing the French to the verge of collapse. But on this day they took up the gauntlet appointing Général de Division Philippe Pétain, of the reserve II Armée, to command the sector. As France's best general he reorganised the defences and within days stopped the Germans. On 6 March Falkenhayn sanctioned the extension of 'Gericht' to the western bank of the Meuse and for two months there was a ferocious struggle around the key heights of Dead Man (Mort Homme) and Hill 304 (Côte 304 Metres). The Germans, led by Falkenhayn's brother, Eugene eventually took the heights but artillery fire ground down Hill 304 by seven metres[3]!

Verdun was an artillery duel involving up to 3,000 guns (1,300 heavy) in a struggle reduced to the formula 'artillery conquers the ground, the infantry occupy it.' The Germans were bleeding the French Army but Pétain's rapid rotation of divisions – 40 by the beginning of May compared with 26 German – eased the burden. It also undermined French Army commander Maréchal Joseph Joffre's plans for a summer offensive, and to salvage it he moved Pétain out of the driving seat by promoting him on 1 May to command GAC and brought in replaced him with Général Robert Nivelle who was less demanding in resources.

Nivelle's appointment coincided with a failed French counter-attack to retake Fort Douaumont from 22–25 May followed by another German assault upon the eastern bank on 1 June. After initial success the attackers were sucked into a week-long siege of Fort Vaux and made little progress. The bloody pattern of bombardment, attack, counter-bombardment and counter-attack continued until 11 July when a last German push was held and Crown Prince Wilhelm was ordered to go on the defensive as Allied pressure mounted on the Somme. Germany had lost half a million men (80,000 dead and missing), undermining Falkenhayn's position and on 29 August he was replaced by the Eastern Front commander *Generalfeldmarschall* Paul von Beneckendorff und von Hindenburg who, with his chief-of-staff *Generalleutnant* Erich Ludendorff, was happy to close the Verdun front[4].

It rumbled into life again in early autumn as Joffre faced growing political opposition. Nivelle was in the public eye but supreme power required a success and only in October, as the Somme offensive wound down, did resources became available. For tactical and publicity value, the eastern bank of the Meuse was selected and the task of retaking Forts Vaux and Douaumont assigned to the ferocious Général Charles Mangin. Following days of merciless bombardment by 600 guns and 15,000 tonnes of shells, he struck on 24 October taking Douaumont and, after a fortnight's bloody squabbling he compelled the enemy to abandon Vaux on 3 November[5].

The recaptured ground was exposed to enemy fire and to secure it Nivelle launched another offensive using the same tactics of thorough artillery preparation, a creeping barrage and an attack upon a narrow front. Some 670 guns were assembled but appalling weather made it impossible to range them until the skies cleared on 11 December, the subsequent bombardment allowing the French to take most of their objectives four days later. The same evening Nivelle left II Armée on the first step to relieving Joffre while on 22 December Mangin was given VI Armée bringing to an end a battle which had seen the lines little changed after 10 months' savage fighting which had cost some 650,000 men, the French suffering 377,231 casualties including 51,600 dead and missing.

Both sides' morale was shaken and the battle had an insidious effect upon French battle doctrine, convincing many the policy of forward defence was viable even under the heaviest bombardment. The practice continued into 1918 and would lead to a severe defeat that summer[6].

On both sides air power was fragmented with squadrons dispersed among ground commands (army groups, armies and army corps) that retained operational control, the generals' blinkered views counting more than the experience of air officers who were often regarded as mere technical advisors. A comment on the German Army applied on both sides as one observer noted: 'Each *Stofl* had to establish his own position and it became apparent the success of an army's aviation depended upon his personality[7].' Verdun was an opportunity to increase the status of the air services for both sides' air leaders but neither was able fully to exploit the opportunity.

France's Lieutenant-Colonel Édouard Barès, aged 43, qualified as an aeronaut in 1911 before earning a military aeroplane pilot's license and flying with the Greeks in the Balkans War. A short, dapper man with neatly trimmed beard, tremendous charm and a capacity for hard work, he was born in a frontier town on the Argentine pampas[8]. The family returned to France when he was four and rather than follow its legal tradition he entered the military academy at St Cyr.

Seeking active service, he joined the overseas infantry (Infanterie de Marine) and served in Africa winning glowing reports from his superiors that offset the personal tragedies of the deaths of his wife in 1907 and his daughter four years later leaving him with a son. As the ranking pilot in the French Army at the beginning of the First World War he commanded IV Armée aviation with such success that in September 1914 he became director of the Western Front air service (Chef du Service Aéronautique des Armées du Nord et Nord-Est)[9].

Facing him was *Oberstleutnant* Hermann von der Lieth-Thomsen, who was based at Charleville and was a shrewd, bull-necked, staff officer who resembled a successful inn-keeper. A protégé of Ludendorff, he had been interested in the aeroplane since 1907 and the two had been the first staff officers to fly in an aeroplane. Thomsen never earned a pilot's licence but was appointed *Feldflugchef* in 1915 to improve the performance of the *Fliegertruppen* after their disappointing performance in the war's opening months. The carmine stripes of a Greater German General Staff officer compensated for his technical ignorance and he benefited from the technical expertise of his visionary chief-of-staff, the bird-like *Major* Wilhelm Siegert, who had lost several fingers stopping a runaway aeroplane before the war[10].

Thomsen made the first bid to raise *Fliegertruppen* status when, on 10 March, 1916 he vainly proposed an ambitious rationalisation of air power which would combine the resources of the Army and Navy[11]. Across the lines, Édouard Barès was less ambitious but also wished to raise his service's status and on 2 May suggested expanding the Aviation Militaire into an arm like the infantry and artillery. On 21 May he repeated the idea to GQG's organisation branch and also proposed that officers of the rank of colonel or lieutenant colonel be given total command of all squadrons at army and army group level[12]. Both proposals were promptly rejected by staffs determined to maintain their prerogatives in the military hierarchy[13].

The two bids reflected a surge in self-confidence among each side's airmen but it rarely lasted long for their perception of air superiority differed greatly from that of the staffs. Staff officers equated the absence of enemy aircraft with control of the skies and they were slow to accept the airmen's view that the air would never be totally clear of enemy aircraft. Staffs perceived surges of enemy activity as the loss of air superiority when they were really responses to the tactical situation and, from the start of the battle, the staffs' hysterical reaction to these 'crises' would shape air operations.

On the German side the task of supporting the Crown Prince's troops was assigned to the *Stofl 5. Armee*, the 40-year-old *Hauptmann* Wilhelm Haehnelt. Haehnelt was an infantryman who became an aeronaut in 1908 and a few months later was detached to the General Staff. He then became an infantry company commander before gaining his pilot's licence in 1913 being appointed commander of FFA 4 at the outbreak of war and *Stofl 5. Armee* in September 1914. After the war he was prominent in light aviation and aviation history becoming the Luftwaffe's historian but retired in March 1942. He would be taken prisoner by the Russians at the war's end and died in captivity in March 1946[14].

At the end of December 1915 Haehnelt was ordered to deny enemy aircraft the air space over the Meuse. With barely half-a-dozen squadrons this was a difficult task and only one or two patrols were flown, but the assignment of *Kagohl 1* and *Kagohl 2* created as multi-role combat formations, eased his problems. Most of Haehnelt's 168 aeroplanes were C-types but there were also a couple of twin-engined G-types and 21 E-type fighters, many of the single-seat fighters being transferred from neighbouring armies and organised under the *Kagohls* into *KEK Nord* on the eastern bank and *KEK Süd* on the western[15]. Haehnelt also had 14 balloons, which he controlled through a dedicated telephone network, while the air defences were augmented by 71 anti-aircraft guns and 40 field guns with a secondary air defence role. Also available were seven 7 squadrons of the neighbouring *Armee Abteilung Stranz* holding the St Mihiel Salient east of Verdun which added some 40 aircraft to overall German strength as well as six 6 balloons. The importance of artillery in the forthcoming battle meant that 20% of the *Artillerie*

Feldfliegerabteilungen would be committed to the battle[16]. Facing this armada of 200 aircraft were RFV's three corps squadrons with 30.

Pétain's arrival saw a rapid reversal of French fortunes both on the ground and in the air because he possessed a symbiotic approach to warfare based upon the integration of all the arms and services, including aviation[17]. After resolving the initial crisis at Verdun, he sought to drum his ideas into the minds of sceptical subordinates with varying degrees of success. His interest in air power was pragmatically confined to its direct contribution to the terrestrial struggle, yet he stimulated a renaissance of French air power helped by Barès who hurried to Bar-le-Duc to establish a command post and commuted daily to Pétain's headquarters at Souilly[18].

With Pétain's defence based upon the rapid rotation of army corps, continuity was achieved by creating four (later eight) permanent corps sectors (groupements) temporarily occupied by army corps headquarters with a reserve of seven squadrons (four fighter) which he deployed in key sectors[19]. The army had a permanent support force (heavy artillery, engineers, communications, logistics) which included an aviation liaison officer under Capitaine Paul Gérard, the II Armée's stocky, bespectacled aviation officer who had been hastily dispatched from VI Armee on the Somme.

Gérard, aged 38, was an infantryman who had switched to aviation in 1911 and would lead squadrons at army and army group level throughout the war, being promoted Commandant in May 1917. As a squadron commander he led the first night bomber mission in 1914. After the war he helped organise the Czechoslovak Air Force and held senior positions in French military aviation until his retirement in 1936. He died in November 1964[20].

On 21 February Barès had a total of 100 squadrons on the Western Front with 856 aircraft, of which only 59 were unserviceable[24]. Yet by 28 February the reinforced Verdun front had less than 150 aircraft (see Table 1-2), rising to 226 in mid April and achieving numerical superiority only in May with 250[21]. With industry unable to replace losses the squadrons had to retain machines with warped airframes (many rebuilt after crashes) and strained engines long after they should have been consigned to the scrap heap. Many crashes were due to poor pilot training yet it was only on 21 May, after Nivelle assumed command of II Armée, that Pétain proposed replacing tired and inadequate pilots with men from other armies as well as providing new aircraft from the reserves[22].

Table 1–2:
II Armée squadrons 28 February – 15 December, 1916

Date	Caudron	Farman	Voisin	Sections	Nieuport	Total
28 February	3	5	-	2	6	**16**
26 March	5	6	-	5	4	**20**
16 April	7	10	-	4	6	**27**
14 May	7	8	2	6	6	**29**
15 June	6	7	1	6	6	**26**
20 July	4	9	1	6	5	**25**
20 August	3	9	1	5	5	**23**
15 September	4	9	1	4	5	**23**
15 November	4	7	-	5	5	**21**
15 December	7	8	-	-	5	**20**

Source: *Armées Françaises X/1*, II Armée entry

In quality French aircraft generally remained inferior to the enemy with the majority being 'pushers' with engines at the rear of the fuselage 'pushing' the aircraft forward, while the Germans used 'tractors' with engines at the front of the fuselage with propellers 'pulling' them through the air. This made all the French corps and artillery aircraft vulnerable to fighters because of 'dead spots' behind, and below them which fighters could exploit and French corps squadrons continued to be shackled with 'pushers' until the late summer of 1917. However, for most of 1916 the French fighter squadrons (escadrilles de chasse) had superior aircraft in the nimble Nieuport 10 and Nieuport 11 Bebés (as well as Nieuport 12 two-seaters) creating unease on German airfields and with Barès regarding air superiority over Verdun as vital he committed 66% of his Nieuports to the battle[23].

In the first days of the attack French airfields were targeted by German guns, driving the squadrons to safer nests. With enemy aircraft literally driven from the field during the first few days of the offensive the Germans flew unchallenged and claimed mastery of the air[24]. Reconnaissance smoothed the way for the capture of Fort Douaumont, but soon German airmen were reporting that the French were strengthening both their defences behind the battle front and those on the eastern bank of the Meuse[25]. As the original French squadrons settled into new airfields and reinforcements arrived, there was an increase in activity (see Table 1-3), although the norm seemed to be one sortie per aircraft per day[26].

Table 1-3:
II Armée sorties 27 March – 2 April 1916

Day	Fighter	Corps	Bomber	Total
27 March	-	4	-	4
28 March	-	2	-	2
29 March	57	36	-	93
30 March	48	83	-	131
31 March	73	105	-	178
1 April	102	92	-	194
2 April	79	99	7	185
Total	**359**	**421**	**7**	**787**

Source: SHAT 19N488/4.

While the attackers appear to have lost only about two aircraft, this surge so unsettled Crown Prince Wilhelm's corps commanders that within two days of *'Gericht'* opening they were demanding aerial reinforcements. *OHL* promptly despatched *Kagohl 5* (and eight *Kasta*) together with 10–20 Fokkers raising Haehnelt's strength to 230 by the beginning of March yet the nagging feeling of inferiority remained[27].

For once this feeling of inferiority had some substance as Barès picked up the gauntlet within days of arriving at Bar-le-Duc. On 29 February he demanded his fighter squadrons fly 'armed reconnaissance' missions in force, covering pre-arranged routes at specified hours. He added with a flourish: 'The squadrons' missions are to seek out, to engage and to destroy the enemy.' Yet this was more an article of faith than a statement of doctrine and failed to specify the size of 'armed reconnaissance' formations which soon operated in a splendid isolation[28].

To overcome this hurdle, Barès concentrated all his fighter squadrons in one group following an experiment first conducted in 1915 by Capitaine Paul du Peuty who had created a combined fighter-reconnaissance group to improve command and control[29]. The groupement de chasse was created at Bar-le-Duc on 13 March under Commandant Charles de Tricornet de Rose, the commander of MS12 and France's first military pilot. Rose now co-ordinated the fighters' efforts to clear the skies of enemy reconnaissance aircraft using 'armed reconnaissance' sweeps by small formations (usually four fighters), although selected pilots made lone patrols. From 13–19 March his fighters clashed with enemy aircraft on some 70 occasions flying more than 215 sorties, a third being 'armed reconnaissance' missions, and claimed about six victories although it appears only two German aircraft were lost[30].

But the French corps commanders, who had lost control of the fighter squadrons, believed this led to the continued appearance of German aircraft and their bitter protests led to the groupement's disbandment within a week. On 19 March the squadrons were again dispersed among the corps sectors and the Aviation Militaire's low status meant it was months before fighters were again concentrated[31].

In compensation Capitaine Auguste le Révérend, former commander of Garros' squadron MS23, now arrived to co-ordinate fighter operations under Pétain's staff and continued to emphasise offensive missions with his six squadrons. But co-ordinating operations between the various corps was difficult and offensive operations were hindered by the diversion of fighters; on 18 March, for example, each fighter squadron flew three or four reconnaissance sorties[32].

Gradually, Révérend's work would see some reduction in enemy activity and Barès was able to build upon this to recreate the groupement de chasse on the Somme in the summer leading in the autumn to the first permanent groupe de chasse (GC 11) on the Verdun front under Révérend. By then the staffs in their châteaux were reluctantly beginning to accept that the key to air superiority was the offensive use of fighters and there would always be both 'leakage' and casualties[33].

The aggressiveness of French fighter pilots meant German aircraft were increasingly harassed on both sides of the line while the French were less troubled. The Germans were hampered by the dispersal of combat aircraft and the absence of a cohesive tactical doctrine, commanders followed their own inclinations[34]. But the *Fliegertruppe*'s passive defensive tactics were the prime problem as aircraft patrolled sectors like sentries in barrage patrol sorties (*Sperrflüge*)[35]. This became the *Kasta*'s prime role when the German offensive switched to the western bank of the Meuse early in March forcing Haehnelt to abandon a bombing programme he had planned a week earlier[36].

Even the Fokkers, 66% of them dispersed among the *Kastas* or *FFAs* were used for *Sperrflüge*[37]. But the rotary engines were not suitable for these sorts of missions as the aircraft had to be flown full throttle (see below) reducing endurance to 90 minutes and even then their cylinders needed constant replacement. The *Kagohls* remained the backbone of the aerial defence because they were based upon C-types with greater endurance (five hours for a LFG Roland C.II) and higher fire power (two machine guns) than the Fokkers. It was Boelcke who recognised the Fokkers were better in the interceptor role. When he created a third Fokker unit, *KEK Sivry*, on 11 March he had a telephone line laid from the forward observer network to his airfield to warn him when enemy aircraft were crossing the lines and apparently introduced the concept of attacks by teams of two or three fighters. He added four victories to his total, but within a fortnight he was warning Thomsen that the Nieuports outclassed his Fokkers[38].

The German staffs again took counsel of their fears during March and claimed the *Fliegertruppen* had again lost air superiority even though losses were less than six aircraft[39]. The arrival of the newly-formed *Kagohl 4* allowed Haehnelt on 12 April to arrange patrols covering the whole Verdun battlefield both to relieve pressure upon the troops and to neutralise enemy air reconnaissance. The front was split in two with each sector covered by two *Kagohls* operating on alternate days to maintain a *Kasta* combat air patrol over each sector. Crown Prince Wilhelm's officers believed this methodical use of air power would neutralise enemy air activity but it proved a waste of resources[40].

Worse still, it was costly with the *Kagohls* losing nearly half the German aircraft shot down over Verdun and some 75% of the fatal casualties, many to increasingly aggressive French patrols of two to four Nieuports roaming as far as the enemy balloon line. Although many of his pilots preferred 'lone wolf' missions, Révérend certainly established a degree of air superiority by the end of March flying up to 100 sorties a day[41].

Yet the French success was due as much to technology as tactics. The Nieuports, like the Fokkers, had engines where the cylinder block, with the propeller bolted to it, rotated giving an excellent power/weight ratio and great torque which helped manoeuvrability. But the engine could not be controlled and ran at a constant high speed consuming fuel rapidly forcing Nieuport and Fokker pilots to be aggressive to exploit their small fuel tanks.

By contrast the C-types had water-cooled engines based upon the automotive tradition with a fixed cylinder block and rotating crankshaft driving the propeller. Ultimately they were more powerful than the rotary and, more importantly, they possessed a throttle to adjust engine performance and fuel consumption in flight. These were ideal requirements for patrolling but they made response times slower and their mass inevitably made the two-seaters more sluggish in battle giving the initiative to the enemy[42].

The Nieuports were also used for aerial sentry duty with numerous 'barrage patrols' until April and were augmented by the corps squadrons. On 24 February, N23 and N67 flew eight such sorties while MF63 and MF72 flew five, although during March fighters assumed a more offensive role. Strike squadrons were also diverted to fighter duty: VB109 and VC111 flew six offensive 'cruising sorties' on 20 March and the following day seven barrage sorties over the eastern bank of the Meuse[43].

Numerical superiority and the decline of the Fokker helped to tighten French control of the skies from April, symbolised on 30 April when the machine gun of *Rittmeister* Erich *Graf* von Holck of *AFA 203* (attached to *KEK Sivry*) jammed after shooting down a Voisin from a formation. Von Holck was then pursued and shot down by Sergent Buisse and l'Adjutant Travers in a C27 Caudron watched by a helpless Manfred von Richthofen. German accounts indicate that the *Landsers* were becoming resigned to see the enemy flying overhead, shooting down their aircraft and directing artillery fire [44]

Yet during April German aircraft began to penetrate French air space. Incomplete French records indicate that during February and early March there was a daily average of three clashes as the weather improved while the commitment of more squadrons saw the figures during April rise to 16 or 17. Simultaneously, German pressure steadily increased, spearheaded by bombers and on 27 April many enemy aircraft were reported over French batteries although the majority remained over their own trenches. By mid May French reports note the enemy were 'very active' with an average of 30 combats a day[45]

Pétain's successor, Nivelle, retained a vestige of the Napoleonic spirit and encouraged aggressiveness throughout his command. He was concerned about the German resurgence and one of his corps commanders warned on 3 May that briefly concentrating fighters at one point would not prevent enemy air superiority. Whatever his faults, Nivelle was realist enough to recognise the impossibility of preventing individual aircraft operating over French lines[46]

Yet he was clearly uneasy about the air situation and on 19 May the loss of two aircraft over French lines was the excuse for a bitter complaint to Pétain. He claimed the enemy had achieved air superiority with a new type of fighter operating in squadron strength and which were using the same offensive tactics as the French. This occurred precisely as Barès was trying to raise the status of airmen and his optimism, together with Nivelle's pessimism, indicate just how much air superiority was a matter of perception[47].

Perhaps Nivelle was venting steam while under pressure to retake Fort Douaumont, but he was clearly more concerned about German aircraft flying over his own lines than any real or imagined failure of his own airmen over enemy lines. There were no new German fighters and while the *KEK*s may have been slightly expanded most Fokker monoplanes (augmented by a few Fokker single-seat biplanes) were scattered across the front. There is also no evidence of excessive losses, indeed during the week only four French aircraft fell (one in an accident) while aircrew casualties totalled eight men[48].

Despite this Pétain reprimanded Barès for failing to support Nivelle and demanded new men and machines for Verdun, although the only reinforcements which did arrive were eight fighters of the N124 whose pilots required three months' intensive training before they were combat ready. However, William Thaw, who would command the squadron when it transferred to the US Air Service, claimed his first victory five days after Nivelle's letter[49]). While French fighters continued to fly patrols in May leading to numerous clashes between the escadrilles and the *Kagohl*, solo sorties remained the norm. There appear to have been few major dogfights and by the time of the last German attacks in June the French appear to have imposed a degree of control over the battlefield[50].

Surges in activity occurred with each new German attack, their airmen usually being active during the afternoon before the *Landsers* advanced and during French counter-attacks[51]. During one of the latter in late May, as Nivelle sought to regain Fort Douaumont, French fighters and some Farmans attacked balloons with giant Le Prieur rockets in the first use of air-to-air missiles to claim six of the eight balloons on the front[52].

In contrast to the slaughter on the ground the airmen's casualties were relatively light. From 24 February to 30 June, some 60 French aircraft failed to return to base and there were 100 casualties, including 51 killed and missing. The Germans lost 24 aircraft from January to the end of

August and suffered some 70 casualties, of whom about half were killed [53].

The struggle for air superiority, like most air operations over Verdun, was largely at the Tactical level and bombing was one of the few expressions of Operational level activity. At first both sides used aeroplanes and airships to bomb communications but lighter-than-air operations were quickly abandoned. To support the initial attack Falkenhayn, who had planned the operation, wanted the airships to stage 'an extremely intense night offensive' against the rail system behind Verdun but his hopes were dashed by high winds and snow storms. Worse, *Hauptmann* Alfred Horn's LZ 77 was shot down and in the aftermath airship operations were quietly abandoned[54]).

An *OHL* ban on night-bombing led Haehnelt on 26 February to order daylight attacks upon the Meuse bridges and camps around Verdun and the *Kasta* dropped 2.32 tonnes of bombs without effect. Within a week demands for air space denial meant the *Kagohls* largely abandoned bombing, although attacks were occasionally made upon the rail system supporting II Armée and positions west of Verdun which meant Haehnelt missed a significant opportunity to choke Pétain's forces[55]).

German artillery fire had cut the railway north of Bar-le-Duc leaving the French only a narrow road to channel supplies and reinforcements. They extemporised a fleet of trucks passing at 14-second intervals for the task, becoming the first army to rely exclusively upon the internal combustion engine for support, and by 7 March had sent 190,000 men and 25,000 tonnes of supplies up to Calvary along what they called the Sacred Way (La Voie Sacrée). To defend this vulnerable target the II Armée had 12 static anti-aircraft guns and 4 mobile sections but they were rarely tested[56]).

Only from late April did the Germans return to daylight bombing, beginning on the morning of 25 April when an estimated 17 aircraft dropped 50 bombs upon Brocourt airfield although the defenders' fighters and anti-aircraft guns claimed a quarter of the attackers. Another 25 bomber sorties were flown around Verdun by the end of April but all these attacks were within 10 kilometres of no-man's-land and upon the battlefield[57]).

During May the *Kagohls* tried to shield the front but they returned to bombing on 1 June when 15 struck Bar-le-Duc from bases in the St Mihiel Salient dropping another 50 bombs in the face of fierce fighter attacks, including the Lafayette Escadrille, which disrupted a second raid. There were 5 more major raids involving a total of 100 sorties during June with targets including Nivelle's headquarters at Souilly on 19 June. These raids stirred a hornet's nest and were frequently intercepted, defending fighters on 16 June being 'alerted by radio'. They ended when the Germans closed down the offensive on 22 June [58].

To aid air defence both sides had observer posts along and behind the front to monitor enemy air activity. Those in the rear guided friendly aircraft using arrows made of white cloth which were laid out to show in which direction the enemy were flying. The ground-based systems at Verdun were poorly integrated with the squadrons but during the year both sides established reporting centres linked to the observers by a telephone system which was later extended to fighter bases[59]).

The German bombing was retaliation for the growing intensity of French raids although at the beginning of the Verdun campaign the French bomber force was in turmoil. Disputes within the Aviation Militaire about the value of day- and night-bombing saw Barès supporting daylight attacks while others, including X Armée air, commander Peuty, regarded such missions as a waste of effort. The disputes undermined the status of the bomber and during February half of GB 1's squadrons were converted to fighters while from February GB 2's units were gradually converted into corps squadrons. It is possible that Verdun saved the French bomber force[60]).

GB 2 opened the Verdun bombing campaign on 21 February by dropping 110 converted shells but by the end of the month it had flown barely a dozen bomber sorties. MF 25 joined the sporadic campaign in late March but in April was converted to the night-attack role because the French began to believe these were more effective. They believed, wrongly, that bomb damage could be repaired more easily in the day and that night missions could also provide a bonus of information on enemy activity behind the lines[61]).

When GB 2 disbanded in March it was replaced by GB 5 with the new Bréguet-Michelin BM 2 and BM 4 which flew their first mission on 14 March. They were augmented by MF 25 but both the Farmans and Bréguet-Michelins carried feeble loads and in May the latter were replaced by the reformed GB 2 with two Voisin squadrons and the independent VB 101. With their arrival in May the French switched exclusively to night-bombing flying 6 to 12 sorties through the gloom with each bomber carrying a 200 kilogramme load. Yet on 2 July Pétain bitterly complained about the 'flagrant inferiority' of French bombers and demanded a stronger force, ideally two groupes for each army group[62]).

Corps squadrons occasionally augmented the bombers from 21 March, C11 opening their campaign by dropping 10 bombs on rail targets[63]). The use of corps aircraft in the bombing role was not confined to the French for FFAs on the British front also flew such missions at this time (see Chapter Two).

Both sides made only token efforts to fill the bombers' target folders as most reconnaissance was at the Tactical level with relatively little at the Operational level. Before launching 'Gericht' the Germans required only a few sorties because the Verdun area was thoroughly photographed throughout 1915 since OHL feared a French thrust towards Germany's main east-west rail link between Sedan and Metz. With so much detailed information only a handful of sorties were needed before 'Gericht' although some aircraft had to travel as far as Bar-le-Duc 45 kilometres southwest of Verdun, to update files[64]).

By contrast RFV's squadrons were usually grounded by the region's notoriously poor winter weather and even in the brief respite of January they took barely six photographs. Unfortunately, there was no one at RFV who could interpret them and when GAC finally sent someone to calm an increasingly anxious leadership this officer, while admitting there were signs of increased German activity, concluded they were a feint[65])!

In the following months, occasional long-range reconnaissance sorties were flown and for photographic missions both sides sought safety in numbers by using large formations. Sometimes the French could assign a shield of a dozen fighters for a couple of Caudrons or Farmans, although three or four was the normal escort for both sides. Alternatively up to eight Caudrons or Farmans might be used on deep probing missions lasting up to four hours. Surprisingly, the French regarded night reconnaissance by Voisins as more effective than day missions which were sometimes assigned to lone Nieuport fighters[66]).

Tactical level reconnaissance missions by corps squadrons dominated air operations. At first each army corps entering the line brought its own multi-task corps squadron to monitor the tactical situation through lone reconnaissance sorties[67]). The observer noted the condition of the fortifications as well as hostile and friendly artillery fire then wrote a report upon his return. Although the pilot and observer acted as a team, (the German nicknames were 'Emil' and 'Franz' for pilot and observer), it was the latter who was the superior and even in 1918 a British report on French corps squadrons noted with astonishment and underlined text that '…the pilot is generally a mere chauffeur[68]).'

French reconnaissance was very specialised with 'avions de surveillance' and 'avions de commandement'. The former conducted general observation and were specifically denied any fire control mission. They were augmented by one or two 'avions de commandement' per corps front which radioed directly to corps headquarters on the battle's progress and especially about artillery activity[69]).

The French guns were directed by special squadrons (Sections d'Aviation d'Artillerie Lourde or Sections d'Artillerie Lourde) but here, and in the corps squadrons there was a unique French system[70]). The front was divided among commandants de secteur who provided squadrons with observers thoroughly familiar with that sector, and these sometimes made up half the artillery observers.

Discovering the location of friendly troops in the cratered wilderness was increasingly important but required flying low, under fire from friend and foe alike. Both sides built upon the experience gained the previous year but such missions, contact patrols in British terminology, depended upon the willingness of the troops to indicate their positions with flares or cloth panels. The French Poilu (literally 'hairy', the French equivalent of 'Tommy' or 'Doughboys') developed greater confidence in his airmen than the enemy Landsers, who feared attracting the airmen's attention and this led to many German deaths through 'friendly' as well as enemy artillery fire[71]).

French contact patrols at Verdun began with exercises by XII Corps d'Armee's MF 22 from 30 April and it was soon joined by MF 33 and C4, the last supporting Mangin's III Corps d'Armee. The first contact patrol missions were reported on 24 May, and a few weeks later the Germans flew their first Infanterieflieger missions[72]).

The corps squadrons played a lesser role in the great artillery duel, occasionally registering for counter-attacks but their main contribution was through photography, the French stating: 'Fire was controlled by photography[73]).' Photographs not only detected targets but also monitored the gunners' effectiveness through images taken with bulky plate cameras fixed to the aircraft's side using rubber dampers to reduce vibration.

Photographs were taken vertically, with the camera looking straight down on the target, or obliquely with it facing forward but downward to provide troops with an image of their objective. Each corps headquarters had a photographic developing and printing facility which received the plates within an hour of their being exposed. The French would produce up to 100 prints from each negative and a British observer reported 5,000 prints a day might be produced. To support counter-attacks the French built airstrips near divisional headquarters so photographic plates could be delivered direct to motorised dark rooms for rapid developing of the negatives. During the attempt to retake Fort Vaux some prints were parachuted directly to Mangin's corps headquarters[74]).

Each army headquarters also had a photographic reconnaissance squadron to help staffs monitor enemy activity along the whole battlefront. They were assisted by special officers operating under Gérard and Haehnelt who correlated the squadrons' accounts to provide detailed written reports on the overall tactical situation. During 1916, the French expanded this into the Service de Renseignements Aériens (Aerial Reconnaissance Service) which brought along the day's photographs and worked every night with the army's intelligence organisation (Deuxième Bureau) and the gunners to produce a detailed picture of the enemy batteries as well as planning the following day's fire plans. The concentration of each groupement's squadrons on one airfield made this easier and the groupement air advisor would spend the day debriefing pilots and sifting through reports before driving down to Souilly at dusk to report at army headquarters[75]).

Most French and German fire direction missions were flown by dedicated squadrons, the German *Artillerie-Fliegerabteilungen* and the French Sections d'Artillerie Lourde, whose priority was neutralising enemy artillery (counter-battery operations). When an observer detected a target, he would transmit, in Morse, an alert to radio stations operated by heavy batteries or groups of batteries. Gunners ready for business would lay out cloth panels in a pre-arranged sequence and the observer would select the most suitable guns. He would radio a warning to them and, when they responded with a second cloth signal, he would begin directing fire[76]).

Directing fire was a time-consuming business. Even if the trailing wire radio antenna was not cut by shell fragments and if the radio worked perfectly, enemy counter-battery fire might drive friendly gunners into the dugouts. The mere presence of enemy aircraft dissuaded many British batteries in 1915 from opening fire and this also occurred at Verdun. Another problem for artillery observers was that the drum fire gradually obliterated almost every feature on the landscape while smoke, mist, haze and cloud frequently obscured targets. With the French alone firing 80,000 shells a day by mid April, ranging a battery's fire was like following a drop of rain during a downpour. Sometimes French gunners were too exhausted to respond to the airmen and this probably also applied to the Germans[77] .

The narrow waveband of the 'spark' radio sets limited both the numbers of missions on each corps front and the batteries served by each aircraft. The aircraft supported individual heavy batteries, heavy or field artillery groups and in the early days of Verdun no more than one fire direction mission involving one or two artillery units could be flown on each corps front. Tight radio discipline and careful timing meant that by March the French could simultaneously operate two artillery fire direction missions on each army corps front while two aircraft could support heavy artillery groups[78]).

When not used for correcting artillery fire, the French gunners used their radios to intercept enemy radio signals in what came to be called communications intelligence (Comint). Every 10 days the French listed the location of every enemy radio, its associated units and the volume of traffic; indeed it was the increase of radio traffic which first alerted the French that something was planned for Verdun. Although jamming of radio frequencies is not mentioned in any accounts of Verdun, the Germans had already demonstrated their capabilities against the British on 12 July 1915 during routine artillery missions and it was an option which remained open [79].

French organisational skill overcame their guns' numerical and qualitative inferiority and allowed them to smash innumerable attacks, while German air-artillery co-operation at Verdun was found wanting [80]. The Germans were unable to exploit their superiority either in guns or corps aircraft, while throughout the year their army corps were rarely supported by more than one *AFA*.

The French, on the other hand, would have at least two Sections equipped with twin-engined Caudron G3 and G 4 'tractors' and Maurice Farman MF.7 and MF.11 'pushers', pre-war box-kite designs whose engines were barely capable of getting them airborne with their crews and equipment. Supplementing the groupements' squadrons, Pétain's army artillery was divided into Eastern and Western Sectors each with a Section d'Artillerie and a reconnaissance squadron ([81]).

In the first weeks of Verdun, French aircraft conducted very few fire direction missions. A small number of artillery patrols and registrations were carried out but until mid April most fire direction missions were conducted by the kite balloon companies. On 26 April for example, aircraft conducted 28 registrations and fire missions but balloons conducted 174 with 74 batteries while from 1–4 May, aeroplane and balloon registrations were 42 and 224 respectively [82].

The Germans also placed greater emphasis upon the tethered kite balloon which rose and set with the sun to supplement forward observers on the ground. Each side's army corps had four hydrogen-filled balloons, dubbed 'sausages' (saucisses) by the French and 'dragons' (*Drachen*) by the Germans, organised into compagnies d'aérostières and *Feldluftschifferabteilungen* respectively. They were literally plugged into the ground telephone system and tended to support the lighter batteries, for direct destructive fire and the isolation of sectors by barrages, although they also proved a valuable source of tactical oblique imagery [83].

The balloons were occasionally shelled, but although it was easy to pierce their gas cells it was far more difficult to ignite the hydrogen. When hit they would sink to earth like a tipsy dowager as their observers exploited life-saving static-line parachutes to reach the ground safely. Despite their limitations, German gunners regarded them as the lesser of two evils compared with the aeroplane, but throughout the war they preferred to opt for terrestrial observers. The exception was the west bank of the Meuse where the numerous ridges meant ground and balloon observers could see little, allowing the aeroplane to blossom ([84]).

During the summer the Somme became the prime aerial arena and many French squadrons, together with most of the *Kagohls*, were sucked into the maelstrom. As Joffre cut Nivelle's ammunition allotments and diverted them the new campaign the II Armée was urged to 'get more bang for the buck' through aircraft and in directives issued in early July, Nivelle arranged that only batteries whose locations the enemy had detected would fire when enemy aircraft were overhead. Pétain himself remained concerned about the situation in Verdun's skies and pressed on 2 July not only for improved aircraft, including fighters with machine guns or even cannon, but also for an aerial doctrine and the creation of an aerial reserve ([85]). He also wanted the fighters concentrated into groups, and with support at this level, Barès was able to create, on 19 October, three groupes de chasse, two under army groups. But the first, GC 11, was under II Armée with Révérend controlling 4 squadrons reinforced by 12 fighters taken from the squadrons on Pétain's quiet fronts bringing total strength to the equivalent of 6 squadrons ([86]).

These supported the first of Nivelle's attacks with standing patrols of five or six fighters and quickly cleared the enemy from the sky. Eight corps and artillery squadrons (with six balloons) were then able to direct the guns assisted by the best observers. Simultaneously two squadrons were assigned to bomb targets beyond artillery range [87].

The Germans began to concentrate their fighters in August, initially creating three squadrons, but two were sent to the Somme front in September leaving *Oberleutnant* Fritz von Bronsart-Schellendorf's *Jasta 7*, reinforced in mid October by *Jasta 14* from *Armee Abteilung 'A'* ([88]). They acted as a catalyst upon French air doctrine for, like an anxious mother hen, the French Army wished to keep an eye on its chicks. The desire to clip the airmen's wings found expression on 10 October when GQG demanded that where the enemy was active, fighters provide 'direct protection' (protection immédiat) both to the ground forces and the corps squadrons [89].

The policy was not completely defensive. Fighters would fly shallow sweeps along the enemy front as well as barrage patrols and escort missions, but with fighters largely confined within the enemy balloon line it meant the French outer air battle was far closer to the front and during the Verdun counter-offensives air operations were largely restricted to a Tactical level inner air battle. As the French made their preparations the *Fliegertruppe* were expanded on 8 October into a more comprehensive organisation, the *Luftstreitkräfte* under *Generalleutnant* Ernst von Hoeppner as *Kogenluft* and Thomsen as his chief-of-staff (see Chapter Three) but there was no time to influence events on the Meuse where the Germans were overwhelmed.

On 23 October alone the French flew 160 sorties, including 65 fighter and 6 bomber, with 50 fire missions of which 28 were counter-battery. From 21–25 October French corps squadrons flew 305 observation and

39 photographic sorties and on most days the fighters flew 60 sorties. Yet it was only Nivelle's infantry attack on 26 October which convinced *OHL* that *5.Armee* needed aerial reinforcements with all available squadrons, including those of *Armee Abteilung Stranz*, being sent to the eastern bank of the Meuse. Yet: 'Strong enemy squadrons arrogantly flew overhead, sometimes up to 45 aircraft against six German'. In addition, the *5.Armee*'s rail network was struck by French night bombers before, and after, the attack.

With the arrival of *Jasta 10* from the British front on 28 October the Germans claimed a noticeable weakening of French air activity ([90]). But this owed more to the weather with Nivelle's preparations for the second attack during November hindered by cloud and rain which grounded both sides' aircraft for days[91]. Yet, once again: 'The noticeable superiority of the French artillery and air force caused the almost total destruction of the positions at the front and in the rear, very bloody casualties among the infantry and heavy losses of guns [92].'

These operations helped Hoeppner hammer the last nails into the coffin of fighter fragmentation and passive air defence[93]. The *Luftstreitkräfte* raised the airmen's status and established their own chain of command while allowing fighters to be used more aggressively. Another of Hoeppner's objectives – improving co-ordination between the airmen and the ground forces – was also achieved but this proved a poisoned chalice by actually encouraging the fragmentation of resources with squadrons dispersed under multiple commands to support the *Landser*.

Barès' achievements were less substantial. He had reorganised and expanded both the fighter and bomber forces but could do nothing to improve Aviation Militaire status leaving it at the generals' beck and call. The dispersal of squadrons and the reluctance of their masters to allow them to operate out of their sight made it easier for the Germans to contain French air power and they were to rate the more aggressive British as the significant foe. Worse still, despite all the promises from the politicians and the rear services, there was clearly no prospect of giving the squadrons modern aircraft for the following year's spring offensive.

By then Barès had become a victim of political cross-fire. In 1914 as the Germans had advanced upon Paris the politicians fled and Joffre's victory on the Marne had given him undisputed moral authority over the politicians for two years. His failure to repeat the success ultimately allowed the politicians to engineer his replacement by Nivelle. Like drug addicts seeking a 'fix', the politicians sought new issues to strengthen their status and one was the obsolescence of French aircraft. A bureaucratic battle of attrition developed between GQG and the politically-dominated War Ministry which gradually tightened its control and on 15 February 1917 secured the dismissal of Barès ([94]). He rejoined the infantry and fought with distinction as a regimental commander, including service at Verdun. After the war he returned to the air corps helping to convert it into the Armée de l'Air and became its first chief of staff in 1931 then served again in 1933 and 1934. He would live another 20 years and see air power help to crush his country in 1940 and to liberate it in 1944 ([95]).

The spring offensive of 1917 failed to meet Nivelle's grandiose objectives and the politicians who had lauded him now replaced him with Pétain (See Chapter Four). The new commander's strategy was based upon limited offensives, set-piece battles and short advances, but to execute them he needed to stamp the need for integration and organisation upon the French Army through a root and branch reform which extended to the Aviation Militaire which, he believed: '...was indispensable for the success of limited offensives ([96]).' Barès' successor, Commandant Paul du Peuty (see Chapter Four) was himself replaced on 2 August 1917 by Colonel Maurice Duval, a slim 48-year-old who had risen, like Pétain, from infantry brigade commander to VI Armée chief-of-staff.

Duval was born in Bayonne in 1869, the year before France's humiliating defeat by Prussia and perhaps growing up in the shadow of these events led him to enter St Cyr when he was 19. He joined the infantry but his career suffered the swirls and eddies of political and army factionalism in turn-of-the-century France. Perhaps the defining moment of his life came in 1907 when he went to Japan and embarked on a two-year study of the Japanese Army during the Russo-Japanese War. His conclusions (and those of Pétain) emphasised the importance of fortification and fire-power in an army obsessed with Napoleonic concepts of manoeuvre and for these reasons he was not promoted to major until 1911 ([97]).

As an infantry brigade commander he was wounded during the bloody offensives in Artois and Champagne during the Autumn of 1915 but distinguished himself and was appointed an Officer of the Légion d'Honneur. Promoted colonel in June 1916 he became chief-of-staff first of VI Armée on the Somme, then of I Armée and the combination of background and efficiency did much to recommend him to Pétain.

For Duval the new appointment may have helped overcome grief for the loss of his son, Robert, during the Nivelle Offensive and he became a regular member of Pétain's early morning conferences. Compensation for his lack of aviation experience was achieved by appointing the experienced Commandant Bertrand Pujo, former Chef d'Aviation of GAN, as his chief-of-staff and Pujo remained an eminence grise until the end of the war ([98]).

After the war Duval resigned his commission but retained an interest in commercial aviation as well as joining the board of the newspaper *Figaro*. His only contribution to the defence of the Fatherland after 1919 was to act as an unofficial observer in Spain during the Civil War which led him to produce two books ([99]). He died, at the age of 89, in 1958.

Yet the appointment of an infantryman to command air squadrons seemed to many, including Peuty, the ultimate humiliation. While both Pétain and Duval tried to retain him, promoting him Inspecteur des Formations et du Matériel Aéronautique on 2 August, Peuty opted to join the infantry and perished as a regimental commander the following spring.

Duval, like Hoeppner, was one of the best sort of staff officers, hard-working but with an intellectual curiosity which sought to harness air power with the army holding the reins. While Pétain's views of air power were blinkered (See Chapter Five) leading to a Tactical level doctrine being written on tablets of stone with his directives for the future conduct of operations, gradually they would be expanded under Duval's guidance ([100]).

But first Duval had to find ways of executing the new doctrine because Pétain's priority was to restore morale and confidence among the Poilus. He intended to achieve this through a series of limited offensives to strengthen his defences in 1918 for the German offensives which he regarded as inevitable. His offensives would be limited in scale but with almost limitless resources to guarantee victory and Verdun was to be the first laboratory.

Pétain had inherited a 40-division flight of fancy from Nivelle but reduced it to a more pragmatic level to retake key terrain on the western bank of the Meuse, especially Mort Homme and Hill 304 with their evil memories. The II Armée still held the Verdun front but was now under Général Adolphe Guillaumat who appears to have been somewhat reluctant to seek La Gloire. Prodded onward he was given the resources he sought and on 12 August his gunners began eight days of systematic bombardment with nearly 2,255 guns expending 110,000 tonnes of shells upon 5. *Armee*, now under *General der Artillerie* Max von Gallwitz.

The bombardment pulverised the defences, decimating and exhausting the defenders who lost 14,000 casualties (of whom more than half were captured) and were unable to prevent the French retaking Mort Homme and Hill 304. But the attackers were too widely dispersed and Pétain underestimated the vigour of the enemy response leading to an unwelcome, but mercifully brief, battle of attrition which helped push the butcher's bill to nearly 15,000 Poilus, of whom a third were killed, before the operation was closed on 25 August [101].

When the die was cast in June, Guillaumat had only 8 air squadrons, including two fighter, and with his intelligence staff identifying 23 enemy squadrons in the Verdun region (including 5 fighter and 3 bomber) his initial reaction was to demand more fighters[102]. He promptly received a group from Pétain's growing reserve while during the next few weeks the number of corps/reconnaissance squadrons was tripled. He then received another 2 fighter groups, indeed such was the operation's importance that GC 13 was transferred from Flanders in mid August to join GC 14 and GC 15 bringing total fighter strength to 16 squadrons (see Table 1-4) and overall strength to 410 aircraft.

In the aftermath of the Nivelle Offensive, the fighters' apron strings were loosened. On 19 July 1917 Pétain published his '*Note on the use of aviation during limited attacks*' which was split between the artillery and infantry phases. The fighters were now to operate offensively at both high and low altitude although their zone of operations would still be determined by the army commander[103].

At Verdun the front was split into two with GC 14 covering the right bank and GC 15 the left bank, the remaining group acting as reserve. They saturated enemy air space at high and low altitude and quickly clipped the Germans' wings with only 10 combats reported in the first 7 days of August, yet Gallwitz was unable to convince *OHL* of the seriousness of the threat until two days before the bombardment began [104].

With Haig maintaining pressure in Flanders, *OHL* was reluctant to provide any reinforcements and Gallwitz had to make do from the handful of squadrons scraped together by *Heeresgruppe deutscher Kronprinz*. These included three *Jasta*, each supporting a corps sector, which were augmented by *Jasta 23* on 20 July but this was the limit of reinforcement[105].

Reconnaissance proved difficult and to defend German air space the *Kofl 5.Armee*, *Major* Alfred Streccius, who had been *Stofl* of the Eastern Front *9.Armee* the previous summer, relied upon brain rather than brawn using an experienced pilot to control the fighters. He selected *Rittmeister* Konstantin von Braun, who had led the Saxon *Jasta* 24 against the French during the spring and was now anxious to return to the front after 'flying a desk' in *1.Armee Flugpark*[106].

Jagdgruppe von Braun was created on 5 August and controlled not only Gallwitz's fighters but also two *Jasta* of *7.Armee* in the west and one of *Armee Abteilung 'C'* east of Verdun. On 8 August the French recorded 14 combats and more than 80 over the next six days while French corps squadrons, unimpeded until now, were attacked 6 times in the same period despite strong escorts which were retained throughout August as enemy resistance grew[107].

The corps squadrons flew more than 600 artillery co-operation sorties while more than 160 photographic reconnaissance sorties were flown and 1,000 plates exposed from 12–19 August to support artillery fire direction. In the face of stronger enemy defences N23 was forced to fly two photographic sorties on 8 August and from then until 19 August the two army fighter squadrons flew 20 such sorties. As usual enemy balloons were a last minute target with 20 attacked on 18 August[108].

During the bombardment II Armée aircraft flew 2,539 sorties, of which 1,176 were by the fighter squadrons, and in accordance with Pétain's new doctrines, GB 1 entered the lists on 16 August but flew a disappointing 43 sorties and dropped fewer than two tonnes of bombs without loss. Despite the scale of French fighter operations, 2,034 sorties (606 in the three days before the assault) for the loss of five aircraft to 20 August, only a pair of German two-seaters were lost in the period 12–22 August, both before the French assault[109].

When the French attacked on 20 August, Streccius had 37 squadrons (including four *Staffeln* of *Kagohl 2*) with twelve squadrons and *Reihenbildzug 3* under his direct command, the largest concentration of forces supporting *Maasgruppe West* (*VII.Armeee-Korps*) where *Hauptmann* Seraphim's *Grufl 14* had eight squadrons including three *Schusta*. The German airmen fought hard and the French, who flew 610 sorties on the first day, reported 150 combats of which 30 involved corps aircraft but they were well shielded for nearly 39% of all fighter sorties were escort missions. Streccius' fighters and *Flak* claimed seven French aircraft while his contact patrols continued to monitor the situation[110].

The scale of air fighting steadily declined after 20 August, the Germans losing five aircraft by 25 August, and the only intervention of their bombers was a heavy attack upon Verdun on the night of 22/23 August. The defenders' activity may be gauged by the record of *FA 254* (*A*) from 19–22 August when it flew 39 sorties and dropped 763 kilogrammes of bombs while claiming three victories. On 21August the squadron also participated in a new mission which was to grow in importance when *Hauptmann* Seraphim created an ad hoc ground-attack force described as a *Schlachtgeschwader* with *FA(A) 274* to support a *Maasgruppe West* counter-attack on Hill 304 during which it expended 575 kilogrammes of bombs and 7,600 rounds of ammunition[111].

Compared with the previous year's campaign, air operations in 1917 displayed greater specialisation of both squadron and machine. Corps aircraft rarely flew bomber missions or barrage patrols, the bombers concentrated on bombing and the fighters on achieving air superiority. Yet at Verdun both air campaigns were largely confined to the Tactical inner battle with few attempts to strike beyond the balloon lines. An alternative, and more ambitious, approach was developed by the British and in 1918 would be demonstrated in this region by the Americans.

Table 1-4:
Air strength II Armée 15 June – 15 September, 1917

Date	C	F	R	N	GC	GB
June 15	2	4	-	2	-	-
July 15	5	13	-	2	1	-
August 15	6	9	3	2	3	1
September 15	9	8	3	2	3	1

Source: *Armées Françaises X/1*, II Armée entry

Chapter Two

The Foundations of Air Power

Between the first shots of the Verdun bombardment and the guns falling silent at the Armistice, the fortunes of the airmen swung wildly within a framework bounded by organisation, mission and infrastructure. The airmen's successes and failures were also influenced by production and training although these elements lie outside the scope of this book.

Both sides organised their air power around squadrons assigned to each army corps but the corps squadrons' roles varied between the combatants. While the French and Germans organised specialised reconnaissance and artillery squadrons to improve unit efficiency, other combatants combined these functions in their corps squadrons for greater flexibility. Most air services, except the British, had specialised army squadrons augmenting the corps squadrons for deep reconnaissance and to direct very long-range guns of the type described by the French as Artillerie Lourde a Grande Puissance (ALGP)[1].

The British and the Americans also had an air command layer between army and corps level; from 30 January 1916 the British created separate wing headquarters for corps and for army (combat) squadrons, some of the latter including secondary deep reconnaissance roles. Two years later the US Army would establish separate corps and army observation groups to meet its reconnaissance requirements[2].

The Americans had the largest squadrons for corps and army operations while the Germans had the smallest, size being dictated by policy rather than production. German corps (and fighter) squadrons, like most units in their air force, also lacked homogeneous equipment, using several different aircraft models despite the logistical problems. The rationale appears to have been to have the best aircraft for specific tasks but in practice the vulnerable new pilots tended to fly the oldest aircraft[3].

Uniform equipment helped formation flying and eased logistical problems with British and American squadrons having different aircraft models only when they were being re-equipped. While paying lip service to the homogeneity principle, the French did not always follow it: corps squadrons often had several types even in 1918 when Spa-Bi20 had seven Spad 11A2, two Sopwith 1A2 and three twin-engined Letords. In 1917 many 'Nieuport' fighter squadrons had Spad S7 and in September 1918 SPA 167 was created with Spad S7 and Spad S13 ([4]). Barès planned to add four Letords (2A3, 4A3, 5A3) or Caudrons (R4A3, R6A3) to corps and five to artillery squadrons for long-range reconnaissance with secondary bombing and escort missions. At least 54 squadrons received 2 or 3 of them while 3 army squadrons were entirely equipped with the Caudron. The last French wartime attempt to create a three-seater reconnaissance aircraft (A3) led to the Caudron R11 long-range escort[5].

The German philosophy of numerous small squadrons reflected new army doctrines adopted in the autumn of 1916. Flexibility was the key word for the German Army with battlefield missions assigned to divisional task forces using infantry regiment Battle Groups (*Kampfgruppen*). The traditional cumbersome army corps were now headquarters to co-ordinate divisional operations in a sector, becoming giant battlegroups which were often designated Groups (*Gruppen*). These units and commands were augmented by myriad artillery and specialist units under *OHL* control while *Gruppen* and divisions also controlled sub-headquarters such as *Artillerie-Gruppen* and *Artillerie-Untergruppen* (each with a radio), air squadrons as well as kite balloons and *Flak* units[6].

Ideally each army corps/*Gruppe* had a *FA(A)* for both reconnaissance and artillery fire direction and a *Jasta* to shield it, with each division being supported by a *FA(A)* and a *Schutzstaffel* (*Schusta*) or escort squadron. Recognising that in hard-pressed corps sectors the army air commander (*Kofl*) could not control both army and corps air and *Flak* units the Germans came to delegate this task to a *Grufl*. The *Kofl* controlled long-range reconnaissance, fighter and bomber forces but their resources reflected their front's importance and many had only a handful of squadrons[7]. Under Pétain the French adopted a similar approach, although most corps (and artillery) squadrons were directly under army corps or even autonomous divisions on a semi-permanent basis. Operationally the squadrons would be assigned to support specific divisions for a mission such as an offensive[8].

Table 2-1:
Aviation Militaire Française Orders of Battle 1916–1918

Date	Fighter	Bomber	Army	Artillery	Corps	Interior	Escort	Total
January 1916	16	11	15	11	33	4	-	90
November 1916	26	25	9	21	47	7	-	135
February 1917	30	19	15	25	47	13	-	149
April 1918	58	27	4	77	54	15	1	236
November 1918	64	32	11	80	54	10	3	254

Source: Davilla & Soltan 6, 8–9, 10–11, 15–17, 19–20. SHAA A109.

Table 2-2:
RFC/RAF Orders of Battle

Date	Fighter	Bomber	Corps	Total
February 1916	7	-	14	21
July 1916	13	1	15	29
January 1917	21	1	19	41
July 1917	26	6	20	52
January 1918	29	7	19	55
July 1918	40	23	20	83
November 1918	43	24	20	87

Source: Jones VI Appendixes. Appendices XXVIII & XXIX
Note: Fighter includes Fighter-Reconnaissance. Excludes Independent Force and naval support but includes RNAS squadrons attached to RFC wings.

Table 2-3:
USAS Orders of Battle

Date	Pursuit	Bombardment	Observation	Total
May 1918	2	-	2	4
July 1918	7	1	6	14
September 1918	14	1	12	27
October 1918	14	4	14	32
November 1918	20	7	18	45

Source: Maurer. *I*: 18.

'Finding, attacking and destroying' – Fighters

Table 2-4:
German squadron Order of Battle

Date	Fighter	Bomber	Attack/Escort	Corps	Total
April 1916	-	38	-	81	119
October 1916	13	42	-	101	156
April 1917	37	12 (3)	30	116 (44)	195 (47)
March 1918	80 (3)	33	30	153 (20)	296 (20)
November 1918	81 (2)	35	38	140 (15)	294 (17)

Sources: Neumann:74, 64, 65.
Note: Figures exclude home defence units, those in the Middle East and *Reihenbilderzüge*.
Figures in parenthesis show squadrons outside the Western Front. Compare with Table 7–10.

To shield corps aircraft the other basic element of the force structure was the fighter squadron whose importance was reflected in growing numbers. French fighter squadrons in the Zone d'Armées rose from 18.5% of squadrons in January 1916 to 28% in November 1918, while the British figure rose from 33.3 to 49%, with the USAS not far behind (see Tables 2-1, 2-2 and 2-3).

Across the line German fighter strength rose from about 18% of strength in the autumn of 1916 to about 40% (see Table 2-4) by the end of the war[9].

Fighter aircraft were initially scattered among the corps squadrons but from the autumn of 1915 the Allies concentrated their fighters into dedicated squadrons. Initially every French army headquarters had one or two fighter squadrons but from late 1916 the best were combined into groupes de chasse, each of four squadrons (although they might be augmented) to reinforce armies[10].

Eventually the French created 13 groups; with one attached to each army headquarters leaving the autonomous army fighter squadrons, which also had a reconnaissance role, with inferior aircraft. In March 1918 the Belgians created their own three-squadron group, while on 4 May the 1st US Pursuit Group (ultimately with four squadrons) was created followed later by two more[11].

Pétain and Duval took the concept further on 4 February 1918 by creating a fighter wing, 1er Escadre de Combat under GC 15 commander Chef de Bataillon Victor Ménard with GC 15, 18 and 19 followed on 27 February by 2eme Escadre de Combat with GC 11, 13 and 17 under Major Philipe Féquant. Their missions were described as 'Assuring our observation aviation liberty of action over the battlefield' and 'Finding, attacking and destroying enemy aviation.' They were the foundation for mixed task forces, Groupements Ménard and Féquant, which ultimately became the 1er and 2eme Brigades d'Aviation, with both leaders at first also retaining command of their escadres[12].

The British assigned their fighter squadrons to mixed army wings from February 1916 but, with up to nine squadrons, after two years these became increasingly unwieldy. During the summer and autumn of 1918 a second army wing was added to most existing brigades and usually became an all-fighter unit, although II Brigade and IX Brigade created two mixed (fighter/day bomber) wings ([13]). Until August 1916 the Germans had only ad hoc fighter concentrations or *KEKs* and while some of these were expanded into the first *Jasta*, *Jasta 2* and *Jasta 3* were formed from scratch on 10 August 1916. Hoeppner created 37 *Jasta*, most on the Western Front, but finding more than 500 experienced pilots and leaders was a formidable task and the latter were selected for their organisational rather than fighting skills[14].

Of the 35 officers who led *Jasta* in the first quarter of 1917, two-thirds had no air victories. Most were professional officers, 20 came from two-seater units while a third of all *Jasta* leaders (and many pilots) had previously served in *Kagohls*. Throughout the war the Prussian Army especially preferred to have leaders who came from the professional army rather than reservists. In *Jagdgeschwader I* (*JG I*) during 1918 *Leutnant der Reserve* Ernst Udet (30 victories) twice lost out to professional colleagues: firstly to *Leutnant* Erich Löwenhardt (27 victories), then to the outsider *Oberleutnant* Hermann Göring (22 victories), who was also a friend of the German Crown Prince which may have earned him the Pour le Merité. In August 1918 *Leutnant der Reserve* Joseph Veltjens (35 victories) was briefly superseded as commander of *JG II* by regular *Rittmeister* Heinz *Freiherr* von Brederlow (two victories) although the *Rittmeister* soon departed[15].

The *Jasta* were scattered piece-meal among the armies but the success of French fighter groups led the Germans to emulate them by creating larger formations during the early summer. *Kogenluft* preferred flexible *Jagdgruppen* of two to seven *Jasta* and from 1918 attached at least one to each army headquarters on major fronts. But on 26 June 1917 Hoeppner created a permanent unit, *JG I* with four *Jasta*, which was a mirror image of the groupes de chasse. Yet despite its success, real or imagined, it had little impact upon *Luftstreitkräfte* force structure. *JG II* and *JG III* were not created until eight months later, while the Bavarian *JG IV* (the Bavarian air service was semi-autonomous like the Royal Bavarian Army) was converted from *JGr 8* only on 3 October 1918 a month after naval fighter squadrons were combined into *Marine Jagdgeschwader V*[16].

The fighters' prime role was to achieve air superiority and they usually flew patrols; offensive ones behind enemy lines or defensive ones over friendly trenches the latter either active (especially by the *Jasta*) or passive such as barrage patrols which continued to be flown in small numbers until the end of the war. Fighter formations in 1916 were little more than a pack of individual wolves seeking their own prey in swirling dogfights but by the following year pilots tended to operate in pairs. The formation commander, who would sometimes have special markings or fly streamers, would control his men by rocking the aircraft or by using hand gestures, but once battle was joined anarchy reigned. Strongly defended kite-balloons were also attacked but such missions meant that balloon-busting aces, such as Heinrich Gontermann and Frank Luke, were the bravest of the brave[17].

The nature of air combat meant the manoeuvrable biplane or even triplane was the preferred airframe while the faster monoplane, which was structurally suspect, rarely appeared on the Western Front after 1916. Ground-controlled interception appeared from 1916 but did not stimulate development of the faster monoplanes which made better interceptors. The French did briefly re-equip three Nieuport squadrons with Morane-Saulnier MoS 29/27 parasol monoplanes from February 1918 but their unreliable engines meant they too were replaced within three months by Spads. In August 1918 the Germans introduced their own monoplane, the Fokker E.V/D.VIII, but it too was plagued with structural problems[18].

With fighters came the 'aces', a term apparently coined by a French newspaper for any man who had brought down several aircraft although the Germans used the term '*Kanone*' (canon). Between 1915 and 1918 more than 1,550 men (including those in land-based naval fighter squadrons) qualified to become aces on the Western Front by being officially credited with five or more victories. They included four sets of brothers; Germany's Walter and Harry von Bülow-Bothkamp, the Americans August and Paul Iaccacis, Britain's James and John McCudden as well as the renowned Manfred and Lothar von Richthofen. About 1,200 of the aces survived the war, some by only a few weeks, although a few almost saw the second millennium. Several fought in the Second World War during which German naval ace Theodor Osterkamp added six victories while Britain's Gerald Maxwell and American Reed M. Chambers would ultimately fly jets[19].

Most 'aces' victory scores were in single digits, although some claimed double figures, led by the great Manfred von Richthofen, but all shared aggressiveness, bravery and fast reflexes. Some carefully stalked and picked off their prey with a handful of bullets but others were reckless brawlers who would cheerfully examine their bullet-riddled aircraft if they made it back to safety. The careful pilots tended to live longer but ultimately luck played a part. Ernst Udet reportedly clashed with France's greatest ace Georges Guynemer who ran out of ammunition during their battle and Udet avoided Death's boney grasp again a year later when he parachuted to safety from a fatally damaged fighter.

The aces tended to be in their early 20s although, at 18½, Britain's Ridson Bennet may have been the youngest, while Adolphe duBois D'Aische (a Frenchman born in Belgium who achieved six victories), was the oldest at 43. He was one of 175 two-seater pilot and gunner aces including the Iaccacis who each scored 17 victories in Bristol Fighters with No 20 Squadron RAF. The British had the largest number of two-seat aces and two, Mathew Frew and Thomas Harries, became aces firstly on two-seaters and then again in single-seaters. Youth did not automatically mean health: some pilots were physically mutilated and several (including Guynemer) suffered combat fatigue while it is difficult to believe how some men managed to get through the stringent physicals to become pilots. The American William Thaw suffered 20/80 vision, a hearing defect and limited movement in his knee; Germany's Otto Kissenberth wore spectacles to fly, while Britain's Sydney Carlin had a wooden leg!

The aces were drawn from all strata of society; the fathers of Orlando Bridgeman and Robert Grosvenor were English lords, Albert Ball and

Elliot W. Springs were the sons of wealthy manufacturers, while Frederick Libby was a cowboy. Most were of middle-class background which ensured the essential combination of health and education as well as a greater affinity with machines. Virtually all aces were bachelors and of Western European origin during an epoch in which racial superiority was almost the 11th Commandment. An exception was Indra Lal Roy, India's only ace, who was credited with 10 victories in 170 hours flying time (one month) while *Leutnant* Karl 'Carlos' Meyer was born in Venezuela of a German father and Venezuelan mother[20]!

Fuelled by newspapers the air ace phenomenon peaked in 1917 as French and German (but not British) military leaders encouraged public adulation to deflect questioning about the war's overall conduct. Newspaper publishers recognised that their readers required heroes in an age of mass slaughter and the phenomenon may also have been the last flickering of 19th century Gothic romanticism with its images of knightly valour and virtue widely displayed in both art and architecture before the war. When the war's rhythm increased in 1918, the phenomenon seemed to fade although the number of aces on the Western Front doubled. This increase reflected improvements in British training, for they had numerous minor aces, and the appearance of the Americans many of whom had earned their spurs with French and British squadrons.

Allied, but rarely German, fighters were used as escorts but could shepherd their charges little more than 25 kilometres behind the lines. A long-range escort fighter, the Martinsyde Buzzard Ia, was developed by the British but did not enter service before the war's end. Multi-engined escort fighters were used by the French to support their bombers with Groupements Ménard and Féquant having two Caudron R11 escort squadrons, R46 and R246, manned by the best gunners in the Aviation Militaire[21]. There were never more than 40 'gun ships' but they inspired a generation of airmen and designers who failed to emulate the Caudrons' legendary success, the last attempt being the 8th US Air Force's YB-40s in 1943.

The British had more success with two-seat reconnaissance-fighters; first with the Royal Aircraft Factory's FE 2 (which became a valuable light night bomber from the spring of 1917) and then the famous Bristol F2A/B Fighter both of which extended battlefield fighter cover. The Aviation Militaire sought to emulate their allies and issued requirements for a two-seat fighter (C2) aircraft in November 1916 and May 1917 but while the Breguet 17, Hanriot-Dupont HD 3, SEA 4 and Spad S20 were all selected for production only the HD 3 reached the front line in October 1918[22].

The robustness of the Bristol Fighter saw two assigned to Captain Charles Portal's No 16 (Corps) Squadron with I Brigade in March 1918 to provide fire direction for long-range guns. They were so successful that there were plans to add a Bristol Fighter flight to each corps squadron and ultimately to re-equip all corps squadrons with these superb machines. Shortages of aircraft meant only five dedicated flights were created, starting with I Brigade's detachment on 2 July, and no corps squadron was exclusively equipped with the Bristol Fighter. During 1918 radio-telephones allowing two-way voice communication were introduced into a pair of Bristol Fighter squadrons (No 22 and No 88) but a post-war study noted the near impossibility of a formation leader controlling all his men in a dogfight[23].

The Germans used C-types as two-seat fighters quadrupling the numbers in this role during 1916 when the *Kagohls* were the foundation of air defence. By the autumn there were seven *Kagohls* but their failure to defend German air space meant they were replaced by the *Jasta* to whom many *Kagohl* aircrew migrated as *Kasta* numbers contracted to meet a radical role change.

Siegert wanted the *Kagohls* to become specialist bomber units but most crews by late 1916 were not trained for this role. *Luftstreitkräfte* chief-of-staff Thomsen, seeking to salvage something from the wreck, persuaded Hoeppner and *OHL* to convert most of the *Kasta* into escort units for the corps aircraft leaving a cadre for a more effective bomber force and on 1 January 1917 four *Kagohl* (see below) together with half the *Kasta* in *Kagohl* 2 and 4 were disbanded to create 30 *Schusta* with 8 more formed later from the *FA*. By subordinating the *Schusta* to the *FA*, with whom they shared airfields, liaison became closer, raising morale in the corps squadrons. From July 1917 they were re-equipped with manoeuvrable Light C-type (CL) aircraft for which a requirement had been issued a year earlier[24].

The *Schusta* were not a success. They claimed 34 victories in the West during the first half of 1917 but *FA* crews claimed to have shot down 54 enemy aircraft, and the ratio was 1:2 in the FA's favour during April and May. In July and August the *Schusta* were credited with 12 victories and their charges with 29 yet a role change from escort to ground-attack saw the *Schusta* claim more victories against low-flying aircraft, 34 in September compared with 24 by the *FA*[25].

The role changed again as the *Luftstreitkräfte* began its second major expansion programme. Hoeppner quickly recognised that America's entry into the war on 6 April 1917 would ultimately enhance Allied air power. Within two months he persuaded *OHL* to expand his forces in the *Amerikaprogramm* which focused exclusively upon fighters and corps aircraft. He planned to add 57 squadrons and to double the number of *Jasta* but shortages of seasoned timber and scarcities of materials such as copper, nickel, aluminium, zinc and rubber (which would plague German air staffs in the 1930s), hampered execution and only 47 squadrons were created[26].

Although the fighter force was doubled (one *Jasta* was sent to Palestine), Hoeppner was reluctantly forced to accept a dilution of its quality. Fighter pilots were no longer required to have previous front-line experience and instead green recruits were sent directly from the schools. Surprisingly, the failure to expand the *Luftstreitkräfte* proved a blessing in disguise because *Kogenluft* was forced to recognise the value of stronger squadrons and a quarter of the *FA* were expanded to nine aircraft[27].

Ground-attack

Although not part of the *Amerikaprogramm*, ground-attack forces were also strengthened during this period. During the Somme campaign in 1916 both sides had strafed (machine-gunned) ground forces using corps aircraft which the British augmented with fighters. The *FA* were given a tertiary ground-attack role after the winter 1916/1917 but had little spare time while the *Schusta* were specifically instructed to attack enemy troops 'when not employed on the protection of artillery aeroplanes[28].'

Ground attacks grew in importance from the spring of 1917 and by the summer it was a regular feature of air planning, especially for British fighter squadrons. Carrying up to four 20–25 pound (9–11 kilogramme) bombs the fighters operated around the forward-edge-of-battle area (FEBA) and also struck airfields in ever growing numbers. About the same time new regulations encouraged French fighters to emulate their British allies, although they rarely carried bombs[29].

Schustas became increasingly involved in ground-attack missions from the summer of 1917 later forming ad hoc *Schlachtgeschwader* with single-engined bombers to provide close air support and also to strike behind the FEBA as far as the gun line. By November 1917 ground-attack was their prime role and on 23 March (or 27 March) 1918 they were formally renamed *Schlachtstaffeln* (*Schlasta*)[30]. Initially they were dispersed among corps headquarters, but in April 1918 four permanent *Schlachtgeschwader* (*A-D*) were created, each with four *Schlasta*. Their organisation was flexible, although a cadre of *Staffeln* was retained by each *Geschwader* which were joined from the summer by three or four ad hoc *Schlachtgruppen* (*Schlagru*). Simultaneously the *Schlasta* were expanded by about a quarter, new *Staffeln* being created either from *FA* (some direct from the Russian front) or from cadres supplied by other *Schlasta* which were themselves being expanded nominally to nine aircraft. Yet the *Schlachtflieger* failed to strengthen *Luftstreitkräfte* strike power because, even compared with British fighters, they delivered a derisory offensive load. They were essentially aerial Storm Troops whose machine guns were augmented by 12 or so hand grenades or, from June 1918, by five 2kg *Fliegermaus* anti-personnel bombs[31].

British and American ground-attack operations were spearheaded by fighters but their vulnerability to ground fire was widely recognised. With the British the task was monopolised by squadrons whose fighters had poor high-altitude performance such as the Airco DH 5 and Sopwith Dolphin. The British rejected an armoured Sopwith Camel for fear of disrupting production and instead developed the purpose-built Sopwith Salamander which appeared during the autumn of 1918 although few reached the front before the Armistice[32].

In the Aviation Militaire Française independent fighter squadrons attached to armies were sometimes used for tactical ground-attack missions but were augmented during the latter stages of the war by day bomber-squadrons and occasionally the corps squadrons. Duval recognised the need for dedicated ground-attack squadrons and considered producing the Dolphin as the Dauphin before issuing a requirement for two-three seat armoured ground-attack aircraft (S2/3) and Ab 2 (equivalent to German CL) to equip corps squadrons. Only the latter was met by the Lioré et Olivier (LeO) 5 which became the post-war LeO 7[33].

'The most precious intelligence source' – Reconnaissance
Reconnaissance remained the fundamental role of air operations and army leaderships required their 'eyes' to look deep behind enemy lines as well as over the battlefield and record it with photography, described by the French as 'the most precious intelligence source.' Strategic reconnaissance in the Second World War sense barely existed because aeroplanes had limited ranges (although Spad S13 fighters of VIe Armée's SPA 49 flew up to 200 kilometres into enemy territory on photo-reconnaissance missions in 1918) but certainly from 1916 Operational Level reconnaissance became a valuable tool for the generals[34].

High performance aircraft were the key but the Allies had few and their scarcity during the winter of 1916/1917 meant the Franco-British forces suffered the war's worse air reconnaissance failure when they failed to detect the *Siegfriedstellung*. This position was built across the base of the Somme Salient centred upon St Quentin from the autumn of 1916 as part of a strategic move to strengthen the German defence of the Western Front. It was a remarkable feat of military engineering involving 540,000 men and 1,250 trains of engineer stores, although the Rail Troops orchestrated this so carefully that only eight trains a day were added to the rail network, too small an increase to be noticed[35].

Rumours of activity filtered across no-man's-land the airmen were asked to investigate. At this time the French had some 50 unreliable Caudron G6 while the British had 150 FE 2s and the fast new Sopwith Strutters, although even the latter had to operate in formations of four to six as the German fighter threat grew from the autumn of 1916[36].

III Brigade detected work 20 kilometres behind the lines in late October and on 9 November FEs followed what proved to be the northern section of the new line down to Bourlon Wood, south-west of Cambrai. The British concluded it was a switch line, a position at an angle to the original front to protect a flank, and dubbed it the 'Cojeul Switch' although an escaped Russian prisoner reported work south of Bourlon Wood[37].

For intelligence the greatest problem is not gathering information but assessing it and Allied intelligence was confused by the covering positions *Riegel 1, 2* and *3 (R1–3)* which were also discovered on the Somme battlefield close to the frontline. Whispers through the wire still referred to defences south of Cambrai but they were ignored and it was only on 27 November that Trenchard asked 9 Wing to investigate, but from 13 December the Strutter-equipped long-range reconnaissance squadron, No 70, was detached to I Brigade north of the *Siegfriedstellung* and did not return until 2 March 1917[38].

The wing also had to meet GHQ demands to monitor the rail system, supplementing an extensive intelligence network in Belgium. The rail system was also the focus of the IV Brigade's No 22 Squadron which flew more than half the photographic reconnaissance sorties by the four British southern wings. An added complication was the 35-kilometre extension of the British front on New Year's Day 1917 to assist the spring offensive which increased Trenchard's search area to 1,630 square kilometres while his FEs were now based 35 kilometres west of the trenches[39].

The problem of finding the remainder of the *Siegfriedstellung* was due neither to enemy fighters nor to inadequate commitment. Despite snow, sleet, rain, fog, mist and low cloud during the 121 days from December to March the British flew visual and photographic reconnaissance sorties on nearly half (59) especially at the end of winter. Some 405 reconnaissance sorties were flown and 30 aircraft (including 10 escorts) were lost, a rate of 4.9% (see Table 2-5) with the greatest effort and highest losses occurring as the Germans retreated[40]. The losses reflected

Table 2-5:
Reconnaissance sorties by RFC over *Siegfriedstellung* sector

Month	III Brigade	IV Brigade	V Brigade	9 Wing	Total
December 1916	13 (8)	8 (7)	5 (2)	7 (1)	33 (18)
January 1917	23 (18)	46 (35)	16 (12)	-	85 (65)
February 1917	15 (13)	44 (34)	14 (9)	-	73 (56)
March 1917	56 (15)	55 (38)	30 (24)	73 (-)	214 (77)
Total	**107 (54)**	**153 (114)**	**65 (47)**	**80 (1)**	**405 (216)**

Source: RFC brigade work summaries. Note: Parenthesis is photographic.

the nature of the missions, for if aerial reconnaissance is a form of robbery then the Allies at this time were crude muggers relying upon firepower to hack their way through the defenders. FE flights would take some two hours to make the round trip to the *Siegfriedstellung*, up to 105 kilometres behind the original front line, and they ran the gauntlet of the shark-like *Jastas* who could not be kept at bay indefinitely.

The brunt of the search fell on British shoulders and while one of Nivelle's first acts was to order his airmen on 2 January 1917 to co-operate with his allies to seek out the new German fortifications, this brought no concrete results. It was not until 26 January that Brigadier John Charteris, Haig's Intelligence Officer, gave official credence to the existence of what the Allies would call the Hindenburg Line between Arras and Laon. A week later, on 2 February, Nivelle received similar reports from his intelligence service and ordered renewed aerial reconnaissance. The same day British airmen provided the ominous news that the 'Cojeul Switch' extended to St Quentin[41].

This news was later confirmed by No 70 Squadron (which returned to 9 Wing on 2 March), but during February the RFC began to produce a more detailed picture of the fortifications. New work east of Arras caused more confusion, initially being dubbed the 'Drocourt-Quéant Switch' until it was realised it was actually the *Wotanstellung* designed to protect the northern end of the *Siegfriedstellung*. Its proximity to Douai (home of Manfred von Richthofen's *Jasta 11*) made reconnaissance hazardous and it was not completely photographed until the beginning of April with more time elapsing before the discovery that it extended northwards into the *4.Armee* zone.

At least Haig had a fairly accurate trace of the new positions, which was more than Nivelle did. By the time GQG introduced the Strutter it was on the verge of obsolescence and unable to provide effective long-range reconnaissance. Haig, on the other hand, was better served and the replacement of the FE by the DH 4 from the spring of 1917 revolutionised British reconnaissance allowing a single aircraft to perform the task which had once taken gaggles of FEs.

As German ace Kurt Wolff noted in an official memorandum issued by *Kogenluft* for squadrons in the West: 'For long-range reconnaissance, mostly (the British) use a fast machine which, through its speed alone, is almost impossible to shoot down.' On 25 May, for example, Lieutenant F. McD. C Turner and 2nd Lieutenant R. de R. Brett of the DH 4-equipped No 55 Squadron flew a 320 kilometre photographic mission from Le Cateau to Maubeugre to Mons to Tournai to Lille at a speed of 130 km/h taking photographs with a wide angle camera from a height of 5,200 metres. However Wolff was pessimistic about the aircraft's invulnerability for on 10 May No 55 Squadron lost two DH 4s to *Flak*[42].

The DH 4 allowed Trenchard to resume photographing those

airfields that had been neglected due to the Arras campaign, and May Day alone saw new pictures for files on 10 airfields. Lone reconnaissance missions usually evaded the defences and during the Flanders campaign in 1917 only four were lost on such missions. But because these missions were the responsibility of British bomber squadrons, the reconnaissance effort diluted Trenchard's bombing campaign and in September 1917 accounted for nearly half the 100 sorties flown by No 57 Squadron. Even FE bomber squadrons were drafted with the first-night reconnaissance being flown by No 101 Squadron on 26/27 August [43].

The Germans converted a dozen *FA* into dedicated photographic reconnaissance units, *FA (Lichtbild)*, which were expanded from six aircraft to the higher (nine aircraft) organisation during the *Amerikaprogramm*. They were usually attached to *Armee Oberkommandos* to monitor activities especially rail and troop movements, in order to discern enemy intentions. A typical three-hour mission, flown by *Hauptmann* Baron von Lowenstern of *FA 270 (Lb)* on 24 March 1918, followed the major railroads between Reims and Belfort and such missions were flown on every flyable day[44].

From the winter of 1916/1917 the *FA (Lichtbild)* began to receive Rumpler C.V high-altitude reconnaissance aircraft supporting *Heeresgruppen* and acting like cat burglars compared with their Allied contemporaries. They had modified electrically-powered movie cameras, *Reihenbilder*, which used slowly-moving celluloid films instead of photographic plates to take single images. Such was their success that they began to be concentrated in special units, *Reihenbilderzüge*, with the first two created in July 1917 and five more in the following months [45].

The Rumplers could photograph a strip 100 kilometres long and several kilometres wide flying high above Allied fighters with impunity; indeed only eight appear to have fallen in combat[46]. In the bitter cold and thin air the crews survived with the aid of electrically-heated suits and oxygen from a compressed-air cylinder sucked through a straw, in aircraft which were the predecessors of the U-2 and SR-71.

The *Reihenbilderzüge* cued the *FA (Lb)* whose plate cameras produced sharper and more detailed images. The importance of these specialised units grew during 1918 as the *FA*'s expertise in photography declined as the growing strength of the Allied Blockade reduced supplies of key chemicals which meant the Empire's dwindling stocks of photographic plates had to be exploited more efficiently. Long-range reconnaissance resources may have been further concentrated for by 21 March 1918 there existed an *Aufklärungsgruppe* under an *Oberleutnant* Fricke[47].

Preparations for the spring offensive of 1918 saw German reconnaissance activity intensify from the New Year and on 26 February *OHL* demanded even more missions especially around the Anglo-French boundary although extra sorties were flown along the whole front to confuse the enemy. Balloons were used to take photographs up to 30 kilometres behind the enemy lines, while to collate the information Hoeppner had 4,000 cartographers[48]. They discovered that Haig's weakest defences were in the Somme valley, formerly occupied by the French, and here the Germans concentrated overwhelming strength. Silent as a snake, the assault forces assembled at the last minute using 10,400 trains with men and material dispersed from stations immediately upon arrival.

Concealment was vital, and by day troops were to be marched in every conceivable direction in a vain attempt to confuse 'the cunning English'. Some German aircraft and balloons even monitored their own lines to ensure camouflage was maintained and that no new tracks were created. However, once the German Army launched its first two offensives the *Luftstreitkräfte*'s long-range reconnaissance squadrons were unable to keep track of Allied movements, although there was some compensation with the discovery of weak French defences in the Chemin des Dames leading to a third offensive which smashed through VI Armée late in May[49].

Aerial reconnaissance influenced fundamental changes in defences during 1918 with growing emphasis upon concealing positions from preying eyes. At Arras, British machine guns were protected by 'spider web' wire ,which was invisible in photographs, and in March these defences helped to smash the German offensive *Unternehmen 'Mars'* within a day. When the Germans attacked in the Chemin des Dames, two months concealed positions built by British troops escaped the hurricane bombardment and were discovered intact four years later. Across no-man's-land during the autumn of 1918 the Germans increasingly relied upon scattered and concealed positions with hidden wire barriers[50].

For the French, the Chemin des Dames debacle in May 1918 was partially due to the failure of their long-range reconnaissance squadrons whose reports had earlier helped convince Pétain that the German main offensive would be in Champagne, causing him to hold back troops who should have reinforced Haig. During 1917 Caudrons and Letords, augmented by camera-equipped Nieuports and Spads of army fighter squadrons, probed up to 60 kilometres behind the lines but during the second half of the year they were augmented by high performance Bréguet 14A2s. In May 1918 the VI Armée commander, Général Denis-August Duchêne, had been diligent in dispatching his reconnaissance aircraft (see Chapter Six) but German preparations were well concealed and shielded by bad weather in the final days[51].

As the German troops flooded towards the Marne, the French opted for a radical change in long-range air reconnaissance. For some time Capitaine Paul-Louis Weiller, former commander of BR224 and now the reconnaissance advisor at Général Ferdinand Foch's inter-Allied headquarters, had claimed that long-range reconnaissance could detect enemy intentions up to a month in advance. A former gunner, Weiller was a pioneer both of aerial photography and cartography, having been an observer then a pilot, but his claims had been contemptuously ignored until sheer desperation forced Foch to listen[52].

Following the Chemin des Dames debacle BR220, attached to the recently established Division Aérienne, was assigned the long-range reconnaissance role specifically for Foch's headquarters. Flying almost daily, initially in trios and later with single very-high-altitude sorties, BR 220 examined the front. For detailed analysis the SRA delivered prints to 30 graduates of the École des Beaux Arts, who each specialised in one of six sectors. Weiller was especially looking for hospitals and hangars whose presence, together with those of fighters and bombers, indicated an imminent offensive.

These techniques helped to detect and to smash the last German offensive in July 1918 and Weiller was given his own groupement with two squadrons. He would meet Foch's chief-of-staff, Général Maxime Weygand, almost daily to provide clues on German plans to withdraw. Appropriately, Foch made him an officer of the Legion d'Honneur on 11 November but also classified the whole project top secret in a vain attempt to maintain the national technological lead.

As the Allies advanced during the late summer and autumn their airmen probed German defences, discovering they existed in name only. Much of this work was in daylight and was generally a secondary task for bombers. Visual night reconnaissance had appeared at Verdun in 1916 and required flares whose quality was vital; indeed a post-war study concluded that short-burning flares hindered British night reconnaissance[53].

Spies and Pigeons

Allied aircraft also supported the espionage network which included the rail-watchers. Ordinary combat squadrons delivered agents and France's Jules Charles Toussaint of MS 3 received a Légion d'Honneur for flying seven missions from March 1915 onwards as well as three daylight retrievals. The hazards of night landings and take-offs meant that from 1916 agents were also parachuted behind the lines from Nieuport 12 or Strutters. A damaged Strutter of N62 was burned by its crew on 5 April 1917 but the 'observer' was later captured carrying a rucksack with eight carrier pigeons and their food, a signal lamp and a money-belt with French and German currency[54].

By the first half of 1915 the French had flown 28 special operations missions, some with saboteurs carrying cases of dynamite, and only one aircraft was lost. In the spring of 1918 Spa-Bi215 supporting 311e Regiment d'Artillerie Lourde was also involved in special operations landing agents at one site and evacuating from another after four or five days. Unmarked Dorand ARs were also used for these missions and French Intelligence may have activated Escadrille 137 in the Nancy area as a dedicated special operations unit[55].

The British effort is better documented beginning in November 1914 using volunteer pilots from various squadrons although the task was gradually assigned to 9 (GHQ) Wing. Initially agents were landed behind the lines but after losing four aircraft in mid 1916 Trenchard refused to commit any more, although GHQ pressure forced him to change his mind the following spring[56].

An alternative way of delivering agents was demonstrated on 8/9 March 1917 Lieutenant William Reed of No19 Squadron dropped an agent from a Spad S7 'by Guardian Angel parachute.' But parachuting was unpopular with agents as they had to sit on the wing strapped to a strut then slide off it when signalled. It was also difficult to hide the parachute after landing and, when unconcealed parachutes signed several men's death warrants, Intelligence demanded a return to landings.

Despite Trenchard's opposition a Special Duty Flight with six BE 2 and BE 12 (one for parachuting agents) and 30 men was created in late April 1917 under Captain John Woodhouse as a dedicated special operations unit. During the first half of May three agents were landed and there were three or four sorties a month during July and August with mixed success. On 9/10 August Woodhouse returned with his passenger after a six-hour mission plagued by searchlights while a BE 12 was lost after becoming trapped in mud after landing an agent[57].

An alternative was to attach agents to balloons, which exploited the prevailing westerly winds and floated across the lines where the men landed by parachute. With Trenchard's support, at least seven men, some carrying lightweight radios, drifted over the trenches, but the radio receivers were defective and at least one agent was caught and executed[58].

In the absence of reliable lightweight radios, homing pigeons offered a more reliable means of communication with the advantage that pigeon-rearing was common in northern France and Belgium allowing birds to be concealed in local lofts. By the spring of 1916 agents were receiving baskets of pigeons, one of the first being delivered by III Brigade's Captain Morton of No 8 Squadron west of Havrincourt, where there would be heavy fighting during the Battle of Cambrai in November 1917. On the night of 7/8 July 1916 there were experiments to see if pilots could be guided to the drop zone by electric torch and these proved so successful that a month later it was used to drop more birds west of Havrincourt[59]. Aircraft on reconnaissance missions would also parachute baskets of birds with a copy of that day's French newspapers to show this was not a German ruse. This encouraged daring civilians to fill in military questionnaires and return them attached to the bird's leg. The average rate of return was 40%, of which half had useful military information.

From March 1917 baskets of pigeons were also dropped by balloon into areas of particular interest and from a flock dropped on the night of 8/9 April, a quarter returned by midday many with useful information. German counter-measures and tighter controls reduced the effectiveness of this intelligence source during 1917. By June 1918 pigeon drops were carried out only on bright moonlit nights and, according to the last commander of I Flight, Captain Percival Lawrence, these were the only special duty operations carried out during the latter stages of the war.

German aircraft were used for special missions on the Eastern Front (including dynamiting a railway) and in Palestine. A German directive on the use of aircraft in support of armies published in May 1917 stated in Paragraph 102: 'One worthy mission is for aircrew who land far to the rear of the enemy to blow up important rail lines with explosives. ...Escort will be provided by one or more aircraft which, during the sabotage mission, will shoot enemy posts and rural citizens from the air.' A hint of German special operations flown on the Western Front is suggested by a French decree on 23 July 1918 ordering citizens to report to the authorities immediately if an aircraft landed outside a military airfield and, if possible, to detain the occupants although, this may relate to damaged military aircraft forced down (Chapter Six) in French territory[60].

Table 2-7:
Bombing on the Western Front in 1917 (tonnes)

Month	French tonnage		British tonnage		Totals	
	Day	Night	Day	Night	Allied	German
January-March	–	72.0	77.0	5.2	154.2	114.0
April	0.5	37.8	22.3	9.3	69.9	6.5
May	8.6	72.1	26.3	14.1	121.1	66.8
June	6.8	46.2	27.3	23.7	104.0	84.5
July	9.9	56.5	35.7	69.8	171.9	186.8
August	8.2	40.2	41.1	74.3	163.8	153.0
September	28.6	125.8	58.0	147.9	360.3	269.0
October	8.1	28.7	53.4	118.6	208.8	461.4
November	3.1	5.6	17.6	28.1	54.4	210.3
December	15.3	40.5	13.2	48.6	117.6	94.0
Total	**89.1**	**525.4**	**371.9**	**539.6**	**1,526.0**	**1,646.3**

Sources: UKNA Air 1 881/204/5/600–599. SHAA 129 Dossier 1. *Nachrichtenblätter*. Figures from latter are incomplete after March 1917. RFC brigade/wing work summaries (III Brigade incomplete for May and June). British figures include RNAS operations in support of land forces but exclude Independent Force. Note. Figures below 500 kilograms rounded down, figures above 500 kilogrammes rounded up.

'A definite moral and material effect' – Bombing
Intelligence and air reconnaissance helped to fill bomber target files for bombers with most of the bombs dropped in western Europe being in direct or indirect support of armies and navies. Other bombs were expended on strategic attack; the destruction of the enemy's political

will and sinews of war, but while this would dominate post-war writing and influence air power doctrine it is a subject outside the scope of this book [61].

The 25,000–30,000 tonnes of bombs dropped by Western Front bombers between 1916 and 1918 (see Tables 2-7 and 2-8) were mostly on Operational (*Operativ* in German) level missions. These were succinctly described by I Armée headquarters which on 1 July 1917 ordered its bomber squadrons 'to destroy by means of systematic bombing hostile airfields (so as to compel squadrons to move continually), bivouacs (especially artillery), depots, stations, highways, roads, railroads and any kind of establishment in the enemy's rear zone.' They were Operational both because of the nature of the missions and because they were conducted at, and commanded by, army/army group level, although the supreme command (GQG, GHQ and *OHL*) provided overall direction and co-ordination[62].

Table 2-8:
Allied bombing on the Western Front in 1918 (tonnes)

Month	French		British		US (day)	Total
	Day	Night	Day	Night		
January	35.8	26.3	14.3	28.5	-	104.9
February	62.9	50.4	26.3	44.2	-	183.8
March	66.0	104.6	145.1	145.1	-	460.8
April	71.8	73.3	211.3	110.2	-	466.6
May	137.1	347.1	240.1	157.0	-	881.3
June	222.4	383.9	290.2	181.7	2.7	1,080.9
July	189.6	293.2	215.7	216.2	-	914.7
August	268.7	336.7	146.5	331.7	19.5	1,103.1
September	132.3	208.9	159.2	248.2	35.6	784.2
October	287.3	248.2	169.1	207.9	32.3	944.8
November	182.1	37.7	13.4	48.0	10.6	291.8
Total	**1,656**	**2,110.3**	**1,631.2**	**1,718.7**	**100.7**	**7,216.9**

Sources: SHAA A116. SHAA A128. British brigade war diaries supplemented by wing work summaries but figures missing for IX Brigade in May and November. 1st Day Bombardment Group history, US NA M990/14.
Note: Bombs in tonnes with figures below 500 kilogrammes rounded down, figures above 500 kilogrammes rounded up. French night bomber tonnage includes Italian GB 18. During 1918 the Germans dropped 5,800 tonnes of bombs. *Weltkrieg XIV*:723.

The distinction between Operational and Strategic attacks was blurred because the former included individual factories and utilities while the latter could have a direct impact upon operations. For example, from the summer of 1917 until March 1918 the French dropped more than 155 tonnes of bombs on factories and the rail system between Metz and the Saar valley. The objective was to disrupt steel production but the attacks also threatened the German Army logistics system for which Metz was the eastern hub[63].

Early in December 1916 *OHL* ordered the *Heeresgruppen* and *Armee-Oberkommando* to use *Kagohl* purely for bombing, noting that industrial targets would be attacked and it might also consider attacks upon Paris. The first campaign was a strategic assault with Operational benefits upon the French rail network from 2/3 February 1917 to support the unrestricted U-boat blockade which ultimately brought America into the war[64]. Believing the British would unload ships in France's southern ports and move cargoes by rail, the whole German bomber force was used to interdict the main lines running parallel to the front until the spring. Paris was another grey area being both the heart of France and a major production centre, especially of aircraft, and during 1918 there were 483 bomber sorties against the city although only half the 22 tonnes of bombs lifted from the airfields seem to have struck the metropolis[65].

The German bomber renaissance from December 1916 sought to enhance its capability to strike the enemy throughout his operational depth, a concept which *General* Walter Wever made the raison d'etre for the *Luftwaffe* two decades later. Hoeppner was undoubtedly advised by Siegert and *Kagohl* leaders such as *Oberstleutnants* Alfred Keller and Ernst Brandenburg to make the 'Big Bird' twin-engined bombers (*Grossflugzeuge* or G-types) the foundation of the new arm. Recognising that the seven *Kagohls* lacked both the training and equipment for bombing, Hoeppner, like a good gardener, slashed dead wood to stimulate growth and began a considerable investment in both time and resources[66].

The reorganisation of the *Kampfverbände* was due to take place on New Year's Day 1917 but for some reason – possibly to assert its independence – the Bavarian War Ministry jumped the gun by a day and its *Kagohl* 6 was split into *Schusta* 22–28. *Kagohls* 5 and 7 were disbanded on schedule while *Kagohl* 3 became *Gruppenflieger* 3. The remaining *Kagohl*s were reduced to half their former size; three in the West (*Kagohl 2, 4* and half of *Kagohl 1*) and the other half of *Kagohl 1* in the Balkans from whence it returned to the West in late April to become the new *Kagohl 3* on 3 April[67].

The complex 'Big Birds' were slow to arrive and single-engined C-type two-seaters were used as bombers by both *Kasta* and corps squadrons in 1917. The latter had triumphed during the summer of 1916 when *Hauptmann* Hempel's *FFA 40* (later *FA (A) 257*) destroyed 9,000 tonnes of British ammunition at the Audicq depot, north-west of St Omer on the night 20/21 July. The British lost 6% of their total monthly ammunition consumption leaving some heavy guns dangerously short at the height of the Somme campaign. GHQ then redistributed ammunition among smaller sites which proved less vulnerable to bombing[68].

The *FA*s' bombing role declined as the flock of 'Big Birds' grew and by late 1917 the single-engined bombers were confined to retaliatory attacks upon targets in eastern France. Yet in the first quarter of 1917 the corps squadrons contributed 62% of the 114 tonnes dropped by German aircraft on the Western Front. Of 70.7 tonnes dropped by the *FA*s in this period, 66% was delivered by squadrons supporting the four armies opposite the BEF. Meanwhile *Kagohl* strength grew and by the end of April 1917 the *Feldheer* had some 70 twin-engined bombers including reserves although about half the 85–90 front line bombers appear to have been single-engined. British intelligence claimed each *Staffel* of *Kagohl 4* had only two G-types; *Kagohl 1* certainly had C-type aircraft in June and during that month both *Kagohl 3* and *Kagohl 4* still had only five *Kasta*[69].

It was not until the summer of 1917 that the majority of the German strike force were 'Big Birds' but just as this was being achieved the *Kagohl* were again expanded. Consequently there were never enough 'Big Birds' so C-types were retained, especially after another reorganisation of the bomber force into *Bombengeschwader der OHL* (*Bogohl*) on 18 December 1917 when *Bogohl 5, 6* and *7* were formed although, possibly to clip the Bavarian War Ministry's wings, its *Bogohl 8* was not formed until 15 April. From spring 1917 giant R-type (three engines or more) bombers began operational evaluation in the East and they arrived on the Western Front in mid August. There were never more than 16 in the West and they were used both for Operational

Table 2-6:
Night operations over the British front May–October 1918

Month	Nights	Sorties	Bombs dropped	Casualties Killed	Injured	Victory claims
May	22	896	3,720(2,028)	530	1,353	27
June	25	572	2,313(1,226)	103	406	9
July	22	564	2,177(590)	179	424	14
August	21	854	3,287(745)	179	501	23
September	21	512	3,001(253)	120	259	24
October	16	316	1,587(-)	41	61	20
Total	**108**	**3,714**	**16,085(4,842)**	**1,152**	**3,004**	**117**

Source: UKNA Air 1/2267/209/70/38.
Notes: Bomber sorties are contemporary estimates. Bombs dropped figures in parenthesis are upon lines of communication. Claims figures in parenthesis are for night fighters.

Level missions and for strategic attacks upon England flying 102 sorties and delivering nearly 104 tonnes of bombs[70].

With more than 160 bombers the Germans inflicted great damage, especially upon the BEF's logistics infrastructure which was crammed into a narrow triangle bounded by the front line, the River Somme and the Channel. During the Ypres campaign of 1917 it was even more compressed behind the city and for German bombers it was like shooting fish in a barrel. Edmonds later wrote: 'Seldom, if ever before, had bombing from the air produced such a definite moral and material effect[71].'

In the following year the attacks '. were more numerous, were made in greater force, extended over a wider area, and the bombs dropped were much heavier.' The railway system came under especially heavy pressure with lines cut, bridges hit, locomotives and rolling stock damaged yet the trains continued operating even as bombs fell. Although French railway authorities adjusted traffic to the raiders' movements, a single aircraft could still disrupt traffic for four hours without dropping a bomb while successive alarms could paralyse movements all night with an inevitable impact upon supply movements, often at crucial periods[72].

The problem grew worse during the shorter summer nights in 1918 (see Table 2-6) as the rate of bombardment increased. From the night of 21 May until dawn of 2 June there were 100 raids in which some 80 tonnes of bombs were dropped causing 663 casualties, including 245 dead. The raids, combined with the land advance, forced the British to move facilities, 600,000 tonnes of stores and 250,000 personnel westwards beyond bomber range and GHQ even considered evacuation to England[73].

The calmness of women soldiers and nurses under air attack (19 were killed on the British front from 21 May to 2 June) deeply impressed men in those sexually chauvinist times and contributed to the cause of post-war women's suffrage in both the United States and Great Britain. Although hospitals were not deliberately targeted, nurses perished because they were working close to legitimate military targets as at Etaples where 182 medical staff and patients were killed and 643 wounded during May 1918. Bombs were no respecter of rank, with Haig's and Pétain's headquarters both being targeted; three nights of attacks by *Bogohl 2* in late March forced GQG from Compiègne to Provins east of Paris[74].

Until mid summer 1918 more than half the German bombs dropped on the British (see Table 2-6) struck communications. But from July only a quarter of the bombs fell on communications targets because bombers were increasingly used as substitute artillery, a pattern repeated by the *Luftwaffe* on the Russian front from the autumn of 1942. Yet the rail network still suffered and the Allies feared serious disruption, indeed by October attacks upon junctions hindered their movements while railheads were sometimes rendered unusable. Haig's supplies fell far behind the rapidly advancing front line and poor roads meant motor traffic could not take up the slack[75].

Germany's use of aeroplanes rather than airships for Operational and Strategic missions seems surprising given Germany's pre-war technological advantage. Before the war Count Ferdinand von Zeppelin developed effective dirigibles, airships with gas cells encased in an aluminium or wooden framework. But they were vulnerable to the elements and defences while Thomsen's scepticism about them was confirmed by their failure during the Verdun bombing campaign (see Chapter One). The German Army flew only a few dirigible missions over France in 1916 and 1917 with the last on 16/17 February 1917 when *Hauptmann* Sommerfeldt's *LZ 107* flew a 1,300 kilometre 9½ hour round trip to Boulogne to drop 1.4 tonnes of bombs. Count Zeppelin died just as Army airships were transferred to less demanding fronts and a few months later *OHL* dissolved its airship service to conserve and to recycle scarce resources[76].

Allied experience with semi-rigid airships, whose gas cells were attached to an aluminium or wooden frame, mirrored that of their enemies. During 1916 the French flew 14 sorties, some to support the Verdun defenders, and two airships were shot down. The loss of a third on 23/24 February 1917 led GOG to transfer the survivors to the Navy the following day[77].

The French were quicker than the Germans to recognise that the aeroplane was a more reliable bomb platform and by the summer of 1916 had six bomber groups (GB 1–4, GBM 5, 6) and the equivalent of a seventh. But the day bomber-force was shackled with poor aircraft and between May and October 1917 nearly 81% of bombs (see Table 2-7) were delivered at night. Yet despite many setbacks by the summer of 1918 Duval had developed substantial day (GB 3, 4, 5, 6, 9) and night (GB 1, 2, 7, 8, 10, 51) forces[78].

The growing importance of bombers led Duval to concentrate them into powerful strike forces by creating, in March 1918, 12e Escadre (GB 5, 6 and 9) and 13e Escadre (GB 3, 4) together with a night force consisting of Groupements Villomé (GB 2, GB 18), Chabert (GB 1, 7, 51) and Laurens (GB 8, 10), the last two formally designated 11e and 14e Escadres. Duval influenced US bomber development and the two American day bombardment groups activated by the Armistice mostly followed French doctrine[79].

However Duval lacked heavy bombers, receiving only one squadron of licence-built Italian triple-engined Caproni Ca 1/3 from February 1916 and assigning them in July 1917 to GB 2 where they operated with VB 101. A second squadron was formed in February 1918 and GB 2 became a dedicated heavy bomber unit the following June. Consequently, in December 1917 the French eagerly accepted an Italian offer of the Caproni-equipped Gruppo Bombardemento 18 (Capitano Renato de Riso) only to discover that its three squadrons had only 12 bombers between them and even then they did not become operational until March 1918. Général Noël Éduard de Castelnau, the driving force behind French strategic bombing, would complain on 22 August 1918 about the lack of Italian commitment compared with the French and by November the two groups were operating independently, with Gruppo 18 (known to the French as GB 18) having been transferred to 11e Escadre. By the Armistice GB 2 had flown 660 sorties and dropped 600 tonnes of bombs, some in support of the AEF. From August 1918 the Capronis were augmented by two Farman F 50 BN 2 squadrons of GB 1 while the Caudron C23 BN 3 was about to enter service at the time of the Armistice[80].

The British were slow to form bomber squadrons and usually dispersed them because bombing was regarded as a tool to split enemy air power, the only concentration being 9 Wing which augmented brigades in major operations. In 1916 the RFC lacked a purpose-built day bomber and until the DH 4s introduction in 1917 it relied upon a combination of multi-task 'combat' aircraft (such as the Martinsyde G102 Elephant) and corps aircraft. The latter were usually flown solo which made them even more vulnerable to fighters although they continued to augment the dedicated bombers even in 1918. Another problem for RFC commander General Hugh Trenchard was the Army's belief that single-engined day bombers were better than heavy night bombers which persisted until evidence to the contrary was produced by the Royal Navy in August 1917[81].

Some RFC leaders were especially enthusiastic about using corps squadrons for bombing, notably I Brigade commander Brigadier Gordon Shephard who, at a conference on 21 November 1916, proposed assigning half of each squadron to bombing. There were no objections and Shephard, the first British 'bomber baron', practised what he preached with his squadrons dropping 6.7 tonnes of bombs or 75% of the total delivered by the RFC during the first quarter of 1917. The brigade continued this policy even after he was killed in an air crash on 19 January 1918, and on 16 February 1918 four lumbering RE 8 'bomb trucks' were lost to fighters[82].

But British day bomber strike power was diluted by the despatch of small formations – indeed even in the first half of 1918 most bomber missions were flown in flight or half-squadron strength with six to nine aircraft. Demands for reconnaissance also undermined the offensive policy, even during crises and these missions accounted for 24% of 216 sorties by 9 Wing's bomber squadrons in the period 1–20 March 1918. In these circumstances it is not surprising that during late 1918 Bristol

Fighters were sometimes pressed into the day bomber role[83].

Trenchard believed he was aiding airmen and soldiers by striking all along the line and delegated targeting to brigade commanders. This policy was first questioned during the Third Ypres campaign in the summer of 1917 when Haig's intelligence staff considered surgical strikes against the enemy rail network but there was no commitment to concentrate forces on specific targets. Despite growing disquiet in London about the use of Trenchard's strike arm, Haig refused to interfere but the pressure for a revision of bombing policy grew early in 1918[84].

The details are obscure and may have reflected the Army leadership's growing alarm at the emergence of the RAF and fears that the new service would ignore the ground struggle. On 16 February with a major German offensive imminent the Chief of the General Staff, General Sir William Robertson, condemned 'spasmodic bombing' and demanded a concentration of effort. He wanted marshalling yards, rail repair facilities as well as large logistics centres to be attacked, while rail traffic would be interdicted only when major ground operations had begun to ensure maximum impact upon enemy strategy[85]. It was Trenchard's successor, Major-General John Salmond, who implemented this directive but only partially and the bomber squadrons remained dispersed. In April Salmond's chief-of-staff, Brigadier Philip Game, was separately approached by Colonel Maurice Wingfield (the logistics commander for the 2nd Army's General Sir Herbert Plumer) and transportation expert Major-General Sir Philip Nash about cutting rail lines supporting German offensives. Game, who preferred striking rail junctions rather than cutting individual lines, tried to fob off Nash by claiming he lacked bombers, but Nash and Wingfield were persistent and the latter had Plumer's support[86].

Changes were forced upon the RAF during the summer as a result of improved inter-Allied command arrangements including Foch's appointment as supreme Allied commander. During April the Inter-Allied Transportation Council studied plans to disrupt the enemy rail network by striking key marshalling yards, stations and sections of track within 80 kilometres of the front. The council drew up a list of suitable sites and sent its recommendations for the British front to Salmond who again dismissed the scheme as impractical. Plumer disagreed, and with the enemy concentrating opposite him in June as *OHL* prepared a new assault ('*Hagen*') on the British lines, he pleaded with Haig for massed attacks upon rail 'choke points'. Although in favour, Haig delayed a decision because IX Brigade was supporting the French on the Marne Salient but with its return imminent Salmond was summoned to a meeting which included Haig's chief-of-staff Major-General Sir Herbert Lawrence on 19 June (Haig's birthday)[87].

Haig had long been a loyal supporter of his airmen provided he felt they were giving him adequate support and at this meeting he appears to have been quite critical of the RAF. He demanded that Salmond's bombers concentrate on a few decisive targets day and night because 'we have squandered our tons of bombs on many trivial objectives.' On 23 June, two days after IX Brigade returned, Haig demanded a carefully monitored experimental offensive upon rail targets opposite Plumer's front. IX Brigade dropped 106 tonnes of bombs within a week but had to break off again to support the French and the experiment was not repeated, although Salmond does appear to have used the brigade as a concentrated strike force in later operations[88].

Pétain took the concept of paralysing the enemy rail system further on 5 September 1918 when he presented Foch with a plan to exploit Allied numerical superiority. To support the great offensives later in the month he proposed concentrating his own night bombers on targets opposite the central front while Salmond's attacked those opposite the Allied left and Trenchard bombed rail junctions in Alsace-Lorraine. Because air commanders were granted considerable autonomy and discretion the plan appears to have been only partially executed during the autumn but it would herald the kind of air offensive which would wreck western Europe's rail systems from 1944[89].

The fears of both the British and French generals that the creation of strategic bombing forces would deprive them of air support were partially justified. Duval was especially sceptical and when he learned of plans to establish the Independent Force in eastern France he famously asked: 'Independent of whom, of God?' By the time of the Armistice, the Independent Force had five of the eight RAF heavy bomber squadrons in France but its reluctant commander, Trenchard, ensured it flew mostly Operational Level missions, many supporting the AEF[90].

Big bombers usually meant larger loads and bigger bombs. In 1916 most bombs were about 10 kilogrammes which remained the mostly common ordnance, although both the Germans and the British quickly introduced 50- and 100-kilogramme munitions. During 1917 the Germans introduced even larger ordnance, the first 300- kilogramme bomb being dropped on the Western Front by the beginning of September 1917 while Giants occasionally dropped 1-tonne bombs in 1918. British single-engine day bombers carried up to twelve 200–25 pound (9.11-11.3 kilogramme) then either two 112-pound (50.8 kilogramme) or a single 230- pound (104 kilogramme) bombs. Night bombers carried heavier loads: the FEs might carry three 112-pound or up to twelve 25-pound bombs or a mixture of one 112-pound and eight 25-pound while the Handley Pages frequently carried 100–16 112-pounders. During late 1918 larger ordnance was introduced with a 1,600-pound (725 kilogramme) bomb dropped by No 207 Squadron on 6/7 August and a 1,700-pound (816 kilogramme) one month later [91].

The French used large day bomber formations not only because of doctrine and the need for protection but also because they lacked bombs larger than 50 kilogrammes. In 1917 the Sopwith 1B1 Strutter carried only eight 10-kilogramme (120mm) bombs while the Voisins could carry eighteen of them or a dozen 25-kilogramme (155mm) or six 50-kilogramme (200mm). Even the formidable Bréguet 14B2 carried only twenty-eight 10-kilogramme or a maximum thirty-two 8-kilogramme (115mm) bombs[92].

The Cloak of Night
Both sides' formations were rarely over enemy lines for more than two hours because most targets were between 15 and 70 kilometres from the front and many within 40 kilometres, this proximity of targets allowing some German pilots to fly six sorties a night. Navigation was a combination of map, compass and dead reckoning, although on all but the darkest nights it was possible for low-flying aircraft to follow rivers and roads and to identify towns and villages. Starlight and moonlight were augmented by flares to aim bombs although on 8 June 1918 one RAF officer suggested using bright flares to blind searchlight teams, possibly the genesis of 'Window'[93]. From 1917 visual navigation aids supported both sides' night bombers through networks of static and mobile beacons ('lighthouses') augmented in the German case by searchlights, flares and tracer bursts. By the end of the war the RAF planned to use Royal Navy radio beacons in eastern England and French ones around Paris and Lyons for long-range missions into Germany[94].

The cloak of night protected many bomber crews but they were not invincible and from 1917 the defences were strengthened with guns, searchlights and sound locators. Night fighting and night interdiction sorties were also flown by both sides from spring 1917 using modified day fighters. The British and French created night fighter squadrons for strategic defence but they were not deployed to protect the armies until the summer of 1918[95].

In mid June No 151 RAF Squadron arrived in France with Sopwith Camels which were scrambled from their airfields by radio and which then patrolled two 'barrage zones', orbiting beacons and intercepting any enemy they saw, a concept the *Luftwaffe* would use with great effect from 1940. Attached to 54 Wing, the squadron flew 392 night fighter and 18 intruder sorties from 1 September to 10 November 1918. It recorded 26 engagements from September to November and 20 victories from July while 645 kilogrammes of bombs were dropped. A few Western Front pilots became night fighter 'aces' including No 151 Squadron's commander Major Christopher Quintin-Brand and *Leutnant* Fritz Anders of *Jasta 73*[96].

Infrastructure and Technology
The effectiveness of the defences was reflected in growing German losses. During 1917 more than 50 bombers fell in combat in the West, many in daylight tactical missions, although *Kagohl 3* attacks on England accounted for a third including 55% of known 'Big Birds' losses. During the first half of 1918 at least 40 bombers were lost (see Table 2-6) and 45 in the second half with 62% being 'Big Birds' and Giants. Such was the threat from intruders that both sides built dummy airfields as bomb magnets. They were also used to control landings with returning bombers signalling the landing-code by flare or lamp, receiving authorisation from the controller then landing at the real base[97].

The air force infrastructure was of growing importance to the bombers as a target from the second half of 1916 initially on an ad hoc basis. But by the summer of 1917 these had become routine, especially by night bombers although the British also used fighter-bombers extensively. Runways were cratered and windows were broken but damage to airfield facilities, increasingly protected by sandbags, was limited.

An airfield was usually near a main road and consisted of a minimum 250 square metres of open and level space covered short grass or stubble. Up to four or five squadrons might use a single site with the men accommodated in farms, châteaux or wooden huts while the aircraft had wooden or tented hangars[98]. The infrastructure also included supply depots and workshops, the latter important because combat and accident ensured aircraft had a very short life, averaging four months[99].

Maintenance was eased by use of materials and technology based largely upon domestic life; timber was usually used for the airframe (some manufacturers used metal tubes in the fuselage) and braced with wire similar to that used in domestic pianos, while most aircraft had linen (used in clothing) dipped in acetate for strength to cover the airframe. The internal combustion engine used by automobiles was similar to that of the aeroplane and the wheels used in undercarriages were structurally identical to those of bicycles. Plate cameras were a common sight in the pre-war world while popular interest in radios grew for both sexes before the War following a series of maritime disasters in which radio-operators became international heroes, beginning with the White Star Line's John Binns and the loss of the liner *Republic* in 1909[100]. In each air force, the squadrons maintained aircraft either in the open air or in hangar with a mechanic for the engine and a rigger for the airframe.

The squadrons were at the end of a logistics system based upon the air park, a flexible organisation of between 300 and 1,000 men. The air park was a collection of repair shops, machine shops and store rooms which supplied new aircraft, spares and equipment to major commands usually at army level, although the French also assigned one to each escadre and autonomous group. The Allies also had separate depots at army group-level for major repairs of aircraft and engines and in 1918 both sides were forced to create advanced depots to keep pace with the advance[101]. As aircraft were vulnerable to wind and weather they were often sent to the air park in crates by rail to ensure they arrived intact in the combat zone. This was not without risk and while being conveyed to a prison camp in September 1918 American ace Lieutenant Howard C. Knotts, already credited with six Fokker D.VIIs, had the unique achievement of destroying another seven on flat cars by setting them ablaze[102].

Aircraft and aircrew losses on the Western Front steadily rose to reach a bloody peak in 1918 with more than 8,300 casualties (see Table 2-9) representing 53% of all Allied and 56% of all German aircrew casualties ([103]). In all more than 15,000 airmen were killed, disappeared, taken prisoner or injured supporting the ground forces on the Western Front of whom nearly 40% were British for whom the great blood-letting began on the Somme in 1916.

Table 2-9.
Aircrew combat losses on the Western Front 1916–1918 by Quarters

Quarter	French	British	Other	Allied Total	German
1916 Q1	127 (80)	69(50)	3(2)	199(132)	83(58)
1916 Q2	161(98)	69(42)	-	230(140)	142(110)
1916 Q3	242(145)	296(213)	1(1)	539(359)	196(135)
1916 Q4	153(97)	212(146)	-	365(243)	154(110)
1917 Q1	117(71)	302(203)	-	419(274)	187(143)
1917 Q2	260(134)	845(592)	7(7)	1,112(733)	535(401)
1917 Q3	298(183)	759(541)	6(5)	1,063(729)	518(344)
1917 Q4	298(89)	482(347)	6(6)	786(442)	452(334)
1918 Q1	255(182)	533(342)	3(3)	791(527)	597(448)
1918 Q2	631(409)	768(498)	49(42)	1,448(949)	1,126(868)
1918 Q3	689(423)	1,174(820)	308(242)	2,171(1,485)	972(721)
1918 Q4*	232(134)	523(355)	171 (115)	926(604)	292(234)
Total	**3,463**	**6,032**	**554**	**10,049**	**5,254**
	(2,045)	**(4,149)**	**(423)**	**(6,617)**	**(3,906)**

Notes: Main figure is total with permanent losses in parenthesis. Other is Belgian and US. No data is available on Italian losses
* October 1–November 11 only.
Sources: Bailey & Cony: 33–327. Franks et al *Casualties*:182–327, 339–379 & *Jasta War Chronology*:8–284. Henshaw:65–455, 459–472. Pieters:Appendix XII. Sloan: 49–53,56–59,61–63, 211–217.

Victory Over The Somme:
June–November 1916

If air superiority at Verdun was a matter of perception, then on the Somme it became an undeniable reality. Indeed, for a brief period air superiority became air dominance which befitted the higher status of airmen in the British Army due to a fortunate combination of the circumstances of expansion and Trenchard's relationship with BEF commander General Sir Douglas Haig who would reap the benefits during his 1916 offensive.

Haig's offensive was planned for August as a joint enterprise along the Somme valley with the French to break through the German lines and end months of bloody deadlock. Yet the ink was barely dry on the agreement when the Germans struck at Verdun drawing the French like moths to a flame.

Haig reluctantly brought forward the operation to late June to relieve pressure on Joffre who halved his contribution, leaving the British to make the main thrust north of the Somme. General Sir Henry Rawlinson's 4th Army was to make the breakthrough which would be exploited by the newly created Reserve Army (5th Army from 31 October) under Lieutenant-General Hubert Gough. Assisting them would be GAN under Foch who would commit only VI Armée (Général Emile Fayolle) on Rawlinson's right with X Armée (Général Alfred Micheler) to the south, playing initially a passive role. Facing them were two positions, five kilometres deep, on the Pozières-Guillemont Ridge manned by *General der Infanterie* Fritz von Below's *2. Armee*. This ridge lay between the deep, marshy valley of the Ancre and the broader plain of the meandering Somme and its three trenches were strengthened by village and farm strong points as well as batteries concealed in valleys and depressions.

The British 1,400-gun bombardment began on 24 June but with only 630 heavy guns and unreliable ammunition it neither cut the barbed wire nor crushed the defenders' deep dug-outs. When the infantry advanced on 1 July, poor tactics compounded the failure, with the attacking waves suffering 60% casualties in exchange for securing a toehold in the first German line[1].

For four-and-a-half months Rawlinson and Gough, who entered the line on his left, inched forward in a grinding artillery battle similar to Verdun. There were two brief flares of hope, the first when Rawlinson followed a hurricane bombardment with a pre-dawn attack from no-man's-land on the night of 13/14 July to take most of the German second line in seven hours. The success was not exploited and neither was the next one on 15 September when tanks spearheaded an attack at Flers to secure the Pozières-Guillemont Ridge. The campaign continued until mid November when a blizzard brought it to a merciful end with the Allies occupying a wasteland 40 kilometres long and twelve kilometres deep at a cost of 498,000 casualties (63,600 dead and missing). The defenders lost 300,000 men.

During the battle British pressure forced the Germans to reorganise. On 19 July, Below and *2. Armee* staff were given responsibility for containing the British north of the Somme and redesignated *1.Armee*. A new *2.Armee* was created facing the French south of the river under *General der Artillerie* Max von Gallwitz who doubled for a month as overall commander of the Somme front which was designated *Heeresgruppe Gallwitz*. His successor was Crown Prince Rupprecht of Bavaria the former commander of the *6.Armee* (Arras sector) whose *Heeresgruppe Generalfeldmarschall Rupprecht, Kronprinz von Bayern* (more commonly *Heeresgruppe Kronprinz Rupprecht*) had *6., 1.* and *2. Armees*.

Prince Rupprecht's appointment was Falkenhayn's last act as Chief of the General Staff, for the slaughter on the Somme and Verdun fuelled discontent leading to his replacement at the end of August by Hindenburg and Ludendorff. On 5 September they met the Western Front commanders at Cambrai and informed them that, for the next 18 months, the German Army in the West would stay on the defensive in new fortifications, the first of which would be the *Siegfriedstellung* behind the Somme front.

The RFC success on the Somme helped influence the German decision because its air superiority for much of the campaign, and aerial domination during the summer, greatly aided British progress. This success owed much to the mutual confidence between Haig and

Trenchard, the RFC commander in France, which had been sealed a year earlier when the former refused to attack until the latter was sure his airmen could provide the right level of support. The 43-year-old Trenchard responded, like many of Haig's subordinates, with fierce loyalty which was as important to the British commander as the air leader's professional competence and was repaid with support against political and Army critics[2]. The statement '…the air service had no more whole-hearted supporter' was justly quoted to such a degree that on 21 May 1917 Haig would successfully resist a Government demand for Trenchard's recall to England[3].

Trenchard visited GHQ frequently and submitted daily reports on air operations upon which Haig would crayon comments as well as parroting Trenchard's views in his diaries. They met regularly to discuss operational matters and one of Haig's aides, Major Desmond Morton, noted that they seemed to read one another's thoughts and expressed themselves with gestures and grunts rather than with words[4].

Haig also had a psychological insight into his air commander when he wrote: 'It is the greatest strain of any man always to be planning how others were to be killed[5].' It was a strain evidently felt by both men for neither was a butcher. Yet the support was not slavish and Haig would dismiss Trenchard's ideas if he felt they compromised support for the Army.

This would be a rare setback for the RFC and its leaders, who were all airmen and treated more than technical experts a situation which Trenchard exploited to the full. This unique situation evolved because the pre-war British Army was small enough to develop familiarity and confidence among its leadership who now faced the daunting intellectual demands of modern warfare. As the British Empire's armies expanded to unprecedented levels it became the most egalitarian meritocracy on the Western Front and seemed to break many bonds of conservatism and bureaucratic inertia.

Trenchard was tall and lanky, his nickname 'Boom' being mocked by a dry-sticks voice, the legacy of a bullet through the lung during the Boer War. Like Barès, he was the son of a lawyer whose family had served King and Country for 800 years, and he entered the Army more by default than ambition. Trenchard seemed lazy and his mediocre career reflected the absence of challenge, although he always strived to ensure his men were the best and he felt the strong loyalty which British officers have for their regiment[6].

His indomitable spirit speeded recovery and he returned to active duty in the Boer War becoming a trouble-shooter to the legendary British commander Lord Herbert Kitchener. Afterwards he found challenges aplenty in West Africa but the White Man's Grave, as the region was called, exacted its revenge and he was seriously ill when he returned to England[7]). As he neared retirement age his career took off, both figuratively and literally, in 1912 when he became interested in the aeroplane.

Determination overcame the hurdle of age and he won his pilot's licence in August 1912, just after his 39th birthday, although he was an indifferent flier. He became an instructor and as an observer during the 1912 army manoeuvres he detected all the 'enemy' movements, including those by Haig's division then joined the Central Flying School (CFS) where he received his nickname and quickly became de facto commander, thanks to a demanding nature and a talent for administration and rapid improvisation. Unfortunately, his success meant that when the BEF went to France in 1914 he remained at home in an administrative role aiding Kitchener[8].

With the New Year he was given the new 1 Wing which was assigned to Haig's 1st Army. In August 1915 Trenchard was promoted Acting Commander of the RFC in France when his predecessor, Sir David Henderson, returned to Great Britain to become General Officer Commanding RFC and to cleanse the Augean Stables of the RFC's logistical system[9]. Henderson never returned to France but the close relationship he had established with BEF headquarters was maintained and strengthened. This was because of a shared view of air power. On 9 July 1916, Trenchard told Haig his prime objective 'is to try to keep German machines from crossing our lines or interfering with photography, contact patrols, or wireless work with artillery,' to which Haig wrote 'I agree[10].' To achieve this goal Trenchard believed in offensive tactics which he regarded as the mark of a good commander and woe betide any whose resolve appeared to fade in the face of mounting casualties[11].

Notes in work summaries show he carefully monitored operations but had a loose-rein style of command. The lack of uniformity even with basic reports reflected both Trenchard's impatience with bureaucracy and his indifference to operational analysis, a surprising feature in a man with a flair for mathematics. The brigade commanders effectively ran private fiefdoms with monthly conferences at RFC headquarters, and Trenchard's command style was displayed when air-artillery co-operation was first discussed on 7 March 1916.

On this occasion corps wings commanders described their experiences but only during the last months of his leadership was any attempt made to hammer out a common doctrine following serious problems at Ypres[12]. Curiously, records of these conferences were not included in brigade war-diaries. Planning between the army headquarters and brigades often appears to have been organised verbally and the avoidance of paperwork sometimes reduced the effectiveness of British air power[13].

An early problem for Trenchard was the 'Fokker scourge' for despite the fact that most British aircraft were the Royal Aircraft Factory's BE 2 'tractors' these had no advantage over the French 'pushers' because the observer was in the front seat where his field-of-fire was restricted by struts and rigging wire. The pace of air combat increased steadily with Trenchard's former command, I Brigade, having an average 54 combats per month (Table 3-1) from February to April 1916[14].

Table 3-1:
I Brigade operations February–April 1916

Date	Sorties	Combats	Losses	To Fokkers	Total RFC losses
February	675	31	2 (1)	-	8 (9)
March	1,032	68	2 (2)	1 (2)	19 (25)
April	1,013	64	1 (2)	-	8 (10)
Totals	**2,720**	**163**	**5 (5)**	**1 (2)**	**35 (44)**

Sources: Henshaw. *The Sky Their Battlefield*:70–82; I Brigade war diaries February-April 1916, PRO Air 1/2174/209/14/2–3 & 1/2176/209/14/12.
Note: In Losses figures in parenthesis are aircrew.

The brigade actually escaped the worst of the Fokkers, which appear to have downed 13 aircraft (and 18 aircrew) on the British front, most while on long-range reconnaissance missions. From October 1915 onwards these reconnaissance aircraft were escorted by at least one aircraft but by 14 January 1916 Trenchard was demanding they be escorted by at least three 'fighting machines in close formation.'

Formation flying became essential for bomber missions which were restricted to essential targets from February 1916[15].

The commander of No 24 Squadron, Major Lanoe Hawker, a seven-victory 'ace' even before the first British fighter with interrupter gear reached France on 25 March 1916, highlighted another problem when reporting a successful engagement in his Airco DH 2 on 29 April 1916. Almost peevishly he noted: 'This pilot remarked how much harder it was to fire at this machine when it started dodging instead of diving. This information might be useful to B.E.2C pilots[16].'

But it was eight months before most RFC 'tractors' had interrupter gear forcing the British to rely upon 'pusher' fighters such as the Airco DH 2 and Royal Aircraft Factory FE 2 and FE 8. Their growing numbers together with the poor weather, which grounded the Germans during April, saw the crisis ease and morale was boosted when the inadequacies of a captured Fokker E.III were displayed to pilots. Yet on the Somme front, IV Brigade twice (1 and 9 June) ordered reconnaissance FE 2s of No 22 Squadron to be escorted by four aircraft [17].

The crisis was rapidly passing and the changing fortunes were symbolically demonstrated on 18 June when *Oberleutnant* Max Immelmann, Germany's leading ace and a lapsed vegetarian who chose to eat meat to keep up his strength, was killed over the *6.Armee* front. Fearing plummeting morale the Kaiser ordered Germany's other great ace, *Leutnant* Oswald Boelcke, sent eastwards to relative safety on an 'inspection tour.' But nothing could be done to restore confidence in the Fokker and there were demands for Halberstadt D.I biplane fighters[18].

Trenchard's preparations for the Somme offensive began on 1 April with the creation of IV Brigade under Brigadier Edward 'Splash' Ashmore, former commander of I Brigade, to support Rawlinson who had recently taken over the southern part of 3rd Army front. Ashmore received the 3 (Corps) Wing under radio specialist, Lieutenant-Colonel Edgar Ludlow-Hewitt's wing from Brigadier John Higgins' III Brigade and the newly activated 14 (Army) Wing under former Indian Army officer, Lieutenant-Colonel Cuthbert Hoare[19]. They would provide most of Rawlinson's air support together with Trenchard's own strike/reconnaissance force, Lieutenant-Colonel John Hearson's 9 (Headquarters) Wing. However, just before the artillery preparation began there was a last-minute change and on 22 June, Lieutenant-

Colonel Hugh Dowding relieved Hearson who created the Reserve Wing to support Gough[20].

All of these men were junior officers, with Ashmore being only a major at the outbreak of war, while the bible of precedence, the Army List, showed those who *acted* as Brigadiers (brigades) or Lieutenant-Colonels (wings) were actually captains in their early thirties. As none was the scion of a wealthy family they had to live on the small wage by which parsimonious governments ensured they could live like officers, but not gentlemen[21]). Before 1914 promotion was slow, especially after the conclusion of the Boer War in 1902 following which there were no major colonial campaigns or expeditions to provide either opportunities for advancement or the excitement and challenges which compensated for the monotony of garrison life. These were now offered by the new Royal Flying Corps (RFC).

Ashmore was a gunner who joined the Army in 1891 and became a staff officer in 1908 serving around the Empire before joining the backwater that was the Central Force, Home Defence. A desire to get to the front meant that in November 1914 the 42-year-old major transferred to the RFC, was rapidly promoted and distinguished himself on the Somme. He then became a divisional artillery commander but in July 1917 was given command of London's air defences which would benefit from the technological advances developed in France. By 1919 he was an Air Vice-Marshal but returned to the Army in September as an air defence specialist until he retired in 1929. He died in 1953 at the age of 81.

Higgins was 40 and was commissioned in June 1895, having been a Gentleman Cadet in the Royal Military Academy, Woolwich, and then served in the Royal Field Artillery but in 1912 became one of the first students in the CFS and switched to the RFC. Before the war he was involved in firing guns from aircraft and then commanded No 5 Squadron before being wounded and returning home. He returned to the Western Front in June 1915 as a wing commander and then commanded II Brigade before briefly returning home in January 1916 to command VI Brigade, but at the end of the month he was given III Brigade. He remained with the brigade until April 1918 when he was given a home defence command. He stayed in the RAF after the war to retire as an Air Marshal in 1930 settling in India where he retained aviation interests. At the outbreak of the Second World War he commanded air forces in India for a year then returned to Great Britain where he died in 1948.

When Gough's arrival extended the battle north of the Ancre, Ashmore was unable to control air operations along the Somme front and V Brigade was activated on 27 August under 33-year-old Brigadier Charles Longcroft, one of the most experienced aviation officers in the British Army[22]). He was commissioned in the Welsh Regiment in 1903 but transferred to the Air Battalion, Royal Engineers in April 1912 a month before it became the RFC. He remained in the RAF until 1929 becoming the first Commandant of the RAF College, Cranwell, and in 1958 he presented the RAF's first standard to No 1 Squadron which he had commanded when it was converted from an airship unit in 1914. Initially he had only Hearson's wing reinforced by a squadron each of DH 2 and FE 2, both from 9 Wing, but 22 (Army) Wing was activated on September 14 under 30-year-old Lieutenant-Colonel Felton Holt[23].

The Somme air campaign differed from Verdun because Trenchard was willing, and able, to project his offensive operations deep into the enemy's Operational level air space. Trenchard believed this outer air battle both on the main battle front and on its periphery was the key to success in the Tactical Level inner air battle to keep the enemy air force at arm's length. This was no coherent air doctrine but reflected a determination to carry the battle to the enemy at all times with both fighters and bombers[24].

Success in the outer battle helped give Trenchard dominance in the early stages of the Somme campaign and reduced corps squadron losses, but in the latter stages the skies were fiercely contested. He credited the success to his men's offensive spirit and the defensive, almost passive, tactics of the enemy. In reality his success was due to a more subtle combination of factors (see below) but especially the supremacy of his own two-seat fighters over enemy two-seaters25). When the Germans introduced high-performance single-seaters the pendulum slowly swung back.

Throughout the campaign the British fighter screen created a net to ensnare enemy hawks before they could fall upon the lumbering corps aircraft. The fighters flew Offensive Patrols (OPs), usually at flight strength (four to six aircraft), with the squadrons supporting Rawlinson and Gough being augmented by those of the neighbouring III Brigade. Trenchard was also fortunate because half the British aircraft on the Somme were high-performance fighters, both single-seat DH 2s and two-seater FE 2s. By operating in formation they overwhelmed the

Germans' two-seaters and Fokkers, which still flew Lone Wolf missions. However, the OPs had to shield a great volume of air allowing the enemy to avoid them, especially in cloudy conditions, and they worked best when covering small areas or when there was a strong fighter force[26].

The opening shots of the air campaign were fired on 29 May but it intensified from 25 June when the RFC attacked 15 of 23 observation balloons along the whole British front and claimed five (three by Ashmore's men), blinding *XIV. Reservekorps* opposite the British. German balloons were now attacked on every occasion and during the first days of the battle, the Somme front lost six out of nine with eight observers killed (some when their parachutes failed) while the demoralised aeronauts saw their 'Dragons' confined to heights of 500 metres. They regained confidence only in August after German fighters engaged and shot down a number of potential balloon-busters and were recipients of a more effective parachute[27].

Yet aircraft remained the prime target with Hoare using Major Rutter Martyn's No 22 Squadron FEs to fly OPs as far east as the German second position attacking the enemy on every opportunity. Pressure increased on 30 June when Ashmore ordered Hoare to keep at least three OPs over the enemy rear areas during the morning leaving French Nieuports to protect the front during the afternoon[28].

The FEs spearheaded Trenchard's offensive. In the eight weeks from 3 July No 22 Squadron flew 628 sorties (Table 3-2) of which 94% were OPs compared with only 46% of the 893 sorties flown by the nimble DH 2s of Hawker's No 24 Squadron. Although the single-seaters outclassed the Fokkers they were used more for escort and defensive missions, and from 7–27 August half of IV Brigade's single-seat fighter sorties were Defensive Patrols. Occasionally Higgins' fighters claimed a victory over the battlefield leading to a distinct note of pique in the IV Brigade war diary, as if a guest on a grouse hunt was claiming someone else's bird[29].

Table 3-2:
14 Wing fighter operations

Week	DH 2/FE 8			FE 2		Total
Total	Total	OP	DP	Total	OP	
3–9 July	141	32	33	101	90	242
10–16 July	113	44	-	77	77	190
17–23 July	88	43	11	43	41	131
24–30 July	105	61	20	64	60	169
31 July-6 August	152	106	42	130	121	282
7–13 August	104	35	66	90	90	194
14–20 August	74	21	49	53	50	127
21–27 August	116	68	37	70	61	186
28 August - 3 September	90	40	40	55	50	145
4–10 September	134	103	13	52	42	168
11–17 September	137	94	37	68	56	205
18–24 September	144	107	26	68	59	212
5 September-1 October	196	130	71	79	65	275
2–8 October	45	13	31	55	24	100
9–15 October	17	-	17	54	18	71
16–22 October	166	154	8	121	50	287
23–29 October	58	41	17	36	24	94
30 October-5 November	96	30	37	50	40	146
6–12 November	84	23	55	44	32	128
13–19 November	79	26	41	33	26	112
Total	**2,139**	**1,171**	**651**	**1,343**	**1,076**	**3,464**

Source: 14 Wing war diaries and summaries.
Note: OP = Offensive Patrol, DP = Defensive Patrol.

From 21 June Ashmore assigned Hawker's squadron the task of intercepting aircraft which slipped through the net and both 3 Wing and No 22 Squadron were ordered specifically not to intercept the enemy. Two days later Hawker was told to fly defensive patrols along the line but was permitted short-range OPs to the German second position when these chores were completed[30].

Because of the FEs, most air combat until mid September took place at least three kilometres behind the German lines and often behind the original third position. Fighter casualties were light, Ashmore's loss rate in July and August was less than 1% (Table 3-2) with nine FEs falling (four were destroyed) and five DH 2s (two destroyed), most being forced to land in friendly territory through combat damage or mechanical failure and later being recovered[31].

The Somme net might have been even stronger if Trenchard had concentrated resources in key areas rather than spreading them evenly along the front. Although he had six squadrons of FEs, and was expanding the Strutter-equipped No 70 Squadron piecemeal, only one reconnaissance-fighter squadron was on the Somme front flying about two missions a day[32].

Hoare's efforts meant Ludlow-Hewitt's corps squadrons enjoyed freedom of action (Table 3-3) pushing east of the enemy second position and meeting little opposition while from 1–25 June Ashmore's men flew more than 1,600 sorties. When the British attacked on 1 July there were only nine combats which cost one aircraft, while *Flak* brought down a second[3]. Low casualties allowed Trenchard to create reserves of men and machines for he was determined there would be no empty chairs in squadron messes, no matter what the casualties[34].

On 1 July he had 185 aircraft, including Higgins' No 8 Squadron covering Rawlinson's left, to which the French added 100. The Germans believed they faced 309 aircraft. Falkenhayn had sent *Kagohl 3* to strengthen the defences giving Below 15 squadrons (Table 3-4) and 104 aircraft by 1 July but only three squadrons, including *KEK Nord* (also known as *Abwehrkommando Nord* or *AKN*), and 14 anti-aircraft guns faced the British while the majority, including *KEK/AKN Süd*, faced the French. There were only 16 German fighters on the Somme front, including 2 Halberstadt biplanes, while piecemeal reinforcement in the early days, including expanding *AKN* to 6 Fokkers, failed to relieve pressure[35].

The eight weeks following the opening of the British offensive were the RFC's halcyon days, despite the fact that half the 134 aircraft and 123 aircrew which the British lost over the Western Front in July and August fell on the Somme battlefield. Even with the RFC flying more than 9,000 sorties (Table 3-3) over the Somme, the hours/aircrew casualty (killed and missing) ratio were 226 in July and 295 in August, figures equalled only in July 1918[36].

Table 3-3:
British Operations Over the Somme June 19 – August 27, 1916

Week	3 Wing	15 Wing	14 Wing	9 Wing	Total
19–25 June	425 (-)	-	360 (-)	35 (-)	820 (-)
26 June -2 July	525 (1)	45 (-)	225 (4)	100 (2)	895 (7)
3–9 July	290 (2)	255 (3)	250 (3)	110 (6)	905 (14)
10–16 July	255 (4)	230 (-)	230 (2)	135 (-)	850(6)
17–23 July	230 (1)	190 (1)	140 (-)	115 (4)	675 (6)
24–30 July	305 (1)	230 (1)	175 (-)	120 (5)	830 (7)
31 July -6 August	400 (-)	405 (1)	340 (2)	180 (4)	1,325 (7)
7–13 August	280 (-)	385 (1)	215 (4)	90 (3)	970 (8)
14–20 August	255 (-)	300 (-)	160 (1)	70 (1)	785 (2)
21–27 August	305 (-)	440 (3)	215 (2)	105 (9)	1,065 (14)
Total	3,270 (9)	2,480 (10)	2,310 (18)	1,060 (34)	9,120 (71)

Source: Brigade and Wing war diaries; Henshaw 86–104
Note: Figures in parenthesis are aircraft losses.

Table 3-4:
German air strength on the Somme

Date	FFA/AFA	Kasta	Jasta	Strength
24 June	8	6	-	100
4 July	12	8	-	140
10 July	1	9	-	150
1 August	24	12	-	300
2 September	29	21	4	350
20 September	34	28	4	420
1 October	46	28	4	490

Sources: *Weltkrieg X*:349, 361, 362; *Weltkrieg XI*:59, 62, 81.

But there were exceptions, notably Dowding's 9 Wing whose loss rate rose to 3% (15 aircraft) in the three weeks from 3 July, its Morane-equipped No 60 Squadron losing six aircraft and 11 aircrew including the squadron commander and two flight commanders. The abstinent Dowding possessed more than his fair share of British reserve, hence his nickname 'Stuffy', and successfully requested the withdrawal and re-equipment of the squadron with Nieuport fighters. His justified requests irritated Trenchard who came to regard him as a 'Dismal Jimmy' and marked his card for return to England once the campaign ended. However, 'Stuffy' was no desk-bound bureaucrat and flew a number of missions over the Somme[37].

Some new pilots were barely able to take off and land and No 60 Squadron's new commander, Major Robert Smith-Barry, refused to rush boys with only seven hours flying experience into combat. Having been injured in an air crash himself, he recognised the inadequacy of both pilot and observer training and considered how it might be improved. At the end of the campaign he wrote to Trenchard proposing a more demanding syllabus and in 1917 was posted back to England to revolutionise British and, eventually, the world's air training[38].

Despite 'green' aircrew, during the first two months of the offensive, the British established air superiority so absolute that before Rawlinson's mid July attack he moved field guns into the front line and assembled supplies in No-Man's Land without detection[39]. However, rain, mist and low cloud restricted operations during most of the summer and into the early autumn and even when the battlefield dried out, smoke and dust created a murk which obscured vision.

Falkenhayn reluctantly sanctioned substantial reinforcements to the hard-pressed Somme front following a visit to Below's headquarters on 3 July. Within a fortnight there were 150 aircraft, a figure doubled (Table 3-4) by the end of the month when Gallwitz assumed command. Elements of *Kagohl 6* arrived from Verdun and the interceptor force was strengthened by the creation of *Kampf-Einsitzer Kommando Nord, Süd* and *Vaux*, while *AKN* was expanded to 16 Fokkers, placed under 2. *Armee* and led by the 'ace', *Leutnant* Otto Parschau, being renamed *Kampf-Einsitzer Staffeln B(ertincourt)* in mid July[40].

Yet despite this, the morale of Below's airmen evaporated and the star of *Hauptmann* Alfred Mahnke, *Stofl 2. Armee*, waned at army head-quarters. On 17 June Mahnke had provided Below with photographic proof of Allied preparations, but the British tightened their control of the air preventing further photographic sorties until their infantry attack[41]). Many of Mahnke's airmen were also 'green' while some aircraft such as twin-engined 'Big Birds' and AGO C. I/II twin-boom 'pushers' of *Kagohl 3* were useless for air defence which was further handicapped by fragmentation of command as well as fuel and spares shortages.

The reorganisation of the front saw Haehnelt brought up from Verdun to become *Stofl 1. Armee* while Mahnke retained his position on the quieter French front. But during late July, both men began bringing order out of the chaos keeping some *FFA* under their own command for long-range (Operational Level) reconnaissance which, like the RFC during the Fokker scourge, received very strong escorts. On 29 July, No 24 Squadron engaged a reconnaissance aircraft escorted by seven Rolands over Martinpuich and drove them back, but the following day the IV Brigade war diary noted 19 enemy aircraft had crossed the lines. An added problem for the Germans was that morning haze confined their reconnaissance to the afternoon, a time when the British were especially active[42].

Fokkers and single-seat biplanes were used as interceptors but, as at Verdun, the backbone of the defence remained the *Kasta* flying sentry duty (*Sperrflüge*) barrage patrols over the gun line around the third position. Two or three *Staffeln* were assigned to each army corps sector which they patrolled alternately in the morning and afternoon. It was to no avail and *Generalleutnant* von Stein of *XIV. Reserve-Korps* opposite Rawlinson complained on 23 June: 'Enemy squadrons are now patrolling up to the Arras-Bapaume-Peronne road (i.e. some 20 kilometres behind the German lines). Until quite recently they were restricting themselves to near the front[43].'

Even when German staffs recognised reluctantly the illusory protection of barrage patrols, they were still retained to boost morale of the *Landsers*, while the gunners demanded the aerial shield protect them from counter-battery fire. The British also flew these missions and on 28 July No 22 Squadron was recorded by the 14 Wing work summary as flying four defensive patrols 'Forming air barrage for reported sighting of hostile raid returning[44].'

The *Fliegertruppe*'s failure severely strained relationships with the staffs, although not to breaking point as has been claimed by many historians. The German airmen suffered badly during July and August with 51 aircraft lost over the Somme. More than half the aircraft lost from 1 January to 30 September also fell there, compared with only a quarter over Verdun. By contrast a third (81) of the 205 confirmed German victories in the same period were on the Somme front. The *Fliegertruppe*'s heaviest losses of 1916 (190 men) were in July, but recent research suggests total losses of 168 men, including 132 dead[45].

The slow German recovery began on 7 August with a meeting between Gallwitz and *Feldflugchef* Thomsen who was informed that only 156 of the

176 (88%) aircraft assigned to *1.Armee* and 95 of the 123 (77%) assigned to *2.Armee* were serviceable and they assumed they were facing '500 aircraft'. Total Allied air strength on the Somme was, in fact, some 385 aircraft, or 470 if III Brigade was included. The Fokkers were increasingly augmented by Halberstadts and by some Fokker D.I so that by the end of August a third of the 60 German fighters were biplanes. However, the Fokker biplane suffered from wing failure (like so many Fokker designs) and they would be withdrawn from service by the end of the year[46].

Gallwitz had already received substantial air reinforcements while his *Flak* force was increased to 100 pieces, although they lacked a dedicated communications network. Meeting Thomsen in August he noted the impact of enemy air superiority: 'The heavy losses of guns cannot be replaced…This leads to a…remorselessly severe weakening of our artillery which…makes our infantry suffer.' He also reported enemy bombers were striking rail stations and camps with little success. By contrast the pressure was increasing upon the observation balloons with six destroyed in 30 attacks since the beginning of the month, the Germans destroying only one[47]).

Gallwitz requested high-performance fighters as good as the Nieuports to re-equip *Kagohl 3* and *6* together with improved radios which would allow the *AFA* to support more batteries. Thomsen offered little comfort; he would provide 48 single-seat fighters and five *FFA* as well as strengthening *Flak* defences for balloons. He also agreed to an experiment with *2. Armee* aviation opposite the French, changing the *Kagohl* missions from air defence to escorting the *AFA* because the French sector was quieter than the British, although *2.Armee's* use of fighters was criticised[48].

Gallwitz had already ended the rotation of *Armee-Korps* (with attached squadrons and *Flak* units) and, as with the French at Verdun, the front was sub-divided into sector commands or *Gruppenkommandos* each with *Fliegertruppe Grufl*. The new German organisation brought much needed continuity to the defence and the *Grufln* were credited with boosting morale by improving air support, which was better integrated with ground operations[49]). But during August rain, mist and low cloud largely confined German airmen to their own lines as the war diary of the British 4th Army's No 44 Anti-Aircraft Section shows. In June the gunners engaged enemy aircraft on five occasions, firing 172 rounds, and in July they were more active with 23 engagements (428 rounds) but in the next two months they fired upon the enemy only 17 times (340 rounds)[50].

Before Boelcke departed on his 'inspection tour' in late June he had discussed with Thomsen creating permanent fighter units and he later expanded these ideas into a memorandum on air fighting which Thomsen read as the Somme crisis grew. The air ace was a thoughtful man who wanted single-seat fighters used as interceptors and, having criticised their dispersal among the *Fliegerabteilungen* or *Kampfstaffeln*, he proposed replacing ad hoc groupings such as the *Kampf-Einsitzer-kommandos* and *Kampf-Einsitzerstaffeln* with larger, permanent units to hunt the enemy. This was not new and Immelmann's mentor, *Major* Friedrich Stempel, the *Stofl 6.Armee*, had made a similar proposal earlier in the year. Whether or not Boelcke was aware of Stempel's ideas he now proposed concentrating new fighters into *Jagdstaffeln* (abbreviated to *Jasta*)[51].

Thomsen accepted these ideas and three days after meeting Gallwitz he ordered, on 10 August, the creation of seven *Jastas*, four on the Somme front. They were based some 20 kilometres behind the lines to allow time for the ground observation organisations to detect and track enemy formations and then scramble fighters by telephone. Most early *Jasta* were raised by renaming ad hoc Fokker/Halberstadt units; *AKN* becoming *Jasta 1* on 22 August although the squadron's Kurt Wintgens (the first Fokker victor) was killed in a Fokker E.IV on 25 September. Boelcke was recalled to the West from the Ukraine on 11 August and assigned to *Jasta 2* with Albatros D.I, but spent six weeks training his hand-picked 'cubs' to act as a wolf pack while flying solo missions in a Fokker D.I to add seven victories and bring his score to 26 by mid September[52].

The *Jasta* score book was opened by *Hauptmann* Martin Zander's *Jasta 1* on 24 August when two pilots shot up a Strutter of No 70 Squadron that had been previously damaged by *Flak*, with *Offizierstellvertreter* Leopold Reimann forcing it to land behind British lines. The *Staffel* claimed three victories but ended the month spectacularly when it bounced Martinsydes of No 27 Squadron which had just bombed camps in Havrincourt Wood, east of its airfield at Bertincourt, and shot down three while *Kagohl 1* claimed a fourth[53].

British losses rose from 62 in August to 102 in September but the elite *Jasta 2*, which began operations only on 17 September, played a minor role in these. Of 123 victories claimed by the Germans in

September only 10 (all bombers) were by Boelcke's men at the cost of three 'cubs' (see below). The Germans certainly paid heavily for their success with 27 aircraft out of 350 lost and 53 aircrew casualties (including about 35 dead and four taken prisoner) out of a total aircrew strength of 680 (both figures representing nearly 8% of the machine and personnel establishment)[54]. Still the German fighter force grew and during October, the Somme front had eight *Jasta*, one for each *Gruppenkommando*, although they were mostly used to shield rear areas and rarely flew over the front line.

Meanwhile Ludendorff and Hindenburg's Cambrai Conference in September acted as a catalyst in improving the *Fliegertruppen*'s fortunes. Ludendorff demanded a closer integration between air and ground units, blaming the *Fliegertruppe* for the failure and noting: 'An understanding of the great importance of artillery spotting is something which can be awakened only over the course of time.' Yet Ludendorff's protégé Thomsen was not under serious threat and deftly transferred his loyalties to the new regime which sanctioned the abandonment of *Sperrflüge* and ordered the *Fliegertruppen* to carry the battle behind British lines in large formations[55].

Through technical foresight and happy coincidence a new generation of aircraft were also being deployed including the Albatros D.I/II fighter and C-types with 220 hp Mercedes and Benz engines such as the Albatros C.V/16, DFW C.V, LVG C.IV and Rumpler C.III which could fly reconnaissance missions with impunity above enemy fighters at altitudes up to 6,400 metres. The Albatros and the Halberstadt were powered by bulky in-line engines but these were attached to light airframes which meant their loaded weight was only 896 kilogrammes and 728 kilogrammes gave an excellent power/weight ratio with higher speeds than their adversaries.

The evening before the Cambrai Conference, 12 squadrons (including seven *Kasta*) were sent to the Somme in response to an air situation described as 'very serious'. Some came from Verdun, including *Kagohl 4* and half of *Kagohl 1* (later *HalbKagohl 1*), helping to raise *1.Armee* strength to 42 squadrons and a nominal 270 aircraft (Table 3-4) by the end of September[56].

The importance of the Somme front meant it was absorbing a quarter of the *Fliegertruppe*'s strength including 44% of the *AFA* and 58% of the *Kasta* even before the new wave of reinforcement. The *2.Armee* was stripped to reinforce *1.Armee* giving it 55% of the 346 aircraft on the Somme front by 13 September although the handful of 21 new biplane fighters were divided equally. A month later German air strength had increased to 508 aircraft of which two thirds were with *1.Armee* with Haehnelt's 'prudent proposals' and 'energetic influence' later praised by Hoeppner[57].

With growing numbers of superior aircraft the Germans were able to strike back against the British supporting the Flers tank attack in mid September. The British surge in losses in the fortnight from 11 September (45 aircraft) reflected the growing obsolescence of Trenchard's aircraft. However, the British did claim the world's first air-to-air missile victory on 15 September, an LVG by 2nd Lieutenant A.M. Walters using Le Prieur rockets[58].

Table 3-5:
British air operations over the Somme
28 August – 19 November 1916

Week	IV Brigade		V Brigade*		9 Wing	Total
	3 Wing	14 Wing	15 Wing	22 Wing		
28 August -3 September	350 (2)	175 (4)	275 (3)	100 (-)	135 (9)	1,035 (18)
4–10 September	275 (1)	255 (6)	230 (2)	160 (3)	125 (3)	1,045 (15)
11–17 September	410 (-)	320 (7)	305 (2)	195 (1)	160 (10)	1,390 (20)
18–24 September	245 (1)	230 (10)	255 (-)	175 (4)	95 (10)	1,000 (25)
25 September -1 October	370 (2)	275 (3)	375 (-)	430 (-)	155 (6)	1,605 (11)
2–8 October	175 (-)	125 (1)	145 (1)	45 (-)	10 (-)	500 (2)
9–15 October	215 (1)	200 (3)	345 (1)	170 (-)	60 (2)	990 (7)
16–22 October	295 (2)	350 (5)	410 (1)	270 (1)	160 (6)	1,485 (15)
23–29 October	130 (-)	120 (3)	175 (5)	110 (-)	10 (2)	545 (10)
30 October -5 November	180 (2)	155 (4)	265 (2)	230 (-)	15 (3)	845 (11)
6–12 November	190 (1)	160 (1)	290 (-)	340 (-)	45 (3)	1,025 (5)
13–19 November	135 (-)	120 (2)	260 (1)	290 (-)	45 (3)	850 (6)
Total	2,970 (12)	2,485 (49)	3,330 (18)	2,515 (9)	1,015 (57)	12,315 (145)

Sources: RFC Brigade and Wing work summaries. Casualties from Henshaw. Figures in parenthesis are failed to return to friendly airfields.
Note: * 22 Wing was operational from 19 September. Previous figures for Nos 23 and 32 Squadrons. No data for V Brigade operations on 7 October.

The Flers attack coincided with the delivery of six shark-like Albatros D.I fighters to *Jasta 2* and two days later Boelcke led five 'cubs' on their first patrol encountering eight BE 2cs of III Brigade's No 12 Squadron which were to bomb Marcoing rail station escorted by six FEs of No 11 Squadron. Superior German training and aircraft claimed two British bombers and four escorts, one of the latter by *Leutnant* Manfred von Richthofen, the survivors escaping only through the timely intervention of a No 60 Squadron OP. Another three aircraft were lost during 15 September but the following day's report by Trenchard to Haig was a masterpiece of obfuscation worthy of any Civil Service mandarin.

Trenchard noted there was little interference with British corps squadrons, and that most air fighting remained well behind the enemy lines while only 14 enemy aircraft had crossed the 4th Army lines during the week compared with '2,000 to 3,000' British sorties. This was disingenuous, to say the least, for a direct comparison (Table 3-5) shows the total sorties on the Somme front was less than 1,400. It is interesting to note the Germans, while recognising the close integration of British corps squadrons into the ground assault, felt by September 21 the air situation was more favourable to them[59].

For all this, Trenchard recognised the magnitude of the threat and on 25 September informed Haig: 'The enemy this morning undoubtedly showed a great deal of activity in the air, although this activity was usually in the region of 14,000 ft (4,270 metres) to which height most of our machines could not get.' The implications for the outer air battle were so serious that on 24 September he organised a massive, but unsuccessful, sweep of 60 aircraft towards Cambrai only to have salt rubbed into the wound with the loss of several of his latest multi-task 'combat' aircraft the BE 12, a derivative of the BE 2 and just as big a turkey.[60]). Reluctantly, he withdrew them from the fighter role, and was soon demanding double the number of fighter squadrons per army, warning he had only three with modern fighters (Nieuports, FE 2s and Strutters). The Royal Navy provided a mixed squadron with Nieuports, Strutters and the single-seat Pup, but this did not become operational until early November[61].

As British losses rose, German aircraft were also beginning to probe behind Haig's lines leading some generals to demand, like the French, that Trenchard's horns be pulled in. Trenchard responded in bullish fashion on 22 September with a vigorous defence of his offensive strategy, drafted by his aide Captain Maurice Baring, and echoing the argument at Verdun that even with an infinite number of aircraft a defensive strategy would not secure the skies. After reviewing the experience at Verdun and on the Somme he concluded: 'The sound policy would seem to be that if the enemy changes his tactics and pursues a vigorous offensive, to increase our offensive, to go further afield, and to force the enemy to do what he would gladly have us do now. If, on the other hand, we were to adopt a purely defensive policy, or a partially offensive policy, we should be doing what the French have learned by experience to be a failure, and what...the enemy, by their own accounts, point out to as being one of the main causes of their recent reverses.' Haig circulated the document not only among his army commanders but also within the War Office partly to answer his critics and to press for reinforcements[62].

Yet Trenchard had to admit the new German fighters were affecting his operations and restricting deep penetration missions although, despite *OHL*'s earlier demands, few enemy aircraft crossed the lines. It was only in the closing days of the campaign that Holt was reinforced by a couple of squadrons including the Pups of No 8 Naval Squadron[63]. The situation on the Somme continued to deteriorate during October, with the greatest pressure on Longcroft's front, and soon combats were taking place less than three kilometres from, or even over, the front line.

The lack of interrupter gear hamstrung British fighters and forced the Allies to depend upon unreliable Lewis guns which could fire only short bursts from bulky 47-round (later 97-round) pan magazines which were quickly expended, forcing pilots to break off engagements to reload. The drums sometimes slipped and struck the pilot on the head and this may have contributed to Albert Ball's death in May 1917[64].

The two Maxims of the Albatros doubled its firepower compared with other German fighters and it was so fast that British fighter pilots and observers had difficulty holding them in their sights[65]. The practical rate of fire for a machine gun was 250 rounds/minute or four rounds/second which meant the Lewis gun had only five seconds worth of fire before reloading, while the Germans with the Maxim had more than 60 seconds.

Like spiders in a web the Germans were able to wait for their victims, claiming 50 over the Somme from 9–29 October including five French machines. Dowding's 9 Wing which flew deep into enemy territory continued to suffer most severely, 57 aircraft failing to return in the 12 weeks from August 28[66].

In the 10 weeks to mid September, Dowding's average loss rate was 3.2% but the new fighters now helped push this to 10.5%, dropping slightly to 9.5% in the last four weeks of the campaign and steadily draining away his strength. His leading strike force, No 27 Squadron began the campaign with 17 Martinsydes and lost the same number while Nos 19 and 21 Squadrons each lost 24 BE 12s. The vulnerability of the long-range aircraft was underlined by No 70 Squadron whose Strutters were the most modern aircraft in Trenchard's inventory but which still lost 19 aircraft [67].

In October No 19 Squadron began to exchange BE 12s for Spad S7s, but these had only a single Vickers gun and were plagued with engine troubles which the British overcame only through a determined effort in the New Year. The reconnaissance-fighters were strengthened numerically by the arrival of No 18 Squadron and the expansion of No 70 Squadron. Hoare's wing benefited most, doubling its strength with the arrival of Nos 18 and 21 Squadrons, while Longcroft's corps wing received a third squadron equipped, like the others, with BEs[68].

The growing potency of the German fighter force dominated the outer air battle during the last 10 weeks of the campaign (Table 3-6). As the pendulum swung slowly in Germany's favour, the obsolescence of British aircraft was an ill omen for the 1917 spring campaign. While new designs were being developed, including the Airco DH 4 reconnaissance-bomber, the Bristol F2A reconnaissance-fighter together with the Armstrong Whitworth FK 8 and the Royal Aircraft Factory's RE 8 corps aircraft, Trenchard knew they would have no impact on the Somme campaign. Few squadrons were reaching France and fewer with new aircraft, although four brought the Royal Aircraft Factory's FE 8 'pusher' single-seat fighter and the BE 12. Captain Ian Henderson, the only son of Sir David, led one of the latter squadrons and survived the battles over the trenches only to perish in an accident in June 1918. Father and son were eventually reunited in death three years later when they were buried in the same grave[69].

Table 3-6:
1.Armee air operations 22 October – 4 November 1916

Week	Artillery	Photo	Ground Attack	Line Patrol	Fighter	Bomber	Total
22–28 October	137	96	87	198	267	31	816
29 October- 4 November	85	72	132	152	261	11	713
Total	**222**	**168**	**219**	**350**	**528**	**42**	**1,529**

Source: UKNA Air 1/9/15/1/27. Line patrols by *Kagohls*. Ground attacks are strafing sorties.

Significantly during the autumn, the *Jasta* clipped the wings of 14 Wing's FEs leading to a sharp decline in their offensive role during late September and October (Table 3-2); the FEs' share of the wing's OP sorties dropped to 27% then 21%. They were diverted to escort duties and even defensive patrols, with OPs dropping from 84% to 43% of their total sorties. By contrast the single-seat fighters were increasingly committed to the offensive role and by October 72% of their sorties were OPs. But the 'pushers' (and especially the FE 8) were increasingly outclassed by the new German fighters, above all the Albatros. British pilots continued to be handicapped by weak fire-power, unreliable engines and inadequate tactical training, rarely fighting as a team and sometimes ignoring their leaders [70].

Meanwhile, the *Jasta* began to filter into the inner battle intercepting eight corps aircraft on 20 October without success. Five days later Boelcke led *Jasta 2* on a sweep over German forward positions opposite Reserve Army's left. They claimed three victims with 2nd Lieutenant A.J. Fisher having the melancholy distinction of being the first British airman shot down by enemy aircraft behind Allied lines. The Germans maintained pressure upon Reserve Army and in the three weeks following 8 October, the corps wings lost 10 aircraft. High winds, bad light, rain, mist and fog hindered air support during October although every bright interval was exploited. Strong westerly winds sometimes meant British aircraft were virtually stationary in the sky while poor visibility reduced the quantity and quality of reconnaissance reports to which the army commanders were accustomed [71].

The defences were further strengthened by a reorganisation of the *Flak* arm to create a second defensive zone which concentrated virtually all the

Table 3-7:
Losses on the Somme September–November 1916

Date	German losses (fighters)	British losses (fighters)	German claims (By Jasta)*
September	27(4)	90(36)	123(48)
October	12 (4)	51 (19)	88 (56)
November	24 (4)	35 (23)	60 (52)
Total	**63 (12)**	**176 (78)**	**271(156)**

Sources: Franks et al. *Chronology*:9–21.Henshaw:105–128. *Weltkrieg XI*:78–79, 92,102.
Note: * Excludes balloons. British fighters include FE as well as BE 12 and Martinsydes on fighter missions.

light motorised weapons (*leichten Kraftwagenflak*) on the Western Front upon the Somme battlefield). Horse-drawn weapons (*pferdebespannten Flak*) were often deployed within five kilometres of the front line while the more mobile motorised guns could change their position (and were probably further to the rear because of ground conditions). Improved telephone networks at *Flak* headquarters (*Flakzentralle*) assisted co-operation with the airmen, the guns often being used to signal the presence of enemy aircraft to friendly fighters [72].

By the end of September Haig was reporting the monthly wastage of fighters and long-range reconnaissance aircraft at 75% and demanding reinforcements. British casualties steadily mounted although Trenchard held onto the initiative with his fingernails until the Somme campaign ended (Table 3-5) but the strain is shown in British hours/fatal or missing casualty ratios which declined from 215 hours/casualty in September to 179 in November. Despite this, RFC overall strength increased by a third between 1 July and 17 November from 410 serviceable aircraft to 550 while there was a corresponding increase in pilots from 426 to 585 [73].

The Germans' improved fortunes were reflected in a dramatic drop in losses between September and October (Table 3-7) although Boelcke fell on 28 October after a mid air collision. They ended the campaign with 540 aircraft (Table 3-4), a third of their strength, on the Somme and might have achieved more by concentrating their resources [74]). Each army headquarters on the Somme now had two *FFA* for long-range reconnaissance and the remainder were assigned to divisions or artillery groups, each having one *FFA* or *AFA* exercising tactical control over an escorting *Kasta* based at the same airfield.

In the closing weeks of the Somme campaign Thomsen finally achieved the radical change in German aviation he had sought since the Cambrai Conference. On 8 October the *Fliegertruppe's* aviation and aeronautical units were combined with the meteorological, intelligence, *Flak*, army dirigible and home defence forces to create the *Luftstreitkräfte* which also assumed responsibility not only for air-to-ground radio communications but also for Comint electronic warfare [75].

The *Kommandierende General der Luftstreitkräfte* (*Kogenluft*) was a tried and trusted staff officer, *Generalleutnant* Ernst von Hoeppner. At the outbreak of war he was Chief of Staff of the Saxon *3.Armee* whose advance westwards resembled something from the Thirty Years War leaving a trail of burned villages and butchered civilians to culminate in the sacking of Dinant. While the army commander, *General* Max von Hausen, bore international odium for these war crimes, under German command philosophy Hoeppner bore the greater responsibility. Nevertheless the career of the 56-year-old former cavalryman was unfettered and at the time of his new appointment he was commanding a division[76].

Hoeppner recognised his own limitations and appointed Thomsen his chief-of-staff while Siegert returned to Germany to supervise production. Although Hoeppner never learned to fly he was a gifted administrator who was soon visiting the Front, acquainting himself with his new command. He delegated tactical control of aviation to *Stofln* (who now became *Kofln*) and from them, and other leaders, he received monthly and later bimonthly reports supplemented by visits to the Front and weekly meetings of *Kofln*[77].

High winds, low cloud, fog and snow during November helped to double German losses while the more robust FEs regained some of their tarnished glory with 77% of their sorties being OPs. The DH 2s were increasingly committed to defensive patrols, possibly at the insistence of Gough and Rawlinson, and these accounted for more than half their sorties with a significant 13% involved escorting FEs. During November the *Jastas* accounted for 86% of all official victories (Table 3-7) compared with 39% in September culminating on 23 November when Hawker was lost on a Defensive Patrol to *Jasta 2's Leutnant* Manfred von Richthofen[78].

Sustained bombing was the other plank of Trenchard's strategy, the aim being to inflict material damage, to divert enemy resources and to dilute enemy air power on the main battlefront. Its effectiveness remains in dispute and even if it was not flawed during the Somme Trenchard certainly lacked the means of implementing this strategy. His objective in 1916 was to interdict the rail network as well as major ammunition dumps supporting the battlefield in an area 90 kilometres long from Lille in the north to St Quentin in the south and 160 kilometres deep from the front line to Namur. Running the gauntlet of fighters and *Flak* the bombers suffered badly and if the weather deteriorated it was rarely possible to recall them, with Trenchard's command post having a rare success just as four Martinsydes of No 27 Squadron on August 18 parted company with their escort[79].

The only dedicated bomber squadron, No 21, had the unreliable and cumbersome Royal Aircraft Factory RE 7, an aircraft so unpopular that the men were delighted by every crash. Unfortunately it was replaced by the BE 12. To augment his minuscule strike force Trenchard turned to the corps squadrons and even drew from III Brigade which lost four aircraft on bombing missions during 1 July. That day two thirds of 9 Wing's sorties were bombing raids which delivered 4 tonnes of bombs but Dowding had to borrow eight BEs from I Brigade[80]). The bombing campaign had a terrible effect upon the corps squadrons accounting for 48% of their losses (15 aircraft) in the first 2 months of the campaign because the BE 2 was totally unsuitable for this role. It was augmented by the single-seat Martinsyde and later the BE 12 while even reconnaissance-fighters were drafted. On the night of 15/16 July No 22 Squadron sent out six aircraft to herald the FE's future role, the squadron flying a few day and night bombing raids the following month[81].

The scale of Trenchard's attacks was maintained into September with airfields added to the target list in response to the growing fighter threat. There was also an ambitious attempt at decapitation on 15 September to support the tank attack when Martinsydes twice struck Below's reputed headquarters at Bourlon, while BE 12s bombed a reported corps headquarters[82].

The bombing effort during the latter stages of the Somme campaign was costly with 23 aircraft (including escorts) lost from 1 September to mid November. Once again it was the corps squadrons which bore the brunt of the losses with nine aircraft falling (six from III Brigade), 'bomber' squadrons losing only five Martinsydes and BE 12s together with two FEs acting as bombers[83].

Between July and mid November 297 tonnes were delivered, mostly during daylight, although there were 110 experimental night bombing sorties. The latter became a regular feature against rail targets from mid October using FEs of No 18 Squadron, BE 2s of No 13 Squadron and BE 12s of No 19 Squadron, leading Trenchard to demand a dedicated night-bomber squadron. These experimental night bombing-sorties in turn provoked the first night interdiction operation on 14/15 November when a German bomber followed a No 18 Squadron FE (attached to V Brigade) and attacked its airfield[84].

Higgins' brigade actually contributed 55% of the total bombing effort in its peripheral support, striking targets not only in the rear of *6.Armee* but also the northern flank of *1.Armee*. *Jasta 2* was stationed across Higgins' axis of attack suggesting that Trenchard's strategy was indeed stretching enemy forces, while *Jasta 11*, later to win fame under Manfred von Richthofen, was formed under *6.Armee* on 28 September. Higgins also flew 2,900 OP sorties (Table 3-8) spearheaded by Major T.O'B Hubbard's No 11 Squadron whose obsolete aircraft and poor tactics led to the loss of 22 aircraft during the campaign, mostly to *Jasta 2*[85].

Table 3-8:
III Brigade Offensive Patrol sorties 1 July – 15 November 1916

Month	Sorties	Losses
July	717	5
August	887	4
September	686	16
October	417	11
November 1–15	207	5
Total	**2,914**	**41**

Source: RFC Headquarters brigade summaries & Henshaw:89–125.

Whatever the criticisms of Trenchard's policies both the outer and peripheral battles certainly ensured Ashmore's corps squadrons were well shielded and they suffered no combat losses in June. Ludlow-Hewitt's wing began registering heavy guns from 17 June flying 20 to 30 sorties daily, each against one or two targets, with an average of 16 regarded as 'successful.' On the first full day of the bombardment (25 June) they located 102 batteries mostly on Rawlinson's left but they were often hindered by rain, morning mist and low cloud[86].

The defenders' only success was on 18 June when Fokkers unsuccessfully intercepted two corps aeroplanes while *Flak* slightly wounded one officer. Below's guns were blinded and subjected to a storm of fire which destroyed or damaged nearly half of them, with the heaviest casualties opposite the British[87].

Each fire direction mission was time-consuming with 60 rounds of 9.2-inch (233mm) ammunition or 100 from a 6-inch (152mm) howitzer needed to destroy a single gun pit. Ludlow-Hewitt had only 98 serviceable aircraft and 97 pilots in mid June, but he helped to pioneer a valuable technical innovation in the 'clapper break' which modified the tone of the aircraft's radio transmitter allowing ground operators to distinguish between aircraft using the same frequency[88]). This doubled the number of batteries/artillery groups which could be supported simultaneously on each corps front, but it still meant only two units could be supported and barely twelve of the 4th Army's 700 batteries might benefit from aerial fire direction at any one time.

As at Verdun, gunners greatly depended upon aerial photographs with nearly 60 photographic sorties from 24 June. The photographs were supplemented by observer's reports, many with worrying accounts of uncut barbed wire aprons, which were accepted or rejected almost at a whim by their superiors. Curiously, Hoeppner would later debunk RFC photography as 'astonishingly out-of-date' and claim the French were superior to the British in artillery co-operation, especially engaging targets of opportunity. The British appear to have been more flexible in engaging such targets exploiting artillery patrols to seek concealed batteries[89].

The 1 July attack began under a cloudless sky but low-lying mist then smoke, dust and haze obscured the German lines. The shells bursting through the murk were described by one No 9 Squadron observer flying above the clouds as being like a large misty lake into which thousands of stones were being thrown. Each corps was supported by five aircraft at any one time; two on contact patrol (one with radio and the other ready to drop messages to corps headquarters), two for counter-battery work and a fifth to observe for the heavy howitzers around the second German position[90].

Ludlow-Hewitt's men flew 115 sorties on 1 July suffering only one observer wounded but the RFC could do little to stop the slaughter of British infantry below. Poor visibility and thousands of exploding shells made counter-battery work extremely difficult with only 51 targets were successfully engaged. Conflicting reports led Rawlinson to telephone Ashmore some two hours after the attack began to say: '...things were going well on the whole[91].'

Harsh reality overcame optimism and when Gough was brought into the line Hearson's Reserve (now 15) Wing was attached to Ashmore in a semi-autonomous role with half of Ludlow-Hewitt's squadrons. The corps wings dominated the trenches until the end of August with devastating effect upon the defenders who lost 88% of their field guns and 45% of their heavy guns from 26 June to 18 August (including captured and withdrawn damaged guns) as Allied artillery interdicted the front. With limited aerial observation the defenders were reduced to 'blind' protective barrages[92].

The experienced Ludlow-Hewitt (who flew several sorties with No 34 Squadron) further improved British artillery fire direction by introducing a figure-of-eight manoeuvre. Radio reception improved when the aircraft flew at right-angles to the ground station so aircraft began the firing sequence as they entered the westerly ('upper') loop and flew away from the target. They corrected as they turned into the easterly ('lower') loop and returned towards the target. Ludlow-Hewitt also analysed every individual failure and in August gave each corps a Central Wireless Station to monitor shoots and to act as a reserve[93]).

Increasingly the British relied upon artillery patrols to pinpoint enemy batteries as they fired, targets of opportunity being engaged using the 'zone call' system developed in anticipation of a return to mobile warfare. Maps were sub-divided into zones covering 2,500 square metres and the transmission of the two appropriate letters could ensure an area of the battlefield came under fire from all batteries within range. Ludlow-Hewitt used his squadrons more flexibly with only a third of his sorties being controlled artillery shoots while Hearson, whose men flew more sorties, focussed upon controlled shoots which accounted for more than half of operations. Both men also visited heavy batteries to explain the zone call system[94].

Here, as at Verdun, the Germans relied less than their enemies upon aircraft for directing artillery fire, often restricting them to sectors prone to haze or fog. This reflected the gunners' prejudice against the aeroplane and their preference for ground observers or kite balloons, even to the extent of ignoring photographs. By November 1916 more than half of Hoeppner's kite balloons in the West were on the Somme and during the first half of September the *1.Armee* aeronauts were usually more successful detecting enemy batteries than airmen, conducting an average 132 shoots a day compared with 93, but only in light wind conditions. The British continued to dominate the artillery battle and their aircraft and balloons helped to destroy the batteries of the *55. Feldartillerieregiment* soon after it entered the line in November[95].

The *Fliegertruppe's* impotence in the inner battle was reflected in the IV Brigade war diary. On 2 August it observed: 'Some enemy aeroplanes came over our lines for the first time for a long period.' Five days later, while recording seven air combats it noted: '… corps machines were not interfered with by hostile aircraft.' But the situation was fluid and on 22 August artillery aircraft of 15 Wing were repeatedly harassed although attacks were rarely pressed home[96].

On both sides the inner air battle saw closer contact with the men on the ground. Emulating the French at Verdun, the British introduced contact patrols with Ashmore developing the tactics through exercises[97]). As the battlefield became a cratered wilderness the patrols provided accurate and timely intelligence on troops' progress and location with the generals often better informed than the men themselves. Infantry companies indicated their positions with flares while battalion and brigade headquarters replied either with signal lamps or cloth panels allowing the airmen to mark maps which were dropped to corps headquarters. The German *Infanterieflieger* operated in a similar fashion, but to support them each sector assigned a field battery to suppress enemy machine guns[98].

Ashmore's men also began strafing roads in June while on the first day of the infantry attack corps aircraft attacked German positions impeding the advance with 20-pound (9-kilogramme) bombs. Although the aircraft were not integrated with the ground battle, they affected enemy morale and by September German troops were instructed to remain motionless when enemy aircraft were in the vicinity and not fire upon them because this would attract artillery fire[99]! By attacking German infantry, artillery positions and columns with bombs and machine gun fire from low altitude, the enemy aircraft created a feeling of complete helplessness among the German troops[100].

Hoeppner noted querulously that the attacks inflicted light losses and were poorly planned while acknowledging the effect upon morale which created what he described as a 'queer mental attitude.' Signs condemning airmen appeared in German dugouts. German airmen were in a Catch 22 situation for whenever they flew over friendly troops the ungrateful groundlings would believe they were the enemy, fire on them and summon German aircraft for protection[101]!

British air superiority acted as a catalyst upon German Army defensive tactics. Until July the German generals packed trenches with men until artillery fire turned these into mass graves. But by early August the Germans were dispersing themselves in the myriads of shell holes using machine guns to compensate for numerical inferiority. Batteries were also dispersed although fire control was centralised.

From late August the air-ground conflict became less one-sided with German contact patrols and artillery aircraft more active, the latter because there was greater reliance upon directed fire to conserve ammunition for counter-battery operations. Preparations for the Flers tank attack were detected and German aircraft helped direct the barrages which contained this brief success[102].

With enemy aircraft more active over the front directing artillery fire, Trenchard strengthened the defences by exploiting the army's radio interception units (code-named 'Compass Stations'). From October they radioed the bearings of enemy aircraft detected either by intercepted transmissions or visual observation to army wing headquarters. The wing would 'scramble' fighters by telephoning the nearest squadron although it was planned to give each fighter a radio receiver so the Compass Stations could communicate directly with them. From November fighter patrols were directed from the ground towards enemy aircraft by cloth panels. These were laid out by forward posts linked by telephone to the Compass Stations and indicated the sector (numbered for the enemy side and lettered for the Allied), the number of aircraft and (when the enemy aircraft crossed the line) the direction of the flight[103].

Both sides' radio organisations also monitored the airwaves for counter-battery activity so that threatened gunners could take cover. A captured *6.Armee* document showed that by late July there were two communications interception stations reporting to army headquarters, and the more active Somme front would have followed suit[104]. The Germans differed from the British in having a jamming function used against enemy transmissions only upon the authority of a senior gunner, a technique now known as 'spot jamming' but one which was rarely powerful enough to drown out the signals. The French were also involved in radio interception and exchanged views on it with the British on 8 December[105].

The British did not try to jam enemy radios but they were happy to confuse the enemy. To support Rawlinson's attack on 14 July, Haig's headquarters tried to panic the enemy into a hurried withdrawal. An aeroplane radioed in German, presumably using a bilingual radio operator, that the second line had been captured with British cavalry pursuing the routed troops. Unfortunately, when British cavalry did advance during the evening the defenders quickly stopped them. Another attempt was made six weeks later on 5 September when No 9 Squadron dropped five message bags 'with German colours' into the enemy front line while No 34 Squadron dropped messages 'in German streamers'. The messages are not recorded in British records but presumably contained either instructions to withdraw or information to induce retreat, but if recovered they also had no effect[106].

While the tide in the outer air battle slowly began to turn in mid September, the impact upon the inner battle was delayed and from 28 August to 8 October British corps squadrons flew more than 3,400 sorties and enemy aircraft shot down only three machines (Table 3-5). But in the following weeks the German incursion rate accelerated with 4th Army reporting 33 on 20 October although this declined two days later. German airmen also increased the number of ground attacks (Table 3-6) although few were reported by the British[107].

Despite mounting pressure Trenchard continued to provide adequate Tactical Level air support until the end of the campaign but this did not deflect criticism, especially as the expectations raised by air support in the early stages were dashed. On 30 October Rawlinson wrote to Haig reviewing artillery support for his troops since the start of the campaign and proposing that army corps assume operational control over the corps squadrons in the same way as other support services such as engineers and signallers.

In a spirited riposte on 2 November, Trenchard sought to blind his critics with science and rebuked them for their ignorance of basic air-ground co-operation. Ironically, Trenchard's complaint that the constant rotation of batteries hindered closer relationships with RFC observers ignored his own failure to develop a uniform system of artillery co-operation. Perhaps this is why Haig backed the critics and on 30 November the army corps received operational control of the squadrons with the RFC responsible only for the execution of orders, the worst defeat of Trenchard's career on the Western Front[108].

The peripheral struggle around Trenchard included the French on Ashmore's southern flank. VI Armée began the campaign with some 165 aircraft including 7 fighter squadrons concentrated in Chef de Bataillon Antonin 'Felix' Brocard's Groupement de Combat de la Somme, also called Groupe Brocard and later GC 12. Corps squadrons flew night bomber missions during July but it was not until August that GB 3 arrived. Fayolle benefited from the presence of Capitaine Gérard who was transferred from the Verdun front where he had distinguished himself[109]).

With only a handful of Nieuport 12 two-seat fighters and no day bombers the French lacked both the means and the will to prosecute the outer air battle as vigorously as the British and their doctrine did not permit them to roam deep behind enemy lines. At the beginning of June Foch, commander of GAN, demanded OPs by the fighters with their scale determined by the enemy response. But because the French, as at Verdun, focused upon the inner battle even in the face of increasing enemy strength, (Table 3-9) the Germans were able to concentrate opposite the British.

Tables 3-9:
French strength during the Somme campaign 1916 (mid month)

Escadrilles	June	July	August	September	October	November
Caudron	4	5	10	11	11	12
Farman	4	9	9	15	16	19
Voison	-	-	5	5	5	5
Nieuport	7	7	7	14	14	12
Strength	140	165	250	350	360	360

Source: *Armées Françaises X*/1. GAN, VI & X Armée entries.

Unlike Pétain, Foch displayed little interest in air support during the campaign and certainly did not seek greater pressure within the enemy rear areas. From 6 July, VI Armée assigned small numbers of fighters to defend sectors or for specific operations, while attacking corps demanded fighter support from Brocard. As early as 7 July solo fighter sorties were banned but French fighter pilots continued to be wilful[110]). Gérard was constantly battling the fighters' tendency towards Lone Wolf missions; on 8 July he demanded they operate in patrols of four, while seven weeks later he reminded Brocard's men that pairs of fighters were officially to operate as teams. In practice, as with the British, once battle was joined it was every man for himself while Brocard was further hindered by the extension of the French battlefront to X Armée which diluted the effort despite raising overall air strength by 150 aircraft[111]).

This extension meant Fayolle lost operational (but not administrative) control of the Groupement de Chasse to Foch leaving him with a single fighter squadron while X Armée had two, since GAN had received a stream of complaints from the front about fighter cover. Although Foch had 10 of France's 23 fighter squadrons, he demanded more and Joffre provided him with another from Verdun (leaving four) but simultaneously fighter squadron strength was temporarily reduced to eight aircraft to create more squadrons[112].

Sheer élan and numbers helped contain the German threat but numbers were clearly not the solution. Photo-reconnaissance was a major problem from the start, partly because VI Armée's SRA had only two photographic interpreters. Despite strong fighter escorts the army reconnaissance squadrons could not reach enemy rail heads and photo-reconnaissance by fighters proved an inadequate substitute[113].

Recognising this Duval, Fayolle's chief-of-staff, reverted to using corps squadrons for photo-reconnaissance on 22 July although he sometimes had to assign eight fighters a day to escort them. Trenchard appears to have helped for, on 2 August, six British fighters were assigned to escort a Strutter on a photographic reconnaissance mission but by 4 September Brocard's fighters were being ordered to fly photo-reconnaissance. Barès flew a vital reconnaissance mission over Bouchavesnes on 13 September to raise morale among the two-seater crews[114].

However, German resistance grew steadily and in late August VI Armée complained that the enemy had been reinforced. This led to a steady increase in the scale of air combat; 24 clashes on 7 September, 56 on 22 September and 47 three days later while under growing German pressure, C46 and C106 were flying barrage patrols by 25 September. The situation became so grave that in early September four fighters were required to protect a Caudron of C21 when it flew a long-range artillery (ALGP) mission[115].

The *Jasta* gradually swung the balance and during the autumn, in response to threats by VI Armée's left to the outermost of the *Siegfriedstellung* covering positions, *Riegel 1* (*R1*) the Germans gave ominous demonstrations of their superiority. The British tank attack at

Flers allowed the French to take the village of Bouchavesnes close to *R1* provoking a German counter-attack on 20 September to shield the position. This was supported by 42 squadrons (including 18 *Kasta* and two *Jasta*) or two-thirds of the 66 squadrons on the Somme front with each *Gruppenkommando* for the first time having a *FFA* attached for contact patrol operations[116].

The German Official History recorded: 'German airmen ruled the skies over the battlefield, and in support of the German infantry struck enemy positions and reinforcements with machine gun fire and bombs. The contact patrols provided photographs as well as timely radio and personal reports on the battlefield situation[117].' Although the Germans were driven back to their start line, Fayolle later complained bitterly about the lack of fighter protection, but this appears to be the only French official reference to these events[118].

The second counter-attack was on 15 November near the village of Sailly-Saillisel, south-east of Bapaume and a key point in *R1*. It was supported by 52 aircraft which achieved air superiority and bombed and strafed French batteries. It was '.a sign of the completely changed operational use and effect of the German air squadrons compared with the first months of the battle and was of especial significance bringing to an end the Battle of the Somme[119].'

No information is available about the participants (who may well have been drawn partly from the *Kasta*) but the success is likely to have influenced *Kogenluft's* later decision to give the *Schutzstaffeln* a secondary ground-attack role. Once again French official sources appear silent on the subject.

Despite French air strength growing to 360 aircraft by mid October, mounting 60 to 120 sorties a day, the Germans became more active over the Gallic front lines. While the *Jastas* claimed only six French aircraft by 25 October, the dithering with Brocard's fighters meant both army commanders continued to direct a stream of complaints to Foch demanding better protection. Even the presence of GC 12 in VIe Armée from September and the formation of GC 13 in Xe Armée in November had no effect[120].

On 25 October Foch ordered Brocard to have two line patrols along Fayolle's VI Armée front at medium and high altitude and added: 'Reinforcements will be thrown at the opportune moment in sectors where German aviation shows itself particularly active.' The imposition of 'protection immédiate' completed the hand-over of the initiative to the Germans. Yet the *Jastas* had few successes and from 25 October until the campaign's end they claimed only 6 French aircraft on the Somme front, compared with some 20 British[121].

While the French may have been successful by their own standards their airmen had less direct impact upon the Germans. The experiences of *107. Reserve Infantry/24. Reserve Division*, formerly with *2. Armee* and then sent to reinforce *1.Armee* on 24 September after Flers were typical. The regiment's post-war history noted: '…the pronounced superiority of the enemy in the matter of aircraft and captive balloons was more unpleasant than it had been when we were on the Barleux sector (opposite the French)…[122].'

This activity had no effect upon the Somme air campaign which concluded with the Allies having lost their dominance and on the verge of losing air superiority. Trenchard's airmen had been extremely active flying more than 21,400 sorties over the Somme while between July and mid November they registered 8,612 targets for the BEF (about half of them on the Somme) and had taken more than 19,000 photographs[123].

From late June, 216 RFC aircraft which were supporting the campaign failed to return to a friendly airfield, an overall loss rate of 1% of which 143 were destroyed or captured. Another 592 were written off either due to severe damage or accidents, while 235 were returned to England for repairs or for assignment to training units. The human cost was some 500 men killed, wounded or missing of whom half fell behind the German lines. Trenchard was proud that 164 victories were credited to his men and actual German losses over the Somme were 114 aircraft[124].

The Somme campaign was later described by Siegert as 'aviation's high school'. The most important lesson was that air superiority achieved by offensive operations was of significant benefit to ground forces. Aircraft roles expanded during the campaign which saw the first steps taken towards close air support, counter-air (through attacks upon airfields), interdiction, ground-controlled interception (including non-visual means), electronic warfare (through radio interception), special operations, night-bombing and night-intruding. But the greatest influence was upon the technology of air power for it stimulated demand for more specialised aircraft designs, a trend which had appeared at Verdun but was became even more apparent over the Somme.

Air forces now needed dedicated high-performance combat aircraft rather than the multi-task 'combat' aircraft such as the BE 12 and Martinsyde. Performance was now everything, especially in the outer air battle, both for reconnaissance and bombing to slip through the enemy fighter net. The single-seat, 'tractor' fighter became the arbiter of air superiority and significantly, the RFC's prime fighters, the Sopwith Camel and Royal Aircraft Factory's SE 5, first appeared in December 1916 by which time the French had brought into service an improved version of the Spad S5, the famed Spad S7 which had only a single Vickers gun and was plagued with mechanical problems because the Hispano-Suiza engines were complex, notoriously difficult to maintain and often unreliable. For these reasons Trenchard was reluctant to accept them and also proposed using both the DH 4 bomber and the RE 8 corps aircraft in the reconnaissance-fighter role, while the Bristol Fighter was designed both as a replacement for the BE 2 in corps squadrons and was also to be capable of fighter patrols ([125]).

As the year closed Trenchard realised he faced the prospect of fighting with a bent sword. He was saddened by the losses although he remained unflinchingly committed to offensive operations and, even if he had possessed doubts, as a British officer he believed it his duty to show stoicism. Consequently Dowding, who had complained about losses in August, was replaced by Cyril Newall as commander of 9 Wing on 26 December. Dowding returned to 9 Wing headquarters after 10 days leave to spend the three-day Christmas holiday with his men before going home ([126]). It would be Newall who would command the wing as Allied air forces faced their greatest trial during the following spring.

Chapter Four

Triumph and Tragedy: Spring 1917

The bitter winter of 1916–1917 provided some respite for airmen although the German Army waited with dread for another defensive campaign. Between July and October 1916 it had suffered 800,000 casualties, bruising morale and eroding discipline as well as forcing Ludendorff and Hindenburg to recognise the need for radical measures. They opted for a defensive concept in which the airmen would play an important role[1].

The new doctrine, published on 15 December 1916, reflected enemy air and artillery superiority the previous summer and sought to draw the sting of enemy fire by dispersing the defenders over an area up to 10 kilometres deep. The battlefield was split into broad zones: Outpost/Forward to erode and to channel the attackers, the Battle or main line of resistance, and the Rear. The Battle Zone was usually on a reverse slope exposing attackers to defensive field artillery while denying them similar support being based upon strong points and automatic weapons (many in concrete pill-boxes and bunkers). It was supported from the gun line in the Rear Zone from where Reaction Forces of divisional strength (*Eingreifdivisionen*), or 'counter-attack divisions' would launch a riposte to drive back the exhausted enemy[2].

The new doctrine could be observed from the air since the traditional defensive 'web', based upon three trenches, was replaced by single or double trenches while barbed wire was laid out in deep, zigzag rows. Proposals by *OHL* radicals to eliminate trenches completely were rejected; because trenches eased movement in quieter sectors and provided landmarks for the airmen. By pushing back the balloon line, the Germans extended the outer air battle zone and made the inner one deeper, causing new problems for both sides by exposing their corps aircraft both to fighters and anti-aircraft guns. Counter-battery work remained important but was now especially difficult because the airmen had to cover a larger area. This was less of a problem for the Germans because they were not so dependent upon aeroplanes for counter-battery fire missions. To reduce their batteries' exposure, they also adopted tactics using precise, short-duration, barrages based upon earlier aerial reconnaissance which helped to identify the enemy's likely assembly points and communications hubs. But in the initial stages of an enemy offensive, the *Luftstreitkräfte* was to direct fire upon targets far behind the enemy lines to disrupt preparations[3].

While the German Army adjusted to the new defensive concepts, Hoeppner and Thomsen spent the winter expanding the *Luftstreitkräfte*, absorbing the lessons of the previous campaigns and establishing their role in the new doctrine. *OHL* had created an autonomous service but still expected it to support the ground battle. The *Armee-Oberkommandos* or *Armee Abteilungen* headquarters were to remain vigilant and use long-range (Operational Level) reconnaissance aircraft to accumulate photographic evidence of enemy offensive preparations, monitoring their communications and infrastructure[4].

OHL now recognised that air superiority was gained by concentrating squadrons opposite major threats and by stripping quieter sectors. Fighters in *Staffel* strength were the best way to achieve this goal and *OHL* demanded they operate '.over the enemy lines.' *Flak* operating as single guns would provide several defensive layers and would also engage aircraft and balloons over enemy lines. The *Kagohl* were ordered systematically to strike Operational Level targets such as railheads, troop concentrations, airfields and storage facilities to disrupt preparations for offensives. At the same level *Armee-Oberkommandos* or *Armee Abteilungen* would use long-range reconnaissance aircraft to provide incontrovertible photographic evidence of enemy offensive preparations by monitoring communications and infrastructure[5]. *OHL* also insisted the squadrons be integrated into divisional task-groups and provided each with short-range (tactical) reconnaissance by aeroplane or balloon with photography providing essential evidence. Fighters would secure air space over the front if an attack was anticipated, artillery aircraft would direct fire especially against assembling assault troops, while contact patrols would monitor the front line. New instructions noted: '...bombing attacks and machine gun fire on enemy troops have a great effect upon morale[6].'

By the spring Hoeppner's preparations were almost complete and most of his 1,300 aircraft in the West were modern machines, offsetting enemy numerical superiority of some 2,400 aircraft most of which were obsolete. By 1 April the RFC had grown by a third to 50 squadrons (897 aircraft), and corps squadron strength had risen from 18 to 24 aircraft, but it had only 10 squadrons (two naval) of modern combat aircraft[7]. The modern Airco DH 4, the Armstrong Whitworth FK 8, the Bristol Fighter, the Royal Aircraft Factory RE 8 and SE 5, the Spad S7 and the Sopwith Triplane had joined the squadrons but represented less than a fifth of Trenchard's strength.

In December Trenchard visited London to beg the Air Board for extra fighter squadrons, but the politicians were more interested in the promotion of David Lloyd George to Prime Minister a week earlier. Upon returning to France he complained to the Board that they were asking him to fight the forthcoming battle with the same aircraft as in 1916. He warned he would be hopelessly outclassed as the enemy was becoming more aggressive and demanded action[8]. Publicly Trenchard remained confident. Meeting his commanders on 6 January he said he hoped to receive 21 squadrons of aircraft equal, or superior, in quality to those of the enemy. Haig, who had been promoted a Field Marshal on New Year's Day, supported him and warned the Cabinet he could not expect to win air superiority in April while the enemy might do so. But the industrial foundations were still being laid and production was further hindered by labour troubles[9].

Criticism of the obsolete aircraft found its way through the Press into Parliament irritating Trenchard profoundly. He informed his brigade commanders at a planning conference on 9 March: 'There is too much criticism by officers on leave to irresponsible persons. This does a great deal of harm and must be stopped[10].' But he was less forthright on how this was to be achieved, and perhaps he was venting his own frustrations.

His concerns were shared by his old friend Peuty, who succeeded Barès in February. Nivelle had gone through the motions of protecting Barès but perhaps he wanted his own man rather than Joffre's. Chef d'Escadron Peuty was a 38-year-old bachelor from the outskirts of Paris who was in the top 30 of 550 cadets from the Ecole Spéciale Militaire in 1900. A cavalry man he became, like many of his countrymen, enamoured of North Africa and from 1908 served with regiments from this part of the French Empire. He did not become a pilot until February 1915 but within four months was commanding MS48 and then the Groupement de Chasse et Reconnaissance on the Artois front before becoming the aviation officer for X Armée. He established a warm working relationship with Trenchard and the British, which may have contributed to his selection by the half-English Nivelle on 20 February 1917. But although a good fighter commander and an enthusiastic supporter of air operations, Peuty lacked organisational skills while his reports on Verdun to his allies suggested he had little time for bombers [11].

Peuty embarked upon a series of pointless flying visits to the front rather than address the problems facing his 120 squadrons. Of 34 fighter squadrons on 1 April only seven had the modern Spad S7, half re-equipping only the previous quarter and only 70 were operational on 1 February. Six squadrons had a handful of Spads but the remainder of the French fighter force consisted of the Nieuport 17 or Nieuport 24. Bomber squadrons retained the Voisin which were supplemented by the inadequate Bréguet-Michelin BM 5B and four squadrons of licence-built Strutters as Sopwith 1B with a small (250-kilogramme) bomb load. Most corps squadrons still had Caudrons and Farmans, with two having the bizarre Salmson-Moineau SM 1A whose fuselage-mounted engine drove two wing-mounted propellers. Some squadrons were created with Spad S7, the new Paul Schmitt 7B bomber as well as the Letord 1A and Dorand AR 1A reconnaissance aircraft shortly before the campaign opened, but most of Peuty's 1,500 aircraft were obsolete and the newcomers were too late to influence affairs[12].

The difficulties in detecting and tracing the *Siegfriedstellung* reflected the Allied inferiority, and although the RFC had greater success than the Aviation Militaire (see Chapter Two) it paid a greater price. By the end of February, the Herculean efforts of the RFC ensured Haig had an accurate trace of the new position opposite its own front, unlike Nivelle who had to plan his strategy in a vacuum[13].

The brutal, unequal, struggle continued as the *Luftstreitkräfte* tightened its grip over the Somme where V Brigade suffered 27% of total British losses during December and January. During December virtually all air fighting took place within a three-kilometre strip on either side of no-man's-land, with 17 of 27 British machines falling within their own lines. The situation was so alarming that increasing numbers of line patrols were flown in one- or two-flight formations while in the more dangerous sectors each artillery aircraft was given a pair of fighter escorts[14].

Another 35 British aircraft fell in January and casualties rose to 61 the following month, bringing total aircrew casualties over the three months to 177 men of whom only 40% fell east of the German lines. By contrast less than 60 *Luftstreitkräfte* aircraft appear to have been shot down along the whole Western Front in the same period[15].

As Sherlock Holmes observed in '*The Adventure of Silver Blaze*' the most 'curious incident' was the dog which did not bark and in the skies over the Western Front, 9 Wing was the silent hound. The new commander, Newall, might have been expected to make his mark by encouraging aggressive operations but during the first nine weeks of his command the squadrons were largely grounded, apart from a few line patrols.

The last reconnaissance was by Strutters of No 70 Squadron on 4 December and nine days later the squadron transferred to I Brigade who retained it until 2 March. Four days later it flew its first mission for Newall and by the end of the month it had lost seven aircraft, more than a third of its strength. The bombers were grounded for weeks while Newall's first OP was only on the morning of 17 March. Newall's inertia undoubtedly had Trenchard's support, and possibly orders, for the RFC's leader was trying to conserve his few squadrons of new aircraft so as to achieve tactical surprise when the spring offensive began. Yet other brigades, who were also encouraged to conserve resources, proved more active than Newall and suffered accordingly[16].

Allied pressure upon the Somme front accelerated the German withdrawal into the *Siegfriedstellung*. Prince Rupprecht received *OHL's* reluctant permission to begin the withdrawal on 4 February but first had systematically to lay waste the abandoned territory in *Unternehmen* '*Alberich*' (named after the malicious practical joker in the Siegfried legend). The withdrawal began on 22 February and for the Allies one of the first clues to enemy intentions was detected three days later by Pups of No 54 Squadron who reported fires in every enemy-held village. The Allied 'pursuit' began only on 17 March and by the time the last Allied troops arrived on 4 April, the Germans were secure in the *Siegfriedstellung* with a strong reserve[17].

The RFC was taken by surprise with many squadrons concentrated between Lens and Arras in anticipation of the spring offensive. Trenchard's response to the German withdrawal was vague advice to brigade commanders to maintain contact, to harass the enemy where possible and to seek out further fortifications east of the new defences. But Allied airmen were moving away from their airfields and had to rely upon hastily prepared forward airstrips which squadrons used during the day before returning to their roosts at night. Artillery work virtually ceased and the RFC achieved little, drawing fire to detect German covering parties. The gunners were in such a hurry to move that they rarely erected the cumbersome 9-metre-high radio aerials and when Rawlinson later complained about the lack of air support for his guns he was rebuked by GHQ[18].

Trenchard's losses in March were double those of February at 131 aircraft (187 aircrew), with almost half the machines and 110 men falling in the British lines. The forces pacing the German withdrawal (IV, V Brigades and 9 Wing) lost 32 aircraft and it was little consolation that the Germans made '. no effective attempt to dispute the work of the Royal Flying Corps in the area of the Hindenburg Line ([19]).' Long-range reconnaissance missions suffered the severest losses with 18 aircraft falling in 214 sorties, an 8.5% loss rate, despite the provision of escorts who themselves lost eight aircraft. So serious was the situation that fighters reverted to their nominal scout role and the Spads of No 23 Squadron and DH 2s of No 32 Squadron helped to reassure Haig there were no more surprises east of the *Siegfriedstellung*. These fortifications were systematically photographed, under the watchful eyes of Pups from No 54 Squadron with the IV Brigade's No 22 Squadron being prominent. The degree of German technical superiority is demonstrated by the fact that their total losses during March were some 40 aircraft. Yet rising star, Manfred von Richthofen, had a narrow escape on 9 March when his Albatros was damaged in a clash with FE 8s[20].

The German withdrawal fatally compromised Nivelle's master-plan for the spring campaign. He became Commander-in-Chief of the French Armies of the North and North-East on 17 December (although Joffre did not formally resign until just after Christmas) but was beholden to the politicians, including the new British and French premiers, for supreme power. To break the deadlock he promised new tactics which were a larger scale version of those used at Verdun based on a thorough bombardment and rolling barrage. A command of English inherited from his mother helped him win over the British Government who placed Haig under GQG's temporary operational control.

Nivelle had planned to squeeze out the Somme Salient using the British to strike the northern face between Arras and Bapaume and GAN to attack between the Oise and the Avre in the west. These would suck in the German reserves allowing GAR to deliver the main blow further south from the Aisne valley over the Chemin des Dames (Lady's Road) ridge to break the back of the over-extended defence and pursue their enemy eastwards. The German withdrawal made GAN redundant and left the British, with GAR, to strike on either side of the new German position. But the Germans had already thwarted any hopes of a breakthrough by building more positions deep in their own territory; the *Wotanstellung* opposite the British and *Hunding-* and *Brunhildstellungen* facing the French[21].

On the British front German aircraft exploited every break in the weather to monitor preparations including rising rail traffic (to 200 trains a day), swelling supply dumps and expanding troop accommodation. They were especially effective north of Arras against the 1st Army, but much of 3rd Army's preparation around that ruined city exploited cellars and underground passageways. Consequently, Hoeppner concentrated opposite I Brigade and reacted so vigorously that it suffered a quarter of RFC losses during March. To relieve pressure Trenchard ordered both III and V Brigades on 19 March to provide support with OPs around Douai. The defending *6.Armee* benefited from the presence of four *Jasta* which were credited with 44 victories during the month, the majority by Richthofen's *Jasta 11* with the Master claiming 10[22].

The British planned to advance from Arras to the Douai plain along open spurs of high ground on either side of the River Scarpe. Between Lens and Arras was the seven-kilometre-long strongpoint of Vimy Ridge, a slight rise in the ground when viewed from the British lines but towering like the Rock of Gibraltar over the plain. This was to be taken by the Canadian Corps of Sir Henry Horne's 1st Army but General Sir Edmund Allenby's 3rd Army would launch the main blow around Arras to outflank the *Siegfriedstellung* by an advance upon Cambrai[23].

The German *6.Armee* was under the 72-year-old stiff-necked conservative *Generaloberst* Ludwig, *Freiherr* von Falkenhausen who stubbornly believed in a rigid, forward defence underpinned by Vimy Ridge, which had repelled two major assaults in 1915. He also held the reaction forces too far back and the resulting confusion gave the British their greatest success since 1914. They struck through rain, sleet and snow showers which a high westerly wind drove into the German faces. The Canadians stormed Vimy Ridge while Allenby punched a 10-

kilometre hole through the German line to reach the Scarpe and open country, the defenders losing 5,600 prisoners in the debacle. Many units fled eastwards, a Bavarian battery being rallied by the infectious optimism of *Leutnant* Albert Kesselring whose actions paved his way for entry into the General Staff and after the war a key important role in the development of the *Luftwaffe*. *OHL's* reaction was the immediate replacement of Falkenhausen's chief of staff with *Oberst* Friedrich Karl 'Fritz' von Lossberg, a defensive specialist who reorganised resistance in front of the *Wotanstellung* while construction of *Wotanstellung II* hastily began to cover Douai and to join the *Siegfriedstellung*[24].

Lossberg plugged the gaps and contained the advance as the attackers failed to exploit their success and their communications sank into the mud. After five days Allenby paused to regroup for another set-piece attack launched on St George's Day (23 April) as the Second Battle of the Scarpe, but this was quickly stopped by the new counter-attack tactics. A third attack on 3 May (Third Battle of the Scarpe) was also a failure and effectively ended the Arras campaign. On 30 April Haig informed his army commanders that his objective was simply to reach the *Wotanstellung* by mid May after which Gough's 5th Army would be transferred to Flanders for the 'Northern Operation'. All serious progress ceased on 14 May although the usual bloody squabbling for position meant the campaign officially continued into June. Meanwhile Gough, with frightening ineptitude and at terrible cost, sought a bridgehead within the *Siegfriedstellung* at the village of Bullecourt which fell on 17 May.

On 16 May the *4.Armee* at Ypres reported British preparations for an offensive but while *OHL* knew the Arras threat had declined it was not until 4 June that Crown Prince Rupprecht reported the campaign's formal end. It had begun with such promise for the British before dissolving into the usual battle of attrition to cost them 134,000 casualties (40,000 dead) and the Germans 120,000 including 21,000 prisoners.

The Arras campaign would prove the greatest trial for Higgins' III Brigade, Newall's 9 Wing and, above all, Brigadier Gordon Shephard's I Brigade[25]. Together they had 442 aircraft on 1 April, nearly half Trenchard's strength including three-quarters of his modern combat aircraft, with 89% serviceability[26].

Higgins' wings were commanded by two recently promoted squadron commanders: Lieutenant-Colonels William Mitchell (12 Corps Wing) and George Pretyman (13 Army Wing), aged 29 and 24 respectively ([27]). Shephard, aged 31, was an old colleague of Higgins having been Mitchell's predecessor. In 1912, seven years after being commissioned in the Royal Fusiliers, he transferred to the RFC and by 1915 was commanding No 6 (Corps) Squadron before being promoted to command 12 Wing. He was an ardent bombing enthusiast (see Chapter Two) and was the only RFC Western Front brigade commander to be killed during the war. His wing commanders were Majors Thomas Carthew (1 Corps Wing) and Wilfred Freeman (10 Army Wing), the former supporting the assault upon Vimy Ridge. Between the wars Freeman would help to overcome the inadequacies of the Trenchard years, especially the development of modern combat aircraft notably the Mosquito and Merlin-engined Mustang. He would also establish close relations with the United States aircraft industry and the US Army Air Force through his friendship with its commander General Henry H. 'Hap' Arnold[28].

Facing them was *Hauptmann* Otto Zimmer-Vorhaus, the *Kofl. 6.Armee* who had replaced *Hauptmann* Sorg a few weeks earlier. German balloon observers had detected preparations for the attack upon Vimy Ridge as early as January and he received twelve squadrons (including two *Schusta* and three *Jagdstaffeln*) following the occupation of the *Siegfriedstellung* to bring his strength to 30 squadrons (including seven *Schusta* and six *Jasta*) and 19 kite-balloons (Table 4-1). He delegated most *Luftstreitkräfte* units to the corps sectors (from north to south: *Gruppen Loos, Souchez, Vimy, Arras* and *Queant*) under a *Grufl* with the three central ones, *Grufln 3, 12* and *2* respectively, receiving one or two *Schusta* and one or two *Jasta* as well as a *FA* for each division. Zimmer-Vorhaus retained three *FA* for tactical reconnaissance but he had no bombers because the French front had priority so he was unable to harass British communications at a time when their roads leading to the front were suffering serious congestion[29].

Table 4-1:
6.Armee air Order of Battle 1 April 1917

Corps Group	Grufl Nr	Fl Abt	Schusta	Jasta
Souchez (VI.R)	3	3	2	1
Vimy (I.BR)	12	3	3	1
Arras (XII.R)	2	2	1	2
Total	-	**8**	**6**	**4**

Source: UKNA Air 1/9/15/1/22.

He had a daily average of only 42 serviceable fighters due to shortages of spares and even then they were frequently grounded by bad weather before the assault and this was reflected in light British losses. By 9 April Zimmer-Vorhaus' strength had risen to 195 serviceable aircraft but the increased British pressure meant they were reinforced within two days by 8 squadrons (half of them *Jasta* and *Schusta*). *OHL* assessed the situation on the French front before despatching yet another 10 squadrons (including two *Schusta*) on 14 April, which doubled Zimmer-Vorhaus' *Jasta* to 8. Subsequently there were only minor reinforcements until *Kagohl 1* was briefly attached but it soon joined many of Zimmer-Vorhaus squadrons moving to the Ypres front[30].

With the offensive imminent, Trenchard outlined his usual plan of campaign on 9 March: 'The aim of our offensive will be to make the enemy fight well behind, and not on, our lines.' Given the state of the RFC this was less a plan of campaign and more an article of faith which was severely tested in the outer air battle[31]. At the beginning of April Trenchard had 200 fighters which outnumbered the *Jasta's* serviceable aircraft by 4:1, but the defenders had technical superiority with their Albatros D.II/III and the Halberstadt D.V supplemented by the Roland D.II and Siemens D.I, while the British relied upon the Nieuport 17 with a leavening of Spads, SE 5s and Triplanes[32]. Even when the weather clipped the *Jasta's* wings, British casualties rose during the countdown to the Easter Monday attack by which time Trenchard's strength had risen to 459 aircraft, but numerous accidents meant serviceability had dropped below 82%.

The key to British air superiority, as on the Somme, would be found in the outer air-battle for which Trenchard established an interception zone whose inner boundary was five kilometres beyond the British front line, between Lens and Bullecourt, and whose outer boundary extended 13 kilometres eastwards to the line Henin-Liètard (east of Lens) to Sains (north west of Cambrai) but which would move forward with the flow of battle. During the Somme campaign the FE reconnaissance-fighters had been the spearhead supported by the single-seat fighters, but now the roles were reversed with FEs flying line patrols to provide an inner defensive layer while 105 single-seaters were to roam the outer zone[33].

Ideally the 310-square-kilometre outer battle-area would be patrolled throughout the day by a flight from each of the 14 squadrons; the outer zone by up to 50 fighters and the inner one by 20 two-seaters, a maximum of 300–400 daily sorties being theoretically possible in good weather. With an average 150 serviceable fighters flying two missions a day this objective was barely possible but weather and casualties meant that only on 11 days were more than 250 sorties flown while the 300-sortie level was broken on two days only[34]. In these stark statistics lay the seeds of disaster.

Despite being frequently grounded, the *Jasta* stretched the attackers during the fortnight before the infantry assault, especially the reconnaissance-fighter squadrons which lost 27 aircraft including five from a No 57 Squadron flight on 6 April (Table 4-2). It was not just the ageing FEs (which IV Brigade banned from unescorted OPs on 3 April) and Strutters which suffered – the casualties included five of the new Bristol Fighters which carried Trenchard's hopes ([35]). Four fell on 5 April when the former home defence pilot, Captain William Leefe-Robinson (whose victory over an airship earned him the Victoria Cross), led No 48 Squadron on its first OP and encountered *Jasta 11* led by the now illustrious Richthofen. Interrupter gear problems plagued the early Bristol Fighter and the flight went into a defensive circle which the *Jasta* slashed to pieces. Leefe-Robinson was captured and became a victim of the influenza pandemic shortly after returning home at the war's end.

Table 4-2:
I and III Brigade outer air battle operations
2 April – 27 May 1917

Week	Total sorties	Patrol sorties*	Losses	Loss rate (%)
2–8 April	1,835	115	32	1.75
9–15 April	1,635	155	40	2.45
16–22 April	1,155	100	14	1.2
23–29 April	2,470	225	42	1.7
30 April-6 May	2,495	240	17	0.7
7–13 May	2,230	190	18	0.8
14–20 May	1,265	90	6	0.5
21–27 May	2,030	190	11	0.5

Source: Brigade/wing work summaries
Note: *Daily average of Offensive and Line Patrol Sorties

The disaster was partly due to Leefe-Robinson's inexperience, but two of his experienced flight commanders, Captains David Tidmarsh and Alan Wilkinson, realised that the Bristol Fighter uniquely combined the speed, manoeuvrability and firepower of a single-seater with the observer's Lewis gun providing a sting in the tail. Both men had victories during this period, Tidmarsh's Albatros over Remy on 8 April probably being that of *Leutnant* Wilhelm Frankl, a 20-victory 'ace' with *Jasta 4*, whose Albatros D.III broke up. This was a significant 'scalp' for an aircraft of which Richthofen commented 'the D.III Albatros was...undoubtedly superior'[36].

So desperate was Trenchard for new reconnaissance-fighters that he press-ganged the RE 8s of No 59 Squadron and on 6 April three were lost escorting a reconnaissance mission. The squadron's heavy casualties during April (12 aircraft or 66% of the establishment) reflected the bizarre misuse of these slow, under-powered aircraft for long-range photographic reconnaissance and line patrols. Although nominally a corps squadron it registered no guns for three months between 17 March and 16 June[37]!

Initially Trenchard radiated optimism, writing to Haig on 6 April: 'Our casualties were fairly heavy but not as heavy as I anticipated for the first days of fighting.' He later stated: 'If only we could get three or four fine days I am confident that we shall bring about the same situation as we had during the battle of the Somme.' Yet two days after that he was less optimistic: '... the enemy has not been knocked out to the extent I had hoped. This, I think, is partly due to thick clouds...'[38].

Bad weather on 6 April restricted the British outer air battle effort to some 210 sorties with light losses (Table 4-2). The most interesting event was the crediting of No 48 Squadron's Wilkinson with three Albatros D.III. Brief improvements in the weather exposed the British corps squadrons to the *Jasta* while on 11 April the defensive shield, which involved less than 80 sorties that day (Table 4-3), buckled allowing the enemy to sweep over the lines like wolves in the fold, destroying seven of III Brigade's aircraft to inflict a loss rate (Table 4-4) of nearly 11%[39].

Table 4-3:
Arras Campaign. British sorties 26 March – 3 June 1917

Week	I Brigade		III Brigade		9 Wing	Total
	1(C) Wing	10(A) Wing	12(C) Wing	13(A) Wing		
26 March-1April	110	145	265	175	40	735
2–8 April	180	520	530	605	140	1,975
9–15 April	250	360	445	580	220	1,855
16–22 April	130	300	310	415	150	1,305
23–29 April	285	665	670	850	575	3,045
30 April-6 May	405	585	605	900	540	3,035
7–13 May	400	505	565	760	290	2,520
14–20 May	230	235	305	495	95	1,360
21–27 May	385	575	430	640	350	2,380
28 Ma -3 June	350	480	375	455	85	1,745
Total	**2,725**	**4,370**	**4,500**	**5,875**	**2,485**	**19,955**

Sources: Brigade and wing war diaries, RFC Headquarters summaries of work.
Note: 9 Wing to Flanders on May 31.

Table 4-4: British Losses in Arras Campaign

Week	I Brigade 1(C)Wing	10(A)Wing	III Brigade	9(GHQ) Wing 12 (C) Wing		Total 13(A)Wing
26 March-1April	-	2(3)	1 (-)	4(7)	-	7(10)
2–8 April	3(6)	7 (10)	10 (17)	22 (26)	15 (26)	57(85)
9–15 April	5(8)	4(8)	19(16)	12 (11)	4(6)	44(49)
16–22 April	3(2)	1(2)	1 (1)	9 (10)	-	14(15)
23–29 April	14 (15)	6(8)	9(12)	13 (14)	7(6)	49(55)
30 April-6 May	6(6)	5(5)	3 (4)	3(3)	10 (12)	27(30)
7–13 May	2(2)	5(5)	4 (2)	7(4)	12 (19)	30(32)
14–20 May	-	- (1)	3 (6)	3(3)	3(3)	9(13)
21–27 May	-	6(6)	1 (-)	4(5)	7(7)	18(18)
28 May -3 June	3(6)	4(6)	-	3(2)	2(1)	12(15)
Total	**36 (45)**	**40 (54)**	**51 (58)**	**80 (85)**	**60 (80)**	**267 (322)**

Source: Henshaw:148–182.

Note: Initial figures are aircraft, figures in parenthesis are dead and missing aircrew.

This was repeated two days later although I Brigade again escaped almost unscathed. The British loss rate on 13 April was distorted by the massacre of six No 59 Squadron REs sent unsupported on a photographic mission less than seven kilometres from Richthofen's base. In the outer battle the British flew more than 1,100 sorties during the week following Easter Monday and lost 20 aircraft, the funeral pyre fuelled by attempts to photograph the *Wotanstellung*. Two clashes between experienced units, *Jasta 11* and No 60 Squadron, from 14–16 April demonstrated German technical superiority with eight British Nieuports lost[40].

During the week before Allenby's St George's Day attack there was a brief decline in activity, which marked the watershed in British fortunes after which their casualties fell while claims rose as the air war was finally carried behind the enemy lines. The dispatch of 285 fighter and reconnaissance-fighter sorties into the outer battle zone on that day (Table 4-3) marked the beginning of a more dynamic policy of dragon-slaying which maintained a daily average of 225 sorties, compared with a maximum of 160 a fortnight earlier. Nine British aircraft fell to enemy action on St George's Day, including a pair lost to collision, yet this was only a 2% loss rate[41].

The new tactics were no panacea and the British lost 40 aircraft on the Arras front during the week, the second highest of the campaign, as the *Jastas'* sweeps exploited weaknesses in coverage to savage the corps squadrons. But Trenchard's men remained the more active flying more than 2,700 sorties (Table 4-2) so their loss rate was 1.7% (Table 4-4), compared with 2.45% a fortnight earlier, and the rate fell steadily during the following fortnight to 0.5%. There was more intensive patrolling of the outer zone and from 24 April better planning meant tighter integration of missions[42]. That day Pups of Newall's No 66 Squadron escorted reconnaissance Strutters beyond the enemy lines and then shielded two outward-bound bomber missions before returning to their roost. Other Pups from the same squadron, supported by No 19 Squadron Spads, welcomed the returning bombers and Strutters, which all came back safely[43]. This established a pattern of integrated operations which continued until the Armistice and which the Germans failed to emulate.

Events like this seemed to feed Trenchard's optimism. He informed Haig on 26 April: '…all the pilots seem convinced that a remarkable change had come across the enemy during the last five days.' He even made an unsubstantiated claim that some BE pilots had attacked Albatros fighters, rather like police claiming a suspect had struck their truncheons with his head[44]!

Yet April ended with Richthofen further twisting the lion's tail by leading a mass sweep of 20 fighters (to which *Jasta 3*, *Jasta 4* and *Jasta 33* contributed) to execute a plan which Zimmer-Vorhaus had devised some weeks earlier to compensate for numerical weakness. They shot down six aircraft and escaped without loss leaving Richthofen to ponder the advantages of permanent multi-squadron formations of fighters. The laconic 9 Wing entry for this day noted: 'HA (Hostile Aircraft) very active to-day, the 'Circus' (a hostile formation of 10 Scouts all excellent pilots) being at work[45].'

The British failure to secure the outer air battle area was the prime cause of 'Bloody April' in which Trenchard lost a third of his strength; 253 aircraft were brought down, 180 (71%) over Arras, another 23 damaged when crashing upon landing. Six naval aircraft were lost on coastal or strategic bombing operations. There were 410 aircrew casualties (half of them killed or captured including 188 pilots) amounting to 20% of the total, with 241 lost behind the enemy lines. It was later calculated that only 92 hours were flown for every man killed or missing[46]. The Royal Air Force later concluded: 'It must be stated that the British air offensive, although pushed with the greatest vigour, and supported by great numerical superiority, not only proved exceptionally costly but failed to establish any degree of marked ascendancy over the German Air Service. As a result, its designed object, that of keeping the enemy engaged over his back areas in order that our Corps machines might work unmolested, remained unachieved[47].'

Trenchard was aware that losses shook morale, but his attitude was demonstrated in a visit to No 59 Squadron after it lost a complete flight. He allowed the shaken airmen to let off steam and then ordered them to: '... give the Hun hell in your RE 8s.' Although the RE 8 was still used in the reconnaissance-fighter role during May, none fell to enemy fire. Shephard quietly boosted morale on 24 April by flying a No16 Squadron BE 2e over the Canadian Corps[48].

Accidents added to the casualty lists, accounting for a daily average of 11 aircraft from 4–8 April, and by the end of the month 273 had been lost, of which 175 were on the Arras front. A third was due to mechanical failure, weather conditions accounted for another third with strong winds often tipping over the light airframes, while the inexperience of many pilots caused the remainder[49].

Pilot training was improving but reports on two BE 2c, which No 9 Squadron surrendered on 17 April because they were no longer combat-worthy, make surprising reading. Of the two, No 5733 had flown more than 208 hours and could not fly with a full service load (observer, radio and Lewis gun) while No 5864 had flown more than 241 hours, crashed twice, been badly hit once and substantially rebuilt. The official verdict was that they were '…fit to fly to England and also for school work[50].' Despite the slaughter Trenchard's overall strength actually increased to 909 aircraft by the end of April (84% serviceable) with 854 pilots[51].

Obsolete aircraft certainly helped to boost Trenchard's casualty lists but another factor was his failure to concentrate resources which compromised the fighter screen. By May the lessons were being learned and there was greater integration of operations. However, at the same time there were growing demands upon the fighter squadrons which were flying OPs, line patrols, interceptions, ground-attack and escort missions to strain man and machine as well as diverting them from their prime role.

Most of the British fell to the *Jastas*, the top scorers being Richthofen's *Jasta 11* which was credited in April with 92, followed by *Jasta 12*, first under *Hauptmann* Paul von Osterroht then *Oberleutnant* Adolf von Tutschek, with 32 victories. Richthofen claimed 21 to take his total to 52 and make him the greatest 'ace' leading a nervous high command to send him on an extended leave. The level of achievement may be judged by the fact that during May even with reinforcements the *6.Armee* averaged 56 serviceable fighters each day and lost only eight pilots killed or captured; indeed during 'Bloody April' Zimmer-Vorhaus's total losses amounted to about 30 aircraft with 49 aircrew dead and missing[52].

The I Brigade records, correlating reports from anti-aircraft observers on the 1st Army front, suggest German air power did not exploit the successes. Even with only 100 serviceable aircraft, the German squadrons facing 1st Army were easily capable of between 500 and 700 sorties a week. But in the fortnights preceding and succeeding Easter Monday Zimmer-Vorhaus's airmen averaged only 265 and 220 sorties a week, although the percentage over British lines rose from less than 4% to 14%[53].

Significantly, although *6.Armee* fighter strength rose to 70 serviceable aircraft on 1 May, 'Bloody April' was not followed by 'Bloody May' despite increased British activity. On the contrary, as Tables 4-3 and 4-4 show, during May Trenchard's losses on the Arras front halved (total losses to enemy action on the Western Front were 197) although overall strength declined to 878 aircraft (92% serviceability) and 822 pilots by the month's end. Simultaneously there was a British resurgence noted by both friend and foe and the opposing *Jastas* saw casualties rise to nine pilots[54].

There was no overall improvement in the quality of British aircraft, although their new generation of combat aircraft had overcome teething problems. During May only a few squadrons were re-equipped; two received the DH 4, one the improved F2B Bristol Fighter and a fourth the dubious gift of RE 8s while another two replaced Nieuport 17C with the marginally superior Nieuport 23. It was through superior tactics that the British began to recover air superiority; stronger fighter screens, reinforced by OPs, countered German morning and evening sweeps, although after one such clash on 6 May Britain's greatest ace, Captain Albert Ball (44 victories), crashed[55]. An innovation on 2 May saw No 40 Squadron Nieuports fly through an artillery barrage to attack eight balloons and claim half, and a similar mission was flown a few days later ([56]). The terrain-following tactics ('hedge-hopping') were later refined for use against ground targets and the concept continues with attack helicopters in the twenty-first century.

Trenchard's fighter screen was weakened as his bomber offensive failed to disperse enemy fighters, partly due to the continued shortage of purpose-built bombers. There were only two day-strike squadrons (No 27 and No 55) with obsolete Martinsyde G.102 Elephants and modern DH 4s respectively and these were augmented by the newly-arrived No 100 Squadron (FE 2) night-strike force. Once again corps squadrons, from the neighbouring brigades of Shephard and Longcroft, added nominal weight with a squadron from each drawing the short straw to provide half-a-dozen aircraft. The bomber offensive started a day late, on 5 April and was disrupted by the Weather. This proved a blessing in disguise. Before Easter Monday, 9 Wing and the part-timers dropped some 1½ tonnes of bombs on railroads, supply dumps, barracks and 5 tonnes upon airfields but the loss rate was 7% because unescorted missions were exposed to the *Jastas*[57].

On the night of 7/8 April, Major M. G. Christie's No 100 Squadron, attached to Higgins' brigade, began roaming the night skies using eight FEs to bomb Douai airfield and the town's railway station. Another two, transferred from No 51 Home Defence Squadron two days earlier, strafed ground targets with a 40mm cannon firing a 0.5-kilogramme (one pound) shell; they derailed a train. But they were not invulnerable and on 8 April *Jasta 4's Leutnant* Hans Klein brought down a No 100 Squadron FE 2 raider to enter the history books as the first night-fighter victory[58].

In the fortnight after Easter Monday Newall's bombers flew only once, although the deadly bats of No 100 Squadron dropped more than a tonne of bombs over five nights. In each of the remaining weeks Newall's bombers dropped an average of two tonnes of bombs while corps and reconnaissance-fighter squadrons delivered an average four tonnes, some at night[59].

Higgins' squadrons then surrendered the strike role and Shephard, boosted by No 100 Squadron, dropped 10½ tonnes of bombs in the last three weeks of the campaign. Shephard relied largely upon FEs to divert German attention from growing activity on the Ypres front and suffered neither loss nor injury. The FEs' success made Trenchard revise his opinions about night-bombing informing Haig on May 7: 'According to reports received I think this night bombing is really beginning to do some good[60].'

His optimism reflected the improving situation, especially within the inner battle area where his nine corps squadrons had faced a month of trial. Trenchard had anticipated a different pace of operations within the inner zone and noted on 31 January: '… the tendency nowadays is not to attempt the wholesale destruction of trenches as we used to think necessary; on the other hand the increased importance of counter-battery work is universally admitted.' His ideal ratio of one corps aeroplane for every six heavy guns was achieved at Arras with two aircraft in each counter-battery area and two registering upon trench positions, allowing a squadron with 21 serviceable aircraft to fly 345 minutes a day in good weather[61].

To achieve surprise, Allenby made the radical suggestion that his gunners avoid the time-consuming process of artillery registration and destruction by calculating the ranges of the key positions located from the air then allow for variables such as meteorological conditions and barrel wear. His 1,700 guns could use this pre-registration or 'predicted' technique to reduce the bombardment to two days followed by a rapid advance behind a rolling barrage. But Haig feared many targets would be missed, his guns would be worn out and the volume of fire would be too intense for aerial or terrestrial observers to correct, so a conventional four-day fire-plan was retained[62].

While high wind, sleet and snow hindered air support for the opening bombardment, the snow also served to highlight new targets. Only 45% of III Brigade's 214 artillery shoots on 4–8 April were judged successful and the one-day delay requested by Nivelle to complete his preparations gave the British a clear, sunny, day to wreck the defences. During the five-day bombardment the brigade registered guns upon 228 positions, engaged 157 batteries and flew some 445 sorties, the counter-battery work proving the key to subsequent British success. Carthew's airmen discovered 86% of the 212 active batteries around Vimy Ridge and drove many eastward by 8 April[63].

The operations of No 13 Squadron, supporting XVII Corps, were typical with 92 sorties to register guns (of which 33 were successful) and 38 artillery patrols (15 successful). A few months earlier Trenchard had stated that pilots should direct artillery fire, but this was not always the case and in No 13 Squadron it was the observer who was literally calling the shots and directing most successful fire missions. During this period the squadron flew 21 photographic reconnaissance sorties to monitor the bombardment and 242 photographic plates were exposed[64].

The first phase of the inner air campaign saw the British gain an indisputable victory in the inner battle with corps squadrons flying 1,000 sorties (Table 4-2). The German reaction in the air, as on the ground, was feeble and on 5 April, for example, the I Brigade war diary noted: 'Our artillery machines were able to carry out their work entirely unmolested.' German fighters made only a few forays over the battlefield but succeeded in shooting down 11 corps aircraft (another three fell to *Flak* or friendly fire) and harassed others, but such was the level of British activity that this represented a loss rate of only about 1% while the timid defenders lost a single corps aircraft [65].

By locating forward troops and enemy batteries the corps squadrons played a major part in the British success on 9 April and without Carthew's two squadrons, Vimy Ridge would have remained unconquered. In succeeding days the battle for inner air space became more active as Zimmer-Vorhaus released his three reconnaissance squadrons to the most heavily pressed *Grufln* [66].

With hundreds of shells falling simultaneously it became difficult to range individual German batteries and the *FA (A)* increasingly monitored major bombardments to ensure coverage of the whole target area. A typical signal, intercepted by the British on the morning of 5 May, read: 'Heavy fire Bullecourt…on railway line-south of Riencourt impossible to range owing to hurricane fire.' For targets of opportunity the Germans called down fire from the special alert battery (*Überwachungsbatterie*) earmarked by each division[67].

German contact patrol work was initially poor, and *Grufl 12* noted the *Landsers* still remained reluctant to attract the attention of German aircraft while many units lost their signal panels, possibly deliberately. From February German corps squadrons received radio transmitter/receivers which theoretically allowed them to provide headquarters with instant information on the location of forward troops using codes or frequently changed abbreviations. But the new radios suffered teething troubles and shell splinters frequently cut the trailing aerials while they were also vulnerable to enemy Comint[68].

Only at the end of April did German air-ground co-operation become effective, especially co-operation with the artillery. 'The artillery…at first failed to make complete use of the information gathered by the airmen, the troops lacked the necessary practice and skill[69].' Trenchard noticed this lack of co-operation on 13 April but even a month later the Germans were flying only eight long-range artillery shoots a week and rarely more than two artillery aircraft supported an artillery group in a day[7]).

From 14–23 April British corps squadrons flew some 800 sorties (including 36 bomber) and lost 25 aircraft for a heavy, but absorbable, loss rate of 3%. The Scarpe battles saw another time of trial, especially the week of the Second Battle when 955 sorties were flown with an average loss rate of 2.4%, although I Brigade suffered 5% casualties because the Vimy Ridge area was *Jasta 11's* hunting ground. During this period British inner battle losses were greater than those of the outer battle, underlining the brief and unique failure of Trenchard's fighter screen although it ensnared most of the 15 German corps aircraft which fell between 9 April and 3 May[71].

Trenchard's third failure during April was his counter-battery campaign due to a combination of German fighter pressure, the dispersal of *6.Armee*'s guns and its extensive use of dummy batteries. III Brigade engaged 69 batteries, claimed 23 'OKs', meaning they were on target, and to have directed shells within 25 metres of the target on 89 occasions during the two days before St George's Day although their vision was obscured by mist up to 1,500 metres. Their 'absurdly optimistic' attitude, continued even when the results were monitored by senior officers and clearly did not match the claims[72].

On 6 May Trenchard demanded a solution and suggested 'artillery machines' fly above the mist to conduct shoots, noting that one brigadier had personally flown such missions. Mitchell had already devised an alternative using kite balloons to take over fire direction when aeroplanes had to abandon missions either through combat damage or fuel shortage and by 28 April Higgins had followed suit. The airmen were not always to blame, and Trenchard had earlier complained to Lieutenant-Colonel Stuart Rawlins (who worked for Haig's Artillery Advisor Major-General Sir Noel Birch) about the gunners' attitude. Citing a VI Corps' heavy battery commander who ordered the radio left by the side of the road he warned: 'If the gunners want air observation, they must do their part[73].'

The German reaction forces also placed new demands on the RFC and on 28 April Trenchard proposed strengthening contact patrols to detect and to neutralise them with artillery fire. This was not effective and only after the Ypres Campaign opened were dedicated counter-attack patrols introduced[74].

A feature of the Scarpe battles was the growing commitment of squadrons to ground-attack missions but the question of bullets or bombs divided the RFC leadership. Carthew was clearly a believer in bombs and daily delivered twenty-four 20-pound (9-kilogramme) Hales' bombs bringing his total by the end of the campaign to more than 7½ tonnes. Mitchell relied more upon bullets and by the end of the campaign had delivered less than 2½ tonnes of bombs[75].

German corps squadrons were also active but dropped only 900 kilogrammes of bombs in the first three weeks of April compared with some 8.4 tonnes dropped by British corps wings between 21 April and 11 May. Zimmer-Vorhaus lacked a strike force until 11 May, when he was briefly allocated *Kagohl 1* with some 25 aircraft, but it departed nine days later. The only significant attack recorded by the British was on the night of 3/4 May at Bethune and even German records suggest

Kagohl 1 played no part in the Arras campaign[76].

Air combat was coming closer to the ground; the *Schusta* attacked corps aircraft, claiming several (although *Schusta* would be credited with only eight victories from 31 March to 11 May) while both sides' contact patrols welcomed the opportunity to 'moonlight' by engaging the enemy. German two-seater crews, both *Fliegerabteilung* and *Schusta*, were also increasingly venting their spleens with machine gun fire upon the Tommies, although German records suggest they had been doing so since the later stages of the Somme campaign (see Chapter Three). In fact the *Schusta* were specifically instructed to attack enemy troops '...when not employed on the protection of artillery aeroplanes' and the growing willingness of German airmen to make low-level attacks forced Trenchard to introduce dedicated fighter patrols to intercept them[77].

On 24 April *Hauptmann* Eduard Zorer, possibly influenced by events on the Somme in September, led his *Schusta 7* in a massed attack to support *17. Infanteriedivision*'s attempts to prevent a break-through just north of Gavrelle. He claimed to have disrupted the assault by 15th Division/XVII Corps without loss, although British records make no mention of air attacks. The British were also flying close air-support missions; on 3 May No 43 Squadron observers spotted a reaction force preparing to strike XIII Corps, just north of Gavrelle and a flight of Strutters from the same squadron strafed them. Yet to reduce the risk from low-flying enemy aircraft Pretyman used two Nieuport squadrons supplemented by Newall's Spads to fly low line patrols[78].

German air activity increased substantially during the three weeks following St George's Day rising from 450 to 690 sorties a week of which about a fifth were over the British lines. The record unfortunately dissolves in mid May but German activity probably declined as squadrons moved to the Ypres front[79].

The peripheral air battle around Arras had far less impact than on the Somme because the German withdrawal to the *Siegfriedstellung* contracted Gough's front and made it difficult to find new airfields for V Brigade's 126 aircraft. They flew some 2,000 sorties for the loss of 40 aircraft, mostly supporting Gough's bloody private war around Bullecourt. Captain Charles Portal of No 3 Squadron, later Trenchard's 'favourite disciple' and Newall's successor as Chief of the Air Staff in 1940, played a prominent role directing artillery fire[80].

During this peripheral campaign more than 25 tonnes of bombs were dropped by II, IV and V Brigades from early April to mid May in missions involving some 440 sorties which cost 16 aircraft (a loss rate of 3.5%). More than half this effort was by Webb-Bowen's II Brigade, principally the FEs of No 20 Squadron which lost 11 aircraft on bombing missions although the Squadron developed an expertise which it exploited with the Bristol Fighter 16 months later[81].

The Arras campaign also saw electronic warfare become an integral element of British air defence. On 13 April Trenchard asked his brigade commanders to report any 'jamming' incidents but rejected active electronic warfare. On 6 May he also refused to allow 'spoof' signals to be transmitted from a captured radio set in a British aircraft to confuse enemy fire direction arguing it was impractical when most enemy artillery aircraft operated behind their own lines[82]. He remained under pressure from the brigades to jam enemy air waves but on 19 May informed them: 'It is understood that suggestions have been made to attempt to jam the German artillery wireless by means of a Telefunken set mounted in one of our machines. The GOC does not wish any attempt of this kind made at present.' No reasons were given but, even in the twenty-first century, the British Army tends not to support active electronic counter-measures, believing they have no lasting effect and merely alert the enemy to communications weakness[83].

An unspoken reason for his decision was that it helped the compass stations to exploit enemy radio transmissions so as to locate enemy aircraft for interception; 320 were detected from 4–19 April of which 140 were ranging guns on up to 160 targets (the British ranged on 650 targets in the same period). The interception of *Artillerieflieger* behind their own lines was considered, but the process would take too long and on 24 April it was decided to leave them to OPs[84].

To cut reaction times Trenchard wanted to use radio telegraphy to guide fighters but on 31 January he postponed the plans because they required high-powered transmitters which would interfere with other radio networks. This proved only a temporary setback because radio telephones were at an advanced stage of development and became operational a year later. Meanwhile, fighters easily detected targets visually once guided to their vicinity. To improve detection, the stations along the front were divided into two groups; Northern and Southern. On 19 April it was decided to give each army two compass stations up to eight kilometres apart linked by telephone and these were established within a month but no documents referring to them were allowed to go further forward than divisional headquarters[85].

Each brigade had an interceptor unit: No 8 Naval Squadron (Triplanes) in I Brigade and No 29 Squadron (Nieuports) in III Brigade, but conventional operations had priority. The naval squadron drove off enemy aircraft twice in April and claimed a victory on 9 May while III Brigade had similar success. On 3 May Trenchard reported that III Brigade drove off five aircraft which were registering targets and harassed others. Nine days later he noted III Brigade interceptors '...have recently had considerable success in interfering with German artillery machines in close co-operation with anti-aircraft guns and compass stations.' He also asked his brigades to consider the feasibility of using fast fighters to intercept enemy aircraft as soon as they began using their radios[86].

The I Brigade's naval airmen became dedicated interceptors, these missions accounting for 26 out of their 35 sorties on 7 May. For faster response a flight was rotated daily to an advanced airstrip from 9 May and the next day 22 sorties were flown. The whole squadron arrived five days later. But these missions took their toll of its machines and, despite the delivery of 15 new aircraft, the number of interceptor sorties dropped to a monthly total to 308 during May, with a maximum daily total of 8[87].

By early June attention was turning to the Ypres salient, to which Newall transferred No 70 Squadron in mid May with the wing following at the end of the month. During the Arras campaign the RFC flew nearly 20,000 sorties between 26 March and 3 June, an average of nearly 2,000 a week or double the rate of the longer Somme campaign, but the cost was high with 267 aircraft failing to return and 322 aircrew being killed or captured (Table 4-4).

If April was a trial for the RFC it was a disaster for the Aviation Militaire Française due less to its losses and more to its abject failure to achieve its goals ([88]). Nivelle stubbornly refused to admit his plans had been shattered by the German withdrawal, informing GAR commander Général Alfred Micheler – 'Nothing has changed in the conditions for a rupture.' Micheler, like Atlas, carried the burden of the offensive on his shoulders, but Pétain (whom Nivelle had snubbed) was now asked to conduct a diversionary operation with GAC. Micheler was to strike northwards taking the Chemin des Dames and the enemy gun line in a coup de main with V and VI Armées under Générals Oliviér Mazel and Charles Mangin then pursue the enemy with the aid of Denis-August Duchêne's X Armée. The assault was originally scheduled for 12 April but the enemy withdrawal and poor weather caused a four-day delay.

Although Nivelle had pledged in January never to attack the enemy's strongest point, he now violated that undertaking by his choice of battlefield, a series of parallel river valleys dominated by steep-sided limestone ridges. During their three-year occupation the Germans had fortified the area, quarrying and tunnelling the soft rock with their usual diligence to provide not only shelters but also underground routes, while some 20 kilometres behind the front line lay the new *Brunhild*- and *Hundingstellungen.*

Heeresgruppe Deutscher Kronprinz delegated the defence of the Chemin des Dames to *General der Infanterie* Max von Boehn's *7.Armee* while the Champagne plains were held by *Generaloberst* Karl von Einem's *3.Armee*. Hours before the French attack *General der Infanterie* Fritz von Below's *1.Armee*, redundant after the withdrawal to the *Siegfriedstellung*, was inserted between Boehn and Einem to secure the area north of Reims[89].

Nivelle's margin of artillery superiority, 3,600 guns against 2,600, was inadequate and he lacked howitzers, while Micheler's shock force was outnumbered by the defenders, a quarter of whom were *Eingreifdivisionen*. The Poilus' traditional élan could not carry them through a deep and undamaged defensive system manned by alert and well-trained troops. As they climbed steep slopes overlooked by the enemy they were scythed down by machine gun fire, the heavy casualties swamping the hospitals and leading to ominous signs of low morale by the end of the day. Through sheer force of personality Mangin drove his troops forward, compelling the enemy to withdraw into a switch line but by then the French were exhausted.

Duchêne's army entered the line on 21 April as Micheler's role was reduced to securing the Chemin des Dames and three days later VI Armée was transferred to Général Louis Franchet d'Espérey's GAN. To the east Pétain struck on 17 April using Général François Anthoine's IV Armée after the usual thorough preparation, but his diversionary operation quickly fizzled out. On 29 April he was promoted 'technical advisor' to the War Minister as the politicians circled like vultures over the fading creature that was Nivelle's offensive.

Nivelle sought to hold power by selecting Mangin as a scapegoat and dismissed him on 2 May in an interview which ended with both men screaming insults like fishwives. Mangin was replaced by Duchêne who was, in turn, replaced by Général Maistre but this game of musical chairs could not breathe life into a corpse and with the disbandment of GAR on 8 May, the offensive formally ended. Micheler (like Pétain an exponent of the doctrine of the limited offensive) was given command of V Armée after Mazel became the other sacrificial goat.

On 15 May Pétain finally became Commander-in-Chief of the Armies of the North and North-East with Foch as Chief of the General Staff. Nivelle was scheduled to command an army group but, understandably, Pétain refused to reinstate him as a subordinate and he was later sent to military exile in North Africa. If Nivelle had not touted his operation as a war-winning enterprise and prepared it more thoroughly, it would have been regarded as a success because it secured a bridgehead in the heights dominating the Aisne and inflicted 83,000 casualties. But the French suffered severely, the post-war General Staff admitting losses of 139,600 to 10 May of whom a third was dead or missing although later research suggests as many as 217,000 casualties. Pétain found a resentful army refusing to advance while the well of manpower was drained almost dry. His priorities were to rebuild and re-equip his army (and air force) both physically and morally. This would take time and for the rest of the year the French Army was capable only of short, limited, offensives leaving the British to carry the burden.

Nivelle had known his air support under Peuty was weak but this was just one of a host of problems, of which the most important was the loss of political and professional support. Unfortunately, the air chief was too busy buzzing around airfields to address his own problems of obsolete aircraft, which ultimately depended upon root and branch reform in the interior, and his decision to send poor pilots back to the training schools was poorly timed for it left squadrons undermanned[90].

Peuty's forces were substantially re-distributed following '*Alberich*' with GAN's air strength halved and most of its squadrons being transferred to GAR. The latter's strength doubled to 63 squadrons with a nominal 715 aircraft (Table 4-5), more than half Nivelle's air strength, while Pétain's IV Armée had another 190 but up to half the aircraft deployed were unserviceable[91].

Table 4-5:
French squadron distribution for the Nivelle Offensive

Army	Corps		Army					Fighter	Bomber	Total
	C	F	C	F	R	V	MS			
V	3	2	8	6	2	-	-	5(1)	-	26
VI	4	2	2	7	-	1	1	9(2)	-	26
X	2	2	3	1	-	-	-	3	-	11
IV	1	2	4	-	1	-	-	6(1)	4(1)	18
Total	10	8	17	14	3	1	1	23(4)	4	81

Source: *Les Armées Françaises dans la Grande Guerre X/1*:GAR, GAE, IV, V, VI, X Armée.
Note: C=Caudron G. F=Farman. MS=Morane Saulnier. R=Caudron R. V=Voisin. Fighter and bomber figures in parenthesis are groupes.

Boehn had twice the air strength of Falkenhausen at Arras, some 450 aircraft by mid April, with similar distribution; a *Fliegerabteilung* for most divisions in front of the *Hundingstellung*, a few to support artillery commands and a *Schusta* for every two *Fliegerabteilungen*. From mid February reconnaissance aircraft brought in details of new rail lines, detraining points, spurs for rail guns, camps and airfields south of the Aisne. On 25 February *OHL* ordered the front strengthened and rapidly reinforced Boehn with troops, guns and aircraft[92].

At the beginning of February Boehn had only *Oberleutnant* Kurt Student's *Jasta 9* but reinforcements meant that by mid April he had twelve *Jasta* and also benefited from control of the *Luftstreitkräfte's* strike force, *Kagohl 2* and *Kagohl 4*. They interdicted the main railway down the Marne valley to Paris concentrating upon Epernay (due south of Reims) and Châlons-sur-Marne respectively, often striking major targets several nights in succession for the loss of two bombers, one piloted by *Kagohl 2 Geschwaderkommandeur*, *Hauptmann* Job-Heinrich von Dewall, who was taken prisoner on 24 March. The introduction of *1.Armee*, whose *Kofl* was *Hauptmann* Helmuth Wilberg, took German air strength opposite GAR to some 530 aircraft (Table 4-6) with another 110 opposite Pétain. The German fighters had the upper hand and their airmen closely monitored French preparations for the offensive[93].

Table 4-6:
German Order of Battle for the Nivelle Offensive

Armee	FA	Schusta	Jasta	Kagohl (Kasta)
AOK 7	18	8	6	1(6)
AOK 1	17	9	6	1(6)
AOK 3	7	1	3	–
Total	**42**	**18**	**15**	**2 (12)**

Source: *Weltkrieg XII*:298–299.
Note: For *3.Armee* only right wing units are included.

The French airmen lacked a day strike force and, hamstrung by the generals' demands for 'direct protection', were confined south of the *Hundingstellung* some 15–25 kilometres behind the German lines. The focus of both sides' attention was the Aisne valley where Peuty concentrated three fighter groups (GC 11, 12 and 14) into the Groupement de Combat du GAR with 15 squadrons (including C46). His hopes of concentrating the fighters to dominate the enemy air space were rapidly thwarted. He had only 131 fighters (152 pilots) on 16 April against a nominal 204 and five days later 153 fighters (171 pilots) forcing him to call on the Paris home-defence force for an extra 30 aircraft. In the week before the attack incomplete statistics indicate the groupement flew more than 600 sorties (in flight-strength patrols) and had 138 combats[94].

The fighter screen arrangements also compromised Peuty's plans. The groupement was under Micheler who immediately split its squadrons between the armies; GC 11 supporting Mazel while GC 12 and 14 supported Mangin. He also demanded the generals give 20 hours notice of their fighter support requirements. But the roads were so poor that motorcycle dispatch riders often did not reach the fighter airfields with their orders until 2 hours after the dawn patrols set off! It was hoped to give the troops permanent air cover but poor weather (there were only two good flying days from 6–18 April) and lack of fighters dashed these hopes[95].

With fewer fighters than Trenchard and a front of 60 kilometres compared with 10 kilometres at Arras, the weaknesses in fighter cover became glaringly obvious when Nivelle's bombardment began on 6 April. Immediately complaints flowed into GQG from the front; on 9 April one of Mangin's corps commanders, Général Pierre Berdoulat (II Corps Coloniale), said enemy fighters constantly harassed his squadrons and balloons preventing his guns destroying a single battery and he demanded support from a full fighter group[96].

Peuty had earlier told his fighter squadrons: 'Your task is to seek out, fight and destroy enemy aviation...' but the pressure on Micheler was irresistible. Even as Berdoulat complained, Micheler was demanding a shield for the corps squadrons in the form of eight daily patrols of up to 10 aircraft on each army front[97].

Yet French fighters played an active role; indeed an after-action report noted that in VI Armée (whose airmen were commanded by the Verdun and Somme veteran, Gérard) there were OPs of 4 to 10 aircraft and while there were a few permanent barrage patrols these were usually flown by corps squadrons. But the OPs were restricted to the inner, rather than the outer, battle space; when GC 11 was transferred to GAC in May its 'offensive' sorties, for example, were restricted to an area 6 kilometres behind the enemy lines or between the balloon lines ([98]). This allowed the *Jastas* to approach the front with impunity and of 33 aircraft lost by GAR from 6–25 April, half fell in French lines. Yet the *Jasta* opposite the French front lost more fighters in combat (19) than those opposite the British (14) suggesting the French fighters did not lack aggression; indeed, in the week of the offensive the GAR groupement flew 1,039 sorties and had 278 combats [99].

As the bombardment began the French quickly discovered enemy artillery strength had grown but they could do little to beat down their opponents. From 6–15 April there were 975 registrations by aeroplane, of which 60% were rated 'successful', and 722 by balloon of which 92% were 'successful' leading to a German offensive against the latter which roasted eight of the so-called 'sausages'[100]. During the bombardment, French corps squadrons suffered 108 aircrew casualties, a third in air combat, 17 due to shells striking aircraft or to ground fire and 54 in accidents. The only reason there was no massacre of corps squadrons was because the Germans were operating a passive, rather than active, defence awaiting their victims like spiders rather than hunting for them in sweeps along the front. The *Jasta* claimed only five corps aircraft from 6–15 April (although most fell within the French lines), and also eight enemy fighters all shot down south of the *Hundingsstellung* while the Germans lost only three aircraft[101].

Sadly, the heroism of the French airmen was wasted for the changes in German tactical doctrine meant the bombardment largely ploughed up the nearest trenches (which were virtually empty) and missed the numerous strong points further back. Salt was rubbed into the wound by the army commanders' continued lack of appreciation. On the first day Mangin complained that on four occasions enemy fighters forced his corps aircraft to abandon their missions while several Germans had flown over his positions during the afternoon. His subordinates agreed; Général Mitry of VI Corps d'Armée declared that the guaranteed aerial barrier was a complete illusion, while Général Mazillier, of the neighbouring XX Corps d'Armée said he had lost a R210 Caudron which had been scheduled to take vital photographs for the gunners while a balloon had fallen that evening. He concluded that, unlike the Somme campaign, France no longer held mastery of the air with the result that his corps squadron, F35, flew on only six days and directed a mere 128 shells[102].

Micheler's excuse to his subordinates was that a third of the 12 fighter squadrons assigned him had failed to arrive, while in those squadrons which were available more than half the aircraft were 'unfit for flying'. He also claimed the overall shortage of pilots was exacerbated by the decision to send many of the best men to pick up new aircraft and he was still awaiting their return. Curiously, in his after-action report, Micheler rated counter-battery work on Mangin's VI Armée front as good. Mangin's squadrons lost 42 aircraft from 10–16 April; four in air combat, 15 to ground fire and 23 (nearly 55%) in accidents, but there were only 10 aircrew casualties: one wounded in combat, four wounded by ground fire with five dead or missing in accidents[103].

As the moment of truth, Jour J (16 April) approached, the complaints reached a crescendo although Mazel's corps squadrons flew 849 sorties in the week before the attack. On 13 April the commander of 41e Division (V Armée) reported German aircraft were flying unhindered over his batteries and his trenches were being strafed. He concluded: 'We need planes!' The next day Chef de Bataillon Nicolas, a liaison officer with V Armée's I Corps d'Armée, had photographic evidence clearly showing the bombardment's failure and he also complained the enemy were strafing and bombing the trenches. He claimed German air-directed artillery had caused the destruction of 10 field guns and the loss of some 600 horses whose lines had been hit by gas shells[04].

The German artillery response on 16 April was lethally precise thanks to ground and balloon observers, a major success being the detection of 130 tanks as they assembled to support V Armée's attack upon 54.

Infanteriedivision whose guns blew most of them to bits. During Jour J the French flew fewer than 300 sorties but contact patrols confirmed there had been little progress. The staffs in their chateaux left squadrons ignorant of last minute changes in plans while the absence of any 'zone call' system made artillery support dependent upon inflexible planning.

Micheler's fighter groupement flew 225 sorties and had 67 engagements but the *Jasta* dominated the French front lines losing one but claiming 9 victims. Peuty had demanded offensive sweeps from midday on 15 April but despite the presence of 'strong' French fighter patrols, occasionally of up to 20 aircraft, *Schusta* crews rarely needed to protect their charges and some passed the time strafing trenches. Poor weather restricted the number of French offensive patrols which were usually composed of six fighters ('never less than five' were the instructions) which the defenders easily avoided[105].

During the next few days the weather reduced French air operations to a daily average of less than 200 sorties, rising to 300 as the weather improved (Table 4-7). Mazel's corps squadrons flew 385 sorties during the week of the assault but German pressure strengthened demands upon Peuty for more direct support especially from the hard-pressed Mangin. Belatedly Peuty assigned GB 3 Voisons to GAR but only for line patrols and escort missions, echoing the misuse of the *Kagohls* the previous summer, and it was only later in the month that they assumed their proper role to drop more than 25 tonnes of bombs. While French losses were light, enemy interference caused many missions to be abandoned which meant the *Jasta* of 1. and 7.*Armee* recorded only 14 victories over aircraft together with 6 balloons from 17 April until the end of the month[106].

Table 4-7:
French air operations April–May 1917

Week	GAR		GAC		Total
	Army	Corps	Army	Corps	
2–8 April	615	445	255	295	1,610
9–15 April	1,065	610	635	1,175	3,485
16–22 April	1,165	480	450	565	2,660
23–29 April	2,510	1,115	990	800	5,415
30 April -					
6 May	2,445	1,880	845	1,030	6,200
7–13 May	1,825	985	705	640	4,155
14–20 May	720	160	225	150	1,255
21–27 May	2,115	775	1,180	725	4,795
Totals	**12,460**	**6,450**	**5,285**	**5,380**	**29,575**

Source: Resumés journaliers, SHAA A129/1.
Notes: GAC is based upon Chalons Grouping returns and GAR upon the Chauny, Fere en Tardenois, Jonchery, Noyon and especially the Soissons Groupings. Figures rounded to nearest 5. No returns for April 12, April 19. May 18–20 possibly due to bad weather.

Air operations intensified in May as the ground offensive was fading (Table 4-7) partly because GQG demanded on 10 May a new fighter policy which called for timely concentrations of aircraft to protect the corps squadrons. This helped cut corps squadron losses and increased their effectiveness while the growing pressure forced the Germans to strip other fronts ruthlessly to contain the threat[107].

On the rolling plains of Champagne the *1.Armee* faced not only GAR but also GAC under Pétain who had only 44 aircraft in mid March when he learned his IV Armée would participate in Nivelle's enterprise. He demanded, and received, 145 reinforcements including the newly activated GC 15 under Capitaine Victor Ménard, a former prisoner of war who had escaped with another pre-war airman, Lieutenant Armand Pinsard, to reach French lines the previous April. After a rest Ménard was given command of N26 with Pinsard as a flight commander, the partnership continuing when Ménard was promoted and his friend, who survived the war with 27 victories, was given command of N78[108].

Ménard's fighter squadrons gave adequate support despite facing not only the squadrons supporting the left of *1.Armee* but also 11 squadrons supporting the right of *3.Armee* under Einem's *Kofl, Hauptmann* Ernst Drechsel (later a *Luftwaffe* general). During the bombardment only four French aircraft were lost and there appear to have been few complaints from the front line commanders about support or interference with artillery fire direction. But appalling weather meant that when the Poilus went 'over the top' only 90 sorties were flown, half by fighters[109].

Significantly Pétain also demanded bomber support and received GB 1 which could strike during the day with two squadrons of Strutters and at night with two Voisin units, the Strutters also being used for long-range reconnaissance. The bombing campaign did not begin until 24 April and in six days less than 8 tonnes was dropped rising to a total of 14 tonnes by the end of the following month[110].

The French suffered less in 'Bloody April' than their British allies; only 47 out of 2,100 aircraft (and 71 men) fell in combat but 266 machines were lost in accidents which killed 59 aircrew. By contrast the British, with 900 aircraft in France, lost 253 machines (183 aircrew) on the Western Front in combat and another 270 aircraft destroyed or badly damaged in accidents. *Jasta* victories confirm the pattern; squadrons opposite the Anglo-Belgian front were credited with 231 victories compared with 72 on the French front, including two Royal Navy bombers which fell over Alsace-Lorraine. Richthofen claimed 21 of the 89 victories on *Jasta 11*'s April score book. By contrast the campaign in the West cost the *Luftstreitkräfte* some 65 aircraft and about 130 aircrew[111].

During May 1917 Allied losses declined but the pattern was unchanged with 130 victories credited to Anglo-Belgian front *Jasta* and 69 to those opposite the French. The *Jasta* lost 26 aircraft in action, equally divided between the two fronts, out of a total of about 85 lost in the West. The French would later report their losses during April and May 1917 as 1.86 and 1.63% of their strength, figures which rose to 2.73% to 4.60% from July to September. While Allied losses were heavy during the remainder of the year (Table 4-7) they never reached the level of April 1917 yet German losses in May rose to 150, a peak unmatched until the spring offensive of the following March[112].

Why were British losses so disproportionately heavy compared with the French when both relied largely on obsolete aircraft? The reasons were a combination of factors including more intense operations, with two sorties a day being routine compared to one a day by the French, and Trenchard's demands for offensive operations as deep into enemy air space as possible which exposed them to enemy fighters. Trenchard would later claim his allies flew fewer sorties than the British because of poor maintenance and that they refused to rest tired aircrew[113]. While the long victory lists during April were the cause of much German rejoicing, and dismay among their enemies, the success especially against the British, masked a fundamental weakness in German air power. Hoeppner and his colleagues equated destruction with effectiveness, a common mistake in the twentieth century which was shared with their contemporaries in the Allied High Command, with Bomber Command in the Second World War and with Military Assistance Command Vietnam during the Indochina Conflict. Destruction may indicate success but it is no guarantee of military progress, for while the Germans controlled the skies over the Aisne valley their fighters, contrary to Hoeppner's orders, rarely penetrated beyond the balloon line. The *Jastas'* cut-and-run tactics made them less hunters than scavengers seeking easy prey rather than trying to disrupt the British air programme. It was a triumph of style over substance for while German pilots had the opportunity to build up large scores the British usually restricted them to the outer zone giving Trenchard's corps aircraft the freedom of the skies.

Richthofen's score book illustrates Germany's failure to exploit the spring successes. Between January and June 1917 he claimed 41 aircraft, of which nearly half were corps aircraft and nearly a third were reconnaissance-fighters (some of the corps aircraft were RE 8s executing the same role) and about 22% were fighters. Because of injuries he flew only two months in the latter half of the year and shot down seven aircraft of which 71% of them fighters for he rarely reached the corps aircraft. He would claim only three more corps aircraft (two acting as bombers) in 1917 and 65% of his remaining victims in 1918 were also fighters. This was because he and his comrades rarely hacked through the Allied fighter net for, while the German continued to contest Allied air superiority, they were never able to overcome it[114].

Chapter Five

The Recovery Of Allied Air Power: Summer And Autumn 1917

There is no greater curse than having your wish come true. Haig discovered this when he launched an offensive during the summer and autumn of 1917 from the historic market town of Ypres across the reclaimed swamp that was the Flanders Plain. On the ground the 'Northern Operation' proved indecisive but in the air the campaign confirmed the recovery of Allied air power.

The Germans held the low Ypres Ridge with its miniature ridges that curve east and south of the city, and they fortified both them and the Gheluvelt Plateau to the east. The 2nd British Army held Ypres under the shrewd, pot-bellied Sir Herbert Plumer, with King Albert's Belgian Army on his left and a French corps in the coastal enclave opposite Nieuport. Plumer planned a series of short jabs along the Ypres Ridge to take the miniature heights and began with an attack upon the Messines-Wytschaete (Messines) Ridge.

The ridge fell on 7 June after the explosion of mines with 400 tonnes of explosives but Haig wanted to break through the Ypres Ridge using Gough's 5th Army as the spearhead, while Rawlinson's 4th Army, which had been brought up from the Somme, advanced along the coast from Nieuport. Reorganising his forces and inserting Général François Anthoine's I Armée between the Belgians and Gough caused delays and before the French arrived, the Germans destroyed the Nieuport bridgehead on 10 July in *Unternehmen 'Strandfest'* (Beach Party)[1].

Meanwhile *General der Infanterie* Friedrich Sixt von Arnim's *4.Armee* facing the Ypres Salient strengthened its fortifications. By the time Gough attacked on 31 July von Arnim's *4. Armee* had added another position, *Flandernstellung I,* which crossed the Ypres Ridge at the village of Passchendaele and to the east had begun work upon another two positions. Gough advanced through drizzle which turned into driving rain but German counter-attacks restricted the attackers to the expendable Forward Zone. Gough launched three more attacks in August but gained little ground as the heavens wept and turned the shell-churned ground into paste.

Haig now went cap-in-hand to Plumer who resumed his original plan as the rains eased and the ground dried. Spearheaded by Australian and New Zealand troops, his meticulously prepared advances on 20 September (Menin Road Ridge), 26 September (Battle for Polygon Wood), 5 October (Broodseinde), 9 October (Poelcappelle) and 12 October (1st Passchendaele) inched closer to *Flandernstellung I*. Then the rain returned, although there were later occasional breaks of fine, cold weather, and the exhausted Anzac forces had to be replaced by Canadians who pushed towards Passchendaele through swampy terrain, which sucked down men, horses and guns. The campaign finally expired when they took the village on 10 November.

Cynics said the salient was barely sufficient to bury Haig's dead. His total casualties were around 245,000 while the French lost 50,000 and the defenders 205,000 including 26,500 prisoners. But the occupation of Passchendaele coincided with the collapse of Russia, accelerated by *General der Infanterie* Oskar von Hutier's *8.Armee* victory at Riga on 1 September, to free millions of German troops who streamed westwards. By the New Year Haig recognised that the enemy would regain the ground which had cost so much blood and, on 10 January 1918, he drafted secret plans to abandon the ridge.

Some German divisions went from the Eastern Front to the Austrian-Italian border under *General* Otto von Below's *14.Armee* which spearheaded an offensive that routed the Italians at Caporetto on 24 October. To prop up their allies Haig and Pétain reluctantly dispatched 11 divisions including Plumer and 2nd Army headquarters to northern Italy. Rawlinson's 4th Army was redesignated as the 2nd Army and Gough's 5th Army returned to the Somme.

The British air campaign in Flanders began modestly over Messines with 361 aircraft in 20 squadrons (II Brigade and 9 Wing) but quickly escalated into the largest and most complex struggle over the trenches since the outbreak of war. By the end of July Trenchard had committed 542 aircraft (Table 5-1) and two more brigades (IV, V) supported by 104 Royal Navy aircraft under Captain Charles Lambe together with 270 Allied aeroplanes. With land behind Ypres at a premium, especially in 4th Army's coastal sector, some of Brigadier John Becke's IV Brigade aircraft operated from III Brigade's airfields opposite Cambrai well outside the 'Northern Operation' battlefield[2].

Table 5-1:
RFC Strength in Ypres campaign: 10 May – 18 November 1917

Date	II Brigade		IV Brigade		V Brigade		GHQ	Total
	2 Wing	11 Wing	3 Wing	14 Wing	15 Wing	22 Wing	9 Wing	
10 May	70/10	83/20	-	-	-	-	-	153/30
	(74)	(67)						(141)
7 June	116/5	117/18	-	-	-	-	96/9	329/32
	(116)	(110)					(92)	(318)
7 July	51/2	43/10	36/10	30/8	79/11	81/15	114/8	361/64
	(54)	(56)	(36)	(32)	(63)	(77)	(105)	(423)
31 July	54/1	68/9	36/5	66/-	86/11	82/4	112/8	504/38
	(65)	(60)	(37)	(65)	(92)	(99)	(116)	(534)
1 September								
	57/4	92/8	39/-	54/2	83/3	109/81	29/6	563/31
	(54)	(78)	(37)	(45)	(84)	(104)	(125)	(527)
20 September								
	86/4	105/21	40/3	51/5	59/11	103/17	130/4	574/65
	(85)	(94)	(36)	(51)	(59)	(99)	(124)(548)	
15 October								
	108/5	110/19	40/5	73/12	60/7	108/10	147/12	646/70
	(106)	(102)	(37)	(71)	(59)	(108)	(144)	(627)
1 November								
	108/4	124/7	30/4	69/8	42/4	91/13	149/21	613/61
	(100)	(127)	(29)	(63)	(41)	(84)	(143)	(587)
15 November								
	135/7	196/39	30/2	71/13	-	-	86/8	518/69
	(130)	(170)	(28)	(66)			(90)	(484)
18 November								
	117/7	203/20	29/0	70/13	-	-	93/4	512/44
	(114)	(28)	(165)	(67)			(90)	(464)

Note: Aircraft total/unserviceable (pilots).
Source: RFC summaries.

Although serviceability was excellent, usually around 90%, the rise in casualties caused pilot shortfalls of up to 10% in some commands (Table 5-1). Uniquely, Trenchard had to strip quieter fronts to create a pilot reserve which was barely adequate but kept the Flanders squadrons up to strength. The shortages may have been due to changes in training with the introduction in Britain of Smith-Barry's training methods which exacerbated the squadrons' recovery from the heavy losses during the spring campaign because they were more demanding, which meant they took longer and reduced the flow of new pilots[3].

By 20 September the British had 26 squadrons (including 14 fighter/reconnaissance-fighter and five bomber) in Flanders and until mid October Trenchard maintained an average 650 aircraft (Table 5-1) supported by some 170 French (Table 5-2). Trenchard's campaign was undermined during the autumn when political pressure to retaliate against the German bombing of London meant that the IV Brigade's 14 Wing was transferred to eastern France on 31 October together with two of Trenchard's precious bomber squadrons as the new independent 41 Wing under Newall. Newall was replaced by Freeman but then, from 8 November, the Caporetto defeat forced the Allies to send 14 squadrons (five British) and 190 aircraft to prop up the Italian Front. The top-heavy Flanders command structure was rationalised by disbanding both IV Brigade headquarters and 3 Wing on 13 November with Becke taking command of II Brigade. The following day, V Brigade returned to the Somme leaving Trenchard with 518 aircraft in Flanders when the 'Northern Operation' officially ceased[4].

Table 5-2:
French squadrons supporting I Armée 17 July – 15 November, 1917

Date	Fighter		Bomber		Army/Corps			Total
	N	Spa	V	AR	C	F	Sop	
17 July	2	8(2)	2	-	6	1	-	16
15 August	2	8(2)	3	-	5	1	1	20
15 September	2	4(1)	3	-	6	-	1	16
15 October	2	4(1)	3	-	6	-	-	15
15 November	1	4 (1)	4	1	3	-	3	16

Source: *Armées Françaises Tome X*:I Armée entry
Note: Spa column figures in parenthesis are Groupes de Chasse.

German air strength grew from a nominal 100 aircraft in mid May to some 300 by 7 June (Table 5-3) as the Arras front was stripped, for: '...the British remained our most dangerous enemy and the British front claimed, as usual, the largest part of the German air force[5].' The Germans matched the British build-up and by the end of July had 660 aircraft (10% Navy) supported by 23 kite balloons. After the British offensive became mired in August, OHL withdrew six squadrons (including two *Jasta*) and reduced air strength to under 550 aircraft. This figure was maintained until the end of the campaign despite Plumer's offensives[6].

Table 5-3:
4. *Armee* squadron strength (excludes naval squadrons)

Date	Jasta	Kasta	Schusta	FA	Total
15 May	4	-	2	7	13
25 May	5	-	2	8	15
1 June	7	2	5	15	29
7 June	8	6	5	17	36
15 June	10	6	10	21	47
31 Jul	18	12	14	36	80
20 September	16	12	14	32	73

Sources: Franks et al. *Chronology*:54–113 & *Jasta Pilots*:16–39. *Weltkrieg XII*:452–453, 467. *Weltkrieg XIII*:60–61,72

The men who commanded these forces were, in some ways, a mirror image of their armies[7]. Brigadier Tom Webb-Bowen, aged 38, led II Brigade consisting of Lieutenant-Colonel Cyril Murphy's 2 (Corps) Wing and Lieutenant-Colonel George Stopford's 11 (Army) Wing. Webb-Bowen had joined the Bedfordshire Regiment on the eve of the Boer War after serving a year in the Militia, but until transferring to the RFC in December 1912 his only significant appointment was two years as adjutant to the Indian Volunteers. Within six months he had become an instructor at the CFS and then Assistant Commandant in August 1914. By 1915 he was commanding No 2 Squadron in Trenchard's 1 Wing and became II Brigade's first commander when it was created in February 1916. At the end of the 'Northern Operation', on 16 November, he went to Italy to command the RFC in that theatre[8]. By then Alan 'Jack' Scott, a pre-war New Zealand barrister, was commanding 11 Wing, replacing Stopford who departed for England on 29 July to become the last wartime Commandant of the School of Military Aeronautics[9].

On 1 June Newall's 9 Wing arrived and was soon joined by V Brigade (still under the triumvirate of Longcroft, Hearson and Holt) which absorbed five of Webb-Bowen's corps squadrons on 10 June. Five days later, Becke's IV Brigade, began arriving in a piecemeal fashion led by Ludlow-Hewitt's 3 (Corps) Wing followed by Lieutenant-Colonel Reginald Mills' 14 (Army) Wing, on 1 July[10]. Becke was eight months younger than Webb-Bowen and also entered the Army through the Militia but was commissioned into the Nottinghamshire and Derbyshire Regiment before serving as a rail staff officer during the Boer War. He transferred to the RFC in October 1912 and later replaced Webb-Bowen as commander of No 2 Squadron rising to command I Brigade's corps wing on the Lens front before replacing Ashmore on 20 December 1916. With the disbanding of IV Brigade in November 1917, Becke again succeeded Webb-Bowen, this time at II Brigade. He left the RAF shortly after the war's end.

Wilfred Freeman a 28-year-old northerner, whose civil engineer father paved London's streets, succeeded Newall at 9 Wing in October. He was commissioned in the Manchester Regiment but transferred to the RFC three months before war broke out and joined No 2 Squadron. He became a pioneer of radio transmission (once directing the shells of his brother's battery) before becoming a flying instructor. After serving in Egypt as a squadron commander he took charge of a training school in England until March 1917 when he assumed command of I Brigade's 10 (Army) Wing, being replaced by Smith-Barry[11].

On 18 October Longcroft returned to England to command the Training Division and was replaced at V Brigade by 38-year-old Brigadier Lionel Charlton, a qualified staff officer, who joined the RFC four months before the outbreak of war to escape the boredom of barracks life. The son of an American mother and a British diplomat father, he was commissioned into the Lancashire Fusiliers in 1893, fought the Boer War then joined the West Africa Frontier Force. For nearly five years he served in a region commonly called the 'White Man's Grave' and met John Salmond (Trenchard's successor as commander of the RFC in France), then became aide to the Governor of the Leeward Islands before service in India. Although a confirmed bachelor, his frank memoirs make it clear that his foreign postings allowed him to enjoy negotiating affection with maidens of a duskier hue[12].

Despite being badly injured in a crash early in the war, Charlton was rapidly promoted becoming a lieutenant-colonel in August 1915 and a Brigadier seven months later. In February 1917 he became Director of Military Aeronautics and from 18 October commanded V Brigade. He remained in the RAF after the war, serving as the first British Air Attaché in Washington, but left the service in 1924 in protest against the policy of bombing rebellious Iraqi tribesmen. He became a prolific author, especially of boy's adventure stories, as well as a radio broadcaster and died in 1958.

The *Kofl 4.Armee* during the first two months of the 'Northern Operation' was 33-year-old *Hauptmann* Otto Bufe, who was born in Alsace-Lorraine the son of a doctor. Qualifying top at cadet school he entered the fast track to promotion within the pre-war army and at the outbreak of war was assigned to the *Fliegertruppe*. Initially an observer, he became a squadron commander and developed a reputation as a tactician before becoming *Stofl 4.Armee* in September 1916. Hoeppner would later praise Bufe's energy and vision in effectively exploiting his resources to prevent the British air threat in Flanders becoming as severe as it had been during the Battle of the Somme[13]. It was Bufe who concentrated fighter squadrons into larger groupings but this would ultimately be his downfall. On 28 May he created a *Jagdstaffelgruppe* under *Hauptmann* Gustav Stenzel, the *Jasta 8* commander. The *Gruppe's* history is unclear, but consisted of *Jastas 8, 18, 27* and *28* which were officially awarded 14 victories in the first six days of June[14].

A permanent command of four *Jasta, JG I*, was created under Manfred von Richthofen on 23 June and entered the fray from 2 July in *Staffel* and *Geschwader* strength. Richthofen exploited the observer telephone system to scramble *Jasta* quickly, but he and Bufe clashed from their first meeting and when Richthofen returned to duty after being wounded (possibly by friendly fire) on 6 July he was furious to discover *JG I* being deployed piecemeal. On 19 July he wrote to Hoeppner's Technical Officer, *Oberleutnant* Friedrich 'Fritz' von Falkenhayn (son of the former Chief of the General Staff), demanding that *JG I* be used en masse. This request was echoed on the same day by Arnim and led to sweeps on 21–22 July with 13 victory claims without loss.

Bufe argued that a fighter presence maintained *Landser* morale and Richthofen himself, in his first order of the day to *JG I*, dispatched the *Jasta* piecemeal. But Richthofen's name carried the day and Bufe was scheduled for transfer to the Eastern Front to become *Kofl 8.Armee* [15]. This transfer may have been a face-saving gesture as the army was planning to break shaky Russian morale by attacking Riga and required an experienced *Kofl*, but in the end the imminence of the British attack meant Bufe was retained until the crisis had passed. He departed Flanders only on 7 August accompanied by *FA(A) 202* and *208* [16].

The new *Kofl 4.Armee* was 37-year-old *Hauptmann* Helmuth Wilberg, one of the most experienced officers in the *Luftstreitkräfte* and the son of a Jewish portrait painter at the royal court of Wurttemburg. His royal connections may have helped overcome the potential barrier of prejudice when he entered the Army in 1899 to become a General Staff officer in 1913. By then he had earned his pilot's licence and his first appointment was as adjutant to the newly established *Inspektor der Fliegertruppe*, *Oberst* Walter von Ebrhardt. Wilberg became a squadron commander then *Stofl 11. Armee* on the Eastern Front before becoming *Kofl 1.Armee*. In *4. Armee* he adopted a more aggressive doctrine than Bufe, especially in the field of ground-attack. After the war his service in the East would stand him in good stead, for the *11.Armee* Chief of Staff, *Oberst* Johannes (Hans) von Seeckt, would lead the *Reichsheer* and selected Wilberg to lay the foundation for the *Luftwaffe* in which he would ultimately be, with Erhard Milch, one of two half-Jewish generals[17].

The British aerial campaign followed the traditional pattern with the emphasis upon the outer battle to shield the corps squadrons, whose counter-battery work was vital against German guns sheltering behind ridges and in valleys. The Messine battle was a relatively small scale operation in which Webb-Bowen and Newall sealed off and saturated the compact battlefield (Table 5-4) to reduce the corps squadrons loss rate to only 0.5% (Table 5-5). Their success led the Germans to complain about the enemy's aerial presence and the ability of Trenchard's aircraft to attack men and installations deep in their rear. By 10 June the British had flown some 6,100 sorties for the loss of 93 aircraft, more than half in the last week, 60% being obsolete or obsolescent FEs, Strutters and Nieuports[18].

Table 5-4:
British air operations over Flanders May 7 – July 1, 1917

Week	II Brigade		IV Brigade		V Brigade		GHQ	Total
	2 Wing	11 Wing	3 Wing	14 Wing	15 Wing	22 Wing	9 Wing	
7–13 May	325	365	-	-	-	-	-	690
14–20 May	270	225	-	-	-	-	-	495
21–27 May	680	650	-	-	-	-	35	1,365
28 May-3 June	690	580	-	-	-	-	70	1,340
4–10 June	770	960	-	-	10	-	470	2,210
11–17 June	310	485	75	-	275	245	215	1,605
18–24 June	190	255	110	-	250	285	60	1,150
25 June-1 July	175	245	90	-	220	190	10	930
Total	**3,410**	**3,765**	**275**	**-**	**755**	**720**	**860**	**9,785**

Source: RFC summaries.

Table 5-5:
British casualties over Flanders 7 May – 1 July 1917

	IV Brigade		V Brigade		GHQ	Total
	2 Wing	11 Wing	15 Wing	22 Wing	9 Wing	
7–13 May	1/2	7/7	-	-	-	8/9
14–20 May	-	10/11	-	-	-	10/11
21–27 May	-	13/12	-	-	-	13/12
28 May-3 June	3/2	9/7	-	-	3/5	15/14
4–10 June	7/9	25/23	-	-	15/11	47/43
11–17 June	1/2	7/4	1/-	-	5/3	14/9
18–24 June	1/2	4/5	3/4	8/7	-	16/18
25 June-1 July	1/2	2/1	1/2	1/2	3/3	8/10
Total	**14/19**	**77/70**	**5/6**	**9/9**	**26/22**	**131/126**

Source: Henshaw:171–188.
Note: First figure aircraft shot down or failed to return. Second figure is aircrew killed or captured.

After Messines the exclusion zone fell east of the enemy balloon line now about 12–15 kilometres from no-man's-land. Through-out the 'Northern Operation' the southern boundary of the air offensive remained the River Lys, but the northern boundary was extended to the Channel by the time Trenchard briefed his commanders on 7 July. The fighters' limited range confined the eastern boundary several kilometres behind the balloon line, but the fighter net was cast further by the Bristol Fighters of Becke, Newall and Webb-Bowen although Longcroft had none[19].

As at Arras the fighter net depended upon a complex series of patrols by the single-seat fighters with Trenchard pursuing his well-tried, but unpopular, aggressive doctrine. Conventional Close or Near OPs were supplemented by Distant Offensive Patrols (DOPs) on the outer edge and Line Patrols within the balloon line. But with the *Jasta* able to strike at will, many British airmen criticised the DOP policy as a waste of men's lives and future Air Vice Marshal Arthur Gould Lee of No 46 Squadron, later wrote 'We could see no rational purpose for our coat-trailing DOPs[20].

In 1918 the Allies found they could shield a mobile battlefield by deploying OPs nearer the army's spearheads, but Trenchard could not afford to take this gamble at Ypres. While DOPs appeared to surrender the initiative to the enemy and sometimes exposed small British formations to massed fighters, the OPs' bullet-catcher' role was successful in shielding the inner battle, despite heavy losses. From July to mid November, 63.5% of British aircraft losses were fighters, while 155 pilots (the equivalent of six squadrons) were killed or captured, some by ground fire. By contrast the Flanders *Jasta* lost 38 pilots in combat or accidents and two during attacks upon their bases, the equivalent of four *Staffeln*[21].

During the Gough-led phase of the 'Northern Operation' the air battle became more intense (Table 5-6) especially after Trenchard opened his campaign on 11 July following a three-day delay due to bad weather. The upsurge in British air activity removed any lingering doubts *OHL* might have had about the direction of the main enemy thrust. There were huge swirling dogfights involving 60 to 100 aircraft during July while despite only brief periods of good weather during the August monsoon, there were nearly 1,000 air battles[22].

Table 5-6:
British air operations in Flanders 2 July – 2 September 1917

Week	II Brigade		IV Brigade		V Brigade		GHQ	Total
	2 Wing	11 Wing	3 Wing	14 Wing	15 Wing	22 Wing	9 Wing	
2–8 July	175	350	95	145	260	300	215	1,540
9–15 July	205	195	150	330	325	320	265	1,790
16–22 July	285	335	120	290	510	445	300	2,285
23–29 July	260	295	135	160	645	590	355	2,440
30 July–5 August	60	135	30	80	150	220	105	780
6–12 August	280	400	130	410	510	680	195	2,605
13–19 August	350	545	160	785	690	1,010	420	3,960
20–26 August	305	405	175	610	635	820	260	3,210
27 August–2 September	55	135	50	130	115	230	20	735
Total	1,975	2,795	1,045	2,940	3,840	4,615	2,135	19,345

Source: RFC summaries.

Table 5-7:
British losses in Flanders 2 July – 2 September 1917

Week	II Brigade		IV Brigade		V Brigade		GHQ	Total
	2 Wing	11 Wing	3 Wing	14 Wing	15 Wing	22 Wing	9 Wing	
2–8 July	2/4	9/14	-	-	2/4	1/1	5/5	19/28
9–15 July	1/1	7/2	1/-	2/1	1/2	13/12	12/10	37/28
16–22 July	1/2	4/6	1/-	3/-	1/2	9/5	8/6	27/21
23–29 July	3/5	4/6	2/2	-	2/1	11/15	13/11	35/40
30 Jul–5 Aug	-/1	1/2	1/1	-	5/2	3/2	5/2	15/10
6–12 August	1/1	6/4	3/3	2/3	6/8	12/11	8/7	38/37
13–19 August	2/2	11/10	1/1	1/2	10/12	12/13	29/24	66/64
20–26 August	1/2	2/2	-	2/1	5/5	10/9	14/15	34/34
27 Aug–2 Sept	1/2	-/	-	-	2/-	2/2	1/-	6/4
Total	**12/20**	**44/46**	**9/7**	**10/7**	**34/36**	**73/70**	**95/80**	**277/266**

Source: Henshaw:197–206.
Note: First figure aircraft shot down or failed to return.
Second figure aircrew killed or captured.

Combat experience played a key role in the Germans' favourable kill ratio as shown by No 84 Squadron, led by future Marshal of the Royal Air Force Major William Sholto Douglas and which joined Newall's wing on 23 September. Sholto-Douglas brought 18 pilots; three experienced Captains (Kenneth Leask, E. R. Pennant, and James Child) as Flight Commanders, an American Lieutenant, Jens F. 'Swede' Larsen (who entered the RFC through the Canadian artillery), and 14 2nd Lieutenants, of whom four were Canadian. The squadron flew its first combat mission on 15 October and in the following month lost some 40% of its original strength and four replacements, almost all to aces including *Jasta* 27's *Oberleutnant* Hermann Göring. Yet the flight commanders survived, with Child and Leask each credited with eight victories, while the surviving tyros became as deadly as their foes. Four founder members still with the squadron in April 1918 were all aces and the South African, Anthony Beauchamp Proctor, would ultimately achieve 54 victories[24].

The Germans recognised air combat was reaching new heights of intensity and that they were inflicting heavy losses (Table 5-8) but because they were ensnared in the fighter net they failed to gain air superiority. The vital British corps squadrons suffered some 13.5% of all losses, including by ground fire, and while a quarter of these losses were to *JG I*, even massed fighter sweeps rarely succeeded in cutting through the fighter screen. For example during the last four days of September, the *Geschwader* flew 272 sorties without success, consuming fuel and ammunition when enmeshed in the fighter screen[25].

Table 5-8:
British losses to fighters, 1 July – 18 November 1917

Month	Fighter	Corps	Long range	Total
July	55	14	27	96
August	52	18	32	102
September	88	15	20	123
October	65	8	22	95
November	29	7	3	39
Total	**289**	**62**	**104**	**455**

Source: Henshaw:192–250.
Note: Long range is bomber and fighter reconnaissance.

There were few big dogfights during the Indian summer of September: Trenchard had to respond to growing threats from low-flying enemy aircraft by having two layers of patrols at 3,000 metres and 1,800 metres, with the lower patrols ready to intercept *Infanterieflieger* and *Schusta*. It was the *Schusta* and ground fire, rather than fighters, that increased corps squadron casualties. Indeed during the Battle of the Menin Road Ridge only 6 of 72 air combats involved the corps squadrons[26].

During the Plumer-led phase the overall British loss rate doubled to 2.85% (Table 5-9) but high sortie rates were maintained in deteriorating weather (Table 5-10). The situation was not one-sided and anti-aircraft artillery observers in 2nd and 5th Army reported 1,525 enemy sorties in the week ending 22 September of which 250 crossed the line while the following week the figures were 1,261 and 252 respectively, both figures evidence of Wilberg's dynamic presence[27].

Table 5-9:
British casualties 3 September – 18 November 1917

Week	II Brigade		IV Brigade		V Brigade		GHQ	Total
	2 Wing	11 Wing	3 Wing	14 Wing	15 Wing	22 Wing	9 Wing	
3-9 Sep	3/3	12/12	1/2	1/-	4/4	6/5	9/9	36/35
10–16 Sep	4/8	9/8	1/2	2/2	1/1	14/13	5/8	36/42
17–23 Sep	3/4	22/18	1/-	3/2	5/6	13/11	8/12	55/53
24–30 Sep	1/1	11/9	-	5/5	2/3	13/12	7/8	39/38
1–7 Oct	2/-	6/6	-	-	1/2	5/8	8/10	22/26
8–14 Oct	10/7	9/8	-	5/5	4/4	6/7	10/12	44/43
15–21 Oct	-	3/5	1/2	3/2	-	7/4	16/22	30/35
22–28 Oct	1/2	11/8	1/-	5/5	1/-	6/5	6/8	31/28
29 Oct-								
4 Nov	2/4	2/2	-	-	-	2/2	2/2	8/10
5–11 Nov	6/6	10/9	1/2	3/1	1/2	4/1	10/10	35/31
12–18 Nov	3/4	11/5	1/-	2/3	-	4/3	-	21/15
Total	**61/78**	**227/206**	**16/15**	**39/32**	**58/64**	**162/150**	**202/203**	**765/748**

Source: Henshaw:219–250.
Note: First figure aircraft shot down or failed to return.
Second figure aircrew killed or captured.

Table 5-10:
British air operations in Flanders
3 September – 18 November 1917

Week	II Brigade		IV Brigade		V Brigade		GHQ	Total
	2 Wing	11 Wing	3 Wing	14 Wing	15 Wing	22 Wing	9 Wing	
3–9 September	360	495	105	350	265	560	310	2,445
10–16 September	405	710	120	380	305	585	355	2,860
17–23 September	525	865	130	315	370	770	240	3,215
24–30 September	475	905	170	435	345	825	520	3,675
1–7 October	465	575	95	245	230	515	230	2,355
8–14 October	455	545	105	240	285	565	150	2,345
15–21 October	465	715	155	425	240	650	230	2,880
22–28 October	375	505	125	310	155	520	255	2,245
29 October–4 November	265	340	80	250	110	330	185	1,560
5–11 November	365	755	65	235	65	325	130	1,940
12–18 November	200	605	55	320	30	120	25	1,355
Total	**4,355**	**7,015**	**1,205**	**3,505**	**2,400**	**5,765**	**2,630**	**26,875**

Sources: RFC summaries.

Despite *JG I*'s much trumpeted successes, it remained a unique formation. *Hauptmann* Otto Hartmann, *Staffelführer* of *Jasta 28* and former leader of *6.Armee*'s *Jagdgruppe Lille*, did create *Jagdgruppe 4. Armee Nord* with four *Jasta* north of the Ypres Ridge on 27 August but it had little impact upon the outer air battle. It was disbanded on 3 September after Hartmann's death only to reappear on 30 September with two *Jasta* under *Hauptmann* Constantin von Bentheim followed, 20 days later, by *Jagdgruppe Dixmuiden* under *Oberleutnant* Harald Auffarth, the acting *Staffelführer* of *Jasta 29*, with four *Jasta*. By the end of the Flanders campaign *JG I*'s *Staffeln* were, naturally, among the leading scorers but behind them was *Leutnant* Walter von Bülow-Bothkamp's *Jasta 36*[28].

The success of OPs was rarely recognised by its major beneficiaries. The corps squadrons continued to feel exposed and in early September Trenchard faced down squadron commanders' calls for stronger escorts, insisting the offensive policy would be maintained. By the end of the month he reported to Haig that the RFC had the upper hand but the situation was not always one-sided and, especially over Plumer's spearhead, the corps squadrons occasionally encountered fierce opposition which disrupted their missions[29].

Fighters increasingly joined bomber attacks upon airfields, although some daring pilots had already flown lone missions. The pace accelerated during the Messines operation, possibly influenced by the controversial claim of the Canadian ace, Captain William Bishop, to have shot down 3 aircraft (bringing his score to 25) during a dawn attack upon an unidentified enemy airfield on 2 June ([30]). Two airfields were struck on 7 June but plans for mass attacks on 31 July and 20 September were thwarted by the weather, although on 20 September bombers did strike six airfields including *JG I*'s Marcke and Bissinghem where nine fighters were damaged and five ground crew killed by half a tonne of bombs[31].

Despite the problems of poor morning visibility, Holt continued to demand more fighter attacks against airfields. On 30 September this caused a crisis when the No 10 Naval Squadron commander, Canadian Flight Commander R.F. Redpath, refused an order to strike *Kagohl 4*'s base at Rumbeke. The squadron was returned in disgrace to Royal Navy command at Dunkirk on 4 October while Redpath was given a desk job. Undaunted, Holt organised co-ordinated sweeps (or 'drives') starting on 20 October when 45 fighters struck Rumbeke, dropping 250 kilogrammes of bombs and claiming a bomber. Three fighters failed to return and the Germans lost one machine, with three more pilots wounded[32]. Although he failed to achieve all his objectives Holt was pointing the way to the future as the Allies learned to operate in ever larger formations.

Trenchard did not neglect defensive missions and Line Patrols, together with Ground-Controlled Interception, averaged 20% of weekly fighter sorties throughout July slowly declining to 15.4% by mid-mid November. From 11 July until the end of August, there were 150 interception sorties over the Ypres salient as improvements in the compass station system allowed operators to target particular frequencies and even specific operators. Squadrons operated an interception rota with raucous blasts on a klaxon scrambling the selected flight within two or three minutes in a system whose principles are still used to this day[33].

The Germans had their own form of ground-controlled interception. They had long monitored Allied radios to warn batteries of imminent bombardment, allowing the gunners to take cover or to change position, but under Wilberg a more active response developed. From late August interception stations were linked by telephone to fighter airfields from where by October 'scrambled' fighters were reported to have significantly reduced enemy artillery fire[34]. Yet only in 4 weeks out of 11 did British corps squadron loss rates exceed 1% of sorties (Tables 5-9 & 5-10).

Flak also played a major part in the defence and during the worse week of corps squadron casualties (October 8–14) accounted for a third of the victims. Arnim had eight *Flakgruppen* with 252 anti-aircraft guns and 28 searchlights, most covering the reaction forces opposite the main axes of the British offensive. *Flak* units, which had been under a *Flakgruppenkommandeur*, were decentralised into smaller task groups (*Untergruppen*) of up to six units for improved fire control and they increasingly participated in the ground battle with truck-mounted or tractor-towed weapons used against tanks.

The British anti-aircraft shield was thinner with 2nd and 5th Armies having only 58 heavy guns, 20 searchlights and 56 machine guns[35]. This was too weak to neutralise the marauding *Kagohls* as bombing had a growing impact upon both sides' armies. The Germans alone dropped nearly 660 tonnes of bombs (Table 5-11) from July to November – 100 tonnes by *Kagohl 4* in the 50 days to 22 September, of which half was delivered during daylight. The white canvas of British tents were an excellent target, yet only on 15 September did Plumer's corps commanders request the urgent dispatch of camouflaged tents[36].

Table 5-11:
Bomb tonnages (kilogrammes) during the later Flanders campaign

Week	German	RFC		RNAS		French	Total
	Day	Night	Day	Night	Allied		
3–9 Sept	53,050	3,565	1,645	1,195	2,133	3,160	11,698
10–16 Sept	16,420	6,585	4,235	1,801	12,470	4,705	29,796
17–23 Sept	16,400	5,671	8,372	2,195	6,205	2,195	24,638
24–30 Sept	57,625	5,075	18,727	9,052	11,515	7,500	51,869
1–7 Oct	74,900	8,555	5,120	819	2,873	2,260	19,627
8–14 Oct	18,450	2,825	1,990	785	6,688	1,360	13,648
15–21 Oct	69,725	5,210	4,910	3,583	-	1,080	14,783
22–28 Oct	74,645	4,335	11,375	1,525	14,177	3,245	34,657
29 Oct-4 Nov	73,515	3,285	6,925	1,185	8,412	3,245	23,052
5–11 Nov	46,500	1,275	6,295	590	6,637	2,260	17,057
12–18 Nov	20,140	955	100	1,631	-	-	2,686
Total	**521,370**	**47,336**	**69,694**	**24,361**	**71,110**	**31,010**	**243,511**

Sources: *Nachrichtenblätter*; RFC summaries; RNAS bombing statistics; French resumés.

Arnim ordered his bombers to fly daylight Tactical Level operations and night time Operational Level missions against the enemy infrastructure as far east as St Omer, 50 kilometres behind the British lines. Gradually, the German Army recognised that faster and more manoeuvrable single-engined aircraft were more effective directly over the battlefield and *OHL* ended the misuse of 'Big Birds' on 21 October by overruling Arnim and restricting the heavy bombers to Operational Level targets which now received tonnes of bombs (Table 5-11) almost every night[37].

The *Kagohls*' short, but extremely active, low-level attack role began on 10 July when four *Kagohl 1* C-types fired 3,100 rounds supporting *Unternehmen 'Strandfest'* against the Nieuport bridgehead. During the

Gough-led offensives, German heavy bombers carpet-bombed batteries but the *Kagohl*s increasingly delegated attacks upon artillery to their declining number of single-engined aircraft. On 11 August a *'Schlachtstaffel'* made 20 attacks upon batteries in the Zellebeke area with *'Schlachtstaffeln'* or *'Sturmstaffeln'* from the *Kagohl*s striking over the following days. On 15 August *Kagohl 1's Schlachtstaffel*, supported by *FA 13* and *Schusta 9*, dropped 200 kilogrammes of bombs on batteries in the Ypres Salient while the remainder of *Kagohl 1*, supported by half of *JG I*, struck batteries west of Lens[38].

The *Kagohls* (occasionally escorted by *JG I*) also strafed and bombed forward areas to support the infantry. Corps squadrons helped them and on 26 June *Gruppe Ypern* ordered *FA 45* to support : '...our counter-attacks with two or three aeroplanes. These will fly in front of the assaulting troops, will stimulate the offensive spirit of the men by flying low and will weaken the enemy's power of resistance by dropping bombs and using machine gun fire[39].' The growing low-level threat confirmed that the inner air space had ceased to be a British sanctuary but German corps squadrons were still too weak for the ground-attack role and with declining numbers of single-engine bombers, Wilberg decided to assign this task to the *Schusta* whose escort role was declining.

British air combat reports show the *Artillerieflieger* were frequently operating alone, and from January to August 1917 their observers were credited with 83 victories in the West compared with 46 by *Schustas*. The *Schusta* joined the *Schlachtverbände* during Plumer's first September attack when eight aircraft strafed the Australians. The attacks became more frequent in October when 2nd Army noted the enemy aircraft were 'unusually active' and causing 'considerable inconvenience'. They struck in strength, apparently with paired squadrons or ad hoc *Schlachtgeschwader*, harassing the British usually at dawn or dusk and sometimes supporting counter-attacks. Surprisingly, this low-level role saw *Schusta* victory lists rise with 34 in September compared with 24 for the *FA*[40].

Haig's headquarters gave short shrift to anyone complaining about the plague of German low-flying aircraft and demanding fighter cover. On 5 August Kiggel, Haig's Chief-of-Staff, confirmed that the continuous aerial offensive remained official policy yet Plumer's corps commanders became so concerned that Trenchard was forced to defend this policy when he opened their conference of October 24 ([41]). Noting that it was difficult to detect the enemy in the gloom he said: 'Our best policy in dealing with low-flying machines is to carry out more work of this nature than the enemy does and do it oftener.' The official attitude had been shown the previous day when the orders for the first attack on Passchendaele made it clear the infantry were responsible for shielding themselves from low-flying aircraft[42].

The Allied bombing effort was a mixture of Tactical and Operational Level with Trenchard's bombers dropping only 181 tonnes (Table 5-11) during the Flanders campaign. Lambe's well-equipped squadrons boosted the Allies with another 157 tonnes, or 59% of the total dropped by the Navy from July to November, an effort justified from the Navy's viewpoint partly because a successful 'Northern Operation' would have eliminated U-boat bases on the Belgian coast ([43]). Yet even with the naval contribution the Allies delivered less than half the German total of bombs during the Plumer period and the overall effect was far less. The lack of heavy bombers was a major problem for the Allies although there was slight compensation from 11 August when V Brigade bombers began to deliver larger loads replacing their usual eight 20-pounders (9-kilogramme) with one 230-pound (104-kilogramme) or two 112-pound (51-kilogramme) loads[44].

Longcroft's brigade had a strike squadron, No 57 with DH-4, while Newall and Freeman controlled most bombers, although No 100 (Night) Squadron supported the 'Northern Operation' striking targets south of the Ypres Ridge from I Brigade airfields because of congestion behind Ypres. Lacking a bomber squadron, a frustrated Webb-Bowen reverted to his Messines tactics from 27 October using his corps squadrons for unescorted daylight retaliatory missions. The RE 8s flew 60 sorties and dropped 1.35 tonnes of bombs without loss, reflecting both *Jasta* ineffectiveness and his own desperation[45].

The corps squadrons were also committed to ground-attack which became a growing priority during the campaign as shown by Longcroft's instruction of 30 July that corps squadrons and OPs were to fly low-level attacks against ground targets behind the balloon line. At the last minute some fighters were fitted with bomb racks and 65 sorties were flown but, unlike the Germans' style of deployment, these were not integrated into the ground battle[46].

Haig was always interested in new technology (before the Somme campaign he attended a demonstration of a short-range 'energy weapon' and on 12 August Kiggel demanded an expansion of the fighter-bomber role. A month later Plumer and Webb-Bowen split the 2nd Army front into three sectors each patrolled by a pair of fighters with maps showing the reaction forces' anticipated routes to the front and assembly points, the returning pilots being debriefed at the army reporting centre. Longcroft simply ordered his OPs to spend their last 15 minutes making low-level sweeps for enemy reinforcements, although a dedicated flight would make low-level patrols[47].

While strafing was exhilarating, it was only those certain of their own immortality who did not appreciate the risks. Ground fire probably accounted for 20 strafing British fighters during the 'Northern Operation' and the thousands of shells also took their toll bringing down 19 Allied aircraft, killing 16 aircrew. At least one crew of No 6 Squadron shared the awful fate of many soldiers when their RE 8 came down in a large water-logged shell crater and they were drowned[48].

Longcroft and Hearson were more enthusiastic about ground attacks than Webb-Bowen and Murphy, dropping 10.25 tonnes of bombs from 20 September until the end of the campaign. The II Brigade's corps squadrons rarely carried bombs until 26 October when there appears to have been a change of heart which meant they dropped nearly 3 tonnes to 11 November[49]. The scale of ground attacks forced the Germans to divert anti-aircraft machine guns to batteries, balloon units, airfields and railway stations while 25 Anti-Aircraft Machine Gun Battalions (*Flugabwehr-Maschinengewehrabteilungen* or *Flamga*) with nearly 1,000 weapons were also created.

Meanwhile, Trenchard's offensive doctrine successfully shielded corps squadrons from the *Jastas'* fiery blast throughout the 'Northern Operation' and helped their vital fire direction and photographic missions. Counter-battery work was vital because the British were striking from the centre of an arc of batteries, many of which were behind the Gheluvelt Plateau beyond sight of even kite-balloon observers while the prevailing westerly winds frequently thwarted the excellent sound-ranging systems. Typically in July, No 9 Squadron flew 15 counter-battery and 20 destruction sorties while from 15 July to 2 August, the corps squadrons observed the fall of more than 34,000 heavy shells (Table 5-12) representing some 3–4% of the million heavy rounds expended during that period[50].

Table 5-12:
V Brigade counter-battery work. Shells fired

Corps	Squadron	Jul 13–15	Jul 16–22	Jul 23–29	Total
II	No 4	2,292	3,899	4,247	10,438
XIV	No 9	221	4,663	6,321	11,205*
XVIII	No 7	2,611	2,892	3,797	9,300
XIX	No21	550	1,398	1,305	3,253
Total		**5,674**	**12,822**	**15,670**	**34,196**

Sources: Brigade war diary and RFC summaries.
Note: * No data available for July 30 or 31 or for No 9 Squadron on July 16 or July 29.

Hearson's 'ideal' preparations were singled out for rare praise by Trenchard on 14 July and he urged other corps wing commanders to follow his example. At Ypres, however, the task was greatly underestimated (there were 389 enemy batteries not 185) and the effects overestimated with Longcroft claiming 106 gun-pits and battery positions destroyed and 253 damaged in the fortnight preceding the infantry attack. In fact German batteries were rapidly rotated between a trio of alternative emplacements, which sometimes used only one gun, while their time in the firing line was reduced to limit casualties [51]. Although the defenders suffered considerable losses in both men and guns (especially *Gruppe Wytschaete* which faced the British spearhead) most were replaced and they continued to thrash the British rear areas to inflict heavy losses upon Gough's batteries. By contrast the British gunners failed to destroy Arnim's pillboxes and strong points that were often camouflaged by debris in wrecked woods[52].

After Messines there was growing concern about the quality of the RFC's artillery fire direction and during August it became obvious not only that the artillery preparation had failed but also that Hearson was out of step with his colleagues. When ranging heavy batteries, the observers in most corps wings continually directed fire from individual guns until they bracketed the target at which point they called down the whole battery upon the target. However, Gough's gunners would range the battery then engage the target for a minute before pausing for four minutes for corrections. This could confuse the observer and Hearson, unlike Murphy, did not make the gunners repeat the observer's signal for greater accuracy[53]. Brigadier Philip Game, Trenchard's chief-of-staff and a former gunner, had identified weaknesses in army training even in the

Arras campaign, but the problem was compounded by Trenchard's failure to develop a common fire-direction doctrine. The lack of a 'universal method' was highlighted by 1 Wing commander Lieutenant-Colonel Tom Carthew who pondered the problem during late August [54].

Carthew was influenced by IV Brigade's Ludlow-Hewitt who had been experimenting with aerial fire direction and was now integrating aeroplane and kite-balloon operations. Meanwhile, Game canvassed corps wing commanders and senior gunners and together in early September they thrashed out a common doctrine which became the basis for Pamphlet SS 131 *'Co-operation of Aircraft with Artillery'* which was published in December and proved invaluable the following year, although the delay in producing such a doctrine was a black mark against Trenchard[55].

Throughout this period British observers were reduced to riding shotgun or taking photographs. Pilots were increasingly directing the guns and indeed from January 1918 observers no longer received radio training. Ludlow-Hewitt supported the policy of relying upon pilots, but in September Longcroft complained that new pilots were inadequately trained in radio transmission[56].

Plumer benefited from improvements when he became Haig's spearhead for the Northern Operation and in September British corps squadrons engaged 9,559 targets (mostly batteries) and took 14,678 photographs, of which 27% and 40% respectively were over the Ypres Salient where corps aircraft were 'almost unmolested'. The improvement in fire direction was noted by Brigadier Hugh Warwick, the XIV Corps artillery commander, who verified his counter-battery performance with No 9 Squadron and reported on 16 October that 55% of the air reports were correct and 27% were 'approximately correct'[57].

The *Artillerieflieger* remained less active, having zeroed-in batteries on communications and assembly zones during quiet periods so the *Artilleriegruppen* could shell them at leisure. From 11–30 July only 183 artillery observation aircraft were detected by 2nd and 5th Army Compass Stations, the highest concentration being 54 on 22 July when the British flew 170 such sorties. Plumer's stations detected only 15 reconnaissance aircraft in the same period and the Germans complained they were frequently intercepted[58].

The German Army was increasingly concerned about the poor quality of air-artillery co-operation during the Flanders campaign but it was unable to overcome the gunners' prejudice against aeroplanes and the problem was aggravated by a shortage of experienced radio officers within batteries despite all the *Luftstreitkräfte's* efforts to provide them. The network of terrestrial and balloon artillery observers certainly reduced the need for aircraft while the balloon organisation was improved through decentralisation by creating *Ballongruppen* whose operations were co-ordinated by the *Armee Ballonzentrale*[59].

During Plumer's first bombardment in September, 2nd Army detected 73 enemy 'artillery aeroplanes' during the first 12 days of September but only 32 from 13–19 September and German guns caused only light casualties. The compass stations detected 'artillery aeroplanes' on 25 days each in September and October with a daily average of six aircraft which, from mid October, began registering heavy mortars (*Minenwerfer*) as well as guns[60].

Photographic and visual reconnaissance remained important. Haig's staff officers occasionally flew over the battlefield but it was a photographic presentation by Trenchard on 28 August that brought home to Haig that the German defence was now based upon machine-gunners exploiting shell holes. The most important visual reconnaissance role now was the contact patrol, although 31 July found British infantry unusually reluctant to mark their positions with flares for fear of attracting the enemy. The predictable result was that '...the messages sent back gave no clue to the probable relation to the battle of the enemy formations encountered, and no advantage was taken of the clear period of visibility before midday to search the back area for the expected advance of the counter-attack divisions[61].'

Responding to German counter-attack tactics, each corps received two contact patrol aircraft to detect enemy activity and during late August these missions accounted for 10% of total corps wing sorties. But they achieved little and were augmented by dedicated counter-attack patrols deeper behind the lines to detect the approaching enemy troops. These patrols came into their own during the Plumer phase and on 20 September monitored reaction forces from assembly until they were crushed by artillery fire[62]. Unfortunately, rain from early October grounded the airmen for days while the featureless expanse of water-filled craters made tactical reconnaissance and contact patrols more difficult, often only the shape of the helmets identifying the slime-smeared troops.

Contact patrols, sometimes involving the *Schusta*, were the German divisions' priority requirement although the divisional air liaison officers tried also to ensure that the gunners had some aircraft available. The *Infanterieflieger* radioed the location of friendly troops to divisional headquarters, but British air superiority meant the *Landsers* continued to be extremely reluctant to display signal panels. The *Infanterieflieger* were supported by divisional field artillery with one battery suppressing known machine gun positions and a second ready to engage new ones [63].

Between September and October there was a sharp drop (65–10) in intercepted messages from contact patrols, possibly because the Germans were also severely restricted by the weather. One of the few aircraft to fly was the all-metal Junkers J.1 which arrived on 1 August, although only a pair of the 'Flying Tanks' or 'Furniture Wagons' served in Flanders with *FA 19* and *FA(A) 250* and were reserved for major operations. The restricted use of aircraft did help to reduce German losses although about 60 two-seaters from the *Fliegerabteilungen* and *Schusta* failed to return on the Flanders front with the loss of some 60 aircrew killed or captured[64].

On the periphery, Shephard's I Brigade provided vigorous support with some 2,000 OP sorties (Table 5-13) while Becke's IV Brigade, acting as an operational reserve, flew 800. Shephard's enthusiasm for the bomb remained unabated with 105 tonnes being delivered, 43% by No 100 Squadron until it was summoned to follow the holy grail of strategic bombing with 41 Wing. His prime strike force consisted of No 25 Squadron with DH 4s using only 20-pound bombs while the corps squadrons (especially No 10 Squadron) frequently used 112-pound bombs in bomber missions, some in daylight. The bomber squadrons struck not only the usual communications, accommodation and airfield targets but also enemy gun pits[65].

Table 5-13: I Brigade operations 1 July – 15 November 1917

Month	OP		Bombing sorties			Bomb tonnage (kg)	
	Day*	Night	Corps	Day	Night	Corps	
July	609	75	137	27	3,983	12,534	2,642
August	360	130	184	53	7,058	22,362	4,523
September	568	200	92	75	10,968	10,792	7,659
October	451	130	-	109	11,075	-	8,480
November	103	25	-	12	1,981	-	1,359
Total	**2,091**	**490**	**413**	**276**	**35,065**	**45,688**	**24,663**

Notes: *November 1–15. Day bomber sorties estimated
Operations by corps squadrons are dedicated bombing missions only.

Trenchard failed to win absolute air superiority but he usually controlled the inner air space and maintained the initiative in the outer one. In round terms the RFC, including I Brigade, flew more than 56,000 sorties supporting the 'Northern Operation' and lost some 750 aircraft and 730 aircrew in combat. The Germans continued to demonstrate their ability to cause losses but, compared with the dazzling results of April, the *Luftstreitkräfte's* performance was lack-lustre.

French support on the periphery was limited, despite a strong air presence in I Armée. To avoid 'friendly fire' incidents Trenchard sent 10 British aircraft to the French airfield at Bergues where they were inspected by 200 French and 20 Belgian pilots, the day ending with mock combats between two French pilots (one of them the leading French ace, Capitaine Georges Guynemer) and two British[66].

The French contributed a third of the total bomb tonnage at night and despite restricting their fighter OPs to 15 kilometres beyond the front line they claimed nearly 100 victories. Casualties were relatively light, the most significant being Guynemer who was killed on 11 September, but Général François Anthoine's declining role in the 'Northern Operation' led to GC 13's return to the French front in mid August to support new offensives and it was followed, a month later, by GC 11[67].

Trenchard was disappointed with the French and irritated by praise of them within Whitehall. On 29 August he sent a critical report to the Chief of the General Staff, General William Robertson, complaining that his allies were less active (Table 5–14) than his own airmen for reasons including the tiredness of men too long at the front.[68]. He failed to mention that most of Anthoine's aircraft were Verdun-vintage Caudron and Voisin 'pushers' with a trickle of Strutters and Dorands replacing them by the end of the campaign.

Table 5-14:
French and Belgian Operations
14 May – 18 November 1917

Weeks	French Corps	Belgian Army		Total
14–20 May	5	5	20	30
21–27 May	20	25	50	95
28 May-3 June	10	5	50	65
4–10 June	50	5	120	175

11–17 June	15	15	30	60
18–24 June	-	10	25	35
25 June-1 July	10	5	40	55
2–8 July	25	45	70	140
9–15 July	55/2	245	65/1	365/3
16–22 July	195	300/1	175	670/1
23–29 July	365/2	260/1	215/1	840/4
30 July- 5August	45	55/1	15	115/1
6–12 August	175/2	250	115	540/2
13–19 August	270/1	335/4	290	895/5
20–26 August	90	170	165	425
27 August-2 September	15	65	15	95
3–9 September	60/1	120/3	115	295/4
10–16 September	70	125	185	380
17–23 September	35	95/1	155	285/1
24–30 September	45	160/3	260/1	465/4
1–7 October	25	95/2	75	195/2
8–14 October	115	145	165	425
15–21 October	125	155/1	195	475/1
22–28 October	120	175/1	265/1	560/2
29 October-4 November	30	95	190	315
5–11 November	50	70/1	110	230/1
12–18 November	45	105/1	110	260/1
Total	**2,065/8**	**3,135/20**	**3,285/4**	**8,485/32**

Source: SHAA A 129/1. MRAHM Aviation Aerostation Rapports Boite 13–14 (amended to nearest 5).
Note: First figure sorties. Second figure is aircraft which failed to return.

The Belgians also marked time because of parlous resources in manpower and material forcing the Aviation Militaire Belge (AMB) to operate prudently. The AMB front line squadrons were commanded from 21 February 1916 by Major (Lieutenant-Colonel from 26 September) Roland van Crombrugge whose authority was extended to cover the supply and training organisation on New Year's Day 1917, a week before his 45th birthday. Of his squadron commanders, Ernst Isserentant, commanded the post-war air force's technical service and air brigade before retiring in 1938 while Paul Hiernaux was still serving in 1940 and was taken prisoner, together with Robert Desmet who was commanding the air school. Jules Jaumotte became a distinguished meteorologist but was fatally injured by a bomb in 1940[69].

From July to November Crombrugge's fighters were credited with 17 victories while the AMB lost four aircraft, including two Farmans. Despite the risks King Albert flew an occasional Farman sortie over his troops, including one on 6 July, although in the tradition of the British Admiral Nelson, the pilots turned a blind eye to his demands to cross the lines[70].

In Flanders there were never more than two French divisions in the line, each supported by a reconnaissance and an artillery squadron[71]. This concept of directly supporting the troops on the ground was similar to the Germans and reflected the reforms Pétain was driving through the French Army. Ever-pessimistic he anticipated the Germans flooding into France in 1918 and his priorities were to prepare for these campaigns and to rebuild the Army's confidence by telling the men: 'I am waiting for the Americans and tanks.' In clearing the Augean Stables he re-wrote doctrines, developed new tactics and provided modern equipment before tempering the steel through limited offensives which proved huge tactical experiments or live fire exercises. Ypres and Verdun (see Chapter One) were early opportunities but to exorcise the evil spirits of the Nivelle Offensive he decided also to strike in the Chemin des Dames. Maistre's VI Armée was assigned the honour and the more substantial support of 1,900 guns, tanks as well as a powerful air force. He struck at Malmaison on 23 October, driving the outgunned enemy across the River Ailette and inflicting 50,000 casualties (including 15,000 prisoners), four times the French losses. With their remaining positions in the Chemin des Dames now outflanked, the Germans abandoned the ridge on 2 November ([72]). Pétain planned further offensives at Reims and the St Mihiel Salient but then decided to conserve his forces for the following year's campaigns, creating a general reserve near Paris which included Anthoine's troops withdrawn from Flanders in November.

Pétain's reforms did not ignore air power. He described it on 7 May as of 'capital importance' and noted that success on the ground depended upon winning air superiority. Three weeks later, in a letter to War Minister Paul Painlevé, he described aircraft as the decisive weapon if it could sufficiently hinder the enemy's replenishment for a time. He pointed out that aircraft were vital because they blinded the enemy, paralysed their transportation and destroyed morale[73].

A cascade of instructions reached the generals from June 20 into mid July. Directives 2 (20 June) and 3 (4 July) defined the status of air power and in the latter one Pétain laid out overall operational doctrines. These included the use of aircraft which were to be more closely integrated with the ground battle, a demand repeated in greater detail on 19 July when he spelled out the role of aviation in a limited attack. The airmen would be reined-in and would fly in full view of the Army, Pétain commenting that the troops must 'feel and see it is done' but this was not so much a return to 'direct protection' as the integration of air power into his favoured limited offensive tactics[74].

Artillery fire plans were to be based upon corps squadrons' observations rather than upon notions conceived in the splendid isolation of chateaux far to the rear, and the squadrons were now instructed to intervene directly in the battle by attacking enemy troops. The bomber squadrons would increasingly support the army by striking the enemy throughout his Operational depth. Strategically Pétain required massive reserves for decisive intervention including a balanced fighter/bomber strike force whose creation followed in the New Year[75].

Sadly, Peuty lacked the necessary intellectual and administrative skills to execute his part of Pétain's grand design and on 20 August was demoted to Inspector of Aeronautics Training and Stores and replaced by Duval (see Chapter One). Within a month Peuty transferred to a North African infantry regiment and was posted missing, believed killed, on 30 March 1918[76].

No stroke of the pen could cure the Aviation Militaire's numerical and qualitative inferiority which awaited the maturing of the expanded aero-industry. While reconnaissance and bomber squadrons gradually received more modern machines only in 1918 did the corps squadrons receive excellent aircraft such as the Salmson 2 and Bréguet 14 as the air force expanded[77].

The new air doctrine triumphed at Malmaison where Maistre's air commander was the veteran Gérard, who had been promoted Chef de Bataillon on 24 May ([78]). At first he had 16 squadrons (200 aircraft) but the figure soon doubled to 33, the Verdun experience dictating four squadrons per army corps. Gérard benefited qualitatively as well as numerically with eight corps squadrons equipped with Strutters while the Farmans were replaced by the Dorand AR1, an under-powered aircraft with back-staggered wings[79]. The most encouraging omen was the debut of the Bréguet 14 whose robust airframe and 300hp Renault engine made it a first-class aircraft capable of a wide variety of roles and the backbone of the Aviation Militaire in 1918.

Poor weather hindered French preparations with only five full days' operations before the bombardment began on 14 October, the corps squadrons concentrating upon photographic reconnaissance (Table 5-15) which involved 47 sorties. Despite the omens, across the lines there was no augmentation of 7.*Armee* air strength, only 168 aircraft on 15 September with one of its five *Jasta* dispatched to Italy a week later[80].

Table 5-15:
VI Armée operations at Malmaison 1–28 October, 1917

Week	Groupes de Chasse	Escadrilles d'Armée	Escadrilles de CA	Total	Combats GC/others
1–7 October	176	29	224	429	50/1
8–14 October	174	36	222	432	17/1
15–21 October	764	158	898	1,820	203/14
22–28 October	754	99	397	1,250	227/20
Total	**1,868**	**322**	**1,741**	**3,931**	**497/36**

Source: SHAT 19N1124.

British pressure in Flanders made reinforcement difficult and forced the Germans to rely upon brain rather than brawn. The *Kofl 7.Armee* was *Hauptmann* Walter Stahr, a former artillery observer who had commanded *FA.2* (later *FA (A) 260*) before becoming *Grufl 3* and he had four *Grufln* and 37 squadrons (including seven *Schusta* and *Kagohl 2*). *Jagdgruppe von Braun* returned from Verdun to control seven *Jasta* but the largest concentration was *Hauptmann* Mohr's *Grufl 13* supporting *Gruppe Vailly* with 10 squadrons evenly divided between *FA (A)* and *Schusta*[81].

The air campaign began on 14 October and intensified three days later when the French bombardment began. Gérard's airmen flew 1,340 sorties to 22 October when bad weather curtailed operations. Corps squadrons now directed guns at night following VI Armée's experimental shoots from 6/7 July while the Germans flew similar missions in September, although success depended upon the target being near a distinctive geographic feature[82].

The French fighters split the front into two double-corps sectors (each shielded by a group) and flew 569 sorties up to four kilometres behind the enemy lines and, as at Verdun, there were strong escorts for the corps aircraft. The latter flew 647 sorties, of which 68% were in support of the gunners, and while Braun's fighters counter-balanced French numerical superiority, French corps aircraft were intercepted on only 14 occasions during the bombardment with no losses, while fighters recorded 156 combats. The Germans were also active with 164 two-seater sorties recorded by VI Armée before the assault but only 49 fighter sorties, an indication that the *Jastas* were being held back ([83]).

On 23 October in an overcast sky which restricted operations Gérard's men flew 212 sorties (half by fighters) in support of the assault. Despite 35 combats, five involving corps squadrons, only one aircraft was lost. The operation involved more than 3,900 French sorties, claimed 31 victories and lost about twelve aircraft while the Germans appear to have lost six, but the resurgence of French aviation under Duval's direction would clearly continue[84].

In November the British front at Cambrai provided a foretaste of the future in a hybrid operation conceived as a raid upon the *Siegfriedstellung*. It was exploited by both the Tank Corps and the gunners as a battlefield experiment to demonstrate the radical tactics of massed tank attacks and predicted hurricane bombardments i.e. short, intense bombardments which relied upon calculation rather than ranging[85].

Operation 'GY' involved General Sir Julian Byng's 3rd Army in an advance towards Cambrai supported by 475 tanks and 1,000 guns which overwhelmed the defending *2. Armee* (*General* Georg von der Marwitz) on 19 November to seize a large section of the *Siegfriedstellung*. Byng failed to exploit his initial success and German reinforcements plugged the gap by holding the dominating Bourlon Ridge[86]. On 30 November Marwitz, a former cavalryman, staged a double envelopment counter-offensive supported by 1,200 guns using the same artillery techniques but this riposte was thwarted by poor infantry tactics. Although he gained part of the original British line, he left Byng with most of his earlier prize. The Cambrai campaign cost the British some 44,100 men (9,000 prisoners) compared with 41,000 German casualties (10,500 prisoners).

Air support was left largely to III Brigade's 'Old Firm' of Higgins, Mitchell and Pretyman, with Freeman's 9 Wing barely entering the equation apart from providing Bristol Fighter and bomber support. Pretyman received a bomber squadron and Freeman provided him with two fighter squadrons while Mitchell was given two more corps squadrons to bring Higgins' force to 285 aircraft by 20 November of which 81% were serviceable[87].

Mitchell's corps squadrons flew more than 600 sorties from October 26 to 19 November (Table 5-16) but in the week before the attack only four artillery ranging sorties were flown while 135 photographic reconnaissance sorties laid bare the defences. The British planned to neutralise, rather than destroy, enemy guns with Pretyman assigning four of his seven fighter squadrons in the fighter-bomber role to strike key batteries. However, No 46 Squadron was converting from Pup to Camel and two (No 3 and 68) were novices with the former promptly losing four Camels on November 6 when strong westerly winds and poor visibility forced them to land behind the enemy lines near Reims [88].

Table 5-16:
British air operations at Cambrai
15 October – 9 December, 1917

Week	12 Wing	13 Wing	9 Wing	Total
15–21 October	340	400	-	740
22–28 October	190	215	-	405
29 October- 4 November	160	265	-	425
5–11 November	190	115	-	305
12–18 November	155	160	-	315
19–25 November	345	165	55	565
26 November- 2 December	380	655	160	1,195
3–9 December	280	465	80	825
Total	**2,040**	**2,440**	**295**	**4,775**

Sources: III Brigade and 9 Wing war diaries. 9 Wing operations relate to operations in support of Cambrai offensive only.

Higgins used corps squadrons for some preliminary bombing and in drafting his plans for 'GY' ordered two unescorted missions to be carried out by both No 8 (FK 8) and No 13 (RE) Squadrons against enemy headquarters after zero hour while the DH 4s struck rail targets.

He also intended to strike the nearest airfields around zero hour with Camels from No 3 and No 46 Squadrons shielded by three SE squadrons providing flight-size OPs up to 20 kilometres behind the enemy lines. Special patrols along the southern part of the front would support the bombers and Bristol Fighters would provide continuous reconnaissance in an arc 16 kilometres east of Cambrai [89].

Freeman and Shephard's I Brigade would bomb rail stations while Freeman's Bristol Fighters would patrol the northern approaches to the battlefield southeast of Douai. Shephard also had twelve corps aircraft ready to help Higgins attack enemy reserves. There was strong anti-aircraft support with 28 guns distributed in a checker-board pattern in a belt some 3.5 kilometres behind the front, special protection being provided for the army supply base, while each corps assigned machine gun teams as shields against low-flying aircraft. Some guns would move forward to protect communications if a significant advance was made[90].

Marwitz's 2. *Armee* was a quiet front with twelve squadrons (78 aircraft), his single *Jasta* being augmented by another from Malmaison at the beginning of November. They were supplemented by a number of *Flak* units whose *Flakzentralle* informed Marwitz of increased air activity (Table 5-16) from 18 November but the Germans failed to detect anything amiss because the British imposed tight security. They also made extensive use of camouflage from early November (some 150 new battery positions were constructed), monitored daily by Mitchell's airmen, while supply dumps were filled only a week before the attack. Mist and fog from 10 November blinded German air reconnaissance while the *Luftstreitkräfte* was seemingly lethargic with Compass Stations detecting only 42 aircraft from 26 October to 11 November and a further three in the next eight days[91].

Mist, fog, low clouds and rain ruined the outer air battle plan but Higgins refused to cancel the airfield attack programme. Across the lines *Oberleutnant* Richard Flaschar, *Staffelführer* of *Jasta 5*, was threatened with a court martial before he and his men would climb into their cockpits. Of the three Camels from No 3 Squadron which rocketed from the murk to attack Flaschar's airfield, two promptly crashed and the third was shot down. Weather conditions were so bad that at least one British pilot was briefly forced to land behind enemy lines, and only four out of the six airfields were struck with the attackers suffering a 20% loss rate. This proved an ominous omen for the British outer air battle where bad weather restricted operations to occasional OPs, bomber and reconnaissance missions none of which matched Higgins' ambitious plans. His bombers began work only on 26 November, although Mitchell's corps squadrons flew 13 short-range sorties to drop 964 kg of bombs[92].

The Germans rushed reinforcements (including *JG I* and *Kagohl 4*) to the crumbling front and with 10 *Jasta* matched the eight British fighter squadrons (including Bristol Fighters). When the British were diverted into close air support the Germans were, for the first time in months, allowed to dominate the outer air battle. *Kagohl 4* dropped few bombs before being transferred to Italy while III Brigade's bombers delivered 2 tonnes from 19 November to 2 December (the corps and fighter squadrons dropped another 7 tonnes) with nearly 15.75 tonnes being dropped by Freeman, mostly at night[93].

Perversely, when the weather turned milder, reconnaissance became more difficult for the British faced '...activity in the air so aggressive as almost to prohibit R.F.C. reconnaissance.' Even the Bristol Fighters had to fly missions in double-flight (eight aircraft) and soon triple-flight formations as observers noted extensive rail traffic into Cambrai and 'above normal' road traffic, troop movements, artillery registration and air activity all around the breakthrough front. *Jasta 5* and *36* were the backbone of the defence scoring 13 victories during the lull in the middle of the battle while *JG I* (which arrived on 23 November) had five. The *Jastas* thwarted attempts to interdict communications across the River Sensée to help *Gruppe Arras* hold the Bourlon Ridge as, for once, the RFC focussed upon the inner air battle[94].

Batteries were attacked to protect the lumbering tanks whose deadliest foes were often truck-mounted anti-aircraft guns. *Hauptmann* Hähner's *Kraftwagenflakbatterie 7* distinguished itself on 23 November by which time *Flak* units had claimed 52 tanks causing *OHL* to order *4. Armee* and *6.Armee* to send all their *Kraftwagenflakbatterie* to Cambrai. Higgins supplemented his artillery patrols with Camel and DH 5 attacks which were to strike batteries 15 minutes after zero hour, then disrupt reserve movements in a broad arc around the axes of the offensive before finally supporting the main axes of the advance. The plans were ruined by pilot inexperience and poor execution, while mist, low cloud and drizzle meant the corps squadrons' 56 artillery patrols failed to discover a single gun[95].

Above: Brigadier Charles Longcroft, one of the most experienced aviation officers in the British Army commanded V Brigade on the Somme Front. In 1917 he ordered his squadrons to conduct low-level ground-attack sorties against ground targets behind the balloon line and sweeps against enemy reinforcements. He is seen here to the right in the car's front passenger seat during a visit to York by former RFC officers in February 1919. *Bruce/Leslie Collection via FAAM*

Below: Formations of single-seat De Havilland DH 2 'pusher' fighters served to overwhelm German two-seaters and Fokkers, which persisted in flying 'Lone Wolf' missions during the Somme air campaign of 1916. This machine, 7907, belonged to 2 Squadron. *Bruce/Leslie Collection via FAAM*

Above: Royal Aircraft Factory BE 2c, No. 2648, 'Ashanti No 2' of 13 Squadron. Although used for a wide variety of roles this sheep in wolf's clothing was almost useless. This photograph clearly shows the BE 2's great weakness, the observer's position in front of the pilot which hampered its defence because struts and wire made it impossible to traverse the Lewis Gun. *Bruce/Leslie Collection via FAAM*

Below: A BE 12, No 6652, of 19 Squadron. A fighter version of the BE 2 which was also used for bombing missions it was as inadequate a combat aircraft as the BE 2 and during the Somme air campaign in the second half of 1916, 19 Squadron lost 24 such aircraft. *Bruce/Leslie Collection via FAAM*

Left: The shrewd, bull-necked *Oberst* Hermann von der Lieth-Thomsen, chief of staff of the *Luftstreitkräfte*. A protegé of Ludendorff, he worked tirelessly to both expand and refine German air doctrine at all levels between 1916-1918.

Right: *Generalleutnant* Ernst von Hoeppner, the industrious commanding general of the *Luftstreitkräfte*, worked to improve coordination between Germany's airmen and ground forces and also oversaw the development and growth of the *Jastas* and eventually the *Jagdgeschwader*. *Greg VanWyngarden*

Above: A Fokker E.III, 419/15. Although the first aeroplane to carry a synchronised forward-firing machine gun, it was slow and difficult to fly although able to out-turn most of its opponents. *Greg VanWyngarden*

Above: The Halberstadt D.V flown by *Oberleutnant* Hans-Joachim Buddecke (seen in the photograph), one of Germany's most famous early aces, in *Jasta* 4 at Castle Vaux, circa September 1916. Buddecke had gained his first victories as a Fokker Eindecker pilot with *Feld Flieger Abteilung* 23, then was sent to the Dardanelles (Gallipoli) to fly Fokkers with the Turkish *Flieger Abteilung* 6. He achieved additional victories in that distant theatre, earning the *Pour le Mérite*. He eventually returned and commanded *Jasta* 4 from its creation. Buddecke fell in action as a pilot in *Jasta* 18 on 10 March 1918 *Greg VanWyngarden*

Right: War over the trenches: close to a German fighter, an Allied aeroplane 'slides' through the sky, burning and trailing smoke. It has probably been attacked by another German aircraft which is out of sight and at higher altitude.

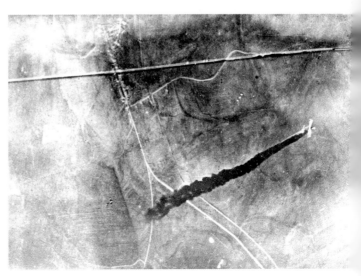

Above: The senior French air commander Édouard Barès declared in 1916 that the purpose of his squadrons was to '…to seek out, to engage and to destroy the enemy.' The following year he was dismissed from his post, a victim of political cross-fire and rejoined the army as a regimental commander.

Left: Parisian Paul du Peuty (right), although a good fighter commander and an enthusiastic supporter of French air operations, lacked intellectual and organisational skills. He eventually transferred to a North African infantry regiment and was posted missing, believed killed, on 30 March 1918.

Above and below: Two photographs depicting a demonstration of the observer's .303in Lewis gun and Scarff ring mounting in a Bristol F.2A reconnaissance-fighter. The F.2A enabled the RFC to extend its battlefield fighter cover and it proved a sturdy and reliable aeroplane. *Bruce/Leslie Collection via FAAM*

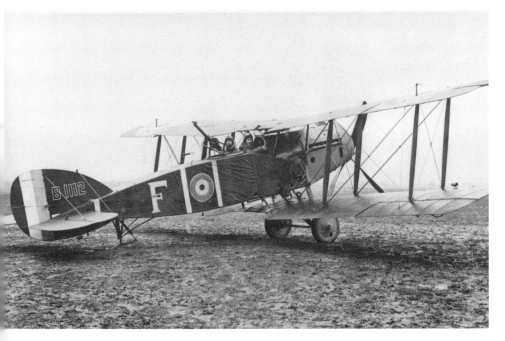

Above: A Bristol F.2B fighter, No B1112, 'F', of 16 Squadron. Powered by a Rolls Royce Falcon III 12 cylinder, liquid cooled inline V, 270 hp engine capable of a maximum speed of 123 mph, the type gave the RFC a battlefield 'workhorse' in which armament was balanced with manœuvrability. *Bruce/Leslie Collection via FAAM*

Above: Major William Sholto Douglas commanded 84 Squadron's SE5s over the Western Front in 1917. Despite gaining a formidable reputation, the Squadron lost 50 per cent of its strength in combat against the German *Jastas* in its second month of operations in November 1917. By the end of the war Sholto Douglas had been awarded the Military Cross and Distinguished Flying Cross. *Bruce/Leslie Collection via FAAM*

Above: Lieutenant-Colonel George Pretyman, who had made the RFC's first photo-reconnaissance sortie on 15 September 1914, later commanded the RFC's 13 Army Wing. Over Cambrai in the autumn of 1917 his fighter squadrons flew in the fighter-bomber role to strike key enemy batteries. He is seen here in the centre of the middle row in a photograph of 1 Squadron's rugby XV in 1916. *Bruce/Leslie Collection via FAAM*

Below: Smiling for the camera, an officer of 15 Squadron hands an observer a drum of ammunition for the Lewis gun which armed the RE 8. 15 Squadron, a part of 12 Wing, found itself continually in action during the battle of Cambrai engaged in low-level attacks and night bombing raids in enemy ammunition dumps. In September 1918, the Squadron dropped boxes of ammunition to forward troops in response to field telephone calls from the line. *Bruce/Leslie Collection via FAAM*

Right: Teamwork: the pilot and gunner of an RE 8 of 15 Squadron. Note the crudely painted roundel. *Bruce/Leslie Collection via FAAM*

Left: Following experience on the Eastern Front, *Hauptmann* Helmuth Wilberg, the son of a Jewish portrait painter, gained recognition for the accomplished way in which he developed German close-support operations on the Western Front. He later became Air Defence Advisor to the *Truppenamt* and ultimately a *Luftflotte* commander before his death in an air crash.

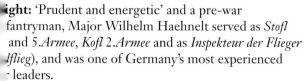

ight: 'Prudent and energetic' and a pre-war fantryman, Major Wilhelm Haehnelt served as *Stofl* and 5.*Armee, Kofl* 2.*Armee* and as *Inspekteur der Flieger lflieg*), and was one of Germany's most experienced leaders.

Above: Albatros D.II, serial number D.910/16. This machine was flown by *Leutnant* Max Böhme of *Jagdstaffel* 5, who was shot down in combat against a DH.2 and F.E.2b captured on 4 March 1917, near Tilloy-les-Hermaville. The large white number '8' was repeated on each side and top of the fuselage, and on the underside in black; at this time *Jasta* 5 used either numerals or letters as pilot's personal markings. This machine was given the British 'captured aircraft' number G.14 in the system of recording captured aircraft. *Greg VanWyngarden*

Below: German ground crew prepare racks loaded with stick grenades to be loaded on to a Halberstadt CL.II escort/ground-attack aircraft. The grenades would be dropped by the observer while flying close-support sorties. Operated by the *Schlachtstaffeln*, they were manoeuvrable, had a good rate of climb and a good field of fire and made their name during the German counterattack on 30 November 1917 at Cambrai. But their physical impact upon the battlefield was reduced by their low bomb loads.

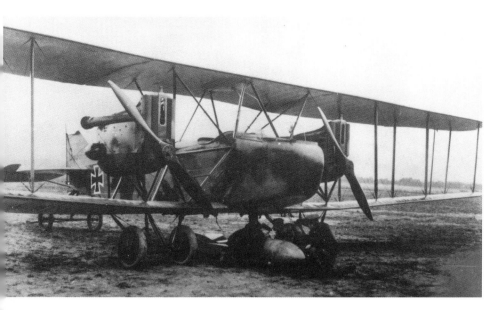

Above: AEG G.IVb bomber of 1917. The AEG Company produced a very successful series of G-types, of which the G.IV was the most prolific. The basic G.IV had two-bay wings, but several aircraft from the first production batch were modified with three-bay wings (as seen here) in order to carry a 1000 kg bomb, and thus becoming the AEG G.IVb version. Loading the 1000 kg bomb usually required a special bomb cart and a shallow pit over which the aircraft fuselage would be rolled into position. However, this photograph is thought to depict five armourers practising with a mock-up bomb to practise loading technique. *Greg VanWyngarden*

Above: Rumpler C.IV C.8476/16. The Rumpler C.IV was a superb reconnaissance aircraft, possessed of high speed, high altitude and long-range capabilities. The first examples reached the front in February-March 1917 and it was still in service at the end of the war. It was delivered with three different engines: the popular 260 hp Mercedes D.IVa, the 245 hp Maybach Mb.IVa 'over-compressed' engine, and the 260 hp BuS.IVa. C.8476/16 was an example of the first production batch, fitted with the Mercedes D.IVa. *Greg VanWyngarden*

Left: French ground crew prepare to load a camera aboard a two-seat Dorand AR1 observation machine ahead of a reconnaissance mission over the lines. Powered by a 190 hp (142 kW) Renault 8 Bd engine, they were underpowered aircraft with back-staggered wings. The pilot sat beneath the leading edge of the wing, with the observer's cockpit being under the trailing edge respectively, and there were cut-outs in both wings to improve the latter's visibility.

Right: A French Spad S7 fighter is prepared for another mission. Armed with only a single Vickers gun, the aeroplane was plagued with mechanical problems because its Hispano-Suiza engine was complex, notoriously difficult to maintain and often unreliable. Several pilots considered it unmanœuvrable. For these reasons Trenchard was reluctant to accept it for the RFC.

Above: In the face of the German advance in 1918, the logistics network of Brigadier Robert Brooke-Popham, seen here in 1912 third from left in the front row and the first man in the RFC to have armed his aircraft, ensured that petrol, oil, spares, ammunition and food was supplied to squadrons and his trucks rushed urgently needed supplies to new airfields. *Bruce/Leslie Collection via FAAM*

Above: In 1918 Major Traffordry led the Bristol fighters of 8 Squadron, RFC, in a corps ar-ground support role in which attempts were made to coordinate support for tanks y the use of radio telephones. Results were mixed. Leigh-Mallory is seen here seated ntre of the front row in this post-war Squadron line-up. *Bruce/Leslie Collection via AM*

Above: The SE5a, C5303, 'X', of Lieutenant L.M. Franklin of 56 Squadron. Despite some early problems with mainplane strength during high-speed dives, the men who flew the SE5a found it to be an ideal gun platform though it did suffer from engine problems. *Bruce/Leslie Collection via FAAM*

Above: *Leutnant der Reserve* Johann Janzen's Fokker Dr.I Triplane 403/17 of *Jagdstaffel* of *Jagdgeschwader* I – the 'Richthofen Circus'. Janzen was a skilled pilot who commande both *Jasta* 4 and then *Jasta* 6, amassing a total of 13 victories. On 9 May 1918 he was shot down in his Fokker Triplane (possibly this one) by a Sopwith Camel of No. 209 Squadron, but survived unscathed. He was captured on 9 June 1918 when the synchronisation gear of the guns on his Fokker D.VII malfunctioned, and he shot off his own propeller while attacking a French SPAD. *Greg VanWyngarden*

Above: A Fokker D.VII built by the Ostdeutsche Albatros Werke, or OAW. This particular machine belonged to *Jagdstaffel* 12 of *Jagdgeschwader* II, or *JG* II (pilot unconfirmed). The surrender of all Fokker D.VIIs was a significant part of the Allies' Armistice demands. *Greg VanWyngarden*

bove: Fokker E.V. 156/18 was attached to the II *Marine Feld Jagdstaffel*. The smiling ilot on the wheel is Theodor Osterkamp; the famous naval ace commanded the II *MFJ* the time the photograph was taken in 1918. He did not fly the E.V. for very long, d probably scored no victories in it. He stated the type was '...too slow to maintain ace with the squadron aircraft (Fokker D.VIIs).' The E.V. was hardly at the front ore than two weeks when fatal wing failures caused the type to be grounded pending vestigation. Osterkamp survived the war with 32 victories and went on to serve a Luftwaffe fighter commander in the Second World War. *Greg VanWyngarden*

Above: The Pfalz D.XII could be considered a robust, rather than outstanding, design. This particular D.XII, 2670/18, was an item of 'booty' handed over to the Allies after the war. It appears here in Canada, with Lt. de Plessier of No. 1 Squadron Royal Canadian Air Force in the cockpit. *Greg VanWyngarden*

Right: Well connected, but known to be arrogant and petulant with his fellow commanders, Major William 'Billy' Mitchell was neverthless a keen proponent of air power and demonstrated his commitment to ground support during his command of the US 1st Air Brigade during the Marne counter-offensive in July 1918 and later during the St Mihiel Offensive of September 1918.

Left: Colonel Frank P. Lahm, a former polo player and commander of the US Balloon School, commanded the American 2nd Army's air units and produced a comprehensive bombing plan for the Meuse-Argonne offensive for the American Expeditionary Force in late 1918.

Although using an advanced airfield 11 kilometres behind the lines, the fighters' ground-attack effort was weak with only 40 sorties flown and 884 kilogrammes of bombs dropped on the first day. Total casualties in low-level missions amounted to 47.5% of aircraft dispatched. The failure of the fighter-bombers against *54. Infanteriedivision* batteries at Flesquières allowed the division to act as a breakwater with its gunners repeating their success against tanks in the Nivelle Offensive (see Chapter Four) by destroying 28 of the 65 tanks which all the gunners claimed on the first day[96].

Close air support dominated the following days' air battles but proved costly for the British who suffered a 30% loss rate on 23 November. With the official end of 'GY' on 27 November, Shephard concentrated upon his own front while the upsurge of German rail and road traffic was interpreted as part of the enemy effort to strengthen the defences so GHQ diverted Freeman's bombers to other targets[97].

To support their counter-offensive the Germans received 8 squadrons (3 *Jasta* and 3 *Schusta*) from Flanders giving *Kofl 2.Armee* 36 squadrons (280 aircraft) of which half (including 3 *Jasta* and 7 *Schusta*) with 125 aircraft would directly support the assault under *Grufl 2* (*Arras*) in the north, *Grufl 3* (*Caudry*) in the northeast and *Grufl 4* (*Busigny*) in the east, the last two also being supported by *Flakgruppen 3* and *4* with 48 guns and 72 machine guns. On 29 November the British noticed *Grufl 4*'s increased activity, but Compass Stations detected only nine artillery aircraft as the Germans planned a 'predicted' hour-long hurricane bombardment[98]. The Germans then attacked led by *Grufl 3* which was assigned three *Schusta* while the other *Grufln* each had two. British generals later claimed the *Schusta* were largely responsible for the collapse of their line and that this was the largest concentration of low-flying aircraft they had encountered. However, the 7 *Staffeln* had only 40 aircraft so the psychological impact must have been considerable. The *Schusta* were most active in the early morning and late afternoon, strafing and bombing the defenders, inflicting casualties and distracting the defenders (especially Lewis-gun teams) at critical moments while *Artillerieflieger* directed fire on points of resistance[99].

Grufl 3's *Schusta* proved 'particularly effective' against III Corps' 29th Division where a battalion of one brigade collapsed under intense air attacks but a neighbouring brigade ignored the *Schusta* and slaughtered a *Sturmtruppen* (Assault Troop) unit. Against the same corps' 12th

Division the *Schusta* proved a double-edged weapon for they inflicted such heavy losses that the infantry fled into a wood which became first a breakwater that split the attacking waves and then became a springboard for a successful counter-attack supported by US Army railway troops[100].

Higgins had 266 aircraft on 30 November. Of these 229 (86%) were serviceable, and they provided equally vigorous close air support mostly against *Gruppe Arras'* anticipated attack, but 70% of the fighter sorties were ineffective OPs. The corps squadrons were equally ineffective because mist shielded the enemy assembly areas, but they did provide close air support and dropped a third of the 1.25 tonnes of bombs expended that day in operations which served notice of the wrath to come in the following spring. British losses (13 aircraft and 10 airmen) – mostly from fighter squadrons – were double those of the enemy. In the following days Higgins' and Freeman's bombers launched a belated campaign against communications to drop 6.32 tonnes with little effect [101].

Cambrai was the last hurrah for both the RFC and Trenchard, who was shortly to return to London as Chief-of-Staff to the new Royal Air Force. By the end of 1917 Trenchard appears to have become 'yesterday's man' and while his strategic principles remained largely sound, he seemed unprepared to adapt them to meet the new aerial situation. During his last six months, his errors of judgement were becoming apparent, especially his continued insistence on spreading his forces equally along the front and the failure to develop a uniform doctrine for artillery fire direction. A new mind was clearly needed, although there is no doubt that Haig regretted the departure of a loyal and previously effective subordinate.

Cambrai was not the RFC's finest hour and left the leadership much to ponder because they had suffered badly and achieved little. The British suffered 115 casualties, including 68 dead and missing, and lost 77 aircraft with No 3 Squadron suffering particularly severely as a lethal mixture of low-level operations and inexperienced pilots cost it 19 aircraft (the equivalent of its establishment) and 15 pilots. Despite optimistic British claims, the Germans appear to have lost only 9 aircraft (excluding forced-to-land) from 20–30 November and 13 airmen killed or captured[102].

The British would learn to plan more flexibly and to integrate close air support with divisional operations while the Army wings learned they must balance commitment to the inner and outer air battle. Curiously the Germans who achieved this balance at Cambrai forgot the lesson and would place too much emphasis upon the direct support of the divisions, perhaps reflecting their autumn triumphs outside France beginning in the East. There, when Bufe arrived from Flanders to become *Kofl 8.Armee*, his two accompanying squadrons helped expand Hutier's air support to 15 squadrons (90 aircraft) including Germany's sole fighter squadron in the east[103]. Some were concentrated into a *Schlachtgeschwader* which helped rout Riga's defenders on 1 September permitting the Germans to begin transferring troops and squadrons westwards. Nevertheless, it was only in March 1918 that the Bolshevik Government effectively capitulated to the rapacious Treaty of Brest-Litovsk and even then nine *Luftstreitkräfte* squadrons remained in the East.

Some German troops, including 11 squadrons, went to the Austro-Italian border and the new *14.Armee* where they smashed the Italians at Caporetto on 24 October. Air attacks spurred the Italian retreat but the *Luftstreitkräfte* then had great difficulty keeping pace with the advancing *Landsers*. The squadrons remained in Italy until summoned to France in 1918 for the great offensive but lost 30 aircraft and 70 aircrew representing 25% and 30% of the respective totals[104].

Riga and Caporetto set the stage as the Germans prepared one desperate throw of the dice to achieve victory in 1918 before America's legions overwhelmed the increasingly weakened and divided Empire. Losses during the year had been heavy amounting in the *Luftstreitkräfte* to 653 aircraft and 136 balloons (20 of the latter to artillery fire) on all fronts, an increase of 195% and 202% respectively on the previous year, while in human terms some 1,850 airmen perished and 175 were taken prisoner ([105]). With enemy air power increasing both in quantity and quality there was no sign that the following year's butcher's bill would fall.

Chapter Six

The German Offensives January – June 1918

The first half of 1918 saw Germany desperately try to break the bloody impasse on the Western Front. The gamble ultimately failed but the opening bombardment upon British lines on 21 March changed the style of both land and air warfare.

Reinforcements from the Eastern Front briefly gave *OHL* numerical superiority and the lessons of Riga, Caporetto and Cambrai opened the window of opportunity a little wider. Shock forces were assembled secretly at the enemy's weakest point to exploit a short, 'predicted', bombardment and to achieve a breakthrough. The offensives were to be spearheaded by *Mobil-Divisionen*, elite units trained in shock troop (*Sturmtruppen*) tactics, called by the Germans *Hutier Taktik* after *General* Hutier, who was Ludendorff's cousin, and given extra horse-drawn transport and radios for greater mobility combined with an attached air squadron. Their initial objective was the gun line but ultimately they aimed to engulf the surviving defenders in double envelopments supported by *Sturm-Divisionen* while garrison units (*Stellungs-Divisionen*) brought up the rear or held the line[1].

The British were the backbone of Allied resistance and *OHL* determined to strike Haig's right (3rd and 5th Armies) in *Unternehmen 'Michael'* which would be extended northward to Arras (*Unternehmen 'Mars'*)). Options existed to attack between Ypres and Lens (*Unternehmen 'Georg'*) while feints and a disinformation campaign fed Pétain's fear of an attack in the Champagne to pin down the French[2]. Ludendorff's gambler's throw involved 70 divisions, including 35 *Mobil-* and 32 *Sturm-Divisionen* (out of 44 and 36 respectively) and 6,500 guns. Originally *Heeresgruppe Kronprinz Rupprecht* was responsible for *'Michael/Mars'* with *2.Armee* (Marwitz), *17. Armee* (*General* Otto von Below) and *18. Armee* (*General* Oskar von Hutier) these last two being breakthrough veterans under their former designations of *14.* and *8.Armee*. Marwitz, supported by Below, would spearhead *'Michael'* and push the British northwards to the Channel covered by Hutier who was Ludendorff's cousin and Hindenburg's protégé. However, the plan was compromised when Hutier's army was transferred to *Heeresgruppe Deutsches Kronprinz* and, at Crown Prince Wilhelm's insistence, given a more active role driving deep into French territory away from the main thrust[3].

Opposite Marwitz and Hutier, Gough's 5th Army had neither the time nor the manpower to improve former French fortifications that had been neglected in defiance of Pétain's orders. The bombardment and fog on 21 March helped the Germans exploit the situation and reach the gun line by noon but at a cost of 78,000 casualties, their highest in a single day[4]. Yet they succeeded in driving a wedge between the British and French forces with Pétain's reinforcements slow to arrive as he kept looking over his shoulder at the Champagne and sought to shield Paris rather than aiding Haig. Determined to maintain contact with the French, Haig agreed at the Doullens Conference (26 March) that Foch (Chief of the French General Staff) become responsible for co-ordinating allied operations in the West in what became the precursor of SHAEF and NATO[5].

Despite this initial success, logistics and defensive power doomed '*Michael*'. Neglect of the former meant *OHL* was unable to sustain the forward troops as they strode through the wastelands created during '*Alberich*' and the first Somme battle. Neither human or equine muscle-power could hope to outpace the defenders' railways and automotive power which moved men and material rapidly to create new defences that the exhausted attackers could not penetrate. Captured supplies did help to fuel the advance; *K.Flak 82* used a British truck to carry them, allowing it to keep pace with infantry and to provide direct support although in its traditional role the gun almost shot down the great Richthofen, being about to fire on an unidentified aircraft recognised as German at only the last minute[6].

A generation later the automotive revolution overcame these problems encountered in France during 1918. In 1937 the British Official Historian prophetically commented: 'One hardly likes to contemplate what might have happened had the Germans pushed up masses of cavalry or mechanised forces to exploit their early success. In future, it would seem that improvised Armies will have little chance, even if there is time to create them, against an enemy who is in possession of aeroplanes, tanks, armoured cars and mechanised troops to exploit a gap… [7].'

To regain the initiative '*Mars*' was launched on 28 March only to be smashed within a day by alert troops in deep fortifications. By early April the embers of '*Michael*' were cooling outside Amiens. The Germans had gained ground and inflicted 230,000 casualties (87,000 prisoners) bruising Haig's army but failing to destroy it, although 5th Army was renamed 4th Army when Gough was made a scapegoat for defeat. This pyrrhic victory cost Ludendorff 303,000 men (20% of the attackers) with the *Mobilverbände* decimated and downgraded to *Sturmverbände*[8].

On 9 April, a scaled down '*Georg*', '*Georgette*', smashed through a Portuguese division between Ypres and Lens, but the British 1st (Sir Henry Horne) and 2nd Armies (the latter again under Plumer) held the shoulders and the Germans were stopped within a fortnight but at the cost of all the ground taken in the 'Northern Operation'. Prompt action by Foch brought two French armies behind the British to dash Ludendorff's Operational Level hopes, although only two corps of Général Antoine de Mitry's Détachement d'Armée du Nord (DAN) needed to be inserted in the line. The front briefly flared to life as the Germans stormed the dominating height of Mont Kemmel on 25 April, but again failed to meet either their strategic or operational objectives[9].

The German offensives saw air warfare reach new levels of bloody intensity. From March to June the Allied air forces suffered 2,128 casualties in combat and the Germans more than 1,400, including Ludendorff's stepson, *Leutnant* Erich Pernert of *FA 29*. The new, fluid, style of warfare relied upon infantry and their heavy support weapons augmented by field guns with occasional assistance from heavy artillery and close air support[10].

The airmen's direct role in the land battle greatly increased with their bombs becoming as much a threat to the soldier as the shell and the machine-gun bullet. The scale of air operations increased as mobile warfare obliterated the distinction between the inner and outer air battles while expanding combat at the Operational level with the air struggle became a huge tornado sucking in aircraft. Where air forces had once operated simply to support army headquarters, their strategic mobility was now exploited and squadrons were switched across the front to act as aerial fire brigades in campaigns involving nearly 2,000 aeroplanes.

The Germans increasingly concentrated fighters into either *Jagdgeschwader* or *Jagdgruppen* while redistributing their bombers into smaller formations, but otherwise there were no significant changes in the *Luftstreitkräfte* when Ludendorff published '*The Attack in Positional Warfare*' on New Year's Day. Here, the emphasis was upon covert assembly and timely commitment of overwhelming force including *Schlachtverbände* made up of *Schusta* and *Fliegerabteilungen*[11].

Kogenluft's war games indicated that no major reorganisation was necessary; the *Grufl* in each corps-size *Gruppe* would have a *FA* as would each *Mobil-* and *Sturm-Divisionen*, even though there were not enough squadrons to support all the latter. *Jagdgruppen, Jagdgeschwader, Bogohls, Schlachtverbände* and some reconnaissance units were attached to *Kofln* to support axes of attack with a *Jagdgruppe* supporting some *Grufln* on prime axes[12].

The *Schlachtverbände* role was psychological, cracking enemy morale through repeated massed attacks synchronised with the infantry assault. Yet *OHL* and *Kogenluft* did not always sing from the same hymn sheet; the former stated *Schlachtverbände* might be supplemented with uncommitted reconnaissance aircraft while the latter told the *FA* they '… should not be employed…as this would be to the detriment of their special work of reconnaissance and observation[13].'

British plans were drafted by Trenchard and published on 16 January, two days before he departed for London. They reflected experience gained on the Somme, Arras and Ypres, but not Cambrai because no breakthrough was anticipated. '*The Employment of the Royal Flying Corps in Defence*' anticipated that the RFC would respond in the traditional manner – army co-operation by corps squadrons, a fighter shield in front of the battle field and bomber attacks upon the infrastructure. The only concessions to new battlefield conditions were that a flight from each Army squadron would augment the fighters' close air support and battlefield interdiction missions while corps squadrons were also to be used for night bombing. The directive's conclusion was pure Trenchard: 'The action of the Royal Flying Corps must…always remain essentially offensive, even when the Army…is standing temporarily on the defensive[14].'

With a steady flow of modern aircraft from British factories, Trenchard's successor, Major-General John 'Jack' Salmond, strengthened his reserve just before the attack. On 6 March IX Brigade was created under the 31-year-old Lieutenant-Colonel Reginald Small to control both Freeman's 9 Wing and the newly formed 54 (Night Bomber) Wing, although the former remained under Salmond's direct command until 26 March[15].

Salmond's reserve of 8 squadrons and 150 aircraft was minuscule compared with Duval whose reserve on 1 March totalled 226 squadrons, including 60 fighter and 28 bomber, with 2,800 aircraft. His fighter squadrons now received the Spad S13 with two Vickers guns and a superior performance to its predecessor, although it retained the latter's mechanical unreliability. Duval's doctrines mirrored those of Trenchard and Salmond but he concentrated resources more ruthlessly with half his fighter groups in the two Escadres de Combat created on 4 February (see Chapter Two) while the day bombers were merged into two Escadres de Bombardement a few weeks later. There were also improvements in fighter and bomber aircrew quality through the creation of an operational training unit, Centre d'Instruction de l'Aviation de Chasse et de Bombardement, which ensured that aircrew were fully trained when they joined their squadrons[16].

Duval's orders of 2 March demanded all available combat units be concentrated for both defensive and offensive purposes. The fighter escadres were to attack and to destroy enemy aviation, but their operations, with those of the day bombers, were to be closely integrated with ground operations. For these reasons he combined fighter and day bomber escadres into task forces: Groupements Ménard and Féquant with 300 and 200 aircraft respectively ready to meet any crisis. Ménard, aged 37, (see Chapter Four) and Féquant, aged 35, would play major roles in the forthcoming campaigns and were both pre-war fliers. Féquant had been one of the first French military aviators, then commanded N65 at Verdun and was later the first commander of GC 13. He would remain in the air force after the war and was the Armée de l'Air chief of staff for 16 months from October 1935. He died in 1938 [17].

On the British front, Salmond was 36 when he replaced Trenchard in January 1918, Brigadier Game remaining as Chief-of-Staff. The son of a general, Salmond entered Sandhurst in 1900 on his second attempt. A year later he joined the Royal Lancashire Regiment and had an uneventful Boer War apart from stepping on the foot of the future Queen Mary! Bored with life in post-war garrisons he joined the West Africa Frontier Force which he was eventually forced to leave on medical grounds after two years. It took him a further two years to recover his health. Having learned to fly privately he entered the CFS in August although he did not join the RFC until November 1912. The first person he met at the CFS was Trenchard and the two became instructors, Dowding being one of Salmond's pupils, and at the outbreak of war he led No 3 Squadron to France where his elder brother Geoffrey was on Henderson's staff. He helped to develop photographic reconnaissance before becoming 2 Wing's first commander then directed a bombing campaign against the railroad network before assuming command of the RFC's training organisation in 1916[18].

With Smith-Barry, Salmond reorganised training in 1917 and in October joined the Army Council as Director General of Military Aeronautics, succeeding Charlton, but remained anxious to return to the front, the more so after his wife died in childbirth. It was only natural that Salmond would replace Trenchard with whom there was both a close professional relationship as well as underlying rivalry. Trenchard appears to have acted as a consultant to Haig even after moving to London and returned to France on several occasions to meet his former 'Chief.' Salmond first met the BEF commander on 22 January and their subsequent infrequent meetings suggest a cooler relationship[19]. Perhaps it was a combination of Salmond's typically British reserve and his relaxed approach to discipline, although he demanded the highest standards. He was intelligent and a good organiser who became Chief of the Air Staff in the 1930s and was briefly succeeded by his brother [20].

With Shephard dying in a crash in January 1918, I Brigade reverted to 40-year-old Brigadier Duncan Pitcher who had been its first commander. He was commissioned in the South Wales Borderers in 1898 but transferred to the Indian Army four years later serving in cavalry regiments but also working with the government and acting as a maharajah's tutor! He was one of the first Indian Army officers sent to England for flying training and was to have established a Central Flying School in India. Joining the RFC in September 1914 as a captain he became Commandant of the British CFS in 1915, but soon afterward went to France. He would remain in the RAF until he retired in 1929 but saw no further service before his death in 1944[21].

Another Indian Army officer, Brigadier Rudolph Hogg, whose 41st birthday was on January 19, assumed command of IX Brigade on 6

March as a belated birthday present. He was a gunner commissioned in 1896 but left the British Army for the Indian Army after five years and in 1911 was King George V's Assistant Military Secretary. He returned to the British Army after the outbreak of war and joined the RFC in November 1915. Within two years he was a colonel and soon after, a brigadier but within eight months of the war's end he resigned his commission and did not serve his country again before his death in 1955.

The winter also saw command changes as former gunners were appointed within III and V Brigades. Pretyman was replaced in Higgins' 13 (Army) Wing by Lieutenant-Colonel Patrick Playfair. Within V Brigade, Holt remained with the 22 (Army) Wing, but 15 (Corps) Wing was now under Lieutenant-Colonel Ivo Edwards[22]. During April, Longcroft returned from England to replace Higgins whose experience was needed for England's air defence.

Meanwhile, Hoeppner was exploiting the network of airfields built along the front during the winter including bomber bases within range of the '*Michael*' 'battlefields. Reinforcements arrived only at the last minute, although aircrew were frequently attached to squadrons at the front to familiarise themselves with the terrain. Some artillery registration was still needed to provide basic ballistic data for the 'predicted' bombardments, and to disrupt defensive preparations. Every effort was made to restrict operations to preserve secrecy, artillery data being distributed to as many incoming batteries as possible, but there was still a noticeable upsurge in aerial activity[23].

From mid February the British noted growing numbers of Germans in the skies over the 3rd and 5th Army fronts, their Compass Stations initiating 40 interceptions in January, 60 the following month and 165 from March 1–20 while in almost 12 weeks the number of air combats rose from 145 to 350. Anti-aircraft artillery observers with the two armies reported 967 enemy sorties during the week ending 19 January (100 crossed the lines) and 1,714 (242) six weeks later including 117 fighters which crossed the lines. British fighters operated 17 kilometres behind enemy lines with Freeman and Playfair flying squadron-size formations while Holt's men flew in flights[24].

The last minute arrival of 47 German squadrons in March brought their strength to 129 squadrons and 1,030 aircraft (Table 6-1) with 90% of the *Schlasta*, half the *Jasta*, 44% of the *Bosta* and a third of the *Fliegerabteilungen*, including 70% of the reinforced squadrons. Haehnelt, one time *Stofl 5.Armee* at Verdun now *Kofl 2.Armee*, had *Bogohl 7* and split his front into two 160-square kilometre zones each with six *Jasta*; the northern under Richthofen with *JG I* and *Jagdgruppe 2* while the southern was under *Oberleutnant* Hermann Kohze with *Jagdgruppen 9* and *10*. Hutier's *Kofl* was Streccius, who had worked wonders at Verdun in 1917 and had *JG II* and two *Bogohl* (*1* and *4*) while Below's *Kofl 17.Armee*, *Hauptmann* Thiemanns, had *JG III* and *Bogohl 5*. There were 17 *Flakgruppen*, one for each corps, while the *Flakwaffe* had assigned 84 batteries, 140 smaller units, 15 *Flamga* (180 machine guns) and 63 searchlights, the largest concentrations being with the flank armies although the threat from enemy ground-attack aircraft meant that Marwitz had six *Flamga*[25].

Table 6-1:

Air support for '*Michael 1–3/Mars Süd*' 21 March 1918

Army	Grufln Nr	Jasta	Bosta	Schlasta	FA	Aircraft	AA Guns
2.	3, 4,12,16	12	3	11	16	340	94
17.	2, 10,14	14	3	7	17	380	99
18.	8, 9,13,17	15	6	9	16	350	131
Total	-	**41**	**12**	**27**	**49**	**1,070**	**324**

Sources: Edmonds *1918/1*:153 n 2. Jones *IV*:Map10. *Luftmacht Teil 1*:33, 35. *Weltkrieg XIV*:42, 104.

Air combat accidentally confirmed the presence of Hutier's army, for the general's note to the mother of a fallen airman was mentioned in a local newspaper's obituary notice published on 5 January. British Intelligence acquired enemy newspapers through Switzerland, realised the airman had fallen on the 5th Army front and concluded that the main enemy blow would land there[26].

Reconnaissance was vital for both sides. Bruchmüller aimed to stun and to decapitate the defenders without repeating the British mistake at Ypres of tearing up the ground to create a barrier for his own infantry. For these reasons his tools of choice were fragmentation and chemical (gas and smoke) rounds, with high explosive limited to the demolition of strong-points, billets, bivouacs, command posts and the telephone network, levelling trenches and cutting corridors through the wire.

Photographic interpreters examined prints carefully to discover buried signal cables through discolorations in the soil. At company-level the *Mobiltruppen* received maps showing deep shell holes and the road network ahead of them as well as numerous photographs to help them advance through the chaos which Bruchmüller hoped to create. Hoeppner also filled bombers' target folders with photographs of railroad stations, road junctions, bridges, camps, supply depots as well as airfields[27].

Salmond improved his reconnaissance by reinforcing V Brigade's Bristol Fighter squadron (No 48) with another eight aircraft on 2 February and sent down a reconnaissance-bomber squadron (No 25) which did not return to Freeman until 6 March. Supported by balloon observation the busy squadrons (Table 6-2) confirmed the blow would land on 3rd and 5th Armies, with dedicated aircraft in each squadron sent to locate enemy guns. From 24 February Salmond demanded evidence to show the exact date of the attack and on 4 March he presented his plans to Haig who described him as '.capable and most pleasant to work with[28].'

Table 6-2: Air operations 3rd and 5th Army front 31 December 1917 – 17 March 1918

Week	III Brigade		V Brigade		IX Brigade	Total
	12 Wing	13 Wing	15 Wing	22 Wing		
31 December -6 January	275	360	120	110	-	865
7–13 January	185	250	135	120	-	690
14–20 January	145	205	175	105	-	630
21–27 January	160	215	140	105	-	620
28 January-3 February	270	230	230	230	-	960
4–10 February	120	135	115	100	-	470
11–17 February	170	185	170	165	-	690
18–24 February	225	255	210	285	-	975
25 February-3 March 3	165	145	180	230	10	730
4–10 March	290	370	295	630	180	1,765
11–17 March	385	680	400	745	410	2,620
Totals	**2,390**	**3,030**	**2,170**	**2,825**	**600**	**11,015**

Source: Brigade and Wing war diaries

On 18 March a German airman shot down near St Quentin revealed *'Michael'* would begin on either 20 or 21 March, a forecast confirmed by deserters and prisoners. But in the last few days there was no upsurge in German air activity because poor weather confined the *Luftstreitkräfte* to patrolling its own lines[29].

Charlton was reinforced and by mid March Edwards had five corps squadrons while Holt had a balanced force of seven squadrons including one reconnaissance-fighter and two bomber. Higgins had Mitchell's four corps squadrons, two supplemented by a single Bristol Fighter, while Playfair also had a balanced force of nine squadrons. Freeman's 9 Wing arrived to support Gough on 7 March with six squadrons[30].

In a vain attempt to disrupt the build-up, the bombers struck airfields, ammunition depots and rolling stock, the last intended to exploit reported enemy shortages. Holt's two squadrons carried the burden from late January before Higgins and Freeman joined them in March and by 21 March some 66 tonnes of bombs had been dropped, mostly in the preceding fortnight. Corps aircraft struck targets of opportunity with 16.75 tonnes of bombs, but although an attack upon *Bogohl 2*'s base at Aincourt in mid February led to all German bomber bases receiving 37mm cannon protection, these efforts had little effect [31].

Salmond had 1,114 aircraft with 111 RNAS on the coast organised into 10 squadrons, split evenly between fighters and bombers, the latter including two squadrons of Handley Pages. More than half his force faced the German onslaught with V Brigade having 219 aircraft (92% serviceable) while III Brigade had 259 (87% serviceable) and 9 Wing had 101. The disposition of anti-aircraft batteries; 11 behind the northern armies and eight behind the southern, reflected Haig's priorities and also protected his key supply facilities[32].

Confident that defence in depth would stop Ludendorff, Haig demanded close air support even for extemporised counter-attacks. He warned Salmond to be ready to switch squadrons suddenly to threatened fronts and to ensure the squadrons received adequate transport. Salmond's reinforcement plan, with logistic arrangements, submitted to Haig on 2 March, subdivided the BEF front into three sectors – northern, central and southern[33].

But on the first morning the air campaign was literally slow to get off the ground due to dense fog and mist which dissolved from north to south like a curtain being drawn back upon a vast stage. As a result even the elite *JG 1* flew only 52 sorties[34]. Early morning vapour plagued airmen throughout the campaign but usually lifted by mid morning, attracting swarms of aircraft to the battlefield (Table 6-3). But the airmen's wings were clipped towards the end of March because drizzle turned to torrential rain. The rain also washed away traditional aerial tactical doctrines which changed radically in the face of the new tactical/operational situation.

Table 6-3:
British air operations during '*Michael/Mars*' 21–31 March 1918

Day	III Brigade		V Brigade		IX Brigade		Total
	12 Wing	13 Wing	15 Wing	22 Wing	9 Wing	54 Wing	
21 March	60	15	25	95	–	20	215
22 March	55	20	80	170	20	25	370
23 March	85	85	45	220	90	20	545
24 March	105	135	65	160	80	25	570
25 March	80	90	50	185	70	20	495
26 March	95	30	75	225	95	45	565
27 March	75	80	35	225	105	45	565
28 March	110	65	40	230	115	–	560
29 March	35	5	15	60	60	30	205
30 March	75	50	75	145	115	–	460
31 March	45	35	25	125	105	40	375
Total	**820**	**610**	**530**	**1,840**	**855**	**270**	**4,925**

Source: RFC work summaries; Brigade and wing war diaries.

Until '*Michael*' air warfare had revolved around corps aircraft whose successful support of the guns had been the criterion for air superiority since Verdun. But mobile warfare saw the traditional air support arrangements collapse to reappear only when the front settled. The key factor now was to strike the enemy throughout his operational depth with bomb and bullet.

The speed of the German advance acted as a catalyst forcing the abandonment of a score of airfields up to 55 kilometres behind the lines during the first 10 days. On 23 March Salmond wrote to Trenchard: 'As you may expect, I am getting extremely hard up for aerodrome space.

Reconnaissances for new aerodromes were sent out today and have returned with quite a few satisfactory results and we should be all right for a time.' Generous vehicle support was a key feature in RFC survival and on the second day of the offensive Salmond informed Trenchard: 'The transport has stuck it all night so far, but I visualise a large number of moves in the future, and shall be much obliged for the extra vehicles of the extra Lorry Park[35].'

Brigadier Robert Brooke-Popham's logistics network ensured a flow of petrol, oil, spares, ammunition and food to squadrons. His reserve of trucks rushed urgently needed supplies to new airfields, but the German advance forced him hastily to transfer threatened facilities. His reluctant last minute decision to fly out 170 aircraft from a depot at Fienvillers on 27 March saved them from destruction during a bombing raid that night. Trenchard also directed a flood of material across the Channel and on 23 March the hard-pressed Salmond wrote him: 'Thanks for the supplies of machines which have kept us going very well[36].' Yet the threat to communications centres and the cutting of wires were a major headache to command and control as Salmond confessed to Trenchard in their nightly correspondence and daily telephone calls.

On 21 March Salmond implemented the southern reinforcement plan and the next day reported that 16 squadrons had moved with another 4 scheduled to reinforce the front. Three days later he reported he was 'out of touch' with III and V Brigades as well as 9 Wing although he anticipated they would all be 'back on line' by the morning of 26 March. 'They will be all on entirely new aerodromes and it will be difficult to keep in touch, and a certain amount of efficiency must be lost. However, they are all out to do their damnedest[37].' The same letter displayed his concern about the situation and he half-jokingly commented that if it deteriorated: 'I shall soon have to apply for floats to carry operations from the sea.' The following evening the joke fell flat: 'I am making preparations for the evacuation, if necessary, of Rouen by sea in case the Huns get through… I propose, if you agree, that the personnel and engines shall be placed in barges and sent by tug[38].'

Yet Salmond's sure handling of his squadrons ensured this remained a contingency plan. Unlike Trenchard, he focussed resources from all the brigades on a single battlefront beginning on 24 March when 10 squadrons of Pitcher's I Brigade began attacking enemy columns, while three days later II Brigade, still under Becke, sent down squadrons from the Ypres front as did Lambe's 5th Naval Group at Dunkirk. To prevent the BEF being driven into the sea Salmond concentrated 64% of his 58 squadrons behind Byng's 3rd Army by 26 March[39]. He benefited from generous French assistance for Duval dispatched both his 'fire brigades', although the arrival of III Armée squadrons was tardier. Ménard with 292 aircraft was sent to support GAR (whose air commander was Commandant L. Picard) on 24 March operating from bases south of Amiens and shortly afterwards Féquant with 289 was ordered to support GAN with attacks around St Quentin [40].

Although the British complained that Pétain's support was too little, too late, he actually committed a third of the French army and a similar ratio of its air power including most of his bombers. By the end of March the French had 75 squadrons (including 36 fighter and 24 bomber) on the Somme front while Humbert's III Armée was reinforced by GC 12 and 14. The French concentrated upon Hutier's *18. Armee* and the groupements flew 1,500 sorties from 25 March to 7 April with Hutier's *Jasta* suffering half of all Germany's fighter losses[41].

Duval's first orders on 28 March emphasised support for the ground forces but on 1 April he switched to achieving air superiority, which meant corps aircraft were escorted only by those fighter squadrons directly under army command leaving the fighter groups to roam. The fighters were supported by a radio network which could scramble aircraft to meet new threats while, in a primitive form of airborne early warning, Ménard had Caudron patrols from R46 reporting enemy air activity in a tactic quickly copied by Féquant using Bréguets[42].

Meanwhile, German air power fragmented with the *Landsers'* every step westwards. Where the British air battle involved large squadrons (each the equivalent of a German *Geschwader*) controlled by three autonomous brigades through six wing commanders, the German control was split between three *Kofln*, each with limited autonomy, 11 *Grufln* and numerous small squadrons (many the equivalent of an Allied flight). The problem grew in magnitude as Hoeppner added to '*Michael*' another four *Grufln* and seven squadrons. The *Grufln* supporting the main axes of the offensive were too weak to project German air power deep into the Allied rear while their strike aircraft carried only small bomb loads. The *Kofln* controlled the *Bosta* but they had few day bombers and this restricted their impact upon the campaign. The problem was aggravated by *OHL*'s failure to address the problems of command and control as the spearheads drew further away from army headquarters[43].

The demands of the new warfare were so great that army staffs largely ignored their airmen, whose leaders were excluded from the decision-making process because the *Luftstreitkräfte*'s status remained on a par with support and service troops. Army headquarters had intermittent communication with the squadrons and issued only the vaguest directives, often leaving their airmen to fight private wars while the *Kofln* frequently left fighter units in limbo for days[44].

Even the prestigious *JG 1* was not immune from these difficulties. On 26 March it occupied the airfield of Léchelle, former home of No 15 (Corps) Squadron, some 25 kilometres from the front. With road congestion strangling the logistics network, it depended upon a meagre 1,500 litres of captured petrol which was barely a tenth of Richthofen's requirements. Yet the following day, despite an acute shortage of water and the need to fly in food (and beer), the *Geschwader* flew 118 sorties and claimed 13 victories. American accounts would later claim no more than 75 enemy aircraft a day were seen supporting the offensive and while this seems a underestimate it certainly indicates the erosion of *Luftstreitkräfte* support[45].

With German air power dispersed and Allied squadrons concentrated, '*Michael/Mars*' was exposed to an air assault on an unprecedented scale throughout its operational depth as the Allied fighters and bombers were augmented by British corps aircraft unable to perform their traditional air support role. They, and the fighters, bombed and strafed the unfortunate *Landsers* while bombers blasted railheads and supply dumps. On 25 March Salmond reported he had 100 aircraft over the battlefield and that they were so thick in the air there was a risk of collision. Gough's front faced the greatest threat, but it was Byng's 3rd Army which received most of the benefit because most of his airfields were not directly threatened by the German advance while, at first, there was little reliable information about the situation in the Somme valley[4].

The scale of ground-attack effort was relatively low at first but dramatically increased in intensity from 25 March when 60 aircraft of I Brigade supported 3rd Army. That day Salmond concentrated his attacks in the Somme valley with orders '…to bomb and shoot up everything they can see on the enemy's side of the line' and he demanded the airmen fly very low and take all risks. On the first day only 5 squadrons were involved in ground attacks but the numbers quickly grew, covered by OP shields in flight or double-flight strength and by 26 March Salmond had committed 27 squadrons to this role. Brigade or wing staffs targeted specific sectors which were attacked at half-hour intervals by the duty flights that were sometimes 'scrambled' by klaxons blaring out the flight letter in Morse. The lack of common doctrine meant the attack tactics varied from brigade to brigade; in some the pilots would split into pairs 8 kilometres behind the enemy lines while others conducted full flight-size attacks. The Americans later criticised the failure to conduct systematic attacks even though the fluid state of the battle made this difficult and the British certainly focussed upon the main axes[47].

Squadrons shuttled into and out of airfields pausing only to refuel and rearm with pilots flying continuously, one making six ground-attack sorties in a day. They probably accounted for up to half the 5,000 sorties flown in the first 10 days of the offensive with V Brigade's squadrons flying 2,101 sorties in March and early April to drop nearly 32.5 tonnes of bombs, while on the whole battlefront at least 150 tonnes of light bombs were dropped by fighters and corps aircraft to 7 April. Almost all Charlton's squadrons were committed to these missions after 21 March but it was three days before Hogg's fighter squadrons abandoned OPs for ground-attack and from 25–26 March he committed all his aircraft to these missions initially west of Bapaume then south of the Somme [48].

The catalyst of mobile warfare accelerated the use of corps aircraft for ground -attack. The hurricane forces of the new tactics blew away the carefully woven web of air-artillery co-operation. British corps squadrons spent a week trying to adapt their traditional roles to the new warfare with little success before seeking a more active role over the battlefield ([49]). Edwards' 15 (Corps) Wing flew occasional ground-attack missions from the first day, but from 29 March flew 'offensive patrols' involving a total of 116 sorties by 3 April. Usually they carried 25-pound bombs, but one RE 8 squadron flew six daylight sorties with a single 112-pound bomb from 28 March-2 April and was unchallenged by German fighters[50].

French bombers flew in escorted flight-size formations dropping down to 600 metres to strafe targets. French fighters (but rarely corps aircraft) strafed the *Feldgrau* columns, occasionally delivering a pair of 10 kilogramme bombs. The greatest contribution of Duval's airmen was massed bomber attacks against troop columns, bridges, supply dumps and the railways ([51]). Because their bases were not usually in harm's way they did not need to waste time and resources on switching airfields. This allowed them to drop more than 25 tonnes of bombs upon Hutier's troops while the British bombers struck the German centre and right. The V Brigade's No 5 Naval (soon renumbered No 205 RAF Squadron), despite being driven from their nests, operated every day: No 101 Squadron flew on seven of 11 nights and during March the two squadrons dropped a total of 50 tonnes of bombs. Hogg's IX Brigade joined in from 22 March and during March dropped 67 tonnes upon a similar range of targets as the French[52].

GHQ clearly appreciated the effort. On 26 March Salmond reported: 'When I was at GHQ tonight I heard a telephone message from (Brigadier) Percy W. Dill (Haig's Deputy Operations Chief) saying that without a doubt the concentration of aircraft in the south had frozen up the attack there temporarily. Similarly (Brigadier C.W.) Cox (Haig's Intelligence Chief) told (Major-General J.H.) Davidson (Haig's Operations Chief) that he considered the concentration of aircraft west of Bapaume had had the same effect.' However, some officers of the retreating 5th Army pointedly remarked to airmen that abandoned airfields were their only evidence of British air power[53].

The Allied air attacks caused casualties and disruption, but the greatest impact was psychological. The *Landsers* were often marching in close order confined to a few narrow, congested roads, deprived of either shelters or *Flak* protection. Allied airmen buzzed around them like 'a swarm of angry hornets' to make lightning, low-level attacks; indeed one officer of *5. Infanteriedivision* was run over while lying prone [54]!

The British focused upon *2. Armee* in the centre and its neighbours' supporting corps (especially *III. Armeekorps* of *18.Armee*). Marwitz reported on 28 March that he was suffering logistics problems and attributing half his casualties to air attack. Below's *17. Armee* opposite Byng also suffered severely, mostly from 'passing trade', but when '*Mars*' was launched on 28 March, Allied airmen were described as extraordinarily active in the *17.Armee* area and bombers blew up a 60,000-shell dump ([55]). The attacks caused hundreds of human and equine casualties and there was some interruption of the logistical system but the degree of damage was probably exaggerated and the overall effect was harassment on a grand scale. Yet if every German infantry and field artillery regiment in '*Michael/Mars*' suffered only 10 casualties in air attacks this would have amounted to about 1% of total German losses during the offensive. The German official record focuses upon the harassment of *2.Armee* from 23 March but such tales of woe cease from 28 March by which time it was conceded the Allies had air superiority which allowed them to strike at will. The fluid nature of the battlefield led to some rare 'friendly fire' incidents, the British 9th Division being struck by four aircraft on Palm Sunday (24 March) leaving a brigadier apoplectic with rage[56].

Schlasta were also extremely active from the beginning of the offensive, frequently operating as *halb-gruppen* (two *Staffeln*) and occasionally as full *Schlachtgruppen* directed by corps headquarters. Flying at 50–60 metres they initially struck infantry concentrations but later attacked batteries, ammunition dumps, reserves, supply columns and vehicles. The manoeuvrability of the Halberstadts and Hannovers meant they suffered less than 40 aircrew casualties. The Hannovers were also used for contact patrol work and one, flown by *Unteroffizier* Johann 'Hans' Bauer of *FA 295* with *Leutnant* Georg Hengl supporting *18.Armee*, would later claim six victories in 160 sorties. The British noted that even in the front line the *Schlastas* caused very few casualties and although they did force men to keep their heads down, their greatest success was to thwart counter-attacks[57].

Retreating troops and fleeing refugees, aggravated by inadequate traffic-control, meant the roads behind the British lines were so severely congested that liaison officers exchanged motor cars for horses to ride across country. The *Luftstreitkräfte* monitored the roads but rarely attacked them: 'Fortunately the enemy's aircraft never appeared to turn confusion into rout, so that by diverting the lightest and best horsed vehicles, such as field batteries and empty ammunition columns, off the roads and across country the greater part of the heavy traffic got clear [58].'

A rare German attack by *17.Armee* aircraft on 21 March caused 'much confusion' on the road supporting IV Corps upon 3rd Army's right. Similar success was recorded on 25 March by *2.Armee* aircraft upon the Albert-Bapaume road while two days earlier the 8th Division headquarters was attacked as it arrived to support XIX Corps in Gough's centre[59]. The later generation of German airmen learned from these missed opportunities, but in the Great War the *Schlastas'* bomb loads were too light to interdict road traffic effectively and in pursuing the logical solution of heavy bombers, the Germans deprived themselves of a powerful daytime strike force.

Night bomber attacks upon the rail system did delay troop movements (although rarely more than half-a-day) and harassed the British logistical infrastructure with some success. Headquarters were also targeted with one significant attack on the night of 22/23 March striking Gough's central XIX Corps, the cork in the bottle providing the only significant barrier to German progress, and apparently disrupted command and control for several days. Only 12 German bombers were lost during *'Michael/Mars'*, although plans for a new attack in the Somme valley were recovered from a *Bosta 17* aircraft forced down on the night of 26/27 March[60].

Both sides used bombers to compensate for the lack of aerial artillery fire-direction because, under the pressure of mobile warfare, batteries failed to erect radio aerials while the airmen's vision was frequently obscured by mist, smoke and dust, as Salmond complained on 22 March. 'It must be emphasised that the organisation for cooperation between the artillery and the Royal Flying Corps failed completely from the first. For long periods, not only in the fog of the first morning but throughout the retreat, there was no communication between the batteries and the aeroplanes, although the zone call system had been introduced primarily to meet the conditions of open warfare[62].' Edwards' 15th (Corps) Wing supporting Gough's retreating troops flew a maximum 24 artillery patrols on 24 March but in the next seven days less than 30 were flown because the gunners failed to respond to their signals. Surprisingly, and despite the fluid battlefield, the RFC lost three corps aircraft to shells during the first five days of *'Michael/Mars'* [63].

The German problem was aggravated both by negligent planning for the new challenges and the transfer of radio operators from *Luftstreitkräfte* to artillery control during the winter. Success was also restricted by the *Artillerieflieger*'s tendency to operate in the afternoon although they had occasional successes notably against VI Corps on 22 March and XIX Corps the next day. Kite balloons remained the backbone of aerial fire direction and the Germans went to considerable trouble to ensure their units kept pace with the troops. By contrast British units rarely had time to fill their gas bags and many aeronauts ended up in ad hoc battle groups. German contact patrols were augmented by a new form of tactical reconnaissance, the *Infanterieüberwachungsflieger* who monitored all aspects of infantry attacks, including the rolling barrage, cueing the *Infanterieflieger* in locating forward positions[64].

Visual reconnaissance was vital in monitoring the battle and Edwards' squadrons flew 67 such sorties on 26 March. With headquarters moving frequently, it was difficult to get information to the staffs and it was not always believed. When No 82 Squadron saw enemy troops pouring through the middle of 5th Army's Battle Zone on the morning of 21 March the news took 140 minutes to reach III Corps headquarters. Three days later No 53 Squadron spotted enemy infantry south-east of Ham but when they tried to drop a message to Gough's headquarters the bag became caught in tail wires. The determined crew landed and reported directly to Gough who cheerfully informed them they had seen French troops who had retaken the village. In fact the Germans had broken through along the Anglo-French boundary[65].

German reconnaissance failed to detect the arrival of French reinforcements on 23 March and their appearance upon the battlefield surprised *OHL*. The German airmen were focussing upon the British and by 25 March they were beginning to send in reports of reinforcements coming south for the Somme front through Amiens. By 27 March *18.Armee* reconnaissance aircraft reported long columns making their way to the '*Michael*' front. More ominously, *2. Armee* air reconnaissance detected new fortifications including a position (the hastily constructed GHQ Line) which secured British communications to the sea beyond artillery range[66].

The *Jagdgeschwader* and *Jagdgruppen* proved less effective than before because the new battlefield covered a greater volume of air space than previously contested while command, control and supply were all failing. There were only 10 aircraft victories on the first day and while the *Jasta* supporting '*Michael/Mars*' were credited with 230 victories (excluding balloons) to 7 April with the loss of 40 fighters this kill rate concealed serious failures. *JG I Staffeln* averaged only five sorties a day while many *Jasta* averaged only two or three and operations were based not upon sweeps but upon interceptions based upon alerts from observers. This may have driven *Jasta 11* to develop operating in three-aircraft *Ketten* formations for more effective interception[67].

The British lost 162 single- and two-seat fighters over the '*Michael/Mars*' front. Of these only 48% fell in air combat, and some of these fell to two-seaters. In 18 days of combat a mere 32 British corps and bomber aircraft fell to fighters while barely a third of overall German victory claims were over these two-seaters, and even this figure was swollen by *18.Armee* fighters' success against the French. The latter appear to have lost about 60 aircraft between 22 March and 7 April, the majority over the Somme, with 74 aircrew dead or missing and 66 wounded or injured[68].

Salmond's airmen flew some 7,000–8,000 sorties to 7 April with total losses amounting to some 263 aircraft. More were burned on their airfields to avoid them falling into enemy hands and hundreds sent to parks for major repairs. Nearly 56% of total casualties (147 aircraft) fell to ground fire. *Luftstreitkräfte* losses in '*Michael/Mars*' appeared relatively light given the importance of the operation, at least 90 aircraft and 135 aircrew. The German figures appear to exclude aeroplanes forced to land or those damaged beyond repair for which up to 60% might be added and many squadrons were reduced to 60–75% of their strength. Worse, the Germans had failed to achieve their objectives giving them no grounds for optimism during the next great trial of strength[69].

In April the storm moved northwards and the air campaign mirrored that of March. For *Unternehmen 'Georgette'* Kuhl's *6.Armee* and Arnim's *4.Armee* received 56 squadrons to bring their total strength to 76 (25 *Jasta*, six *Bosta*, 17 *Schlasta*) with 492 aircraft. They faced Pitcher's I Brigade, reinforced by two of Lambe's squadrons following the creation of the RAF, and supported by Hogg's reinforced IX Brigade (24 squadrons) and Becke's II Brigade (11 squadrons) with a total of 600 aircraft augmented by 100 Belgian, including 45 fighters ([70]).

Rain, mist, fog and even snow restricted operations into early May with German airmen having even less impact than the previous campaign, long range reconnaissance and artillery support proving noticeably weak ([71]). Although the British again lost airfields, and on one fog-bound field a Camel squadron transferred by Lambe had to burn their fighters which could not be evacuated, there was no slacking in the intensity of ground attacks which began even as the *Sturmtruppen* struggled through Horne's wrecked fortifications. The II Brigade flew some 1,900 sorties in a fortnight while fighters and corps aircraft alone dropped 183 tonnes of bombs in France and Flanders, most on the '*Georgette*' battlefield[72].

The British focused upon support forces bringing up supplies partly because the fighting troops, who had been their targets in March, had learned to move in small parties to reduce the risk of air attack. The collapse of the German air defence command control occasionally did allow the British to make devastating attacks. Pressure on *6. Armee* eased only after it ordered on 12 April that 66% of its fighters be used against the low-level attacks. The overall psychological effect appears to have been weaker than on the Somme, but the pressure was severe and on 11 April a desperate *4.Armee* requested another 22 squadrons from *OHL*[73].

Air power proved especially important on the 'very critical day' of 12 April in the battle for the Forêt de Nieppe south-east of Hazebrouck along the 1st and 2nd Army boundary. Fine weather allowed Salmond to commit every available aeroplane against the main axis of advance while *Schlastas* and *Bostas* harassed British reinforcements as well as forcing Plumer to sleep away from his headquarters. Yet the Germans did not have things their own way, and down on the Somme *AOK 18*'s *JG II* at Balâtre airfield was shelled on the night of 12/13 April and 25 fighters destroyed with the *Geschwader* out of action for three weeks[74].

The overall situation was so critical that Salmond's staff, began detailed planning to evacuate the RAF to south-eastern England. Up to 35 squadrons were to be moved and on 12 April Salmond informed the Chief of the Air Staff, Major-General Frederick Sykes (who replaced Trenchard the previous day), that as a first stage 10 naval co-operation squadrons would fly to England while another five would be redistributed to other bases in France, a plan later approved by the Admiralty. Even on 19 April Salmond said it was 'essential' that 5th Group's stores be evacuated as soon as possible and some apparently did cross the Channel[75]. Yet British reports suggest that by this time German air activity was low, a view reinforced by studies of losses, which show some 35 aircraft lost (including a Zeppelin Giant on 21 April) and 85 aircrew casualties. By contrast the I, II and IX Brigades lost 70 aircraft

(III Brigade lost another 14 although not all over the Lys) and suffered 139 casualties but claimed 170 victories. French losses are more difficult to determine[76].

Most *Jastas* were concentrated into *JG III, JGr 3, 6* and 7 but they claimed only 36 aircraft for the loss of eight fighters. During the campaign, 9 Wing experimented with larger OPs involving between three and six flights (the equivalent of one or two squadrons). Full squadron patrols did not become common until the summer and generally SE5s provided top cover while the Camels flew ground attack missions and air combat was largely restricted to some 15–25 kilometres behind the FEBA[77].

From around 20 April there was a five-week-long lull in ground operations with occasional flare-ups. While supporting preparations for a *2. Armee* attack upon Villers Bretonneux, Manfred von Richthofen was shot down and killed on 21 April, but his young cousin *Leutnant* Wolfram von Richthofen survived to command the *Stukas* which spearheaded the *Nazi* conquest of Europe in the Second World War. An omen of this occurred a few days later when the Germans took Mont Kemmel supported by 53 squadrons (17 *Jasta* and two *Bogohl*) and 318 aircraft, much of the success being attributed to the 16 *Schlasta* of *Schlachtgeschwader A, B, C* and *D* who dropped 700 bombs and fired 60,000 rounds, although even here the lack of direction was apparent in *JG I* operations which lacked focus being scattered over the battlefield. Four days later *JG I* helped the Schlasta take the nearby Scherpenberg ridge, on both occasions the Germans claiming 'incontestable mastery of the air[78].'

Mobile warfare brought new hazards to, and opportunities for, the airmen including escape and evasion as the Germans quickly discovered. *Vizefeldwebel* Mülberger and *Unteroffizier* Mall of *Schusta 30* not only escaped their captors on 22 March but reached German lines as did an AEG crew from *Bogohl 7* who were forced down on the night of 16/17 May. For sheer gall, few could match *Oberleutnant* Schunk and *Leutnant* Ross of *FA 40* who force-landed near Amiens on 7 April then persuaded French troops to help them take off by claiming to be Americans ([79])! They were lucky not to meet British troops some of whom were so fearful of spies that they threatened to shoot their own airmen. The confusion also meant that rear-echelon personnel sometimes encountered the enemy and in one such clash on 27 March, the US Air Service's Colonel Raynall C. Bolling was killed when his motor car encountered a German patrol[80].

The Schunk and Ross incident reflected the Allies' longing for American support throughout the crises. Americans were entering France in their thousands but the American Expeditionary Force (AEF) commander, General John J. Pershing, demanded they enter the line in US divisions rather than as cannon fodder in Allied formations. Unfortunately for Pershing, he had few squadrons and many American airmen were indeed assigned to Allied squadrons in which their compatriots had served since 1916. The Americans contributed to the Allied defence from the moment '*Michael*' was launched. While flying with No 41 Squadron on 24 March, 2nd Lieutenant John P. McCone became the first of 10 to be killed in British squadrons during the first half of 1918. By the beginning of June some 180 Americans had served, or were serving in British squadrons, some while seconded from the USAS while others enlisted with the RFC. By June 1918 a further 125 Americans were serving with French squadrons[81].

Until America's industries were adapted to war production its air power depended upon their Allies' over-stretched factories – the old world redeeming the new, to paraphrase President Woodrow Wilson. This created tensions which were summed up by Brigadier Cyril Wagstaff, the British liaison officer with AEF GHQ who wrote on 12 May 1918 to Colonel Walter Kirke, Deputy Director of Military Operations at the War Office: 'The American Air Service are not enthusiastic about their prospects. They feel that their present machines are poor and that America has let them down in the matter of producing machines. They also feel that we have let them down by taking all the raw material and giving all the machines turned out to our own people[82].'

Ultimately the Americans were the authors of their own misfortune. In April 1917 US Army aviation was plagued by internecine disputes and the Signal Corps' determination to control air power had meant its first operational deployment in 1915, the support of Pershing's Mexican expedition by Captain Benjamin D. Foulois' squadron, proved a farce. Doctrinal development was amended through observation of developments in France, but even before the war the US Army knew it lacked modern aircraft ([83]). The internecine struggles continued in

Europe where Pershing was determined to command the AEF unfettered by the War Department but understood both the value and limitations of air power ([84]). By chance he appeared to have the ideal candidate in 37-year-old Major William 'Billy' Mitchell, a man with all the qualifications but few of the qualities for senior air command.

Born in France, the grandson of a banker and the son of a United States senator, he volunteered for the Signal Corps at the outbreak of the Spanish-American War and was quickly commissioned. By 1913 he was the youngest member of the General Staff and was learning to fly, reasons enough to send him to Europe in the spring of 1917 to monitor aviation. Mitchell was a charming, charismatic, intelligent, hard-working and dynamic character whose vision occasionally out-paced reality. He spoke fluent French (the Americans would fight largely on the French front) and was a trained staff officer making him an ideal contender as Pershing's air chief. However, he found staff work a chore and his egocentric, abrasive personality led to childish tantrums. C. S. Forester's comparison of British generals with primitive tribesmen trying to extract a shiny screw from a balk of timber by tugging and striking it rather than turning it, applied to him. His arrogance grew with promotion and he was insufferable to senior staff officers, whom he regarded as fossils. It is possible that not even Pershing fully trusted him[85].

Pershing certainly knew Mitchell's limitations but the choice of his successor saw a tug-of-war with Washington until the appointment in November of Foulois, now a Brigadier General. He had risen from the ranks and was a friend of the Wright brothers, so naturally became one of the first three US Army pilots. Within the Army he was noted as currying favour with his Signal Corps superiors and was consequently distrusted by some airmen but he was a capable officer, although lacking charisma[86].

Foulois' appointment saw Mitchell at his most petulant but he had made many enemies in the AEF and was saved only by Pershing who recognised his abilities as a combat leader. In May 1918 Foulois requested, and received, a combat role as commander of 1st Army Air Service and was replaced by one of Pershing's West Point class mates, the engineer Major-General Mason M. Patrick, who completed Foulois' organisational reforms[87].

Meanwhile, Ludendorff still possessed a powerful reserve, but if the sandglass of time was half-empty the optimistic *Generalquartiermeistergeneral* regarded it as half full. The Allies had a single strategic command under Foch as American reinforcements flooded into France where their strength rose to 651,000 during May to reduce German numerical superiority. Allied material losses were easier to replace and British tank strength actually rose to 600 vehicles. On 1 May *OHL* sent a coded radio message closing down the Flanders theatre (this was intercepted by the Allies who regarded it as disinformation) while Ludendorff considered a radical change in strategy.

To draw the French east of the Somme Ludendorff decided upon a diversionary attack in the Chemin des Dames (*Unternehmen 'Blücher'/'Goerz'*) by Boehn's *7.Armee* and Below's *1.Armee*. The diversion included a later *18.Armee* advance down the western bank of the Oise towards Compiègne (*Unternehmen 'Gneisenau'*) and would be followed by a renewed war-winning assault in Flanders (*Unternehmen 'Hagen'*). The first blow landed on Duchêne's VI Armée whose fortifications again lacked depth and whose occupants were surprised despite warnings from the experienced survivors of the attached British IX Corps.

In the early hours of 27 May 5,200 guns pulverised both defences and defenders so that by noon the Germans were on the Aisne. There they were supposed to halt but a bedazzled Ludendorff, heedless of his own strategy allowed '*Blücher*' to become a horse bolting southwards towards the Marne with the western flank touching the defences of Paris from where a million civilians fled[88].

Pétain's strategic vision and preparations allowed him to rail reserves, including Americans, ahead of the attackers. Maistre's X and Micheler's V Armées arrived from Flanders, the former controlling the western side of the expanding salient while the latter held the eastern side. VI Armée eventually contained the southern thrust and despite a renewed *7.Armee* attack (*Unternehmen 'Yorck'*) to smash the western shoulder of the salient at the end of May, the offensive fizzled out by 6 June.

By May nearly 42% of Duval's 228 squadrons, including most of the bombers, were north of the Somme while 17% were east of the Meuse with GAE together with six American squadrons (including 1st Observation Group) gaining combat experience. Supporting d'Esperey's GAN (IV and VI Armées) in the centre were only 44 squadrons, including Groupement Villomé (GB 2 and the Italian Grupo 18) under Capitaine Joseph Villomé and GC 21 attached to Général Gouraud's IV Armée in the Champagne where Pétain still anticipated an attack[89].

On 14 May came the culmination of Pétain's air force reforms with the creation of a massed strike force, the Division Aérienne (DAé) under recently promoted Général Duval and nominally with Groupements Ménard, Féquant, Chabert and Villomé (although the night-bomber force tended to be autonomous). His chief of staff was 38-year-old Commandant Paul Poli Marchetti, possibly an interim appointment pending the reassignment of Ménard, while Commandant Dorsemaine was at GQG deputising for Duval as acting commander of the Aviation Militaire on the Western Front[90].

In the first half of May Hoeppner maintained intense pressure upon the northern part of the front to divert Allied attention as preparations for *'Blücher'/'Goerz'* were completed. During the month RAF aircrew casualties totalled 340, including 235 dead and missing, while the French lost 211, including 148 killed and missing[91]. Some of these casualties were the result of a rash of 'friendly fire' incidents on the Flanders Front from 3–15 May usually involving British attacking their French allies. The worse was on 8 May when Australian SE 5s 'bounced' French Spads and future ace Captain Gregory Blaxland shot down one, killing the pilot. Salmond soon saw through an Australian cover-up and on 11 May apologised to X Armée air commander Commandant Paul Armengaud but four days later the Chef d'Aviation of DAN, Commandant Morison, complained about further incidents and a British pilot was punished. The squadrons responsible belonged to Hogg's new day strike formation, Lieutenant-Colonel Reginald Mills' 51 Wing, and Salmond demanded improvements in aircraft recognition and threatened severe disciplinary measures if the events were repeated[92].

For *Unternehmen 'Blücher'/'Goerz'*, *Hauptmann* Hugo Sperrle (*Kofl 7.Armee* and commander of *Luftflotte 3* in the future *Luftwaffe*) had 56 squadrons with 13 *Jasta* (including *JG I* and *JG III*), six *Bosta* (*Bogohl 1* and *2*) while some *Grufln* were controlling eight to 10 squadrons. There were 14 *Schlasta* in *Schlachtgruppen A*, *B* and *C* with one for each spearhead corps. The *1. Armee* contributed squadrons under *Hauptmann*

Hugo Geyer, including three *Jasta*, giving the Germans a strength of some 500 aircraft over the front greatly outnumbering VI Armée which had 15 squadrons (one fighter) with some 200 aircraft[93].

German preparations were concealed from intense Allied air reconnaissance by dense woodlands 10 kilometres behind the front as well as by mist and fog in the river valleys. Good visibility occurred only on 22 May and while Duchêne flew 369 reconnaissance sorties as far as 40 kilometres behind the lines from May 10 until hours before the German attack, the SRA failed to detect in the hundreds of photographs, the increased rail traffic or the arrival of more than 1,000 batteries and two million shells. The British No 52 Squadron supporting IX Corps, which had reinforced VI Armée, was no more successful despite operating earlier in the morning, although they did report clouds of dust over roads on 17 May[94].

German air operations provided no clues and in the 17 days before the attack Duchêne's sole fighter squadron (SPA82) flew 131 sorties and reported 43 combats while the *Jasta* supporting 7.*Armee* claimed only five victories for the loss of one fighter. But the *Bosta* were more active, dropping nearly 25 tonnes of bombs in the week before the attack[95].

On 27 May the *Schlasta* completed the destruction of Duchêne's defenders despite dense fog, some supporting the tanks of *Gruppe Schmettow* (*LXV. Armeekorps*) against the British. They also pushed back enemy contact patrols while the *Infanterieflieger* quickly discovered gaps in the defences and helped get the attackers to the Vesle by midday, their shells driving Allied corps squadrons back to safer nests[96].

The British noted the enemy airmen were more effective in May than in March with the *Schlasta* striking road transport and airfields. The first four aircraft dispatched by No 52 Squadron all failed to return. Intense attacks by *Schlasta* and *Bosta* prevented the destruction of the VI Armée air park at Magneux airfield (near Fismes) on 28 May allowing Sperrle to exploit the facilities and 9,000 litres of captured fuel[97]. His bombers dropped 76.5 tonnes of bombs from 27 May to 4 June but were unable to dam the flood of French reinforcements including aircraft. GC 21 and Groupement Chabert were first into the fray from the east and were swiftly joined by GAE's GC 20 while elements of Duval's Division Aérienne began arriving from the west led by Féquant on the evening of 27 May with Ménard following the next day[98].

The German advance forced many French squadrons to change airfields several times, but within a few days the attackers came under the familiar rain of bomb and bullet with the French dropping 200 tonnes of bombs from 31 May to 2 June. Duval struck in 'combined expeditions' using massed bombers against key targets up to 20 kilometres behind the line shielded by fighter groups whose sweeps on either side sought to clear a fighter-free corridor. At the request of Commandant Joseph Vuillemin of 12e Escadre, Ménard's missions received extra protection with bombers escorted by Caudrons of R46 whose crews included the best gunners in the Aviation Militaire[99]. While less effective in the FEBA, the French attacks stretched the German logistics system to breaking point and this was aggravated by the destruction of one of the Germans' few artillery ammunition dumps.

The German advance again outpaced the ability of the *Luftstreitkräfte* to keep pace (apart from the kite balloon units) and there was another slackening of air support. *JG I* moved forward on 31 May but *JG III* took nearly a week from 3 June to move forward piecemeal. To coordinate fighter operations most of the autonomous *Jasta* were placed under *JGr 5* from 30 May. Meanwhile, *JG II* was rarely able to operate in more than *Staffel* strength flying only 25 sorties on 29 May in dense haze and low cloud[100].

At the same time the French were bringing overwhelming strength to bear with some 80 squadrons ((35 fighter, 15 bomber) by the beginning of June, a third of their air force, including 600 fighters and bombers. Despite support from GC 15 the 12e Escadre suffered heavy losses by flying into the lion's den (five bombers to *JG I* on 31 May) but, ultimately, the *Jastas* were powerless to stop French attacks. From 27 May until 6 June the two groupements flew 1,300 fighter and 555 bomber sorties, delivering some 78 tonnes of bombs while Villomé's night-bombers in 440 sorties dropped a further 134.6 tonnes. The cost was high with fighter and bomber groups losing 52 aircraft and 94 men, but French fighters claimed 110 victories[101]. '*Blücher*'/'*Goerz*' provides a rare chance to analyse German offensive air operations. From 27 May to 18 June, the *7. Armee* aircraft flew 6,014 sorties of which 55% were by fighters. Less than 12% (714) were by *Schlasta* which made 2,003 attacks expending 26.6 tonnes of bombs (37.25 kg per sortie) and

407,682 rounds of ammunition. There were a mere 216 artillery cooperation sorties but 565 contact patrols (9%), while a staggering 1,196 long-range reconnaissance and bombing sorties were flown, the latter delivering 106.6 tonnes of bombs. In the course of these operations Sperrle's squadrons consumed 700,000 litres of petrol.

They lost 80 aircraft to enemy action with 117 aircrew (80 killed or missing). The squadrons were credited with 130 aircraft and 23 balloon victories but another 181 aircraft were withdrawn through battle damage or because their airframes were too old. Total German air losses to 6 June were 54 aircraft (46 by *7.Armee*) and some 140 aircrew, of whom about 80 were killed or captured[102].

Once again German staff work on air operations was poor and there were major logistical problems causing undue reliance upon captured supplies. When it occupied Beugneux-Cramaille airfield on 1 June *JG I* was lucky to find a flock of 300 sheep together with cattle, chickens and rabbits, while there was an abundance of wine and cognac leading to 'really wild parties' on otherwise quiet days. Petrol, oil and lubricants were scarcer; French petrol was of poor quality while the rotary engines of the Triplanes became unreliable due to a combination of hot weather and poor quality ersatz castor oil[103].

By early June Germany occupied a swollen salient north of the Marne between Paris and Reims, but Ludendorff's fast-dwindling resources were on the defensive. Indeed to hold the western part of the salient the *9.Armee* was created under *General der Infanterie* Johannes von Eben. To widen the salient the *18.Armee* launched *Unternehmen* '*Gneisenau*' on 9 June from Noyon along the valley of the River Matz, but Général Humbert's III Armée defended in depth and Mangin regained lost ground with a tank-tipped counter-offensive and massive air support [104].

An intercepted radio message about rushing ammunition to the *18.Armee* front led the Allies to increase their air reconnaissance over the Montdidier/Noyon front and detected preparations for '*Gneisenau*'. The Allies concluded the enemy would attack the following day which posed problems for Duval because Féquant was covering the eastern half of the Marne salient while Ménard and Groupement Laurens (25 squadrons) shielded the western side encompassing III Armée whose 22 squadrons included GC 16. On 2 June, Foch requested IX RAF Brigade (eight squadrons excluding 54 Wing) as reinforcements and these arrived the next day. Féquant's 13e Escadre with six bomber squadrons was assigned to Ménard, bringing total strength to some 800 aircraft which ensured numerical superiority against Sperrle's 500 including 21 *Jasta*, two *Bogohls* and seven *Schlasta*[105].

The attack on 7 June was throttled by strong Allied air attacks upon German reserves and transport while Sperrle was unable to protect the luckless *Landsers*. He was equally impotent against Mangin's counter-offensive on 11 June which also had powerful close air support. German reserves and the logistic network were further exposed to Allied bomber attack because Sperrle's priority was to protect the kite balloons. There was no lack of effort by the *Jastas* (*JG II* flying 215 sorties on 10–12 June) but many of its Triplanes were unserviceable and the new Fokker D.VIIs had priority for scarce petrol and oil[106].

Ménard and Hogg flew some 2,000 sorties and dropped more than 82 tonnes of bombs from 7–14 June, British bombers emulating the French to make low-level missions. The air battle proved the wildest on the Western Front with Hogg using half his aircraft for ground attacks flying four daily missions in which fighters dropped up to a tonne of bombs. The confused situation led to another rash of 'friendly fire' incidents with the British bombing French troops and their Allies shooting down, then strafing, a British fighter. Salmond apologised to Duval on 16 June for the British mistakes but the following day Duval replied: 'These mistakes are unfortunately inevitable[107].'

Duval's reply may have reflected preoccupation rather than magnanimity. Pétain's star was waning, especially after the Chemin des Dames debacle for which his chief of staff, Anthoine, together with the latter's brother-in-law, Duchêne, were dismissed[108]. Generals and politicians wanted a more dynamic response and, as with Nivelle in 1917, Pétain's use of air power was one rod with which to beat him.

From April 5 the generals demanded a return to direct support including constant presence over the trenches. When Pétain snubbed them by creating the DAé many generals appear to have boycotted it in protest, despite the fact its operations were generally restricted to 20 kilometres from the front. Even in late July, Duval would complain about the generals' wilful failure to establish proper communications with the DAé and their woeful lack of understanding of its role and value [109].

The Matz battle was the first time the new German Fokker D.VII appeared in strength although they '.did not create such a sensation then as they did later[110].' *JG I* had received the first on 26 May but the fighter's legendary reputation did not begin until the D.VIIf with the BMW IIIa 185 hp engine appeared with *Jasta 11* becoming the first unit fully equipped with them from 22 June. The new fighter had an excellent high altitude performance but was usually issued to the more successful pilots leaving the remainder to use older work horses ([111]). Its impact was psychological rather than physical. During 1918 some 26 Allied pilots who arrived at the front that year claimed at least five Fokkers to become aces while seven aces had victory lists which were exclusively Fokker D.VIIs. This suggests the Fokker's reputation was exaggerated (although it should also be recognised the quality of German fighter pilot was also declining)[112].

The psychological impact upon Allied pilots was all the greater because for nearly a year the Germans had flown inferior fighters. Now they had one whose overall performance finally equalled, or was superior to, their own. Certainly by October there were signs that the Spad S13 was in trouble but by then the escadrilles de chasse were scheduled to receive new aircraft [113].

Nevertheless, the outlook for German airmen was growing bleaker. The Matz campaign cost Germany only 17 aircraft and some 20 aircrew, but it brought total aircrew losses on the Western Front since the New Year to some 1,800, of whom about 1,300 were dead, missing or prisoners. From mid March to mid May *18.Armee* alone lost 459 aircraft, 60% in accidents, with pilot losses averaging 15% per month because fuel shortages in the rear reduced training[114].

These shortages began to bite during the summer preventing the full exploitation of the new Fokkers. During May and June Hoeppner's men consumed 10,000 tonnes of petrol, twice the amount reaching the front and upon the introduction of rationing *Kofl AOK 18 Armee* informed units on 14 June that the *Jasta* would be rationed to 14,000 litres of petrol and 4,000 litres of oil per month. This limited the *Jasta* to 10 sorties a day in some cases. Many aircraft were worn out, indeed *JG II*'s *Jasta 12* and *Jasta 19* had none serviceable on 19 June and while *Jasta 19* soon received Fokker D.VIIs *Jasta 12* had to use Triplanes. On 24 June *Kofl AOK 18 Armee* stated the Triplanes were unfit for further operations and they were all withdrawn leaving *Jasta 12* with four worn out

Siemens-Schuckerts. A hint of the operational problems facing the *Luftstreitkräfte* was the withdrawal of a precious Fokker D.VII from *Jasta 6* and its transfer to *FA(A) 298* where it received a camera to become a high-speed photo-reconnaissance aircraft[115].

By July Germany was in desperate straits for, despite inflicting 392,000 casualties, it had failed to break the Allies while the balance of strength was remorselessly tipping in its favour as the 'Dough Boys' arrived. By contrast, Ludendorff's gambles had cost 795,000 casualties (164,000 dead and missing) since March and these grew as the influenza pandemic, also brought across the Atlantic by the Americans, began to bite among the blockade-ravaged *Landsers* whose sick lists almost doubled during July pushing morale even lower ([116]). *OHL* still pinned its hopes on '*Hagen*' but desperately sought the means to recreate a favourable strategic situation.

Chapter Seven

The Allied Victory in the West: July – November 1918

With the passing of the summer equinox the shortening days were a symbol of Germany's chances of victory. Yet Ludendorff remained determined to launch '*Hagen*', from Flanders on 20 July with 31 *Mobildivisionen* and 1,200 batteries to exploit his latest diversion from the Marne Salient.

Despite dwindling resources this diversion was an ambitious double envelopment of the historic city of Reims by Boehn's 7. *Armee* in the west ('*Marneschütz*') and by *1.Armee*, now under *General der Infanterie* Bruno von Mudra, in the east ('*Reims*'), with Einem's *3.Armee* ordered to destroy Maistre's GAC.

Ludendorff assembled 609 heavy batteries (almost as many as '*Michael*') and 25 tanks, but his desire to strike quickly meant abandoning vital security measures such as camouflage, radio traffic control and deception. He compounded the error by allowing the operation, launched on 15 July, to be referred to as the 'Peace Offensive' (*Friedensturm*) raising his men's expectations[1]. Allied aerial reconnaissance from late June noted preparations for both '*Hagen*' and the '*Friedensturm*' but it was only in early July that the Allies were confident the next blow would come from the Marne Salient. They determined the number of enemy divisions through trench raids and Comint, then used air reconnaissance to determine the scale of artillery support.

Pétain brought Mitry's DAN (redesignated IX Armée) from Flanders as a strategic reserve and tried to persuade his sceptical subordinates to adopt defence in depth while reluctantly accepting Mangin's plan for a riposte from each side of the salient. Most French generals paid lip service to Pétain's defensive philosophy but only IV Armée's Général Gourard, east of Reims, embraced the concept whole-heartedly[2]. When the Germans attacked he held the attackers and their tanks in his battle zone. But V Armée's Berthelot, holding the hills of the Monts de Reims south-west of the city, was more half-hearted allowing 7.*Armee to* crush an Italian corps and advance 5 kilometres[3]. Degoutte's VI Armée on the Marne also paid lip service to Pétain's ideas, but the defenders (including American troops) fought resolutely and within two days *OHL* faced the stark prospect of defeat.

For the riposte, briefly cancelled by a nervous Pétain who was overruled by Foch, Mitry took over part of Degoutte's front as VI Armée joined Mangin's X Armée to attack the western side of the salient at dawn on 18 July supported by 493 tanks and 1,600 guns. The twin nightmares of massed tanks and waves of Americans struck the boundary of Eben's newly introduced 9.*Armee* in the north and Boehn in the south. Boehn conducted a fighting retreat allowing the salient to deflate like a leaking balloon while the Germans fortified the Vesle valley and Ludendorff prepared to launch '*Hagen*'[4].

The second half of 1918 saw the air war reach a bloody crescendo with more than 4,300 casualties (a third of them RAF) as the Allies gradually established control. They achieved this by integrating fighters and bombers into a powerful weapon to strike the enemy infrastructure. Superior tactics also exploited their overall numerical superiority through multi-national operations, especially for the Americans who were supported by French, British and Italian squadrons.

The second Battle of the Marne saw airmen from almost every combatant on the Western Front fight the largest air battle in the Great War involving 2,700 (900 German and 1,800 Allied) aeroplanes. It began inauspiciously, for while the Allies knew *Heeresgruppe Kronprinz Rupprecht* had the largest concentration of forces, their reconnaissance aircraft were grounded by bad weather in late June leaving them uncertain of German intentions. Even when the weather improved from 28 June, reports of enemy preparations came from both the Marne Salient and Flanders[5]. Intelligence finally divined enemy intentions by 7 July, aided partly by Weiller's plotting the location of *Jasta* and *Bogohls*, and any doubts were removed by numerous aerial photographs of uncamouflaged batteries and numerous ammunition dumps.

On 10 July Foch, now certain the enemy would strike from the Marne salient, warned Haig he might want IX Brigade. Hogg's men had returned to Salmond after '*Gneisenau*' and Haig was reluctant to weaken his air forces but loyally assigned nine squadrons (five fighter) to French command when a formal request was made on 13 July. Leaving 54 Wing, they flew south through rain to arrive two days later, just as the German attack began. At the same time No 82 Squadron accompanied XXII Corps which was added to Foch's operational reserve on the Marne[6]. This gave the allies 135 squadrons (Table 7-1) which were stronger and better equipped than Hoeppner's. On 15 June the Division Aérienne received its final reorganisation with the groupements renamed brigades d'aviation; 1er Brigade under Chef de Bataillon (Major) Louis de Goÿs de Mezeyrac and the 2eme Brigade under Féquant each with a staff of 17[7].

Table 7-1:
Distribution of Allied squadrons for '*Friedensturm*'. 15 July 1918

Command	Fighter	Bomber	Other
DAé	24	9	3
Villomé	-	5	-
Chabert	-	6	-
Bloch	-	-	2
IX Brigade	5	4	-
IV Armée	10	-	17
V Armée	9	-	15
VI Armée	6	-	22
Total	**54**	**24**	**59**

Source: Based upon *Armées Française X*:GAC, GAR and army entries. Jones *VI*:412. Maurer *1*:197, 291. Note: Other includes corps, reconnaissance and escort squadrons.

Their orders stated specifically: 'The missions of the brigade command are essentially of a tactical nature' for the DAé was being used increasingly as flying artillery against enemy troop and transport columns. Yet 42-year-old Goÿs was an ardent advocate of strategic bombing who created GB 1 in 1914, and was a former prisoner-of-war like his predecessor Ménard escaping after two years in captivity[8].

A 700-strong strike force was assigned to Maistre's GAC, mostly under Duval with Göys' 1er Brigade based east of the salient behind Fayolle's GAR, while Féquant's 2eme Brigade (supported by Hogg's IX Brigade) was to the west, augmented by Groupement Villomé's heavy bombers and Groupement Bloch's reconnaissance squadrons. On 13 July Duval ordered his fighters to seize air superiority while the bombers would strike any bridges the enemy threw across the Marne. Bloch's squadrons would locate them within the first six hours of the offensive and priority was assigned to the VI Armée front between Château Thierry and Dormans, then the V Armée front[9].

Chef de Bataillon Boucher of IV Armée had 320 aircraft (including GC 21 & 22) and was also supported by Chabert's 11e Escadre while Bertholet's V Armée had some 285 aircraft (including GC 11) under Chef de Bataillon Guillemeney. Gérard had been transferred to Flanders but his successor at VI Armée had 410 aircraft including Mitchell's 1st Air Brigade with 1st Pursuit and 1st Observation Groups, the latter under Major Lewis H. Brereton, a future air force general[10].

Hoeppner had assembled 130 squadrons (Table 7-2) and four *Reihenbildzüge* amounting to 30% of his Western Front strength. However, failing industry meant squadrons were some 10% under strength while the Spanish Influenza pandemic was biting leaving *Jasta 19* with only three healthy pilots on 6 July. The *Jasta* were grouped to maximise effectiveness; 7.*Armee* being supported by *JG I, JG III, Jagdgruppen 4* and *5* while east of Reims was *JG II* and five *Jagdgruppen* (*1, 7, 9, 11* and *Lenz*) all under Berthold who was under *Kofl AOK 3. Armee, Hauptmann* Palmer. The remaining air support was spread evenly like butter on bread with each army having a *Bogohl* and two *Schlachtgruppen*, but the total bomber force was only 50 aircraft[11].

Table 7-2: Distribution of German squadrons for '*Friedensturm*' 15 July 1918

Command	Jasta	Bosta	Schlasta	FA
7. Armee	18	3	9	23
1. Armee	15	3	8	12
3. Armee	13	3	9	14
Total	**46**	**9**	**26**	**49**

Source: *Luftmacht* 4:53.

A fortnight before the German attack, Franco-Italian bombers delivered 107 tonnes of bombs, mostly in and around the Marne salient but rain and storms grounded aircraft most of the following week. The *Jasta* and *Flak* batteries of the '*Friedensturm*' armies were officially credited with 39 victories (all but two by 7.*Armee*) for the loss of nine aircraft but Allied artillery aircraft helped to disrupt enemy preparations, the German lines resembling an ants' nest as they moved in numerous small parties[12].

The Germans struck on 15 July under dull, overcast skies with low cloud which forced aircraft lower, exposing them to ground fire [13]. Poor visibility gave 7.*Armee* a five-hour head start to throw bridges across the Marne and to establish *Jasta* and *Flak* defences, but once the bridges were discovered every *Landser* ran the gauntlet of 'energetic' air and air-directed artillery attack. On the V Armée front Fayolle criticised the DAé for ignoring his desperate situation and Duval would face a similar stream of criticism throughout the Marne battle[14].

The Anglo-French strike force flew nearly 800 sorties on the first day (Table 7-3) and dropped nearly 53 tonnes of bombs in numerous low-level attacks which destroyed many footbridges. That night 15 tonnes of bombs disturbed German rest although the *Kagohls* dropped 47 tonnes. Allied pressure eased the next day when Crown Prince Wilhelm reluctantly sanctioned the bridgehead's abandonment but Ludendorff obstinately refused to confirm the decision and the destruction of the bridges continued for 24 hours, with 70% lost by 17 July, and 'terrifying' casualties among the German engineers before the inevitable evacuation. This was the second success against a bridgehead in a month for Allied air power, the first being against the Austrian bridgehead on the River Piave in Italy[15].

Table 7-3:
Strike force operations. 15–16 July 1918 (bomb tonnage dropped)

Date	1 Brigade	2 Brigade	IX Brigade	Chabert	Villomé	Bloch
15 July	420 (35t)	286 (17t)	92 (0.9t)	30 (7t)	20 (8.3t)	18
16 July	180 (8.9t)	226 (4.8t)	164 (6.0t)	43 (11.3t)	21 (11.2t)	11
Total	**600 (43.9t)**	**512 (21.8t)**	**256 (6.9t)**	**73 (18.3t)**	**41 (19.5t)**	**29**

Source: *Armée Françaises VI/2*:Annexes 2218, 2045. SHAA A128/2. UKNA Air 1/2249/209/46/5. Note: Bomber sorties for Chabert on July 15 and IX Brigade on 16 July estimated.

There were numerous air battles during the '*Friedensturm*'. French brigades recorded 77 clashes with 16 victories, yet Allied casualties were astonishingly low and the strike forces lost only 12 aircraft on the first day while the Germans lost 10 (2 fighters). They lost another 11 during the following two days but were optimistically credited with 94 victories [16]. The IV and V Armées fighter squadrons were extremely active, the latter flying 414 sorties in three days, while VI Armée flew 272 but the pressure was so great that X Armée surrendered GC 12 to IV Armée on 17 July. Both armies were assisted by 1er Escadre whose fighters claimed 15 kite balloons, blinding German gunners, while Allied corps aircraft helped direct fire upon the oncoming hoards. Although reconnaissance and artillery direction remained the prime roles of French corps squadrons, some supporting Berthelot also flew ground-attack missions dropping 81mm Brandt mortar bombs[17].

Even after the *Friedensturm* blew itself out, Allied airmen maintained pressure upon the salient during 16–17 July. This included attacks upon the railhead of Fère-le-Tardenois, an idea which Mitchell claimed as his own vision although it was an obvious target and when in French hands received 19.5 tonnes of German bombs during the night of 27/28 May. The Allied attacks helped divert enemy fighters at the cost of a dozen bombers over two days but the pace of air operations declined during 17 July as men rested for the following day's counter-offensive[18].

To support the assault Göys' and Féquant exchanged positions; part of 1er Brigade went to V Armée in the east bringing its air support to 376 aircraft (Table 7-4). The largest concentration, 1,143 aircraft, was in the west where Hogg and Mitchell helped to support VI Armée while 2eme Brigade covered X Armée leaving IX Armée in the south with only 182 aircraft including one of Göys' fighter groups[19]. Allied air superiority, combined with the last minute assembly of the attackers in woods, prevented the Germans detecting the riposte until it was too late.

Table 7-4:
Distribution of Allied squadrons for Marne counter-offensive.
18 July 1918

Command	Fighter	Bomber	Other
Daé	24	9	3
Villomé	-	5	-
Chabert	-	6	-
Bloch	-	-	2
IX Brigade	5	4	-
V Armée	8	-	16
VI Armée	4	-	15
IX Armée	4	-	7
X Armée	10	-	27
Total	**55**	**24**	**70**

Sources: *Armée Françaises VI/2*:55, 59–62, 64–66, Annex 72. *Armée Françaises X*: Army entries.

On the first day of the counter-offensive, Göys' brigade flew 243 sorties and dropped 14 tonnes of bombs as Allied airmen flew air superiority, battlefield interdiction and close air support missions in a sustained offensive which lasted for another four days (Table 7-5). Rain and low cloud brought relief to the retreating Germans who had endured a 170-tonne torrent of bombs from the French alone[20].

Table 7-5
Allied strike force in the Marne counter-offensive

Date	1 Brigade	2 Brigade	IX Brigade	Chabert	Villomé	Total
18–21 July	666	757	486	106	76	2,091
22–28 July	499	487	593	111	17	1,707
29 July–4 August	8	-	-	143	58	209
Total	**1,173**	**1,244**	**1,079**	**360**	**151**	**4,007**

Sources: SHAA A128/2. UKNAO Air 1/2249/209/46/5. Record books Nos 27, 49,98, 107 Squadrons in Public Record Office.

Allied army squadrons were also active; from 166--31 July, V Armée's aircraft flew 2,458 sorties and lost 15 aircraft while fighters claimed eight victories. Once again the speed of the advance disrupted traditional air operations with many corps squadrons left far behind, 60 kilometres for the inexperienced 1st US Observation Group, but soon bombing and air-directed artillery fire cut the 7.*Armee* rail line at Soissons. Surprisingly, the French found balloons useful in mobile operations by operating in pairs with one ranging guns and directing fire while the other moved forward, a version of the infantry's fire and movement tactics [21].

To support the salient, eight *Jasta* were stripped from *3. Armee* whose *JG II* went to *9.Armee* on 24 July followed by *JGr 11* the next day. Most *Schlasta* were now supporting Boehn and were augmented by all the *Jagdgeschwader* as the evacuation of the eastern side of the salient was given priority. The *Luftstreitkräfte* responded magnificently and by 22 July had established 'a most striking air superiority' over the eastern side allowing 7.*Armee* war diary to describe the crisis as over ([22]).

For the first time German aircraft dominated the skies over enemy lines, some flying seven sorties a day, and Berthelot demanded concealment during the day with movement confined to the short nights. Even then there was no respite as the *Bogohls* harassed communications dropping more than 166 tonnes from 18–22 July and V Armée's advance was noticeably slow even after Pétain sent every available engineer to keep open its roads[23].

Exhaustion, low cloud, rain and poor visibility reduced the pace of air operations within eight days and restricted French reconnaissance of the Germans' new positions north of the Vesle. Only on 2 August, after enemy air activity declined, did the Allies realise the salient had been completely abandoned[24].

The Second Marne campaign demonstrated the potential of air power to influence ground operations with the French alone delivering 421 tonnes of bombs to harass German Army operations from 15 July – 4 August, much of it during daylight hours. Hoeppner had long recognised he lacked such a strike force and he had written to Ludendorff on 6 June: 'Physical and moral success can be achieved only through heavy attacks by massed *Schlachtfliegern*[25].'

Twenty days later *OHL* belatedly demanded the *Luftstreitkräfte* emulate the Allies and focus its resources against communications. The bombers were to strike rail networks while *Schlachtgruppen* and *Schlachtgeschwadern* attacked enemy reserves, especially at choke points, supported by single-engined aircraft from the *Bogohls* and the *Jasta*. *Schlachtgeschwader* performed both Tactical and Operational level missions on 15–16 July but they could not deliver a weight of ordnance equal to the bombers which were confined to the short nights. German airmen had limited influence upon ground operations, indeed on July 18 the *Schlasta* dropped only three tonnes of bombs upon advancing tanks[26].

The Allies had paid for their dominance, the DAé lost some 20 aircraft with 32 aircrew casualties from 18–31 July (although its fighters were credited with 40 victories) while X Armée lost a dozen aircraft in the first five days of the counter-offensive (half on the first day) and suffered 33 casualties. 7.*Armee* reported the loss of 23 aircraft while fighter and *Flak* units were credited with 174 victories[27].

The Germans had little time to recover for on 8 August, at Foch's instigation, the British struck at Amiens using Rawlinson's 4th Army with 530 tanks and Debeney's I Armee. Marwitz's 2.*Armee* collapsed with near-mutiny in the rear, carrying back its southern neighbour 18.*Armee* ([28]). The threat forced a radical regrouping of the defenders on 12 August with Rupprecht's 18.*Armee* and 2.*Armee* being assigned to the newly activated *Heeresgruppe von Boehn* together with the Crown Prince's 9.*Armee*.

The British drove remorselessly onward adapting to the new mobile warfare with a flexibility and tactical innovation that proved more than a match for the increasingly irresolute defenders who abandoned their gains from *Michael* and in early September retreated into the *Siegfriedstellung*. Defeat shook the Empire's social cohesion exacerbating the chaos and unrest, which had existed behind the front lines even before the spring offensive, forcing Berlin to open peace talks as the German Army hoped a resolute defence would bring peace with honour ([29]).

The RAF first shielded 4th Army's lines and aided security by monitoring them for clues which might alert the enemy. The few registration missions were concealed in the routine counter-battery programme. Reconnaissance was carried out surreptitiously but the photographs showed the enemy fortifications were poorly sited and neglected[30].

Plumer's 2nd Army was ostentatiously reinforced to deceive the enemy while II Brigade, supported by I and III Brigades, became extremely active until 6 August to divert German attention from Amiens. V Brigade line patrols worked to contain the Germans, who flew only 37 sorties (seven photographic reconnaissance) from 1–7 August while rain and low cloud grounded most aircraft from 2 August, apart from a brief surge in air combat on 7 August when the British reported 18 clashes [31].

Charlton's V Brigade and Hogg's IX Brigade were augmented by Longcroft's III Brigade and bombers from I and X Brigades (Table 7-6) to give Rawlinson 800 of Salmond's 1,563 aircraft. The French provided 477 aircraft (38 squadrons including GC 12 and GC 16) of Debeney's I Armée and Groupement Laurens (GB 8 & 10) as well as 627 aircraft of DAé while III Armée added 135 aircraft on the periphery. With memories of 'friendly fire' incidents on the Matz, Debeney ordered no attacks upon cavalry behind the enemy lines[32].

Table 7-6:
Allied squadrons for August 1918 offensives

Command	Fighter	Bomber	Other	Total
I Brigade	6	2	4	12
III Brigade	5	2	3	10
V Brigade	9	2	6	17
IX Brigade	7	9	-	16
I Armée	8	6	24	38

III Armée	3	-	9	12
DAé	25	15	2	42
Total	**63**	**36**	**48**	**147**

Sources. *Armée Françaises X*: Army entries amended by *Rapport du Maréchal Commandent*:20. Jones *Appendices*: Appendix XXIV.

For all this the RAF's nominal numerical superiority was offset by battle or accident damage which reduced each squadron's strength as riggers repaired wire or struts, patched and doped fabric while fitters maintained engines. There was a serious shortage of manpower with brigades having barely 1,600 pilots on 1 August and limited reserves. Constant battle drained squadron strengths; No 80 (Fighter) Squadron for example suffered 168 casualties in the last 10 months of the war averaging 75% per month. Within squadrons many pilots were unavailable due to leave, injuries and sickness, especially Spanish Influenza, indeed No 80 Squadron averaged only 22 pilots instead of 24. A quarter of all pilots were novices and before squadron commanders exposed them to combat the newcomers needed to improve gunnery skills, learn formation flying, become acquainted with the countryside and fly-in replacement aircraft. Consequently even a squadron-size mission might involve only 10–15 aircraft[32].

With the well of British manpower drained almost dry perhaps only 50–60% of Salmond's pilots were from the British Isles or British citizens while 20–25% were Canadians. Some 5–10% of Salmond's pilots were Australians who flew not only with British squadrons but in three of the Australian Flying Corps. On 1 August Salmond also had some 210 American pilots, including 45 detached from the USAS to serve in RAF squadrons after receiving training in England, and these accounted for up to an astonishing 13% of his pilots[33].

Salmond estimated he faced 261 aircraft which could be reinforced by 267 in 48 hours, but the British faced *2.Armee*, which had 23 squadrons (190 aircraft) including six *Jasta* and *Bogohl* 7, while the French faced *18. Armee* with 20 squadrons (155 aircraft) including four *Jasta*, the Germans having only 120 fighters on the whole battlefront. The neighbouring *17. Armee* had some 18 squadrons (160 aircraft) including *JGr* 7, *8* and *10*. For the first time in the war most of the *Luftstreitkräfte*, including a third of the *Jasta* and 70% of the *Schlasta*, remained on the French front (Table 7-7), while 850 aircraft (430 fighters) continued to support *9. Armee* and *7. Armee*[34].

Table 7-7:
German air force on the Western Front 8 August 1918

Army Group	Jasta	Bosta	Schlasta	FA
Kronprinz Rupprecht	26	15	9	55
Deutscher Kronprinz	42	9	22	52
Gallwitz	2	-	-	9
Herzog Albrecht	8	3	-	13
Total	**78**	**27**	**31**	**129**

Note: In addition there were five *Reihenbildzüge*, three with *Rupprecht* and two with *deutscher Kronprinz*.
Source: UKNA Air 1/9/15/1/26.

From as early as 26 June the Allies dominated the German front lines to prevent enemy aircraft probing far beyond no-man's-land. The sound of trucks increased and drifted across the lines but the Germans could not discern the reason and a 'clue' from a quick-witted British airman prisoner on 7 August helped to focus German attention well to the north [35].

On 1 August Salmond submitted his plans to Haig but they focused only on the first day and included combined daylight attacks upon airfields within a 50-kilometre radius and night attacks upon the main rail stations. Tactical air support was the main focus of planning which was plagued by confusion within 4th Army as to whether or not the assault would be a limited attack (envisaged by Rawlinson) or a breakthrough battle (Haig's vision) with Charlton naturally planning for the former. Confusion was further fuelled because, unlike the RFC in previous campaigns, RAF planning was largely on an ad hoc verbal basis rather than a thorough and detailed process expressed in written form while a further handicap was the absence of an overall air commander[36].

The bombers were extremely active in the fortnight preceding Rawlinson's attack delivering 288.5 tonnes which sometimes inflicted heavy losses and helped to weaken enemy morale. They also concealed the noisy assembly of the tanks by flying along the front but, as usual, mist and fog ruined the offensive against airfields[37]. The conditions had less impact upon the tactical air support which generally went well. Charlton ensured squadrons were fully informed of each other's activities and, instead of roving around aimlessly, ground-attack squadrons struck specific areas for two hours before moving to new hunting grounds which increased their effectiveness and reduced their casualties. The tanks had their own corps squadron, No 8 under Major

Trafford Leigh-Mallory (later to become the controversial Second World War fighter leader) and their FK.8s had radio-telephones whose reports were supposed to be exploited by command tanks. Unfortunately the radio signals were weak usually being drowned by the roar of the tank engines. Haig's troops were never totally dependent upon either air support or armour and after Amiens could punch through defensive screens without over-reliance upon such luxuries[38].

The lack of overall command, and poor planning, contributed to the battle's most significant failure ([39]). Despite the Marne experience, no thought was given to striking bridges which crossed the Somme behind the German lines. Only when Hogg reported severe congestion at the bridges did Salmond extemporise a plan with Rawlinson's staff (and possibly Haig) to trap a significant element of *2. Armee*. Salmond threw every available aircraft at the crossings until dusk but nearly 10% were lost and the 16 tonnes of bombs they dropped inflicted little damage. The attacks would continue for nearly a week but with diminishing success, an ominous precedent for the Maastricht bridge attacks of May 1940 ([40]).

The dangers to the bombers were exacerbated by the unexplained absence of fighter cover for most of the first day as a low cloud base herded the bombers into the *Jastas'* gun sights. *Kofl 2.Armee* had responded by summoning reinforcements from as far afield as Champagne and these began to arrive during the morning. By happy coincidence the four *Jasta* of *JGr 2* (soon reinforced with two from *1.Armee*) had been ordered to fly low to support the corps squadrons and were able to wreak havoc among the bombers ([41]). Their successes helped bring the *Jastas'* total bag to 30 victories on the first day alone for the loss of twelve aircraft, while the RAF lost 44–45 machines with another 52 damaged beyond repair. This represented 12% of the aircraft committed, and is explained partly by the bombers' Calvary and the severe losses in low-level attacks which accounted for 23% of aircraft lost or wrecked ([42]).

Haig's advance on the ground was maintained by 3rd and 1st Armies supported by III (10, later 12, squadrons) and I Brigades, but despite increased pressure (Table 7-8, 5 August-22 September) Hoeppner continued to maintain powerful forces opposite the French rather like a rabbit mesmerised by a weasel. He dispatched barely 20 squadrons (294 aircraft) to the British front (Table 7-9) of which only a third went to *2. Armee* which also received *Grufl 14* from *4.Armee* ([43]).

Table 7-8:
RAF support for main British offensives August-November 1918

Week	I Brigade	III Brigade	V Brigade	IX Brigade	Total
5–11 August	1,740/7	870/17	2,180/66	885/45	5,675/135
12–18 August	1,765/8	1,060/9	1,880/22	730/6	5,435/45
19–25 August	1,600/6	1,260/24	1,745/10	800/16	5,405/56
26 August–					
1 September	2,180/27	1,265/16	1,405/16	450/10	5,300/69
2–8 September	2,050/32	1,380/21	1,520/11	435/10	5,385/74
9–15 September	635/6	795/3	1,485/8	100/2	3,015/19
16–22 September	1,450/12	1,160/23	1,595/18	435/8	4,640/61
23–29 September	1,675/23	1,345/24	1,630/22	670/22	5,320/91
30 September–					
6 October	1,505/17	1,210/13	2,230/21	475/5	5,420/56
7–13 October	1,070/18	730/9	1,450/8	235/4	3,485/39
14–20 October	465/1	380/5	880/3	215/1	1,940/10
21–27 October	690/6	885/4	1,200/7	100/3	2,875/20
28 October–					
3 November	1,035/18	1,285/7	1,415/7	490/10	4,225/42
4–10 November	700/1	815/17	1,210/20	510/8	3,235/46
Totals	**18,560/182**	**14,440/192**	**21,825/239**	**6,530/150**	**61,355/763**

Sources: Brigade war diaries.

Table 7-9: German air force distribution 15 August 1918

Army Group	Jasta	Bosta	Schlasta	FA
Kronprinz Rupprecht	17	9	3	31
Von Boehn	20	6	11	39
Deutscher Kronprinz	28	6	15	38
Gallwitz	2	-	-	9
Herzog Albrecht	9	3	-	13
Total	**76**	**24**	**29**	**130**

Source: UKNA Air 1/9/15/1/26.

Despite lighter losses the battles imposed an impossible strain upon Hoeppner. *JG I* vigorously defended the Somme bridges after arriving on 10 August but within two days was reduced to 11 serviceable fighters forcing it to collaborate with *JG III* and *Jagdgruppe Greim*, while the strain elsewhere was so great that by mid August two *Jasta*, a *Bogohl* and two *Schlasta* were withdrawn for rest and re-equipment. Hoeppner remained reluctant to denude his forces in the centre even at the end of the month when the *Siegfriedstellung* was threatened by the British advance. He sent only four *Schlasta* (one apparently from the Flanders front) to support the reeling armies while a dozen remained on the moribund *7. Armee* front. It is an interesting comment on *OHL's* priorities that *Heeresgruppe Deutscher Kronprinz* retained the largest concentration of German air power at this time with some 700 aeroplanes, while *Heeresgruppe Boehn* had 600, possibly in response to French pressure and the presence of Duval's aerial task forces. But German bombers helped the *Landser* by maintaining pressure upon the British logistics system with *Bogohls 1,2,4, 5* and 7 together with *Riesenfliegerabteilung 500* dropping 75 tonnes of bombs during the short summer nights of 8–21 August[44].

The French were slow to support their allies at Amiens, with DAé blaming poor weather for only 147 fruitless fighter sorties on the first day. This feeble response may have been due to a struggle for control of French air power with Debeney vainly demanding control over Duval. Spanish Influenza may also have had an effect upon aircrew strength; certainly on 3 September it felled the commander of SPA 3, Capitaine Georges Raymond, who died 4 October. The DAé flew 372 sorties on the second day and dropped 23.5 tonnes of bombs but was then passed southwards like a parcel, first to III Armée and, a week later, to Mangin as he recaptured the Chemin des Dames. Laurens' bombers remained to support the Amiens advance and delivered more than 55 tonnes from 8–11 August but this was little more than a token effort[45].

Allied air pressure eased slightly as the Germans withdrew through the man-made wildernesses of the old Somme battlefield and the '*Alberich*' devastated zone, although the RAF flew some 30,000 sorties. This was due to the dilution of air power as the RAF supported an advance along a 60-kilometre front hindered by a lack of airfields within the devastated zone. Far from their airfields, the British fighters could spend only half-an-hour over the battlefield instead of 45 minutes, effectively cutting air strength by 15–20%. Salmond's numerical strength was further eroded when damaged aircraft attempting to land in the wasteland were smashed, the airmen being lucky to escape with cuts and bruises[46].

At the beginning of September Foch, now a Maréchal de France, issued a directive in which pressure would be maintained along the whole front through successive and supportive advances which would resemble a giant trident plunged into the Germans' line. It began on the Allied right with the Americans striking on both sides of the Meuse, first crushing the St Mihiel Salient on 12 September which brought Allied troops close to the Fatherland, then driving through the Argonne Forest to reach the outskirts of Sedan by the Armistice.

On their left they were supported by Gourard's IV Armée which suffered 41% of France's 147,000 casualties from 26 September until the war's end. The French front was the eye of the hurricane, for the Marne campaign was the last gasp of the French Army and their return to the Vesle valley proved a geographic and a figurative watershed. Now the British and Americans were the spearhead and as they pushed eastwards the French largely adjusted their lines which contracted from 175 kilometres to some 75 kilometres with Fayolle's GAR (I and X Armées) and Maistre's GAC (V and IV Armées) and three army headquarters being disbanded. They were saving themselves for GAE's recapture of Alsace-Lorraine upon whose borders at the war's end GQG was assembling forces including 600 tanks and 174 heavy batteries ([47]).

In the centre the British smashed through the *Siegfriedstellung* on 27 September and the war ended with the Union Flag flying over Mons where, exactly a year earlier, *OHL* had planned its spring offensives. On the left the Allied GAF under Degoutte struck around Ypres on 28 September and despite appalling weather broke through and reconquered the whole of the coastal strip by the Armistice[48].

OHL had hoped to stop the Allies in the defensive systems built in 1916–1917 but as these buckled and cracked, a new strategy was adopted. The German Army would abandon most of Belgium and turn like a door hinged on Sedan to occupy a new position, the *Antwerpen-Meusestellung* which would be held until the Allies granted them a favourable armistice. But chaos reigned behind the German lines with the ramshackle front propped up by only a handful of divisions supported by elite units, including *Flak* gunners. They screened the retreat but the collapse in army morale went to the top as the generals betrayed their political leaders both to secure a ceasefire and to save their own skins. With the American advance compromising the *Antwerpen-Meusestellung* the new German government, with Army support, sent a delegation across the lines in October to negotiate an armistice which was signed on 10 November and came into effect the following day[49].

The pattern of air operations along the whole Western Front from the late summer until the Armistice was shaped by the weather. September was the last month to offer generally good flying weather leading to a peak in victory claims as the Allies claimed some 1,080 aircraft and 166 balloons while the Germans claimed 680 and 96 respectively. The Allies actually lost 580 aircraft and 60 kite balloons while some 120 German aircraft fell although up to 20% might be added, based upon Allied casualties, for aircraft forced to land east of the lines. The RAF accounted for some 75% of Allied claims but its lower victory credit standards partly account for the discrepancy with 40% of British victories last seen 'out of control[50].'

From late September until the Armistice the days were dominated by mist and fog. Air forces were no longer automatically grounded by bad weather but their flying hours were clearly restricted and during the handful of dry, bright, days there were surges in air activity. It was during the autumn that the French, who had long kept a close eye on German radio operations, noted that by plotting the activities of radios supporting the *Luftstreitkräfte*'s *Flak* and meteorological organisations they not only received advanced warning of German intentions to withdraw but also the direction[51].

By the Armistice the Allies had some 5,500 aircraft supported by 125,000 personnel, the largest contributor being the French with 3,222 aircraft followed by the British with 1,799 and the United States with 740[52]. The numerical superiority was skilfully exploited through integrated operations day and night which struck their foes throughout their tactical and operational depth in a manner the enemy could never match. Their air forces were no longer confined to national fronts and at each end of the front, the Americans and Belgians were supported by their allies who helped establish a degree of air superiority over the enemy lines, although it was never absolute.

A qualitative improvement in the German fighter arm partly counter-balanced the Allied threat with growing numbers of Fokker D.VIIs contesting control of the skies. By the autumn the Fokkers outclassed two of the most common Allied fighters, the Sopwith Camel (especially those with Clerget engines) and the Spad S13, but German production could not meet demand and the Fokkers probably never amounted to more than 40% of *Jasta* strength on the Western Front[53]. From July they were supplemented in 18 *Jastas* by the Pfalz D.XII a robust, rather than outstanding, design of similar appearance to the Fokker which entered service with *9.Armee's Jasta 61*. Unfortunately, most of the 900–950 German fighters on the Western Front in August continued to be the Albatros D.V/Va, Pfalz D.III/IIIa and Fokker Triplane – all obsolete or approaching obsolescence and even by the Armistice they still accounted for 40–45% of *Jasta* strength. Some 10% of the fighter force by the Armistice consisted of high-performance fighters such as the Siemens-Schuckert D.IV biplanes and the Fokker E.V (later D.VIII) monoplanes (See Table 7-10).

Table 7-10: German air force distribution. 11 November 1918

Army	Grufl	Jasta	Bosta	Schlasta	FA	Total	Probable strength
4	3	8	6	4	12	30	150(238)
6	1	6	3	-	6	15	60(102)
17	4	8	3	8	11	30	170(274)
2	2	7	3	3	10	23	140(219)
18	4	8	3	4	13	28	160(262)
7	2	4	3	-	12	19	120(179)
1	-	2	-	-	6	8	50(76)
3	-	8	-	5	11	24	140(226)
5	5	15	3	9	15	42	260(381)
'C'	2	1	-	1	12	14	60(92)
19	1	4	3	4	8	19	100(155)
'A'	-	4	3	-	5	12	60(103)
'B'	-	4	-	-	4	8	50(83)
Total	**24**	**79**	**30**	**38**	**125**	**272**	**1,520(2,390)**

Source: Based upon UKNA Air 1/9/15/1/22. Nominal strength in brackets. All strength figures are *Reichsarchiv*.

The Siemens-Schuckerts was first issued to *JG II* from April and were regarded as so secret that pilots were prohibited from crossing the lines and had to operate in a defensive role in the rear. Initially popular because of their phenomenal rate of climb, the aircraft developed a reputation for engine seizures due to the synthetic castor oil Voltol with the rotary engines having lives of only 7–10 hours. There was a similar problem with the Fokker E.V, with pilots making 30 emergency landings in 10 days, but wing structure problems led to their withdrawal in August. They were reissued with strengthened wings in October as the Fokker D.VIII but few saw action. All would soon have faced the new generation of Allied fighters including the Martinsyde Buzzard, Spad S20 and Sopwith Snipe while the outstanding Nieuport 29 was under development together with the American Le Père Lusac 11 which might have eclipsed the Bristol Fighter[54].

The German offensives had also contributed to the problem with the *Luftstreitkräfte* losing 938 aircraft and 352 balloons on all fronts from January to August 1918, an increase of 43% and 158% on the whole of the previous year, while personnel losses amounted to 4,184 men, of whom some 2,500 were aircrew. New aircraft and an effective *Flak* force, aided by a good signals network, could blunt the edge of the Allied sword but could not overcome numerical inferiority and poor doctrine [55].

The erosion of the infrastructure aggravated the situation as Ludendorff combed out men from air and *Flak* units to plug the gaps in ground troops' ranks. Meanwhile the blockade and deteriorating political situation disrupted the logistics system with petrol and spares running out. The *JG II* war diary noted that on 22 September the *Jasta* were restricted to 450 litres per day despite protests to *Kogenluft* but the pace of operations saw each *Jasta* despatch a four-fighter mission four times a day using 3,500 litres. With aircraft losses exceeded replacements by the Armistice, Hoeppner had only 1,520 aircraft instead of 2,390[56].

The starting gun for the Allied offensive was fired east of the Meuse by Pershing on 12 September and his birthday present the next day was the reduction of the St Mihiel Salient which was being evacuated before his guns opened fire, *Generalleutnant* Fuchs' *Armeeabteilung 'C'* having learned the American intentions from newspapers! As the front settled, the Americans switched across the Meuse, the transfer having been organised by a Colonel George C. Marshall whose career would reach a peak 20 years later[57].

The air war would be especially intense on the American front where the Germans concentrated their best fighter units as they desperately fought to thwart the Yankee threat to their key communications centres. The first step in preparing American air support was the creation on 16 August of 1st US Army's air service under Mitchell, with chief-of-staff Colonel Thomas DeW. Milling, while France's Commandant Paul Armengaud acted as a staff consultant. AEF air service commander

Major-General Mason M. Patrick's reforms of the supply chain eased their task while the appointment of Foulois as Assistant Chief of the Air Service allowed Mitchell to focus upon the forthcoming campaign for which he had high hopes[58].

Mitchell had much to prove to his high-ranking enemies who included Pershing's chief-of-staff Brigadier-General Hugh A. Drum and the I US Corps commander Major-General Hunter Liggett, but he was also aware his airmen lacked experience and they went through a frenzy of last-minute training. Low cloud, rain and mist hindered reconnaissance during the first half of September but luckily, given the observers' inexperience, little artillery registration was required. The shortage of airfields due to the hilly terrain around the Salient led to severe congestion; Toul airfield for example was home to both the 1st Pursuit and 1st Corps Observation Groups with 175 aircraft causing concern about the threat from German bombers[59].

To shield the Doughboys and Poilus, Major Bert M. Atkinson's 1st Pursuit Wing split the front in two and from 5 September created a sanctuary extending 5 kilometres behind the enemy lines. Although the Germans could do little initially against this threat to Metz, hub of the German Western Front rail system, the two *Jasta* of Albatros and Pfalz belonging to *Leutnant* Eugen Siempelkamp's *JGr Siempelkamp* were augmented from 2 September by *Oberleutnant* Oskar *Freiherr* von Boenigk's *JG II* with four first-class *Jasta* equipped with Fokkers and the new Pfalz to give a total of 70 fighters[60].

Mitchell would have overwhelming numerical superiority but it no doubt irked to be beholden to his allies for this good fortune. His own 1st Army Air Service had 611 aircraft, of which 78% were serviceable, and 21 of his 51 squadrons were French. The American forces consisted of Atkinson's Wing and Brereton's 1st Army Observation Wing supplemented by the experienced 1st Pursuit and newly created 1st Day Bombardment Groups. The Allies added another 55 squadrons, 47 from the DAé now under Colonel Albert de Vaulgrenant who had 627 aircraft (68% serviceable), and 8 of Trenchard's Independent Force. Trenchard and Mitchell got on well, the former commenting on the draft plans, yet 'Boom' did not learn the offensive had begun until an American liaison officer was shown into his bedroom an hour after the bombardment started! Mitchell could also count upon some Voisins while GAE assigned Villomé's Capronis[61].

While only a third of Mitchell's aircraft carried the US cockade, Americans were flying with Allied squadrons and three would die in Trenchard's squadrons during the operation. Low cloud, heavy rain, drizzle, mist and strong south-westerly winds turned Mitchell's ambitious programme into a damp squib (Tables 7-11 & 7-12) with 4,259 sorties flown (58% USAS) and 75 aircraft lost (56% USAS), this low loss rate of 1.7% due to the German's sluggish response in the first two days. This changed when the Germans reached their new positions and from 14 September the *Luftstreitkräfte* became more active with Allied loss rates reaching 2.3% and on that day *JG II* achieved a *Geschwader* record of 19 victories, the victims including American-made DH-4s of the 1st Bombardment Group who were making the combat debut[62].

Table 7-11:
US operations in St Mihiel Offensive 12–16 September 1918

Day	Fighter	Bomber	Army	Corps	Total
12 September	225/1	10/3	21/-	134/7	390/11
13 September	247/4	11/2	38/-	97/2	393/8
14 September	392/9	77/2	63/1	148/3	680/15
15 September	333/1	53/-	57/-	140/-	583/1
16 September	272/2	49/5	21/-	79/-	421/7
Total	**1,469/17**	**200/12**	**200/1**	**598/12**	**2,467/42**

Sources: US NA M990/13. Henshaw:464–466.
Note: First figure is sorties. Second is combat losses.

Table 7-12:
Allied operations in St Mihiel Offensive 12–16 September 1918

Day	DAé	C.A.	Night	41 Wing	83 Wing	Total
12 September	317/6	17/-	-	9/-	8/-	351/6
13 September	301/1	15/1	-	32/2	12/-	360/4
14 September	273/7	10/2	24/-	53/-	31/1	391/10
15 September	281/2	20/-	20/-	35/4	18/1	374/7
16 September	232/3	19/-	33/-	12/-	20/3	316/6
Total	**1,404/19**	**81/3**	**77/-**	**141/6**	**89/5**	**1,792/33**

Sources: Resumés journaliers, SHAA A128/3. Army Operations Reports 12–16, US NA M990/13 and Maurer *III*. Also Bailey & Cony:298–302. UKNA Air 1/2249/209/45/8.
Note: First figure is sorties, second is losses.

During the first two days US fighters and bombers exchanged roles; the fighters being used for ground-attack and the bombers for line patrols. Allied bombers delivered more than 127 tonnes with the British responsible for nearly 52% of the tonnage against rail and road communications while 15% was dropped by US aircraft. The French bombers flew so low that two were brought down by their own bombs. Attacks upon the Metz area touched a raw nerve and day bombers frequently stirred a hornets' nest with *JG II* stinging the inexperienced American bomber squadrons hard, wiping out a 96th Aero Squadron flight on 16 September and all but one of a 11th Aero Squadron formation two days later[63].

More than a third of Mitchell's losses from 9–22 September were bombers which accounted for 42% of dead and missing aircrew but the bomber threat to Metz forced *OHL* to send down *JG I* on 28 September. There was a mixed reaction from the German strike force; *Bogohl 8* was active and forced Voisin groups to act as night fighters, but *Schlachtgeschwader B* which joined *5.Armee* on 5 September, appeared content to stay on its own airfields[64].

West of Verdun the Americans led the great Allied offensive on 26 September when Pershing's 1st Army and Gouraud's IV Armée struck into the Argonne Forest towards Sedan along the boundary of *Heeresgruppen deutscher Kronprinz* and Einem's *3.Armee* in the west and *Heeresgruppe Gallwitz'* in the east. The *5.Armee* was now under the defensive specialist Marwitz, transferred from *2.Armee* on the British front. This advance threatened both the German rail system supporting Western Front, as well as the last position in Belgium, the *Antwerpen-Meusestellung*[65]. The Americans encountered desperate resistance in the *Kriemhildestellung* which exploited wooded ridges and narrow valleys. The offensive jerked and stopped like an automobile driven by a first-time driver as the inexperienced and badly led Americans endured an infantry slaughter which surpassed Cold Harbor in 1864 with 10% of the 'dough boys' becoming casualties. High morale helped maintain momentum as the army slowly adapted to the new warfare and on 1 November broke through the *Kriemhildestellung*. The offensive cost 122,000 US casualties including 26,000 dead, while the Germans lost 146,000 including 28,000 dead and 26,000 prisoners.

Mitchell failed to repeat the success of St Mihiel where his squadrons largely cleared the skies over American air space, indeed the Germans

(Table 7-13) would prove extremely active during the Meuse-Argonne offensive. For security reasons most of the Allied reconnaissance was conducted by IV Armée squadrons but, as at St Mihiel, American observers were taken along to familiarise themselves with the terrain. French and American fighters prevented the enemy from discovering the build up in 'severe and repeated combats' one of which brought down a German reconnaissance aircraft that had just finished photographing Mitchell's headquarters[66]!

Table 7-13:
Enemy activity over 1st US Army

Week	Observed sorties
2–8 September	285
9–15 September	175
16–22 September	180
23–29 September	765
30 September-6 October	730
7–13 October	641
14–20 October	413
21–27 October	1,302
28 October-3 November	1,614
4–10 November	425

Source: Report from 1st US Army anti-aircraft units, US NA M990/12.

To protect the American assembly, Atkinson's 2nd and 3rd Pursuit Groups flew group-size OPs up to 12 kilometres behind the enemy lines and in barrage patrols. These battles cost the Germans some half-a-dozen aircraft (including two fighters) and they claimed only a dozen victories, an unusually low ratio[67].

For most of the year the Meuse-Argonne front had been a backwater and in mid August had only 14 squadrons (100 aeroplanes) split between *Kofl 3. Armee* and *Kofl 5. Armee*. However, *OHL* was so alarmed by the American presence in the Meuse valley that in the first half of September flocks of aircraft migrated to *3.Armee* and *5.Armee* airfields. The new Franco-American offensive faced 60 squadrons which nominally had 500 aircraft (although Allied intelligence detected less than half) and the front became the focus of *Luftstreitkräfte* operations. The four *Jasta* supporting *3.* and *5. Armees* were reinforced by another

14 including *JGr 1*, *5* and *11* while an ad hoc *JGr Marville* was created to support *5*. *Armee* which was then augmented on 28 September and 9 October by *JG I* and *JG II* which had previously been defending Metz. In mid October five *Jasta* and *JGr 5* transferred from *3.Armee* to *18.Armee* on the Anglo-French boundary but this still left 250 fighters facing the Franco-American onslaught. Hoeppner also concentrated 14 of his 38 *Schlasta* on this front with *Schlachtgeschwader 'A'* assigned to *Kofl 3. Armee* while *Kofl 5. Armee* had *Schlachtgeschwader 'B'* and a *Schlachtgruppe* augmented later in the autumn by *Bogohl 7*[68].

Mitchell still dreamed of demonstrating the value of air power but his initial plans were the conventional air support for a set-piece battle including attacks on enemy troop concentrations, kite balloons and airfields After the breakthrough the airmen would destroy the enemy air service and attack their troops, but with divisions and corps retaining control over their assigned squadrons, his resources were stretched thin. Vaulgrenant's DAé covered the American assembly then returned to GAC leaving Mitchell only four DH 4 bomber squadrons augmented by Villomé's heavy bombers and Trenchard's Independent Force. Most of the 1st Army Air Service's 576 aircraft (54 squadrons including 26 French) and as well as IV Armée's 350 aircraft (34 squadrons including GC 12, 21and 22) were fighters and corps two-seaters[69].

By the Armistice the USAS had 45 squadrons at the front but only a handful of its 740 aircraft were of American manufacture[70]. Internecine struggles prevented the US Army developing its own air power doctrine; indeed this was the bone of contention between Mitchell, who sought, like Trenchard', to carry the fight deep into the enemy rear, and the Army which wished to follow the French example and focus upon the immediate battlefield.

The flood of American manpower saw the AEF expand from an army into an army group under Pershing on 10 October with the creation of 2nd US Army under Major-General Robert L. Bullard while Major-General Hunter Liggett now led the 1st US Army. Mitchell retained command of the army group's squadrons, despite criticism from the upper echelons of the AEF, but the selection of his subordinates at army-level reflected both his views and perhaps those of the disgruntled army leadership[71].

Both the new army air commanders, Milling and Colonel Frank P. Lahm, were former aeronauts who then learned to fly aircraft with the

Wright brothers and both proved more accommodating with staffs than the abrasive Mitchell. To lead the 1st Army's squadrons from 12 October Mitchell selected the former signaller Milling. Milling had been a witness in a legal dispute between the Wright Brothers and Glenn H. Curtiss and was a staunch defender of the Signal Corps' control of aviation joining the Aviation Section's staff in April 1917. He had commanded American squadrons on the quiet Toul front until July 1918 when he became Mitchell's chief-of-staff, his organisational skills proving invaluable in preparing for both the St Mihiel and Meuse-Argonne offensives[72].

Lahm was probably the AEF leadership's choice to command 2nd Army's squadrons from October 14, if only because the former cavalryman was the ranking aviation leader after Mitchell and they loathed each other. The son of an aeronaut with French business interests, Lahm helped acquire the US Army's first dirigible and established heavier-than-air aviation within the Army. In April 1917 he was the Balloon School commander and was immediately despatched to Europe both to assess wartime aeronautical experience and to recover from a polo injury. He created the AEF balloon service but then quarrelled with Mitchell, transferring to the 1st Army staff when his querulous superior became commander of the 1st Army Air Service. Lahm was no reactionary; he produced a comprehensive bombing plan for the Meuse-Argonne offensive, and his appointment undoubtedly owed much to his good relations with his superiors[73].

Perhaps this is why Mitchell appeared to treat 2nd Army air service, admittedly on a secondary front, as second-class citizens. He assigned it only six observation squadrons (half of them French) while the 4th Pursuit Group, created a fortnight later, never had more than two squadrons. The over-strained logistics system provided Mitchell with another excuse leaving Lahm at the Armistice controlling 19 squadrons mostly cadres without aircraft[74].

After morning fog cleared, on 26 September the weather was ideal but during the remainder of the 47-day campaign there was rain on 40 days and good observation conditions on only 10[75]. On the first day Mitchell's airmen flew 814 sorties and lost 16 aircraft while their allies and enemies lost 2 each. During the whole campaign American squadrons would fly 16,700 sorties (Table 7–14) and lose 103 aircraft, a remarkably low overall loss rate (0.6%) for an inexperienced air force facing an aggressive and experienced foe[76].

Table 7–14:
Support for the AEF 26 August – 10 November 1918

Week	Fighter	Bomber	Army	Corps	French	Total
26 August – 1 September	646/-	36/1	3/-	84/-	-	769
2–8 September	889/2	44/-	121/2	268/2	-	1,322
9–15 September	1,261/12	145/6	193/1	619/11	1,027	3,245
16–22 September	1,471/5	86/11	70/-	374/2	810	2,811
23–29 September	1,654/14	135/6	252/-	914/3	40	2,995
30 September- 6 October	2,118/9	199/-	335/3	927/6	14	3,593
7–13 October	1,159/4	102/1	199/2	706/1	21	2,187
14–20 October	571/2	52/-	88/-	336/-	-	1,047
21–27 October	1,039/6	122/2	179/2	651/2	38	2,029
28 October– 3 November	1,332/16	250/-	302/-	1,098/7	49	3,03
4–10 November	993/5	79/5	145/1	846/2	-	2,063
Total	**13,133/75**	**1,250/32**	**1,887/11**	**6,823/36**	**1,999**	**25,092**

Sources: Henshaw:463–472. US NA M990/13, M990/12, M990/14.
Notes: First US figure is sorties. Second is losses. Corps and Army totals include French squadrons supporting US and French forces under US command. 'French' are separate French units (DAé, Groupement Villomé) supporting US forces.

American fighters played an active part but 56 were lost in combat, reflecting the quality of their opponents both in pilots and aircraft. *Kofl 3* and *Kofl 5* fighters were credited with more than 170 victories (excluding balloons) from 26 September-11 November with a loss of 15 but they rarely prevented the enemy from completing their missions. Most American photographic missions were intercepted while 14 of the 27 aircraft lost by the observation squadrons were *Jasta* victims, with *JG I* and *JG II* claiming more than half the total victories.

The 1st Pursuit Group flew the more hazardous balloon-busting missions claiming 10 balloons on the first day and opening a vicious tit-for-tat campaign which would cost the Americans 14 gas bags ([77]). The inexperienced 2nd and 3rd Pursuit Groups were responsible for defending American air space but their OPs rarely encountered the enemy. Pilots frequently vented their frustration by strafing targets and were fortunate to suffer light losses to ground fire. In mid October a night fighter squadron (185th Aero) joined the group but it lacked infrastructure, training and pilots so achieved only one interception.

The German fighters were hamstrung by fuel shortages which grew worse during the campaign and forced the defenders to re-organise with *JG II* taking command of all *5. Armee Jagdgruppen* on 30 September. Over-centralisation did not prove a solution and following a devastating massed attack by DAé on 9 October the front was split with *JG II* responsible for the east bank of the Meuse while *JGr La Ferté* faced the French on the west bank. Bad weather effected both sides during the latter stages of the campaign, *JG II* flying 26 sorties on 21 October and only 8 on November 9[78].

Mitchell intended that 70% of planned bomber missions would interdict the battlefield to break enemy morale and to draw away fighters but neither goal was achieved. Trenchard struck the main rail junctions leaving other communications targets to the Americans, who also made low level attacks upon troop concentrations up to 8 kilometres from the front. Their bomber casualties were heavy as small, unescorted formations were forced low by cloud into enemy gun sights. A formation was wiped out by *JG II* on the first day (one of the captured survivors was 1st Lieutenant Merian C. Cooper who would later direct *King Kong*) but only in mid October did new leaders bring improved tactics. These included larger missions which were difficult to execute due to a shortage of manpower, and the 1st Bombardment Group dropped only 60.75 tonnes of bombs during the campaign. By contrast the French supported Pershing with 91.5 tonnes while Trenchard's bombers delivered some 183 tonnes upon the enemy rail network[79].

It was Vaulgrenant who executed the most spectacular mission on 9 October but its origins are disputed. On 8 October German troops were observed, probably by corps aircraft, assembling in front of the French XVII Corps d'Armée and on the right of Bullard's III US Corps. Mitchell claimed that after the formation was detected (he does not state how) he pleaded for Vaulgrenant's attack. The French state that the attack followed a visit by Pétain to DAé headquarters, apparently in response to II Armée reports, suggesting the mission was to support French rather than American troops. No one informed Pershing's headquarters in time to exploit the situation and Drum could only stand in silent fury as 319 DAé aircraft passed overhead and dropped 32.4 tonnes of bombs upon the enemy[80]. As a result of this attack the Germans developed a more flexible fighter shield.

By contrast the German bombers made little impact upon the campaign, although they were certainly active with the 317th Engineers, who were working on roads at St Juvin, noting that enemy aircraft were overhead every night. It is likely that the fuel restrictions which restricted the *Jastas* had an even greater impact upon the *Kagohls* and it is ironic that, for the second time in two years, they missed a major opportunity to cut their enemies' supply lines in the Verdun region. The need to supply about a million troops along a handful of roads with little attempt at traffic control created monumental traffic jams behind the American lines, as most historians have commented. French Premier Georges Clemenceau was stuck in one and emerged with a strong personal antipathy to Pershing but, as with the Voie Sacrée, the Germans made no attempt to exploit a problem of which they could not fail to have been aware through their reconnaissance aircraft[81].

To the AEF's leaders the DAé attack was another example of Mitchell's grandstanding at a time when the penetration of American air space was increasing and air-ground co-operation was in crisis, contributing to the post-war move in the US Army towards 'direct support' by the airmen[82]. By October many in the AEF were questioning Mitchell's commitment to supporting the army and after the war Pershing's intelligence chief, Brigadier-General Dennis E. Nolan, would claim that Mitchell was opposed to air reconnaissance. Mitchell was reported to have laughed-off a reprimand from 1st Army chief of staff about the lack of reconnaissance sorties and to have resisted change. But it is clear that from October, Mitchell's airmen were trying to establish air superiority over the battlefield, and with Liggett in command of 1st Army there was greater integration of air-ground operations[83].

The level of German air activity actually increased during October exposing the Doughboys partly to air-directed artillery fire but mostly to the 'tender mercies' of the *Schlasta*. Drum would later note that the *Schlasta* had a 'serious effect' upon the infantry's morale. Mitchell is alleged to have dismissed the reports (especially after one of his staff officers made a cursory inspection) concluding that the infantry were being attacked by their own aeroplanes because they failed to display signal panels then fired upon the aircraft. The 'dough boys' often lacked signal panels but even when they were available they were certainly lax in displaying them and consequently they received little sympathy even from General Liggett in a rare act of support for Mitchell. However, it is worth noting that the 1st Pursuit Group was ordered on five occasions between 28 September and 30 October to sweep the *Schlasta* away from the front and on 8 October was specifically told to permit 'no enemy low-flying aircraft to make any attacks on the (troops') positions[84]'

There appears no single reason for this unprecedented loss of air superiority. Factors include the quantity and quality of enemy air strength, which skilfully exploited weather conditions, but Mitchell's handling of fighters, leaving 'green' groups responsible for air superiority, the thinness of the fighter screen due to lack of pilots and the unreliability of the Spad seem to have contributed to the crisis. Bureaucracy also played a part and when the chief of staff of 82nd Division complained to the 1st Army's pursuit 'squadron' that eight enemy aircraft had been over his front for four hours, he was told the squadron objected to receiving information from divisions which should go through the proper channels[85]!

The fundamental problem was the US Army's determination to make the tactics of the previous century relevant on the Western Front, like a toddler hammering a square peg into a round hole. This lethal obsession was especially noticeable in the field of air-ground co-operation where each division had a squadron for artillery fire direction (complementing the balloons) as well as reconnaissance and contact patrol ['infantry liaison'] missions).

The rush to get American regiments and squadrons to the front meant that training was neglected, with most squadrons unable to train with the divisions to which they were assigned. There was also a profound ignorance within the army about air support. Brereton, for example, once received a message: 'German artillery firing on my Post of Command. Stop it ([86])!' The artillery commander of the 35th Division, Brigadier-General Lucien G. Berry who had commanded Pershing's guns during the Mexico expedition, initially ignored aerial observation and told Pershing it was 'no damn good' although he had a change of heart when forced to use it.

The problems were obvious at St Mihiel where batteries moved without informing the very airmen supposed to support them. In the Meuse-Argonne, as with the British Army some 18 months earlier, frequent movements made batteries reluctant to follow the time-consuming process of erecting radio aerials or even informing airmen about changes of location leaving observers to contact empty gun pits. To overcome the problems, gunners received intensive training and retraining while the radio net was carefully monitored to detect those batteries which failed to respond to aerial signals. Yet the fundamental problems still remained. During the final offensive, the 2nd Division's artillery brigade claimed they heard nothing from the airmen and had to fire blindly while German artillery aircraft were always overhead.

Each American corps had a French artillery squadron to whom it appears artillery fire-direction was usually left, but this was not always effective. The 89th Division claimed it received no assistance from BR 214; there were no contact reports, the few messages were devoid of detailed information and many were dropped on the neighbouring 4th Division headquarters while there was no telephone line to the squadron's airfield at Foucaucourt. Air reconnaissance was the prime source of up-to-date information for commanders in the heavily shelled wilderness. The hills and woods made contact patrols indispensable and, to exploit sudden improvements in the weather, squadrons maintained detachments at forward airstrips with crews familiar with the terrain. American corps squadrons concentrated on visual reconnaissance, with few plates exposed, but rarely probed more than 8 kilometres behind the lines. They remained in combat even when the divisions they were supporting were withdrawn and this constant rotation disrupted co-operation with the squadrons having to start afresh with green divisional staffs.

Contact patrols frequently dropped food or ammunition to the more exposed troops and had numerous successes, but it was a hazardous business and in seeking the 77th Division's famous 'Lost Battalion', the 50th Aero Squadron had four DH 4s shot down with two more badly damaged. While experienced troops were willing to reveal their positions the newer divisions did not recognise the cockade markings and regarded the low flyers with suspicion. Public relations, a growing American skill, largely resolved the problem through visits and the contact patrols' unique habit of dropping newspapers and cigarettes to friendly forces as a reward for revealing their positions, although many units lacked signal flares while some had torn up their signal panels.

Low-level 'cavalry reconnaissance patrols' also probed the defences before an attack and reported their findings to the spearheads, a precursor of the scout helicopter. A more active role for US tactical air power developed from 3 November when both fighters and corps aircraft began dropping bombs, delivering 7.5 tonnes in nine days, to bring their total since 26 September to 14.5 tonnes. In addition special counter-attack teams within the corps squadrons probed up to 15 kilometres behind the lines to find reaction forces assembling but ground fire made this hazardous and crews had to be rotated rapidly[87].

Throughout the autumn Hoeppner was mesmerised by Duval's squadrons, most of which were concentrated in GAC, especially IV and V Armées, where 11e Escadres and 14e Escadres were supported by the DAé which seems increasingly to have been regarded by army commanders as something of a comfort blanket. With a front line strength of 3,375 aircraft (1,221 fighters and 407 bombers) and 1,686 in reserve on 1 August, Duval could no longer wear two hats commanding both the AMF and the DAé. Pétain offered him the Operations or Intelligence Bureaux at GQG before Duval opted to remain in charge of air operations[88].

Duval reluctantly transferred the DAé to Vaulgrenant, a staff officer with no previous aviation experience who arrived at Duval's headquarters on 15 August (the Feast of the Assumption!). The new commander did not stand on his dignity and before assuming command on 8 September received a crash course on air power with Göys and Vuillemin as his lecturers. The former focused upon theory while the latter revealed the pragmatic side of air command and with this background, Vaulgrenant was able to exploit his own staff experience to influence the DAé without disrupting it. Surprisingly, this experience made him want fewer bombs dropped on troops and more on the enemy infrastructure and to shield the bombers he was prepared to use OPs to throw cordons deeper into enemy lines[90].

Vaulgrenant briefly supported Mitchell's campaign over the St Mihiel Salient but his primary concern during the autumn was to support IV Armée on Pershing's left (See Table 7-15 for distribution of French squadrons at the Armistice). He made only one major foray over the American front, but occasionally he flew fighter sweeps to support his allies. In the last 14 weeks of the war the DAé flew some 17,500 sorties (Table 7-16), dropped 848 tonnes of bombs and lost about 92 aircraft, a loss rate of 0.5%. This low loss rate reflects a closer fighter support for other missions and a similar pattern can be observed with IV Armée

(Table 7-17) supporting the American left in the Meuse-Argonne offensive[91].

Table 7-15:
Distribution of Aviation Militaire squadrons in November 11 1918.

Command	Fighter	Escort	Bomber Day	Night	Army	Corps	Total
DAé	25	3	15	6	1	-	50
GAR	5	-	-	-	-	-	5
Ier Armée	1	-	-	-	6	14	21
IIIe Armée	1	-	-	-	3	7	11
GAF	-	-	-	-	2	-	2
VIe Armée	7	-	-	-	2	9	18
GAC	-	-	-	12	-	-	12
IIe Armée	-	-	-	-	3	-	3
IVe Armée	14	-	-	-	9	12	35
Ve Armée	5	-	-	-	5	15	25
US AEF	-	-	-	-	7	10	17
GAE	-	-	-	2	-	-	2
VIIe Armée	-	-	-	-	4	11	15
VIIIe Armée	6	-	-	-	4	5	15
Xe Armée	-	-	-	-	3	13	16
Total	**64**	**3**	**15**	**20**	**49**	**96**	**247**

Source: Davilla & Soltan:19–20.
Note: Home defence squadrons excluded but Italian 'squadrons' included.

Table 7-16:
Division Aérienne sorties August–November 1918

Week	Fighter	Bomber	Total	Bombs (kg)
5–11 August	935/7	510/2	1,445/9	80,600
12–18 August	1,125/9	12/-	1,137/9	-
19–25 August	1,319/2	607/4	1,926/6	115,660
26 August – 1 September	1,060/4	359/1	1,419/5	71,645
2–8 September	613/4	195/-	808/4	18,420
9–15 September	974/2	198/11	1,172/13	33,940
16–22 September	1,148/5	-	1,148/5	-

23–29 September	1,138/5	523/1	1,661/6	79,890
30 September– 6 October	1,521/6	617/2	2,138/8	136,439
7–13 October	641/3	284/1	925/4	69,220
14–20 October	308/2	-	308/2	-
21–27 October	725/5	122/-	847/5	23,460
28 October – 3 November	1,061/4	530/1	1,591/5	141,660
4–10 November	568/5	311/-	879/5	77,470
Total	**13,136/63**	**4,268/23**	**17,404/86**	**848,404**

Sources. Bailey & Cony:277–327. SHAA A128/2–3.
Note: First figure is sorties. Second is combat losses. Six escort aircraft were lost from 5 August to 15 September.

Table 7-17:
IV Armée operations 16 September – 10 November 1918

Week	Army	Corps	GC	Total
16–22 September	53/-	240/-	176/-	469/-
23–29 September	113/-	842/1	1,020/	1,975/1
30 September- – 6 October	154/1	963/2	1,253/3	2,370/6
7–13 October	110/-	681/-	649/1	1,440/1
14–20 October	52/-	240/-	496/-	788/-
21–27 October	80/-	176/1	466/-	722/1
28 October – 3 November	73/-	352/-	762/4	1,187/4
4–10 November	77/-	215/-	259/1	551/1
Total	**712/1**	**3,709/4**	**5,081/9**	**9,502/14**

Sources:Bailey & Cony:302–327. SHAT 18N 173.
Note: First figure is sorties. Second is combat losses.

On the French left the most spectacular advance in terms of liberated territory and prisoners was made by the British. On 27 September Haig (augmented by an American corps) smashed through the *Siegfriedstellung* in a day and moved eastwards, remorseless as a steamroller. Covered by occasional tank-tipped counter-attacks, the Germans sought refuge in the *Hermannstellung* based upon the Scarpe and extending into the *Hunding-* then *Brunhildstellungen*. But Rawlinson pushed through on 17

October and by the Armistice Haig had cleared the whole of central Belgium.

This campaign saw the RAF reach its peak, having regained, by mid September, all the airfields abandoned six months earlier, a task made easier by Hoeppner concentrating most of his squadrons on the Franco-American front. Reconnaissance of the *Siegfriedstellung* was hindered until 15 September by low cloud and mist, but this allowed Salmond to rest his weary airmen. When the skies cleared the British set to with a will and by the evening of 17 September Haig and his generals had detailed pictures of the fortifications while the RAF prepared for a traditional two-day artillery preparation ([92]).

Haig's right and centre spearheaded the assault, supported by I Brigade still under Pitcher, together with III, V and IX Brigades while Ludlow-Hewitt's X Brigade covered the quiet 5th Army front. Together they had 57 squadrons and 1,058 aircraft with 87% serviceability, while the armies had 132 anti-aircraft guns. RAF Intelligence calculated they faced between 100 and 120 squadrons (950 aircraft), including units away from the main axes, but this was an exaggeration. They really faced only 60 squadrons (nominally 450 aircraft) including twelve *Schlasta* together with *Bogohls 5, 6* and *7*, the plans of *Kofl 2. Armee* and *Kofl 17. Armee* being fatally compromised by the loss of a third (nominally 100 aircraft) of their fighters a week before the British attack. *JG I* and *JGr 8* were transferred to the American front leaving 15 *Jasta* including *JG III, JGr 2, 7* and *10* facing Salmond[93].

The British numerical superiority proved decisive with nearly 22,000 sorties (Table 7-8: 23 September – 10 November) from 27 September until the Armistice pushing back the German airmen who fought bitterly for every cubic metre of sky. The scale of operations may be gauged by the fact that, despite unfavourable weather in the last six days, from 27 September – 16 October the RAF claimed 231 aircraft and 21 balloons, dropped 681.5 tons of bombs and lost 150 aircraft. The pace of operations remained high even during a brief pause from 25–31 October when Haig regrouped while the RAF reverted to trench warfare missions with aircraft and balloons used to locate artillery for a vigorous counter-battery campaign. It was about this time that Hogg was replaced at IX brigade by 39-year-old former RNAS officer, Brigadier Henry Smyth-Osbourne. Early in the war he was commander of the Royal Navy's Signal School but in 1915 he became air leader for

Commander-in-Chief Nore then in charge of RNAS Manston. He remained in the RAF until 1924 and when Churchill was Secretary of State for Air acted as his secretary. He was briefly recalled to service from 1939–1941[94].

As German fighters operated in *Gruppen* and *Geschwader* formations, the RAF matched this by dispatching paired squadrons. British OPs continued to screen their operations but were often reined-in creating a denser battlefield screen to protect the corps aircraft and fighter-bombers. The Germans often exploited British concerns about high-altitude attack which attracted many of Salmond's fighters above the clouds where they were blind to the struggle below. Pitcher's I Brigade was later criticised for sending fighters out on sweeps rather than holding them back on the ground ready to intercept enemy fighters detected by ground observers[95]. This criticism reflects a confidence not only in the BEF's excellent communications but also British developments in radio technology. While the fluid battlefield rendered the compass station system of ground-controlled interception redundant, advances in radio telephones provided a potential replacement. After a false start in March, 10 squadrons received the new radios between May and August beginning with Bristol Fighter squadrons then extending into three of II Brigade's corps squadrons followed by a bomber squadron[96].

Corps squadrons and No 18 Squadron used their radios to provide up-to-the-minute reconnaissance reports, although ranges were limited and jamming was a problem. The Bristol Fighters squadrons also used their radios to co-ordinate flight formations but the trailing aerials were vulnerable to machinegun fire and were not used in dogfights which were felt to be too wild for a flight leader to control the battle. By the end of the war it was planned to equip all Bristol Fighter and day bomber squadrons with radio telephones while two bomber squadrons were experimenting with co-ordinated escort operations[97].

The fighters augmented increasingly effective massed strikes with bombers against constantly-monitored airfields although the weather thwarted many missions. All brigades organised these attacks and on 30 October X Brigade mobilised every available aircraft of 80 Wing to wreck Rebaix airfield (northeast of Tournai) with two tonnes of bombs in a 62-sortie mission ([98]). Both sides' bombers struck communications targets, especially railway stations and marshalling yards, while German bombs also fell upon bridges, roads and troop assembly areas. However, they rarely struck during the day, with the C-types of *Bogohl* 7 being an exception and even these simply emulated the *Schlasta*. The RAF dropped 425 tonnes of bombs from 23 September until the Armistice, nearly 88% by IX Brigade, supporting Haig's main axes[99].

Salmond was hamstrung by having to transfer bombers to the Independent Force while the unreliability of the BHP engines meant many of the new DH 9s had to abandon sorties. The bombers were a prime target for the *Jastas*, which sometimes forced them to dump their bombs on trenches, and Salmond had to strengthen their escorts, which were occasionally augmented by Bristol Fighters. However, the relentless RAF pressure upon communications forced the Germans from late October to provide the *Landsers* with fighter support in a vain attempt to shield them from a rain of bombs. The *Jastas'* task became harder when Salmond received the DH 9a which proved a formidable opponent thanks to their powerful and reliable American-made Liberty engines[100].

Bombers sometimes flew in at 600 metres against road targets but most battlefield interdiction and close-support missions were flown by the hornet-like fighter-bombers supplemented by corps aircraft. Between them they delivered 242 tonnes of bombs, 59% by the fighter-bombers which dropped an average weekly total of more than 30 tonnes during the first three weeks of the offensive[101]. The emphasis varied between the brigades. The corps squadrons of Charlton (V Brigade) were the most active, delivering 64% of the bombs dropped by corps squadrons from 23 September. Longcroft (III Brigade) also relied upon his corps squadrons but from late September switched to fighter-bombers for ground attacks while Pitcher always preferred fighter-bombers. The fighter-bombers of No 73 Squadron supported tanks by hunting down anti-tank guns, which they detected through carefully studying maps for optimum firing locations. They also sought, sometimes with 'diving attacks,' *Flak* batteries (some with 88mm guns) which proved as deadly a foe to armour in the Great War as they were in the Second World War,[102].

Recognising the failures of command and control at Amiens, on 23 August the British created a radio-equipped Central Information Bureau (CIB) which was an offensive version of the compass station. Based initially at Villers Bretonneux it monitored enemy air activity and was used not only for ground-controlled interception but also as a collecting point for information on ground targets from corps aircraft. It then either radioed details to fighter-bomber bases or used visual signals to direct aircraft in the air[103]. To exploit the CIB the III Brigade kept a flight from each fighter squadron over the FEBA like a taxi rank ready either to strike targets of opportunity or to shield the corps aircraft. The Americans later praised Longcroft's tactical air support and his ability to dispatch a four-squadron mission within an hour, of whom half would attack ground targets at any one time. Such large-scale commitments were rare, however, and fighter-bombers were vulnerable to fighter attacks although by the autumn the British were not only striking infantry and transport but also batteries on the move which Charlton made priority targets[104].

The assault upon the *Siegfriedstellung* demonstrated the absence of an RAF ground-attack doctrine. Pitcher, for example, concentrated I Brigade's five fighter squadrons at the Le Hameau base of No 64 Squadron under the orders of the squadron commander, Major Bernard Smythies, to interdict choke point crossings over waterways. In flight-strength missions involving some 175 sorties, on 27 September Smythies' force dropped nearly 8 tonnes of bombs and fired 26,000 rounds. By contrast Longcroft allocated only one of III Brigade's five fighter squadrons to ground-attack from a forward airstrip. Strong points were their priority followed by either battlefield interdiction in response to CIB reports or attacks upon targets of opportunity[105].

Longcroft and Pitcher allowed their fighter-bombers to roam up to 20 kilometres behind the lines from early October and they caused much confusion. Their improved command and control was illustrated on 9 October when they exploited reconnaissance reports to send every available aircraft against roads crowded with retreating troops. British air attacks meant that from late August daylight movement on German roads became sparse except in crises, while in contrast to the roads behind the Allied lines were crowded. The next generation of airmen would encounter a similar situation in Italy and France but on a much grander scale[106].

The German ground-attack force was also active but while its strength in *2.Armee* and *17. Armee* increased from four to 11 *Schlasta* this represented only 28% of the total force (the same number faced the French) and compares with 14 opposite Pershing. Like the British they continued to operate immediately behind the lines striking assembling infantry as well as horse and transport lines with forward cavalry units being an easy prime target[107]. They largely ignored *OHL*'s demands of 26 June to interdict communications which would have eased the burden upon the *Landsers* by forcing the Allies to use their fighters as a shield rather than a sword. A rare exception was on 6 September when *Schlasta* struck the same Somme bridges that the British had bombed a month earlier, but usually their role was close air support which they occasionally augmented with night bombing and daylight reconnaissance[108].

British tactical air operations adapted to the changing German defence, which was now based upon widely dispersed teams of automatic weapons, mortars, artillery batteries and even individual guns. Artillery registration, while not completely abandoned, became rarer because British gunners preferred pre-registered bombardment supplemented by standing and rolling barrages, harassing and counter-battery fire although the RAF continued to detect 80% of targets[109].

The RAF's artillery patrols not only called down protective barrages upon counter-attacks but also noted both active and inactive batteries, to economise on shells. Aircraft were also used to lay down smoke screens with 40-pound (18-kilogramme) phosphorous bombs dropped in front of active field batteries and suspected observation posts to blind them when there was a shortage of smoke shell. By October, smoke screens were also dropped by relays of aircraft in front of strongpoints to blind machine-gunners[110].

Corps squadrons, which flew a third of British sorties, became more flexible flying their usual combination of artillery, counter-attack and contact patrols although from late August there were subtle differences in each brigade's operations. With dedicated photographic missions largely confined to preparations for set-piece attacks, photography tended to be a secondary task of patrols especially after a break-through to establish the enemy's main line of resistance and the condition of roads behind the lines. When aircraft detected the inevitable counter-attacks they would ignite wingtip flares to warn ground troops, drop smoke bombs on jump-off points and call down protective barrages ([111]).

Reconnaissance was vital for supporting the advance. For example V Brigade, discovered in mid October that the *Hermannstellung* was a fading mirage. Usually the airmen sought out for the gunners the defence's anchor points, such as strongpoints and signal centres, but they were also adapting to mobile operations. They detected routes for the Canadian Corps cavalry-motorised force and reconnaissance battle groups to exploit the *Siegfriedstellung* breakthrough although this task was often hindered by poor visibility. With corps squadrons now probing up to 12 kilometres behind the lines, higher performance aircraft were required and many augmented their strength with one or two Bristol Fighters[112].

The corps squadrons also had a new mission, dropping supplies to forward troops. One of the first was on American Independence Day (4 July) 1918 when Australian and American troops raided the village of Hamel (just north of Villers Bretonneux) and No 9 Squadron dropped boxes of small arms and ammunition to pre-arranged points. By late August this became routine with a few squadrons, such as No 59 Squadron, flying dedicated re-supply missions with two 13.5-kilogramme boxes (each containing 1,200 rounds) but most, such as No 35 Squadron, would deliver a single box during a patrol[113].

There was a mass supply drop soon after the GAF under Degoutte began their attack in Flanders on 28 September. For the Belgians this was the supreme effort and they spearheaded the attack to take Passchendaele on the first day despite torrential rain. With Plumer's 2nd Army and the French VI Armée they advanced eastward pushing back *4. Armee* and exposing *6.Armee* which was forced to withdraw so that by the Armistice northern Belgium was in Allied hands.

GAF received multi-national air support including the RAF and the US Navy/Marine Corps. Webb-Bowen's II Brigade, reinforced by 65 Wing from Ludlow-Hewitt's X Brigade on the night of 20/21 September, contributed 16 squadrons supported by 14 French (including GC 23). The Belgians still under Crombrugge, promoted to Colonel on 26 September, contributed 10 squadrons (including a fighter group) bringing the total air strength to about 700. The liberation of the coast was aided by eight squadrons of Lambe's 5th Group (140 aircraft) and the joint US Navy/US Marine Northern Bombing Group (NBG) nominally with four squadrons, although only one was operational ([114]).

The German Navy contributed 12 squadrons (90 aircraft) of *Kofl beim Marinekorps Flandern* (*Korvettenkapitän* Stubenrauch) to the defence including the recently activated *Marine Jagdgeschwader IV* with five *Jasta*. They were a valuable supplement to Wilberg, still *Kofl 4*, who had lost half-a-dozen squadrons to southern battlefronts leaving him with 20 squadrons (nominally 150 aircraft) including six *Jasta* (*JGr 6*), two or four *Schlasta*, *Bogohl 3* and a unit of Giant bombers. There would be few reinforcements and despite being outnumbered at least 4:1, the German airmen vainly fought to penetrate the Allied fighter screen; by the Armistice the *Jasta* were credited with 134 victories for the loss of 16 fighters ([115]). On the first day the RAF lost 27 aeroplanes in low-level attacks but the campaign followed the earlier pattern with the Belgians claiming 11 aircraft for the loss of eight. British corps squadrons made extensive use of radio telephones but their most significant contribution was to the massed supply drop of 2 October[116].

Flanders mud stopped Degoutte's supply columns, leaving his spearheads, especially the Belgians, dangerously short of supplies. To end the crisis King Albert's generals planned to drop 15,000 rations and 65,000 rounds of small arms ammunition. Plumer's headquarters extemporised support and food was packed at airfields into soil-filled sacks to reduce impact damage. Two squadrons flew 80 sorties in a four-hour period dropping 13 tonnes of supplies and although the US Marine Corps' single DH 9A flew four sorties but much of it was apparently delivered by the French and Belgians themselves[117]. From this small beginning came the aerial resupply capability which has proved a lifeline to modern armies.

By the Armistice, Allied air power was at its zenith in both strength and capability having evolved rapidly during the last three years of the war. Until 1916 air power had changed little since the era of the observation balloon with the aeroplane serving as little more than a free-roaming reconnaissance tool which was also expected to be sword and shield. But from 1916, aided by specialisation in designs, it rapidly progressed from a basic Tactical-level tool into one which could, with increasing effectiveness, strike the enemy throughout his Operational-level depth. During the late summer and autumn of 1918, Allied bombers operating in large formations and covered by dense fighter screens interdicted German communications, bringing them close to paralysis. Tactical air support increasingly focused upon ground-attacks and British experience suggested that the days of the corps aircraft, which carried the banner for multi-task aircraft, were numbered with specialised long-range reconnaissance aircraft capable of performing most of their roles.

Yet in the weeks following the Armistice, Allied air power evaporated like mist on a summer's day. Paradoxically, German air power, like a star going nova briefly expanded, then contracted into extinction early in 1923[118]. Worse, those on both sides who shaped post-war air power followed the cliché that generals never learn the lessons of the last war [119].

Epilogue

By the Armistice, air power based upon balanced forces of fighters and bombers was a key element in the divisional-army corps (Tactical)-level air battle but its potency in the army to army group (Operational)-level was growing. Even a cursory examination of operations during 1918 would have suggested that air power should seek to influence the army-to-army group battle, although the term Operational level was largely unknown to Western armies until the 1960s. Instead the proponents of air power polarised around the Tactical level operations and strategic bombing, with post-war financial stringency acting as a catalyst.

Tactical operations required cheaper, single-engined, multi-task, aircraft and light bombs which were available in abundance even after the post-war munitions sale. Such operations were under army control and reflected the common belief in the continued supremacy of both artillery and the power of the defence. The generals did not expect to repeat the artillery slaughter matches of Verdun, the Somme and the Third Ypres but rather a series of tactical breakthroughs, aided by heavy artillery, with limited Operational level exploitation. The destruction of enemy fortifications was expected to create a barrier across the lines of communication making it difficult to move forward reinforcements and supplies while the defenders' communications would remain largely intact allowing him to create new fortified lines with artillery support to end the enemy advance. All armies therefore were convinced that artillery remained the lord of battles and that the initiative remained with the defender.

The generals were not blind to the value of bombers, which could strike beyond the range of most guns, but both doctrine and limited budgets meant most bombers were single-engined aircraft with limited range and capability. There were fewer multi-engined aircraft because they were expensive but the larger air forces retained them for striking key targets including factories. The generals' most insidious effect upon air power was fragmentation of resources among army corps, armies and army groups[1]. During the 1930s, advances in automotive technology produced improved performance and reliability together with the development of semi-monocoque fuselages to produce more potent and specialised aircraft. This was reflected in the growing autonomy of army air corps notably in France, where the air corps became the Armée de l'Air in August 1933, and the United States where the Army Air Force would emerge on 20 June 1941.

In part, the move towards autonomy was influenced by the advocates of strategic bombing, following the Italian pied piper of General Giulio Douhet, whose writings on the supremacy of future air power were a triumph of hope over personal inexperience. The move towards a 'scientific' method of warfare was part of the wholesale revulsion at the slaughter on the Western Front but soon the advocates of strategic bombing went to the dark side, seeking to destroy not only enemy industry but also civilian morale and bringing the prospect of wholesale slaughter to the civilian population.

Mitchell was one of Douhet's disciples before sacrificing his career on the altar of his own ego but his disciples during the early 1930s turned the US Army Air Corps Tactical School into a strategic bombing seminary[2]. While a strategic bombing force emerged in the United States during the late 1930s it remained under army control as also happened in the Soviet Union where a long-range bombing force was created and its commanders briefly toyed with strategic bombing. Ironically, the new technologies strengthened the case for strategic bombing bringing the prospect of bomber formations too fast for effective interception but capable of fighting off any interceptors which reached them.

In France politicians sought to give the army a strategic bombing capability; indeed, this was the driving force for the creation of the Armée de l'Air. The generals' response was to return to the multi-task warplane of the middle war years with the infamous Bombardement, Combat et Reconnaissance (BCR) requirement which produced another flock of turkeys. Other air forces also sought to use the new aeronautical technology to meet similar requirements; in Germany the problems of a combined long-range fighter/ground-attack and reconnaissance aircraft were quickly recognised and the requirements were split up leading to the Messerschmitt Bf 110, the Henschel Hs 129 and the Junkers Ju 88. Yet the desire for precision bombing led to a dive-bombing requirement in the new strategic bomber which became the

Heinkel He 177.[3] The British also made this mistake and the official specification which led to the Avro Manchester and Handley Page Halifax had the same requirement as well as the ability to act as a torpedo-bomber. Fortunately, the RAF leadership also identified the problems and modified the specification, although the Halifax and the improved Manchester – the Lancaster – retained very strong airframes, allowing many a crew to survive by strong manoeuvres which would have torn apart a lighter airframe.

This was one of the few things which the RAF got right. Trenchard, who in 1917 opposed a strategic bombing force for fear it would fight a private war, was by 1919 advocating strategic bombing as the new service's raison d'etre with the zealotry of a convert. The irony of this situation was underlined in 1927 when Leigh-Mallory, whose squadron had supported the tanks at Amiens less than a decade earlier, and now commanded an army co-operation squadron, was reprimanded for encouraging his pilots to fly ground-attack operations!

Restricted post-war budgets gave Trenchard and Salmond an excuse for not producing an air force capable of true strategic bombing, yet this did not prevent the Americans giving their heavy bombers the vital improved bomb sites, navigators and navigation aids. Single-engined bombers, essentially the grandsons of the DH 4 and DH 9, would remain the basis of British strategic bombing until 1940 with the last in the line being the Fairey Battle, a true sheep in wolf's clothing, and it would be left to Newall and his successors in the mid 1930s to modernise the RAF.

There was no excuse for Trenchard's negligence. A blueprint for a strategic bombing force was drawn up in the aftermath of the war while the experience of many officers was carefully collected and is preserved in the British National Archives. Trenchard had no time for this, his attitude being illustrated when he demanded the official history of British aviation be a chronicle, in sharp contrast to the surviving campaign reports of the Air Historical Branch which coolly dissected operations. The reforms of the RAF began with Air Chief Marshal Sir Edward Ellington (who held administrative posts during the Great War) followed by Newall and Ludlow-Hewitt but they did not take effect until 1942.

A similar approach was taken by General Walter Wever who became the *Luftwaffe*'s first chief-of-staff in 1933, when Salmond was Chief of the British Air Staff, and was to be one of the most influential and least-known shapers of air power. He was a mirror image of Trenchard and had only tenuous connections with the *Luftstreitkräfte* through service as a staff officer. He left no memoirs, so it is not known what effect air power had upon his wartime experience and after the war his most significant contribution to the development of German air power before 1933 was to oppose an independent air force. But he was a reformer and as former Head of Training, was aware of the views of Young Turks, such as *Oberst* Heinz Guderian, that mechanised mobile divisions would succeed where the infantry-based predecessors had failed in France during 1918 to stab at the Operational level of an enemy so rapidly it would be unable to recover.

His proficiency as a staff officer led both to his influential post in the *Luftwaffe* and also to shape his views on its future. To overcome his ignorance he read voraciously and concluded the most effective use of air power was at the Operational level supporting army and army group (as well as battle fleet) operations. Between 1933 and 1934 he successfully demonstrated this to his former colleagues in the army during a series of war games and from then the *Luftwaffe* was shaped to an Operational level doctrine[4]. Tactical level operations were not neglected and the German Army retained its own corps squadrons until 1942 but they were subordinated to the prime doctrine. Nor did Wever neglect strategic bombing, although he was pragmatic enough to reduce the *Ural Bombers* to the status of technology-demonstrators because they were under-powered and unable to achieve their purpose just before his death in an air crash in 1936.

Germany's impressive victories between 1939 and 1942 owed much to the *Luftwaffe* and the doctrines which Wever had conceived. But from 1942 the Allies, especially the Americans and British, began applying the same principles with deadly effect and with great reliance upon fighter-bombers as the British had done in the Great War so that from 1943 the German rear was noticeable for the lack of daylight activity, rather like the German trenches in 1918. By contrast from 1942 onwards the *Luftwaffe* would drift away from Wever's doctrines and the bomber force would largely be reduced to acting as flying artillery, the very role *OHL* had forbade in 1917!

Douhet's disciples ignored the defensive aspects of air warfare, although most air forces retained a Comint capability which Italy's Regia

Aeronautica would raise to new heights in the Second World War. The Italians were able to demonstrate that Comint provided a means of supporting ground-controlled interception, and Major Claire L. Chennault, a fighter heretic ex-communicated by the US Army Air Corps, would demonstrate in China the effectiveness of modern observation networks against bombers. Comint would provide the *Luftwaffe* with early warning of the imminence and scale of bomber attacks, and the Germans would adapt Great War experience to provide an effective night fighter defence. The technology used to create a new generation of bombers would also create a new generation of even more effective fighters, but the bomber barons were reluctant to appreciate the impact of stronger defences. Radar would be the missing link, but in both day and night defence it would prove most effective when harnessed to principles of air defence hammered out on the Western Front.

Reconnaissance, the first role of aviation, was also neglected and left to the bomber-reconnaissance and corps aircraft. The lessons of the Germans with their high-altitude *Reihenbildzüge* and the French with fighters used for photo-reconnaissance were largely ignored until the late 1930s when the *Luftwaffe* re-introduced high-altitude reconnaissance aircraft. The British were quicker to learn the lesson and by the first winter of the war had introduced converted fighters for high-altitude photo-reconnaissance and later for tactical reconnaissance. This has become the norm, although very high-altitude manned reconnaissance aircraft appeared in the 1950s but the principles were the same as in 1917, although it appears unmanned aircraft will bear the burden of future reconnaissance.

Since the Second World War there have been startling advances in technology and superficially there are no lessons for modern air leaders to learn from the First World War. Yet the first decade of the 21st century has seen air power make a significant contribution to major ground campaigns in Afghanistan in 2001, Iraq in 2003 and Georgia in 2008. Not only do these exploit the experience so bitterly gained over the trenches, but also the technology which emerged in the same period. Henri Coand 's jet aircraft appeared at the 1910 Paris air show by which time much of the theory for electronics and radar had also appeared, while during the Great War there were the first steps towards guided weapons, energy weapons and unmanned aircraft. To repeat a very true cliché, those who fail to learn the lessons of history are doomed to repeat the mistakes.

NOTES AND SOURCES

Prologue

1. RAF fighter squadrons frequently flew low-angle dive-bomber attacks which influenced the post war evolution of US Marine Corps dive bombing. The first recorded high-angle attack was by 2nd Lieutenant William Henry Brown of No 84 RFC Squadron who sank an ammunition barge in a canal on 14 March 1918. Some pilots of No 5 Naval/205 RAF Squadron may also have flown dive-bomber missions against canal targets and diving attacks were certainly common in the autumn of 1918. Yet extensive British dive-bombing trials that year concluded it had no practical use! Edmonds. *1918/4*:220. Peter Smith. *Dive Bomber!*:11–16, 22 and *Dive Bombers in Action*:8–11.
2. For the development of military aviation before the Great War see Cuneo. *Winged Mars*.
3. Casualty information throughout this book is based upon Bailey & Cony for the French, Henshaw for the British and Americans as well as Franks, Bailey & Duiven, *Casualties*, (hereafter Franks et al *Casualties*) for the Germans.
4. For technical and tactical developments in air-ground co-operation see Cuneo:154–158, 180–187; Morrow:72–73, 91.
5. SHAA A20; A124/1 & 2. SHAT 19N488.UKNA Air 1/1389/204/25/43.
6. RFC wing war diaries for the second half of the year in the British National Archives contain numerous accounts of aerial combat
7. In a report to the RFC on 25 May 1916 the French Commandant du Peuty noted the inadequacy of the Lewis gun and the need for a proper machine gun. UKNA Air 1/1283/204/11/11.
8. Garros apparently created his deflector in September 1914 but his first success came only on 1 April 1915 and Guttman claims he was brought down after being damaged securing his third victory. Garros escaped in February 1918 and joined a fighter squadron claiming two Fokker D.VII on 2 October but was shot down and killed on 5 October when fighting seven of these formidable fighters. Cuneo:161; Guttman: 17, 115–116; Morrow: 91–92, 104–105.
9. For Wintgens and other Fokker aces see VanWyngarden, *Early German Aces*. Hereafter VanWyngarden, *Aces*
10. VanWyngarden, *Aces*:7–12, 26, 32.
11. Bailey & Cony:19–35.
12. Lamberton, Reconnaissance & Bomber pp.9–10. The US Army would use the French system. The Germans were handicapped by the absence of a uniform grid reference system because each *Armee* produced its own maps and each *Heeresgruppe* had its own grid system.

Chapter One

1. For the background to "*Gericht*" see Herwig:179–183, 193. Horne:42–49.
2. Herwig:187.Horne:79–115.
3. For the battle see Ministère de la Guerre. *Les Armée Françaises dans la Grande Guerre Tome IV Volume 1*:201–536. Hereafter *Armées Françaises IV/1* etc.; *Armées Françaises IV/2*:1–166. *Armées Françaises IV/3*:293–353. Reichskriegsministerium, *Der Weltkrieg 1914–1918. Die militärischen Operationen zu Lande Band X*:54–324, 389–405. Hereafter *Weltkrieg X* etc. *Weltkrieg XI*:117–172. Clayton:.103–116. Herwig:191. Horne:116–184.
4. *Armées Françaises IV/2*:1–166, 307–388. Herwig:184. Horne:210–301. *Weltkrieg X*:54–324, 389–405.
5. *Armées Françaises IV/3*:293–510. Horne:307–318. *Weltkrieg XI*:147.
6. Herwig:198.
7. Hoeppner:49.
8. He was christened José Eduardo but preferred Édouard rather than Joseph.

9. Jean Castex, Louis Laspalles and José Barès. *Général Barès*:20–108. Hereafter Castex et al. Christophe Cony also provided much valuable information.
10. Kilduff. *Germany's First Air Force*:18, 21 and *The Red Baron Combat Wing*:36 f/n 45. Morrow:6, 10–11.
11. Cuneo:276.
12. Castex et al. *Barès*:114.
13. *Armées Françaises IV/2*:Annex 428. *Armées Françaises IV/1*:Annex 2217. UKNA Air 1/1577/204/80/96. GQG's "Organisation générale de l'Aéronautique au armées" of 11 February 1918 defined the role from army corps to army group and explicitly stated the aviation commander received his orders from the command/formation chief-of-staff. SHAA A13/1.
14. For Haehnelt see web site geocities.com/~orion47/Wehrmacht under Luftwaffe General der Flieger.
15. The *Kagohls* had 11 *Staffeln*, including *Kasta* transferred from neighbouring armies, suggesting that some army headquarters had formed their own *Kasta*. *Weltkrieg X*:95. For the *Kagohls* see Hoeppner:40. Kilduff. *Air Force*:17–31; Kilduff. *Richthofen*:43. For an alternative KEK organisation see VanWyngarden, *Aces*:34.
16. Südingen:65.*Weltkrieg X*:63 n1, 71, 90 n3.
17. For the Verdun air campaign see Bülow:67. Christienne & Lissarague:94–98. Cuneo:207–228. Hoeppner:51–54; Voisin:1–5. UKNA Air 1/997/204/5/1241; Air 1/1283/204/11/11;Air 1/1283/204/11/14; Air 1/1303/204/11/169; Air 1/475/15/312/205; Air1/1577/204/80/96; Air 1/2268/209/70/190. SHAA A20; A124; A126. SHAT 19N488. See also. *Armées Françaises IV/1*:448.
18. Castex et al.*Barès*:109–111.
19. *Armées Françaises IV/1*:323–324.
20. Castex et al. *Barès*:111. I am grateful to Christophe Cony for details of this important but little-known officer.
21. Although *Armées Françaises X/1* II Armée entry, shows 16 squadrons present on 28 February a detailed inventory of French army co-operation squadrons on the Western Front for 29 February shows it had only five corps squadrons and 41 aircraft. SHAA A20/1.
22. *Armées Françaises IV/2*:53, Annex 385. *Armées Françaises IV/1*:75.
23. Davilla & Soltan:355–357,360–361. Étévé:193–194.
24. Bülow:67.
25. Hoeppner:49. *Weltkrieg X*:95–96.
26. SHAT 19N488.
27. Bülow:67. Franks et al. *Casualties*:183–184,339. *Weltkrieg X*:127.
28. Voisin. *Doctrine de l'Aviation Française de Combat*:2.
29. Du Peuty had only five fighter squadrons. Franks & Bailey:90.
30. According to Franks & Bailey, Rose was commander of V Armée aviation. A groupement was a temporary task force while a groupe was a permanent formation. Franks & Bailey:85. Morrow:133. The groupement was formed the day after Haehnelt's 41st birthday. Bailey & Cony:40–41. Franks et al *Casualties:* 184–185. SHAA A124. SHAT 19N488.
31. Rose died in an accident during the summer. Christienne & Lissarrague:*94–96*. UKNA Air 1/1577/204/80/96. The desire of French ground forces to see their fighters, even if this actually weakened air defence, effected the Armée de l'Air in 1940.
32. SHAT 19N488. For N67 this represented 17% of total sorties.
33. UKNA Air 1/1577/204/80/96.
34. Hoeppner:50.
35. UKNA Air 1/1577/204/80/96 (entry 6 May).
36. *Weltkrieg X*:127, 127 n1.
37. Richthofen reportedly flew one in *Kasta 8* at Verdun. Kilduff. *Combat Wing*:37.
38. Bülow:67–68. Kilduff. *Combat Wing*:33–34. VanWyngarden, *Early German Aces*:35–37, 50–51, 55. An order for 12 Halberstadt D I biplanes was placed on 8 March.
39. Franks et al. *Casualties*:184–185, 339. Hoeppner:50–51.
40. Bülow:69–70. Cuneo:213–214. Hoeppner:50–51. *Weltkrieg X*:147.
41. Franks et al. *Casualties*:182–192. UKNA Air 1/1577/204/80/96. SHAT 19N488.
42. I would like to thank aviation expert Mr Bill Gunston for his advice on this matter. A fully-loaded C-type at this time had a mass of between 1.2 and 1.3 tonnes.

43. SHAA A124/1 & 2. SHAT 19N488.
44. Cuneo:217 based upon Reichsarchiv.*Schlachten des Weltkrieges XV. Die Tragödie von Verdun 1916. Teil: Die Zermürbungsschlacht*:101, 192. Kilduff. *Combat Wing*:37. Franks et al. *Casualties*:186. SHAT 19N488
45. SHAT 19N488.
46. Voisin. *Doctrine de Combat*:4.
47. *Armées Françaises IV/2*:Annex 385. SHAT 19N488.
48. SHAT 19N488.
49. N124 was the famous Escadrille Americaine, later Escadrille Lafayette, most of whose pilots were from the neutral United States. *Armées Françaises IV/2*:Annex 385. Franks & Bailey:75, 104. Treadwell:37–42.
50. Voisin. *Doctrine de Combat*:3.
51. UKNA Air 1/1577/204/80/96.
52. Christienne & Lissarrague:96. Morrow:133.SHAT 19N488 (entry May 22).
53. Bailey & Cony:37–56. Castex et al:112–113. Franks et al. *Casualties*:182–192, 339–342. Morrow:135. *Weltkrieg X*:624 n1.
54. Hoeppner:52. Robinson. *Zeppelin in Combat*:129.
55. Mortane. *Histoire*:168–172. *Weltkrieg X*:95–96.
56. *Armées Françaises IV/1*:324.
57. Bülow:69–70. Franks et al.*Casualties*:186. Hoeppner:50–51. *Weltkrieg X*:147. UKNA Air 1/1577/204/80/96. SHAT 19N488. The Germans appear to have lost only one C-type from *Kagohl 5*.
58. A *Kagohl 1* aircraft may have been lost in these raids. Franks et al. *Casualties*:340. SHAT 19N488.
59. Cuneo:202–203, 264, 271–273. Voisin. *Doctrine de Combat*:2. The British spotted in August 1915. UKNA Air 1/2166/209/11/10. The technique was adopted by the British and a combat report of 29 April 1916 by No 24 Squadron's 2nd Lieutenant D. M. Tidmarsh. begins: "At 8-15 a.m. when 14,000 foot over Beaumont, I saw our HA (Hostile Aircraft) arrow at Martinsart point S(outh)." UK NA Air 1/2249/209/43/11.
60. Christienne & Lissarrague:100. Davilla & Soltan:554–556. UKNA Air 1/1577/204/80/96.
61. Davilla & Soltan:227. UKNA Air 1/1577/204/80/96. SHAA A 124/1.
62. *Armées Françaises IV/2*:Annex 1875. Christienne & Lissarrague:100–102. SHAA A124/1.
63. SHAA A124/1.
64. Hoeppner:48–49. *Weltkrieg X*:63.
65. Cuneo:218–225 based on Paul-Louis Weiller "L'Aviation Française de Reconnaissance", in *L'Aéronautique pendant la Guerre Mondiale*.63–93.
66. Castex et al. *Barès*:113. On the night of 10/11 April the French flew 15 night reconnaissance sorties. UKNA Air 1/1577/204/80/96. SHAT 19N488.
67. *Armées Françaises IV/1*:Annexes 2217, 2290.
68. Cuneo:143. UKNA Air 1/475/15/312/205.
69. *Armées Françaises IV/1*:Annex 2217. UKNA Air 1/1577/204/80/96; Air1/1283/204/11/14.
70. Christienne & Lissarrague:98. Morrow:139. UKNA Air 1 997/204/5/1241; Air 1/2268/209/70/190.
71. Hoeppner:69. UKNA Air 1/1577/204/80/96.
72. Neumann:424. SHAT 19N488/4.
73. *Armées Françaises IV/1*:Annex 2056; UKNA Air 1/1303/204/11/169; Air 1/1577/204/80/96.
74. Reports from Verdun, PRO Air 1/1577/204/80/96. Prior & Wilson:12–13 note that when photographs were transposed onto maps there could be errors of up to 150 metres on maps due to the angle of the camera or the difficulties in reproducing a three-dimensional location from a two-dimensional photograph
75. *Armées Françaises IV/1*:324. Porch:93.UKNA Air 1/1283/204/11/11, Air 1/1577/204/80/96.
76. *Armées Françaises IV/2*:Annex 1881. Neumann:418–419. UKNA Air 1/1577/204/80/96 & Air 1/475/15/312/205. See also Peter Wright's article *Aerial Photo Coding*.
77. *Armées Françaises IV/2*:327. Hoeppner:49–50. *Weltkrieg X*:237. UKNA Air 1/2166/209/11/12(entry for December 19) & Air 1/1577/204/80/96. It was estimated that 10 million shells amounting to 1.35 million tonnes of steel were expended at Verdun between February and December. The gunners' (and observers') difficulties are described by Prior & Wilson: 13.

78. *Armées Françaises IV/1*:323–324. UKNA Air 1/1577/204/80/96.
79. Hoeppner:49–50. Porch: 81–82. UKNA Air 1/2166/209/11/9 (July 1915).
80. Hoeppner:49–50.
81. *Armées Françaises IV/1*:323 n2. UKNA Air 1/1283/204/11/14.
82. SHAA A124/1. SHAT 19N488.
83. *Armées Françaises IV/1*:448. *Armées Françaises IV/2*:Annex 1881.Hoeppner:39–40, 45. For the difficulties of getting balloons into the air see Cooke:46.
84. Hoeppner:51–52. *Weltkrieg X*:237. The Germans engaged French balloons with pairs of guns. One would fire high explosive to drive away the ground crews while the other would fire incendiary rounds to ignite the gas bags. It is claimed only 128 of the 10,000 men who served in the French balloon service were killed of whom half were observers. Porch: 95–96.
85. *Armées Françaises IV/2*:122–123, Annexes 1824, 1875 & 1881.
86. *Armées Françaises IV/2*:Annex 1875 & *IV/3*:Annex 848. Franks & Bailey. *Over the Front*:85.
87. *Armées Françaises IV/3*:Annexes 866, 892,1048 and 1049.
88. Franks, Bailey & Duiven. *The Jasta Pilots*:18–21, 29.
89. Voisin. *Doctrine de Combat*:17.
90. *Armées Françaises IV/3*:Annexes 1221, 1160. *Weltkrieg XI*:136. Franks et al. *Jasta Pilots*:23. SHAA A126. Quote from *Tragödie von Verdun*:185.
91. *Weltkrieg XI*:152.
92. *Weltkrieg XI*:169.
93. Hoeppner:51.
94. Castex et al.*Barès*:126,130–133. Christienne & Lissarrague:140–141. Cuneo:292–293. Morrow:206–208. Mortane. *Guerre Aérienne*:217–218.
95. Castex et al. *Barès*:135–216.
96. *Armées Françaises V/2*:354.
97. Christienne & Lissarrague:142. Morrow:200. Roman d'Ané.*Dictionaire de Biographie Française Volume XII*. 983. Amended with information from M. Christophe Cony to whom I am deeply indebted.
98. Leon Pujo. *Le Général Pujo et la Naissance de l'Aviation Françaises*:140. Pujo was the son of a primary school teacher and before the war was responsible for assessing German air power. He became the Armée de l'Air chief of staff in December 1935. Christienne & Lissarrague:314.
99. They are shown in Hugh Thomas' definitive work *The Spanish Civil War*.
100. Barnett: 280. Morrow:200.
101. *Armées Françaises V/2*:720–910, Appendix 2. Pedroncini:92–100. *Weltkrieg XIII*:101–109.
102. *Armées Françaises V/2*:Annex 749.
103. *Armées Françaises V/2*:Annex 758. Voisin. *Doctrine de Combat*:51–55.
104. For air operations see *Armées Françaises V/2*:829, Annex 719. Loewenstern:171–178. Martel:217–221. *Weltkrieg XIII*:101. Voisin. *Doctrine de Combat*:57. SHAT 19N489/2.
105. Franks et al. *Jasta Pilots*:31, 37, 38, 47. *Weltkrieg XIII*:101.
106. Franks et al. *Jasta Pilots*:111. Hoeppner:122. Loewenstern:171–178.
107. Franks et al. *Jasta Pilots*:28,37, 34, 319. SHAT 19N489/2.
108. Voisin:58 n3. SHAT 19N489/2.
109. Franks et al. *Casualties*:222–225. Voisin:58 n.3.
110. Hoeppner:122. Loewenstern:178–182, Anlage 6 & 7. SHAT 19N489/2.
111. *Armées Françaises V/2*:881. Franks et al. *Casualties*:224–225, 351. Loewenstern:184–185. SHAT 19N489/2.

Chapter Two

1. These ranged from 200mm to 400mm guns. *Armée Françaises VII/2*:Appendix 1 Table 2.
2. Jones: *II*:148. Maurer: *IV* 512–513, 520–521. This is an abridged and edited publication of the post-war "History of the Air Service, AEF" produced by Edgar S. Gorrell and referred to as the Gorrell Report.
3. *Armée Françaises IV/1*:74. Grosz, *Roland C II*. Hoeppner:86.Imrie: 40–41, 69. Jones: *II*:196 & *IV*:287. Maurer:*IV*: 514–515. Neumann: 304–305.UKNA Air 1/9/15/1/26.The German *AFA* had four aircraft and the *FFA* had six. In the winter of 1916/1917 all corps/army squadrons were redesignated

Fliegerabteilungen (*FA*) with six aircraft and the number of artillery units, *FA(A)*, were expanded. Later in 1917 reinforced (*Verstärkt*) *FA* (*A*) were created with nine aircraft, although by the Armistice only 42% of the *FA* (*A*) were reinforced units. American squadrons had 24 aircraft, while British squadrons at the beginning of 1916 had 12 aircraft but from the summer of 1916 were gradually expanded to 18. The French escadrille had 10 aircraft and the Section d'Artillerie Lourde had five but from October 1916 they both had 10 aircraft. A photograph of *FA(A) 292* taken in May 1917 shows the squadron had the AEG C. IV, Albatros C. V, DFW C. V, LFG Roland C. II, LVG C. IV. Gray, *Albatros D V*.

4. Davilla & Soltan: 291, 486. According to a French prisoner, at the beginning of April 1917 N62 had eight Nieuports, four Spads and four Sopwith Strutters. *Nachrichtenblatt 8/1917* (19 April). French and reflected in squadron designation prefixes with Spad two-seater squadrons designated Spa-Bi, Nieuport squadrons N and Spad single-seat squadrons prefixed SPA..

5. Davilla & Soltan:9–10, 163, 158–167, 290–294.

6. UK NA Air 1/996/204/5/1232. The British identified 70 radios supporting artillery commands in mid April 1917.

7. Bülow:81. Neumann:427–428, 480. The *Stofln* were renamed *Kofln* in November 1916. *Grufln* organised missions with the corps and divisional staffs.

8. *Armée Françaises X/1*. Army Corps entries. UKNA Air 1 881/204/5/593.

9. Neumann. *Luftstreitkräfte*:65. When considering AEF aviation requirements in 1917 General John J. Pershing initially sought only observation and fighter squadrons. Hudson:52

10. *Armée Françaises IV/1*:74. Franks & Bailey:85–109. Hoeppner:102. Jones *IV*:287. Maurer *IV*:526–527. Pieters:14. Squadron strengths were 15 for the French squadrons, 18 for the British 18 (expanded to 24 from mid 1918), 14 for the Germans and 25 for the Americans.

11. Davilla & Soltan: 380, 502–503; Maurer *I*:285; Pieters:17. *Armée Françaises VI/1*:Annex 324. *Armées Françaises VI/2*:Annex 230. Franks & Bailey:86.

12. Castex et al. *Barès*:114.

13. Jones. *VI Appendices*:Appendices XXIV & XXX.

14. Franks, Bailey & Duiven. *The Jasta Pilots:* 14, 16. Hereafter Franks et al *Jasta Pilots*.

15. VanWyngarden, *JG* 1:92, 97 & *JG* II:82–83. See also personal entries in Franks et al. *Jasta Pilots*.

16. Franks et al.*Jasta Pilots*:319–323. Kilduff. *The Red Baron Combat Wing*:101–107. Hereafter, Kilduff, *Combat Wing*.

17. Until late 1917, the patrol had five or six aircraft, the largest number one man could control, and this appears to have remained the basic building block even when larger formations were deployed later. Jones.*IV*:287. For markings see Lamberton. *Fighter Aircraft of the 1914–1918 War*:184–188.

18. For First World War fighter design see Braybrook. Bruce. *Fokker D.VIII*.

19.For Western Front aces see Franks et al. *Jasta Pilots*. Franks & Bailey. Franks et al, *Above the Lines*, Franks & Guest. Pieters. Shores. With victories bringing honours and fame conflicting claims led in German ranks to what was called "the well-known victory squabble" by 12–victory "ace" *Leutnant* Richard Wenzl of *Jasta 11*. VanWyngarden, *JG* I:23. This may have been one reason why German fighters had garish paint schemes and markings.VanWyngarden, *JG* I:9–13. One "down side" may have been resentment among the *Landsers* at the glory-hunting airmen. When *Jasta 6* commander *Leutnant* Hans Ritter von Adam (21 victories) was shot down and killed behind German lines on 15 November 1917 it was found that German troops had removed his body from the wreckage, stripped it naked and dumped it behind a bush. VanWyngarden, *JG* I:59–60.

20. A Chinese pilot, Etienne Tsu of N37, and two black pilots, America's Eugene Bullard and France's Marcel Pliat, appear to have flown on the Western Front with the French. Bailey's article *A Chinese Ace* in Cross & Cockade International. Treadwell:57. Some black aircrew from the West Indies, such as Sergeant William Robinson Clarke, flew with the British (Clarke was wounded while flying as a gunner in a No 4 Squadron RE 8 on July 28. Henshaw; 204) together with one Japanese, Sergeant Harry Fusao O. Ha'ra (sometimes known by the Irish-style name O'Hara). See entries compiled by Devitt and Revell respectively in *Recce*, Cross & Cockade International. A Japanese nobleman, Capitaine Baron Kiyotake Shigeno, served in N26/SPA 26 for most of the war. Although wounded, he survived, only to die of pneumonia in 1924. Guttman:18–19, 33, 58–59. More than 95 Siamese pilots went through fighter, bomber and reconnaissance schools in 1918 and some are believed to have seen action in the last weeks of the war. Meyer (who should not to be confused with 12-victory

naval ace *Oberflugmeister* Karl Meyer) survived the war and helped develop military aviation in Venezuela where he died in an air crash in November 1933. VanWyngarden, *JG I*: 26, 115 caption. See also web site jastaboelcke.de/aces.

21. Davilla & Soltan:167–169. Martel:246. Maurer. *I*:337–338. The Buzzard was scheduled to be built in the United States. Bruce. *British Aeroplane* :314–315. Lamberton. *Fighter Aircraft*:52. R46 had a long had a record of wolves dressed as sheep. Under the leadership of Capitaine Didier Lecour-Grandmaison, it flew aggressively and by the time it was attached to the elite GC 12 in April 1917, its aircraft with multiple machinegun positions had claimed 19 victories.Guttman:34. Davilla & Soltan: 14, 49, 79, 129, 245, 275–277, 524.The majority of Bristol Fighter victories were by observers. Jefford. *Observers and Navigators*:21–22, 22n18, 74–75, 75 n17. Bruce. *Aeroplanes of the RFC*:178. Jefford. *Observers and Navigators*:74, 74 n12. Appendix B. UKNA Air 1/677/21/13/1887, Air2/125/B.11207. The "corps" Bristol Fighters had Sunbeam Arab engines. Portal became Chief of the British Air Staff during the Second World War.

22. *Armées Françaises IV/2*:53, Annex 385. *Armées Françaises IV/1*:75. Davilla & Soltan:355-357,360-361. Étévé:193-194.

23. Bruce. *Aeroplanes of the RFC*:178. Jefford. *Observers and Navigators*:74, 74 n12. Appendix B. UKNA Air 1/677/21/13/1887, Air2/125/B.11207. The 'corps' Bristol Fighters had Sunbeam Arab engines. Portal became Chief of the British Air Staff during the Second World War.

24. Hoeppner:87. Grosz. *Halberstadt CL II*. UKNA WO 157/22. Web site frontflieger.de. According to the last *Schusta 1–6* were formed from *Kagohl 3*, *Schusta 7–12* from *Kagohl 5*, *Schusta 13–18* from *Kagohl 7* and *Schusta 22–28* from *Kagohl 6*. *Schusta 19–21* were formed from *Kasta 19*, *S1* and *S3* while the origins of *Schusta 29–30*, created later in January and in March, are unclear. *Kasta 30* for example became *Schusta 12*.

25. OHL list of destroyed enemy aircraft, Imperial War Museum Accession Number 45104.

26. Hoeppner:139–146.

27. Hoeppner:146.

28.Quote from UKNA Air 1/9/15/1/22. Strafing probably comes from the German verb *strafen*-to punish or the noun *Strafe*-punishment.

29. Voisin:51–55.

30. The dedicated contact patrol aircraft such as the AEG J.I also flew ground-attack missions. Gray & Thetford: 9–11. Grosz. *Halberstadt CL-II*:4 n 5 states the *Staffeln* were renamed on March 23 but the frontflieger web sites on *Schusta/Schlasta 16* & *24* suggest the squadrons were renamed on 27 March. Hoeppner:146, notes that in March the ground-attack units were "definitely known as *Schlachtstaffeln*" while Jones *IV*:Appendix XII reprints *Kogenluft*'s document of 20 February 1918 on "Employment of *Schlachtstaffeln*". Before March 1918 the term *Schlachtstaffel* was frequently used unofficially in German records.

31. Neumann:77 . UKNA Air 1/2124/207/74/3 Numbers 165 (4 August), 168 (7 August), 186 (25 August), 206 (14 September), 207 (15 September), 210 (18 September), 237 (16 October), 239 (18 October).240 (19 October). The website frontflieger.de states *Schusta/Schlasta 32–38* were formed on January 26 from *FA 4, 15, 21, 11, 25, 220 (A)* and *24*. *Schusta 31* was created as a new unit by the Bavarians on February 18. Grenade clusters augmented *Fliegermaus*. Few *Schusta/Schlasta* aircrew were officers. Grosz. *Halberstadt CL-II*.

32. The British planned to have nine dedicated ground-attack squadrons by New Year's Day 1919 and 15 by the following summer. UKNA Air 1/475/15/312/212.

33. Davilla & Soltan: 110, 306, 439–440, 458, 473,502–503.

34. Quote from Porch:94. During 1918 the French took 675,000 photographs. For cameras see Lamberton. *Reconnaissance & Bomber Aircraft*:191–193. See also Davilla & Soltan:502–503.

35. Falls.*1917/I*:87–93.

36. Davilla & Soltan:158, 290. Jones. *II*. Appendix XXVIII. A formation No70 Squadron Strutters was recorded on 1 July 1916 completing a 145 kilometre mission to Cambrai from Fienvillers airfield:"...in the astonishingly short time of 1 hour, 20 minutes." UKNA Air 1/2215/209/30/3.

37. Falls *1917/I*:88. Jones *III*:317–318. In November 1917 British tanks would break through the *Siegfriedstellung* in the areas first probed by the RFC nearly a year earlier.

38. Falls *1917/I*:88. UKNA Air 1 881/204/5/594. Air 1/2215/209/30/8 & 1/2215/209/20/11.

39. For the British train-watching organisation see Occleshaw:186–192. Morgan. Lieutenant-Colonel

R.J. Drake, in his report of 5 May 1919 "History of Intelligence (B), British Expeditionary Force, France from January 1917 to April 1919" (Hereafter, Drake Report on the web site mtholyoke. edu/acad/intrel/ww1) noted that train watching was the prime role of the intelligence organisation in the occupied territories with other tasks such as acquiring information on enemy aircraft and airfields very much a secondary issue. Drake would claim that from October 1917 the British became the prime source of information from behind enemy lines and received no important information from their allies afterwards (Paragraphs 16–17, 36). Some 6,000 people from all walks of life were recruited by British GHQ intelligence, of whom 98 died and 600 were jailed (Paragraphs 95–96). UKNA Air 1/766/204/4/248, 1/767/204/4/249–251.

40. Based upon brigade war diaries December 1916 to March 1917.

41. *Armées Française V/1*:373, 376, Map 30. Falls. *1917/1*:88.

42. Kilduff. *Combat Wing*:93–94. Henshaw:172. UKNA Air 1/245/209/30/13.

43. Henshaw:179–252.UKNA Air 1/1496/204/39/5.WO 158/34. Air 1 1732/204/130/4.

44. During May his squadron flew 11 four-hour sorties taking 96 plates. Loewenstern: 224–231.

45. Bülow:88–89; Hoeppner:108. Details of units from Frontflieger web site. The *Reihenbilderzüg* had four aircraft.

46. Franks et al. *Casualties*: 213–313, 350–368.

47. Bülow:89. Hoeppner:149. Neumann: 478. *Nachrichtenblatt 6/1918* (April 4). The *Luftwaffe* reconnaissance *Staffeln* were organised into *Aufklärungsgruppen*.

48. Herwig:396–397. Hoeppner:151–152, 154. Jones.*IV*:267.

49. Hoeppner:147, 151–152. Luftmacht 1935:*Deutschen Flieger in den letzten Angriffsschlachten. Teil 3*.45 (Hereafter *Luftmacht*).

50. Edmonds *1918/II*:68 n 3; *1918/III*:55 f/n 2; *1918/IV*:258 & *1918/V*:12–13, 96. The trend had begun earlier. On 30 June 1917 instructions on building new defensive positions issued by *4. Armee* in Flanders noted:"...care will be taken that cover against air observation is ensured." UK NA Air 1/1587/204/82/61 (Entry for 18 August 1917).

51. Davilla & Soltan:106, 379, 502–503. Documents planted by the Germans in a balloon which was then allowed to drift into the French lines in late March 1918. Martel:302,317. Yet despite his concerns, Pétain despatched a substantial part of his forces to assist Haig (see Chapter Six draft page 14).

52. For French reconnaissance in 1918 see Christienne:124–125. Christienne & Lissarrague 181,183–184. Martel:268–269. A night reconnaissance squadron, VR 293, was created in October 1918. Martel:241.

53. Fischer:101–113.The Belgian 8. Escadrille was a bomber and night reconnaissance unit with Farman F41. Pieters:120. UKNA Air 1/2268/209/70/200.

54. Davilla & Soltan:383.Mortane. *Special Missions*:15. Maréchal-des-Logis Adolphe Clérisse of N62 was reported missing on 5 April 1917 in Strutter Nr 22. Bailey & Cony: 105. *Nachrichtenblatt 8/1917* (19 April).

55. Chambre:238–242. Mortane. *Special Missions*:11, 13. Occleshaw:227. The unsuccessful pilot in 1914 may have been an America called "Bach" who was lucky not to be shot, but there is no confirmation in Bailey & Cony. Mortane. *Special Missions*: 23–29. *Nachrichtenblätter 14/1917*(31 May), *21/1917*(19 July), *8/1918* (18 April). Neither contemporary nor post-war records mention an Escadrille 137 which should not be confused with VB137 created in September 1918. My thanks to Christophe Cony for bringing my attention to the bomber squadron.

56. Liaison between the airmen and British Military Intelligence was poor. Occleshaw:227–231, 235–237. UKNA Air1/2215/209/30/11, Air1/2215/209/30/4 & Air 1/2399/280/1. The Drake Report (Paragraph 67) states that landings were confined to sites some 15 miles (24 kilometres) of the enemy lines at "a certain period of the moon". He claimed Trenchard rejected landings early in 1917 (Paragraph 64). The agents used static line parachute used by the kite balloon observers and, from 1918, by German airmen. A parachute which opened automatically was demonstrated by René Lallemand at Villacoublay, Paris on July 10 1917. *Nachrichtenblatt 1/1918* (28 February). An account of a Frenchman parachuted behind the lines by 9 Wing on 12/13 April 1917 is in *Nachrichtenblatt 16/1917* (14 June). A lively correspondence in October 1918 between Salmond and Trenchard about parachuting agents is in UK NA Air 1/1997/204/273/245.

57. Henshaw:208. UKNA Air 1/2215/209/30/13–16.

58. Occleshaw:234. For accounts of captured agents see *Nachrichtenblätter 7/1917* (12 April), *16/1917* (14 June), *28/17* (6 September). UKNA Air 1/2399/280/1. The idea of using balloons came from Major B.A. Wallinger, who in many ways was the predecessor of James Bond's "Q", and experimental flights were flown by the Royal Navy's Commander Pollock. The Marconi continuous wave radio, invented by the company's leading scientist Captain Round, weighed 27 kilogrammes. Tragically, it was discovered that the receiver in England was faulty and the Intelligence organisation could do nothing about it (Drake Report Paragraphs 69–73).

59. Occleshaw:218, 233–234, 240–241. Drake Report Paragraphs 66 & 75. NLS AC 3155 No112 (1April 1917). UKNA Air 1/163/15/361/1, Air 1/766/204/4/245, Air 1/1389/204/25/43, Air 1/1513/204/88/38 & Air 1/2399/280/1. *Nachrichtenblatt 10/1917* (3 May) has a photograph of a pigeon basket.

60. Mortane. *Special Missions*: 9, 121–125. Future *Luftwaffe General der Flieger* Hellmuth Felmy was involved in the Palestine operations. Corum & Muller:65 quoting *Weisungen für den Einsatz und die Verwendung von Fliegerverbänden innerhalb einer Armee*, ed.*Koluft* May 1917.

61. See Fredette, Jones.*VI*:118–174. Alan Morris. *First of the Many* and Robinson.

62. UKNA Air 1/881/204/5/593.

63. From mid July to November 1918 there were 2,528 sorties, some by the British Independent Force, against these targets, dropping 634 tonnes of bombs. Martel: 127–136, 157–169,223–238, 264–273. *Armée Françaises V/2*:Annexes37, 123, 156, 175, 209, 313, 343, 512,513, 549, 623, 692, 673, 691,1219,1227, 1135,1143. Jones *VI*:124–125. Martel:127–136, 157–169, 223–238, 264–273. Morrow: 206. Articles by Pesques-Courbier and Nilsson. SHAA A166/2. *Weltkrieg XII*:531.

65. Neumann:445–446. *Weltkrieg XII*:532. *Nachrichtenblätter 5/1917* (March 29), *6/1917* (5 April), *26/1917* (23 August), *32/1917*(4 October), *35/1917*(25 October) & *36/1917* (1 November). Industrial targets in eastern France were also struck by *Kagohl 2* through-out 1917.

66. Hoeppner:87–88. Neumann:428–429, 433.

67. Kilduff. *Air Force*: 69. Frontflieger web site. The new *Kagohls* had three *Staffeln* each of six bombers but by the summer they were expanded back to six *Kasta*.

68. Edmonds *1916/I*:63, 115, 121, 280, 300. Henniker:314–315. Miles *1916/II*:112 n3.

69. *Nachrichtenblatt 9/1917* (19 April). UKNA Air 1/2255/209/58/4. A single-engine night-bomber (N-type) requirement emerged in 1918 but only the AEG N.I appeared before the war's end and few saw combat. Gray & Thetford: xxviii, 245, 383, 549. *Kagohl 3*'s mission was to attacks England and its first daylight raid on London would lead to the creation first of the Independent Force and, ultimately, the Royal Air Force (RAF). Morrow:246–250. One of those "bombed out" during 1917 was the mother-in-law of Field Marshal Douglas Haig, commander of the BEF. NLS AC 3155 No123 (Entry 1 January 1918).

70. Haddow & Grosz. Kilduff.*Air Force*:69. 76 Neumann. *Luftstreitkräfte*:433, 443, 445. Rohrbach's article. *Nachrichtenblatt 7/1918* (April 11). UKNA WO 157/26. The units reformed were *Bogohls 5–8* while *Bogohl 3* retained six *Bosta* but all *Staffeln* still had six aircraft. The Frontflieger web site suggests *Bogohl 8* was activated on 15 April 1918. In early 1918 a prisoner claimed *Bosta 23* had six LVG C.V. UKNA WO 95/251 (17 February 1918).

71. Quote from Edmonds *1917/II*:250. Slessor:54–55. Jones *VI*:161. Bombs caused the American Expeditionary Force's first fatal casualties on the night of 4/5 September 1917 when 1st Lieutenant William Fitzsimmons and three enlisted men of Base Hospital 5 at Danes-Camiers were killed. I am indebted to Mr John Greenwood of the Office of the Surgeon General of the US Army for this information.

72. Quote from Henniker:316. Edmonds *1918/II*:266, 268, 290 & *1918/III*:3–4, 162– 163. See also Henniker: 316–317, 319–321, 324–325, 331–332, 376.

73. Edmonds *1918/III*:3–4. *Nachrichtenblätter 14/1918* (30 May) & *15/1918* (6 June). UKNA Air 1/476/15/312/215.

74. Edmonds *1918/III*:316–17. Macdonald:234–235. Neumann:434. Six-victory British ace Captain John Smith-Grant, heir to the Glenlivet whisky company, was killed on the operating table on 29 May. Shores et al. *Above the Trenches. Supplement*:4. Salmond recognised there was no campaign against hospitals. UKNA Air 1/2267/209/70/35.

75. Henniker. *Transportation*: 317, 321, 325–326460–461; Jones. *Appendices*:Appendix 43. Hooton.*Eagle in Flames*:190.UKNA Air 1/1513/204/58/37.

76. Hoeppner:52, 120–121. Robinson:129 Appendices I & II. *Weltkrieg X*:64. *Nachrichtenblatt* 1/1917 (1 March). Army airships dropped 44.7 tonnes of bombs over France and Belgium and 36.6 tonnes over England. Airships were expensive to build and to operate. At the beginning of the war US intelligence calculated the cost of a Zeppelin at $640,000, the equivalent of $16 million in the early 21st Century. Herbert A. Johnson:83.
77. *Armees Francaise IV/3*:Annex 1053. Christienne & Lissarrague:64. Jones *II*:246–247. *Nachrichtenblatt 1/1917* (1March). UKNA Air 1/1283/204/11/14. Three night reconnaissance missions were flown by a British airship in 1916.
78. For French bombers see *Armée Françaises VI/1*:Annex 363. Davilla & Soltan: 91–92, 110–113, 135–137, 153, 238, 455–456, 469–471, 559–561, 563–564. Martel:105–114, 169–175, 243. Patrick Façon's article on Duval. UKNA Air 1/881/204/5/ 599 & 600. Each groupe had three escadrilles of 10 and later 15 bombers.
79. US Army bomber groups had three squadrons of 25 aircraft. Maurer *I*:357–375. The US Navy planned a Northern Bombing Group with six squadrons of 10 Capronis and six of 18 DH 4. UKNA Air 1/925/205/5/912.
80. For heavy bombers and the French see Davilla & Soltan:19–20, 133–138,173, 251–252. See also Nilsson's article on the Caproni and SHAA A187. The Capronis carried a maximum bomb load of 450 kg and from 1 April to 16 August 1918 GB 2 flew 629 sorties and GB 18 183.
81. For British bombers see Bruce. *British Aeroplanes*:274,280–285, 697–704. Jones.*II*:182–183, 251 and Appendix IX. The Elephant bomber was not withdrawn until the end of 1917.
82. UKNA Air 1/920/204/5/884. Air 1/767/204/4/249–251. Air 1/1443/204/36/2 & 3. Corps squadrons in other brigades were also used extensively for dedicated bombing missions. See UKNA Air 1/2223/209/40/20 (1–4 July 1918).
83. UKNA Air 1/1596/204/83/38 (8 September - 26 September and 10–29 October. Air 1/2176/209/14/19 (1August and 26 August 1918), Air 1/2223/209/40/20 (3–22 July 1918), Air 1/2215/209/30/23. It is worth noting that until the spring of 1918 French bomber groups sometimes flew barrage patrols. SHAA A166/2.
84. Jones *II*:181–184. Jones *IV*:143. Slessor:127.
85. Jones *IV*:278–279.
86. Slessor:76–77, 76 n1., 112–115, 128–129. See also brigade war diaries.
87. Jones *VI*:407–409. Slessor:112–113, 130–131.
88. Jones *VI*:409–411. NLS AC 3155 128.
89. *Rapport du Maréchal Commandant en Chef les Armées françaises du Nord et du Nord*:36. Hereafter *Rapport du Maréchal*
90. Jones. *War in the Air VI*:101–174 & *Appendices*:Appendix XXX. Wise:296, 298–299, 301. UKNA Air 1/1977/204/273/63. Air 1/2198/209/1–5. Air 1/2249/209/45/1–10. By the end of the war the RAF had about 80 Handley Page 0/100 and 0/400 heavy bombers many with American aircrew, especially in the Independent Force. During the war Trenchard was no enthusiast of strategic air power. In September he identified a dozen rail targets, including Luxembourg, Metz, Saarbrücken and Thionville, which also supported operations west of the River Moselle. Of nearly 797 tonnes of bombs dropped by the Independent Force only 42% fell on purely strategic targets while railways and airfields west of the Rhine attracted some 459 tonnes.
91. Based upon brigade, wing and squadron records. Gray & Thetford:7. Lamberton. *Reconnaissance & Bomber Aircraft*:188–189. UKNAAir 1/2249/209/46/6 & 7. *Nachrichtenblätter 28/1917* (September 6) & *25/1918* (August 15).The AEG G-IV could carry five 50 kilogramme bombs.
92. Lamberton. *Reconnaissance & Bomber Aircraft*:188–189. Martel:101–105.
93. Fischer:25–62.Jefford. *Observers and Navigators*:56–57, Appendix D. Wise:295–296. *Nachrichtenblatt 34/1918* (October 17. Entry for October 19.). SHAA A 166/2. UKNA Air 1/475/15/312/189. French bombers generally flew only 35 kilometres behind the line.
94. The British had 24 beacons, of which a quarter were in reserve, divided at Lens into the Northern and Southern Sections under II Brigade and 54 Wing respectively. Jefford. *Observers and Navigators*:Appendix F. UKNA Air 1/475/15/312/189. Air1/1914/204/230/1. Air1/2153/209/3/307.Air 2/17/207/58/2.
95. Aders:2–5. Davilla & Soltan:11–20. Jones.*II*:168–171 & *V*:196–198. NLS AC 3155 No 192. SHAA A129/1. UKNA Air 1/1513/204/58/39. Air 1/1587/204/82/63. In July 1916 the BEF had 113 anti-

aircraft guns, 169 in November 1916. The BEF's anti-aircraft artillery strength rose from 285 in April 1917 to 735 in November, 905 in August 1918 and 1,118 by the end of the war. British Pups and Camels were used from 1 October 1917 in experimental night intruder missions using 25-pound bombs while the French flew 16 night fighter sorties in Flanders from 28–31 October 1917. The French had about a dozen home defence squadrons which were occasionally attached to army groups.

96. Aders: 4, 10–31. Fischer:89–99 Franks et al. *Above the lines*:61–62 & *Jasta Pilots*:76 Hooton. *Eagle in Flames*:122–129. Hudson:283–284. Jones.*VI*:428–429 & *Appendices*:Appendix 43. Shores et al:310–311. UKNA Air 1/1914/204/230/3–5. Air 1/1914/204/230/7. Quintin-Brand would command 10 Group during the Battle of Britain.

97. Franks et al. *Casualties*:199–327, 343–379. Based upon the loss of aircraft with three or more crew. However, some multi- engined bombers were flown by just two men. Gray & Thetford.:113, 129. The bombers had their own landing lights which were supplemented by runway lights and visual cues. UKNA Air 1/1914/204/230/1.

98. Hoeppner:92. Jones.*II*:184–187. Before the Germans retreated to the *Siegfriedstellung* they built a network of 70 airfields. A captured document describing proposed sites is in NLS ACC 3155 No 347.

99. Herwig:357.

100. The *Republic* was by the Italian liner *Florida* off the North American coast on January 22 1909 and began to sink. Unable to contact nearby ships directly Binns, was able to relay a signal through a more powerful transmitter in the United States and then he acted as a radio beacon until help arrived. The *Republic's* passengers were transferred in her lifeboats with the radio operator being one of the last to leave before the liner sank. The incident convinced the British Board of Trade that the density of shipping traffic meant rescue could always be summoned swiftly to transfer the passengers of any stricken ship. Lifeboats were therefore reduced to the number needed to transfer passengers rather than rescue them and the ill-fated *Titanic* was one of the first affected by the new rules. Binns was the obvious choice to be the *Titanic's* chief radio operator but declined and went to work on land in New York. He monitored radio traffic of ships steaming to the stricken *Titanic* and gave a New York newspaper a world exclusive.

101. *Report of the Military Board of Supply*: 742–746, 736–741, 748–749, 764–778. Hoeppner:148.

102. Shores et al. *Above the Trenches*:227. Up to 10% of aircraft flown to parks were lost in accidents. *The Allied Armies under Marshal Foch in the Franco-Belgian Theater of Operations. Volume 2. Report of the Military Board of Supply*:748–749.

103. The casualty figures are, so far as possible, purely for men lost on the Western Front in combat missions while supporting ground operations. Casualties in strategic bombing and naval co-operation operations as well as in accidents have been excluded. Difficulties distinguishing between RAF Independent Force strategic and operational missions mean all its casualties are excluded. Permanent losses are those who were killed, missing, mortally wounded or taken prisoner. Losses are for members of air forces and in the case of American casualties members of the USAS serving with the RAF have been included in American losses while Americans holding commissions in the RAF are included in British losses.

Chapter Three

1. For the Battle of the Somme see Clayton: 116–118. Edmonds *1916/I*.; Miles *1916/ II*.; *Weltkrieg X:325–388 & X:53–116. Armée Françaises IV/ 3*:79–291. Total British casualties on the first day were 57,000 compared with 15,000 at the Battle of Waterloo where the combined casualties of both sides were 52,000 including 7,000 French prisoners.

2. Boyle:134, 178–179.

3. Jones. *III*:309.Haig's diaries May 1917, NLS AC 3155 No 113.

4. Baring:138. Boyle:249. Bond & Cave:16–17. NLS AC 3155 No106 (16 May, 23 May, 14 June, 19 June, 24 June 1916). NLS AC 3155.No108 (18 September 1916) UKNA WO 158/34. But Haig met his Artillery Advisor, Major-General Sir Noel Birch, more frequently and Trenchard's visits were always in on the same day as Birch's.

5. Bond & Cave. *Haig*:15.

6. Boyle. *Trenchard*:15–42.

7. Many of the RFC's senior officers, including Charlton, Hearson, Higgins and Salmond, also served in West Africa at this time.

8. Boyle:43–123
9. Ibid:124–161
10. UKNA WO 158/34.
11. Jones. *II*:164–168. His doctrine was thrashed out in association with Peuty.
12. UKNA Air 1/920/204/5/884.
13. Slessor:127.
14. Cuneo:230–234 remains the best overall source on this era. See also Bruce. *British Aeroplanes*:361. Jones*II*:149–164. Kilduff. *Air Force*:33–48.
15. Henshaw:70–82. Jones. *II*:156–158. UKNA Air 1/2166/209/11/12.
16. UKNA Air 1/2247/209/43/11. Hawker commanded the first DH 2 squadron. See also Jones. *II*:162 n1
17. Cuneo:233 Lewis:47. Jones.*II*:158–164. UKNA Air 1/2248/209/43/12.
18. Franks et al. *Above the lines*:134. Hart:72–73. Kilduff. *Air Force*:46–47. VanWyngarden, *Aces*:59–61. For Immelmann see VanWyngarden, *Aces*:58–59.
19. UKNA Air 1/2247/208/43/11.
20. UKNA Air 1/2248/209/43/12. Air 1/2215/209/30/2 (21 June 1916).
21. Details of all careers from *Quarterly Army List: 30 June 1914* and *Quarterly Army List: 30 September 1919*. Web site: rafweb.org/Biographies.
22. Jones. *War in the Air II*:246.
23. UKNA Air 1/2225/209/40/22.
24. For Trenchard's views see his "Future Policy in the Air" of 22 September 1916. Jones. *War in the Air II*:Appendix IX.
25. For the Somme air campaign see Hart. Also Bailey & Cony:56–85. Bülow: 70–80. Cuneo:229–270. Franks et al *Casualties*:188–197,340–343, *Jasta Pilots*:14–36 & *Chronology*: 8–19. Henshaw:86–127. Hoeppner:71–81. Jones *II*: 203–334. Voisin:5–20. Wise:358–392. UKNA WO158/34. Air 1/9/15/1/27. Air 1/762/204/4/165, 244–247. Air1/1548/204/78/2–1. Air 1/1557/204/80/1 & 2. Air 1/1558/204/80/6–8. Air 1/2215/219/30/2–7. Air 1/2224/209/40/22–24.Air 1/2248/209/43/12 & 15. SHAA A126. SHAT 26N42 Dossier 4.
26. Slessor:43.
27. Duffy:316.Hoeppner:79. *Weltkrieg X*:374–375.UKNA Air 1/2215/209/30/2. Air 1/2248/209/43/12. Ludlow-Hewitt's corps squadrons provided the "balloon-busters".
28. Edmonds. *1916/I*:268–268; UKNA Air 1/2248/209/43/12.
29. UKNA Air 1/1557/204/80/2. Air 1/2248/209/43/12.
30. UKNA Air 1/2248/209/43/12.
31. Henshaw:90–105. UKNA Air 1/2248/209/43/12.
32. UKNA Air 1/1557/204/80/2 & 6.
33. UKNA Air 1/2248/209/43/12.
34. Boyle:181.
35. Edmonds *1916/I*:268–269. Kilduff. *Air Force*:48–49. Stosch:Anlage 1.*Weltkrieg X*:240, 340 n.1. UKNA Air 1/2248/209/43/12. For the German fighter forces the most detailed picture is in VanWyngarden, *Aces*:26,32, 62–63.
36. Henshaw:89–105. Jones. *Appendixes*: Appendix 37.
37. Hart:113–114. Henshaw:89–98.9 Wise:376. UK NA Air 1/2215/209/30/3. WO 158/34.One replacement was future ace 2nd Lieutenant Albert Ball. Trenchard's attitude might also have been coloured by Dowding's eccentricities, for he was a vegetarian with an interest in spiritualism.
38. See Tredrey:79–80 and the *RAF Flying Review* article "He taught the world to fly".
39. Miles *1916/II*:45 n1, 58–89
40. Kilduff. *Air Force*:48–49. VanWyngarden, *Aces*:64–65.*Weltkrieg X*:359, 374–375. Parschau was the first pilot to use a Fokker with interrupter gear and was closely associated with the Fokker company. However, he was flying a Halberstadt biplane when he was mortally wounded on July 21. VanWyngarden, *Aces*:9, 66.
41. *Weltkrieg X*:343–344. Mahnke became a *Luftwaffe* general and distinguished himself on the Eastern Front.
42. VanWyngarden, *Aces*:64. *Weltkrieg X*:364–365. UKNA Air 1/2248/209/43/12.
43. *Weltkrieg X*: 343, 385–6. UKNAAir 1/2248/209/43/12.

44. Hoeppner:71–72. UKNA Air 1/1557/204/80/2.
45. Hoeppner:70. *Weltkrieg XI*: 428, 624 n1. Franks et al. *Casualties*:182–194, 339–342.
46. VanWyngarden, *Aces*: 67, 69, 75.*Weltkrieg X*:374–375. UKNA Air 1/762/204/4/244.
47. *Weltkrieg X*:374–375, 385–6.
48. Hoeppner:74, 79. *Weltkrieg X*:374–375. Interestingly, at least two German "aces" on the Somme front actually flew captured Nieuports. *Leutnant* Gustav Leffers (nine victories) was shot down over the Somme on 27 November 1916 in a Nieuport 16 while *Leutnant* Kurt Student (who achieved six victories including five Nieuports and would later command Germany's airborne forces) used a Nieuport 11 he had forced down over the Somme on 6 July. Franks et al, *Above the Lines*: 154, 213–214. VanWyngarden, *Aces*:64, 72,75.
49. *Weltkrieg X*:385–386.
50. UKNA WO 95/483.
51. For the origins of the *Jasta* see Franks et al.*Jasta Pilots*:13–27. Kilduff *Combat Wing*: 39–40,43–45 & *Air Force*:49. Morrow:150–151. VanWyngarden, *Aces*:70 & *JG I*:17, 19
52. Franks et al.*Jasta Pilots*:13–18. Guttman:56. Kilduff. *Combat Wing*: 45–52 & *Richthofen*:48–51.VanWyngarden, *Aces*:69–70, 77, 81.
53. Duffy:309–311 (quote from p.309).Henshaw:104–105. UKNA Air1/2215/209/30/4. Zander became the first commander of the fighter-pilot training school (*Jagdschule*) on 10 November 1916. VanWyngarden, *Aces*:74.
54. Henshaw:99–115. *Weltkrieg XI*:78–79.
55. Duffy:309. Hoeppner: 78.
56. Hoeppner:76. *Weltkrieg XI*:59, 67–68.
57. Hoeppner:79. *Weltkrieg XI*:67–68. 83, 88.
58. Jones. *War in the Air II*:279. There is no confirmation from surviving German records.
59. Duffy:272, 310, 311, 317. Jones *II*:283–284.
60: Henshaw:113. UKNA WO 158/34.
61. Jones *II*:296–297, 313–314.
62. Jones *II*: Appendix 9.
63. Jones *II*:296–297. UKNA Air 1/2225/209/40/23–24.
64. Shores et al.*Trenches*:59.
65. Jones *II*:302.
66. Franks et al. *Chronology*:13–16. Henshaw:104–127.
67. Henshaw:104–127. UKNA Air 1/2215/209/30/4–7.
68. UKNA Air 1/2215/209/4. Air1/2215/209/30/7 (17 November). Air 1/2248/209/43/12.
69. Jones *II*: 254 n2.
70. UKNA Air 1/170/15/160/8 (11 September 1916). Air 1/1557/204/80/1 & 7.
71. Henshaw:116–122. UKNA Air 1/2248/209/43/15 & Air 1/2225/209/40/23.
72. Cuneo:263–264; Hoeppner:80–81.
73. Jones. *Appendices*: Appendix 37. UKNA Air 1/762/204/4/165 & 1/766/204/4/247.
74. *Weltkrieg XI*:93. Morrow:149. Boelcke's death was witnessed by hundreds of German troops. Duffy:312
75. Cuneo:276–280. Hoeppner:82–84.
76. Tuchman:248, 308–309. Jones *II*:304.
77. Hoeppner:99–101.
78. Kilduff. *Richthofen*:62–63. UKNA Air 1/1557/204/80/8.
79. Jones *II*:215–217. Slessor:44. Wise:366–368. UKNA Air 1/2215/209/30/4.
80. Wise:368n1. UKNA Air 1/2215/209/30/3.
81. UKNA Air 1/2248/209/43/12.
82. Jones.*II*:278. UKNA Air 1/765/204/4/244–245, Air 1/2215/209/30/5.
83. Henshaw:105–125. UKNA Air 1/765/204/4/245, Air 1/766/204/4/246–247.
84. UKNA 1/762/204/4/165, Air 1/765/204/4/244–247, Air 1/766/204/4/246–247.
85. Franks et al. *Jasta Pilots*:24–25. UKNA Air 1/762/204/4/165, Air 1/765/204/4/244–247.
86. Edmonds *1916/I*:30, 87–88, 246–249, 273, 280, 283. Jones*II*:172–178. UKNA Air 1/2248/209/43/12.
87. Henshaw:85–86 *Weltkrieg X*:349, 352–353. UKNA Air 1/2248/209/43/12.
88. Jones *II*:174–175. Miles *1916/II*:566 n 1. UKNA Air 1/2248/209/43/12.

89. Jones *II*:176–177. Hoeppner:68–69. UKNA Air 1/2248/209/43/12. Hoeppner may have been confused. Early in 1916 British cameras used individually-loaded photographic plates but by the summer they had 18-plate automatically-reloading magazines Duffy:314–315. For German descriptions of French and British cameras see *Nachrichtenblätter 14/1918* and *15/1918* (May 30 & June 6).
90. Middlebrook:116. UKNA Air 1/2248/209/43/12.
91. UKNA Air 1 2248/209/43/12.
92. Miles *1916/II*:229. *Weltkrieg X*:385–386. UKNA Air 1/1547/204/78/2, Air 1/2248/209/43/12.
93. Jones *III*:310–313.
94. Jones *II*: 175–176. UKNA Air 1/1547/204/78/ 2–1, Air 1/2248/209/43/12.
95. Duffy:256. Hoeppner:75–76. Neumann:321, Appendix 3.
96. UKNA Air 1/1547/204/78/1, Air 1 2248/209/43/12.
97. UKNA Air 1/2247/209/43/11 (9, 12, 16–19 May). British contact patrols used sirens to request troops to mark the front. For a German comment on these eerie sounds see Duffy:315.
98. Edmonds *1916/II*:88–89, 286. Jones *II*:179–181. UKNA WO 157/22.
99. Duffy:117–118, 228, 310, 317.Jones *II*:213–214. UKNA Air 1/2248/209/43/12 (Entries for June 18, 22 & 23).
100. *Weltkrieg X*: 385–6,.380, 383.
101. Bülow:76.Hoeppner:69–70,74. Neumann:475.
102. Cuneo:257. Miles*1916/II*:205, 353.
103. Jones *III*:319–320.
104. UKNA WO 157/21.
105. UKNA Air 1/996/204/5/1232, WO 157/21. The author would like to express his thanks to Mr Martin Streetly, Editor of *Jane's Radar and Electronic Warfare Systems* for his advice.
106. Occleshaw:127. UKNA WO 158/328. RFC headquarters early in 1916 appears to have included a renegade German officer.
107. Jones *II*:300, 315. *Weltkrieg XI*:83. UKNA Air 1/9/15/1/27, Air 1/2248/209/43/15.
108. Jones *III*:307–310, 326 n 1.UKNA Air 1/2268/209/70/190.
109. Davilla & Soltan:556. SHAT 26N42/4 (2 July). I am indebted to Mr Mike Pearce of Cross & Cockade International for Brocard's Christian name.
110. Davilla & Soltan:485. Franks et al *Over the Front*:170–171. SHAT 26N42/4. The latter has an entry on 7 July querulously demanding: "Why is Lieutenant Guynemer flying solo?" Guynemer would claim 17 of his 53 victories over the Somme many in his Spad S5 "taxi".
111. Cuneo:268, 270. SHAT 26N42/4 (8 July).
112. *Armées Françaises IV/3*: 162–163,Annexes 675, 947, 1199. Cuneo:268–270. SHAT 26N42/4 (5 August).
113. Porch:93 quoting Commandant Paquet.
114. Castex et al, *Barès*:117. SHAT 26N42/4 (4, 22, 24, 27, 28 July).
115. Morrow:135. SHAT 26N42/4 (22 August, 8 September).
116. Cuneo: 259. *Weltkrieg XI*:73–74.
117. *Weltkrieg XI*:73–74.
118. Armées Françaises IV/3:143–145.
119. *Weltkrieg XI*:102. *Armées Françaises IV/3*:268–270. One of the few instances of French ground attacks was on 10–11 November when GC 12 attacked horse-drawn transport with flechettes (steel darts) Guttman:24.
120. Franks et al. *Chronology*: 8–13. Guttman:22.Voisin:17. SHAA A 126. GC 13 was known for the first two months of its existence as Groupe de Combat de Cachy VI e Armée in September.
121. Franks et al. *Chronology*:16–20. Voisin:17.
122. Duffy:312
123. Jones *II*:Appendix VIII.
124. Henshaw: 86–126,Appendix I. *Weltkrieg XI*:111.
125. Bruce. The aeroplanes of the Royal Flying Corps:50–51 & British Aeroplanes: 126. Davilla & Soltan: 337–340, 485, 502. Guttman: 29, 62. Guynemer's Spad S7, with a high-compression Hispano Suiza 8Ab never had an engine change possibly because he had expert fitters whom he used to assist.

By contrast the Spad S13 of 1917 was less reliable and engine problems forced him to land twice on 10 September 1917, the day before he went missing.
126. UKNA Air 1/2215/209/30/8.

Chapter Four

1. Herwig:246–253, 325. Schwarte:287, 299. *Weltkrieg X*:624 n 1. In 1916 the German air service lost 221 aircraft and 45 balloons while personnel casualties from April 1916 to March 1917 were 2,100.
2. Falls *1917/I*:87–93.
3. Herwig:247.*Weltkrieg XII*: 33–34, 40–51.
4. *Weltkrieg XII*:428, 531. *Luftstreitkräfte* strength rose to 1,600 aircraft on all fronts by April, with 500 aircraft in reserve.
5. *Weltkrieg XII*:531.
6. *Weltkrieg XII*:48–50.
7. Falls *1917/I*:13–14. UKNA Air 1/768/204/4/252.
8. Boyle:206–212.
9. Boyle op cit. UKNA Air 1/920/204/5/884.
10. UKNA PRO Air 1/920/204/5/884.
11. This is based upon Paul Ferdinand du Peuty's personal file, SHAT 142.056, examined for me by Ms Laura Soyer to whom I am deeply indebted. Further details were provided by Christophe Cony. His career had some similarities with Ernst Udet. See also Christienne & Lissarrague:141. Franks & Bailey:90. Morrow:198.
12. Davilla & Soltan: 95–97, 435–437, 465–471. Franks & Bailey:89–109. Morizon. This booklet has no page numbers. On 1 February 1917 only 70 Spads were operational.
13. Falls *1917/I*:87–93. *Armée Françaises V/1*:373, 376. Map 30.
14. Jones: *III*:320. UKNA Air 1/766/204/4/248.
15. Franks et al. *Casualties*:198–202, 343–344. Henshaw:Appendix 1.
16. Henshaw:141–148. Jones *III*:323. UKNA Air 1/881/204/5/594, Air 1/766/204/4/248, Air 1/2215/209/30/8–11.
17. Falls *1917/I*:90–170. Herwig:250–251. Porch:104. The withdrawal of radios alerted the French to unusual German activity and on 23 February they learned of the "Alberich" plans.
18. Jones *III*:325–326, 329–330. The British briefly attached corps squadrons to divisions.
19. Henshaw:Appendix 1. Jones *III*:322 n 1. Quote from Jones *III*:325.
20. Franks et al. *Casualties*:202–206, 344–345. Jones *III*:331. Kilduff. *Legend*:79–80, 83. German casualties included *Rittmeister* Friedrich Karl Tassilo, *Prinz von Preussen*, a cousin of the Emperor who commanded *FA (A) 258* but, in his spare time, flew an Albatros with *Jasta 2*. He was captured on 31 March 1917 and mortally wounded during an escape attempt. See Bean:189–190, 190 n124.
21. Falls *1917/I*:26–27, 46. *Armée Françaises V/1*: 599–803.
22. Falls *1917/I*:52–53. Franks et al. *Chronology*:33–40. Neumann:478. UKNA Air 1/767/204/4/251.
23. For Arras Falls *1917/I*:171–471, 507–524. *Weltkrieg XII*:183–278.
24. Mitcham:18.Although a qualified balloon observer, Kesselring never flew during the Great War, unlike one of his Second World War opponents Major Arthur Tedder who commanded No 70 Squadron at Arras. Lossberg's nephew, *Oberst* Viktor von Lossberg, played a key role in reforming the *Luftwaffe* night fighter arm in the summer of 1943. *General der Flieger* Ulrich Grauert, who helped conquer France in 1940, was apparently a cousin of General von Lossberg.
25. Shephard's name is misspelled Sheppard in the Army List. This spelling is taken from RFC records which include his signature.
26. UKNA Air 1/767/204/4/252.
27. Pretyman made the RFC's first photo-reconnaissance sortie on 15 September 1914.
28. Furse:117–126, 211–233.
29. Falls *1917/I*:196. Kilduff *Combat Wing*:74–75, 78, 86. *Weltkrieg XII*:187,190. UKNA Air 1/9/15/1/22.
30. *Weltkrieg XII*:212 n1. UKNA Air 1/9/15/1/22. *Jasta 11* was often reduced to seven serviceable fighters. VanWyngarden, *JG I*:9

31. For the air campaign see Franks et al *Bloody April, Chronology*:41–67 & *Casualties*: 206–214, 345–347. Henshaw:148–183. Morris. Wise:398–409. UKNA Air 1/21/13/1777, Air 1/767/204/4/251–254, Air 1/2177/209/14/24–27, Air 1/2215/209/30/11–13, Air 1/2219/209/40/4–7, Air 1/2238/209/42/3–6. WO 158/35 No 2. *Nachrichtenblätter der Luftstreitkräfte 6–15/1917* (5 April -7 June). Quote from UKNA Air 1/920/204/5/884.
32. Jones *III*:333. UKNA Air 1/9/15/1/22.
33. Jones *III*:331.
34. UKNA Air 1/767/204/4/252.
35. Henshaw:146–155.
36. Shores et al. *Trenches*:364,384.
37. Trenchard had originally proposed using the DH 4 bombers in the reconnaissance-fighter role. Bruce. *Aeroplanes of the Royal Flying Corps*:50–51. Henshaw:153–164. UKNA Air 1/1780/204/150/11.
38. UKNA WO 158/35 No 2.
39. Shores et al. *Trenches*:384. UKNA Air1/767/204/4/252.
40. Henshaw:158–160. UKNA Air 1/767/204/4/252.
41. Henshaw:162–163. UKNA Air 1/767/204/4/252.
42. Henshaw:154–166. UKNA Air 1/767/204/4/252.
43. Jones *III*:360–361.
44. UKNA WO 158/35 No 2.
45. Jones *III*:368–369. Kilduff. *Combat Wing*: 60, 86.UKNA Air 1/2215/209/30/11.
46. Henshaw:Appendix I. Jones *Appendices*: Appendix 37.
47. UKNA Air 1/21/13/1777.
48. Boyle:214–215. UKNA Air 1/1343/204/19/15. Four days later a senior member of the 1st Army staff, Lieutenant-Colonel William Twiss, used a BE from No 10 Squadron for an afternoon reconnaissance. UKNA Air 1/1367/204/22/24.
49. UKNA Air 1/847/204/5/381–381.
50. Ibid
51. UKNA Air 1/767/204/4/252.
52. Franks et al. *War Chronology* & *Jasta Pilots*. UKNA Air 1/9/15/1/22.
53. UKNA Air 1/768/204/4/252.
54. Franks et al. *Chronology*:54–65. Henshaw:168–179, Appendix 1. UKNA Air 1/768/204/4/253. *Jasta* 27's daily serviceable strength dropped from nine to two on 2 May after Roland D.II pilot *Offizierstellvertreter* Franz Hilger was injured in an accident and all these fighters were withdrawn for unspecified technical reasons. UKNA Air 1/9/15/1/22.
55. Jefford. Jones *Appendices*. Appendix XXVIII. Kilduff. *Combat Wing*:95. Shores et al. *Above the Trenches*:59. Ball may have been knocked out by a pan of Lewis gun ammunition.
56. Jones *Air III*:371.
57. Henshaw:150–155. UKNA Air 1/767/204/4/252.
58. Jones *III*:342. UKNA Air 1/21/13/1777, Air 1/676/21/13/1849. Klein had 22 victories in the First World War and would be a distinguished fighter commander in the *Luftwaffe* dying in 1944 as a *Generalmajor*.
59. UKNA Air 1/767/204/4/252.
60. UKNA WO 158/35 No 2.
61. Jones *III*:313–314. UKNA Air 1/918/204/5/879.Mitchell had two squadrons with modern aircraft; No 35 Squadron with the rarely used Armstrong Whitworth F.K.8 (the squadron was assigned the Cavalry Corps) and No 59 Squadron with REs. One of Carthew's squadrons at Vimy Ridge and all of Mitchell's were expanded from 18 to 24 aircraft.
62. Falls *1917/I*:177.
63. *Weltkrieg XII*:200, 202. UKNA Air 1/2239/209/42/4.
64. UKNA Air 1/1626/204/90/4. From 1916 more pilots were receiving radio training and 3 Wing's Ludlow-Hewitt was especially enthusiastic about pilots directing artillery shoots. Jefford. *Observers and Navigators*:42, 52–53.
65. Franks et al. *Casualties*:206–207, 345. Henshaw:149–155. UKNA Air1/2177/209/14/25.
66. Falls *1917/I*:270,311. UKNA Air 1/9/15/1/22.
67. Quote from UKNA Air 1/996/204/5/1233. UKNA Air 1/9/15/1/22.

68. UKNA Air 1/9/15/1/22. However, engine noise could sometimes make wireless reception impossible. Duffy:315.
69. UKNA Air 1/9/15/1/22.
70. UKNA Air 1/9/15/1/22. WO 158/35 No 2.
71. Franks et al. *Casualties*:207–210. Henshaw:158–167. UKNA Air 1/9/15/1/22, Air 1/767/204/4/252. On 25 April Haig's Chief-of-Staff Lieutenant-General Sir Launcelot Kiggell reported that where I and III Brigades flew 842 sorties and ranged on 767 targets from 4–19 April, the German figures for the whole British front were 320 and 160. UKNA Air1/522/16/12/5. OB 1837 S1.
72. Falls *1917/I*:296–297. UKNA Air 1/2239/209/42/4.
73. UKNA Air 1/918/204/5/879. The brigadier who flew artillery missions was not identified.
74. UKNA WO 158/35 No 2.
75. UKNA Air 1/2177/209/14/25–27, Air 1/2238/209/42/4–6.
76. *Weltkrieg XII*:265, 268, 27. *Nachrichtenblätter 12–13/1917* (17–24 May). UKNA Air 1/9/15/1/22, Air 1/767/204/4/252–253.
77. UKNA Air 1/9/15/1/22, WO 158/35 No 2.
78. Falls *1917/I*: 395. Jones *III*:369, 373. Zorer, with *Kasta 1*, was shot down and captured on 1 September but later escaped. *Nachrichtenblatt 17/1918* (20 June). Franks et al. *Casualties*:351.
79. UKNA Air 1/767/204/4/252–254.
80. Falls *1917/I*:171–176. Henshaw:148–175. Jones *III*:331–334, 341, 360. Wise:398–400. UKNA Air 1/767/204/4/252–253. Air 1/2219/209/40/5–6.Longcroft flew over the battlefield in a BE 2 and in May took Captain William "Billy" Mitchell with him to observe an Australian attack upon "Bertincourt" (actually Bullecourt). They were forced to land hastily when enemy fighters appeared. Mitchell:113–115.
81. UKNA Air 1/767/204/4/252–253.
82. UKNA Air 1/918/204/5/879. Air 1/996/204/5/1232.
83. UKNA Air 1/918/204/5/879. I am indebted to Mr Martin Streetly, Editor of *Jane's Radar and Electronic Warfare Systems* for his advice.
84. UKNA Air 1/996/204/5/1232.
85. UKNA Air 1/996/204/5/1232.
86. UKNA Air 1/918/204/5/879. WO 158/35 No 2
87. UKNA Air 1/1441/204/35/8.
88. For the French air campaign see Franks & Bailey. Franks et al. *Bloody April*. Morizon (No page numbers). Bailey & Cony: 104–127. Christienne & Lissarague:110–112. Franks et al. *Chronology*:41–67 & *Casualties*: 206–214, 345–347. Martel:206–208, 211–214. Voisin:20–43, 47–50. SHAA A129 Dossier 1. SHAA A130 Dossier 1. SHAT 18N171 Dossier 3. SHAT 18N412. *Nachrichtenblätter 6–15/1917*.
89. For the French spring offensive see Falls *1917/I*:482–506. Goes. *Chemin des Dames*. *Les Armées Françaises V/2*:36–601. *Weltkrieg XII*:279–284, 289–424. The 7.*Armee* Head of Operations from February 1917 until the end of the war was *Major* Werner Blomberg. As the last *Reichswehr* Minister of Defence in 1933 he helped *Nazi* ambitions by aiding the creation of an independent German air force. He was to be dismissed in a scandal in 1938 and died in Nuremburg in 1946. His son served in the *Luftwaffe* and died over Iraq in bizarre circumstances.
90. Étévé:224.
91. On 1 April 1917 l'Aviation Militaire had 1,233 aircraft. Morizon.
92. *Weltkrieg XII*:280, 282.
93. *Weltkrieg XII*: 281,298–299, 532. *Nachrichtenblätter 5* & *6/1917* (March 29 & April 5). In the Second World War Dewall became a *Luftwaffe* general. Mention should be made that the reinforcements included *Major* Erich Hönemanns' *Jasta 22*. In February 1940 Hönemanns with Student's air support liaison officer accidentally landed in neutral Belgium where the liaison officer's documents fatally compromised Hitler's plans to strike westward. The plans were redrafted with spectacular success ripping apart the French Army, now under Général Maurice Gamelin who was Micheler's chief-of-staff in April 1917. Hooton. *Phoenix Triumphant*:195.
94. Voisin:21. SHAA A 130/1 (No data available for 9–13 April). GB 3 was re-equipping with Paul Schmitts. Martel:206–208.
95. Morizon. Voisin:22–24.

96. *Armées Françaises V/1*:Annex 1226.
97. Voisin:25–27.
98. Voisin:49. SHAT 18N171/3.
99. Christienne & Lissarague:112. Franks et al. *Chronology*: 41–54. SHAA A 130/1.
100. *Armées Françaises V/1*:Annex 1883. From 1917 French balloon crews began to receive radios which allowed them to co-operate with aircraft. Porch:96.
101. *Armées Françaises V/1*:Annex 1883. Franks et al. *Chronology*:43–48.
102. *Armées Françaises V/1*:Annexes 1215, 1218,1238, 1883. SHAT 18N171/3.
Mazillier's Caudron fell to *Leutnant* Josef Jacobs of *Jasta 22*
103. *Armées Françaises V/1*:Annexes 1215, 1218, 1238, 1883.SHAA A 130/1. SHAA A108 Dossier 2.
104. *Armées Françaises V/1*:Annexes 1266, 1324. SHAT 18 N 412.
105. Christienne:145. Franks et al. *Chronology*:48–49. Morizon. Voisin:32.
106. Davilla & Soltan: 560. Franks et al. *Chronology*:49–54. SHAA A129/1. SHAT 18N412.
107. Morizon.Voisin:34. *Nachrichtenblatt 17/1917* (June 21).
108. *Armées Françaises V/1*:625. Pinsard led a fighter group in 1939–1940 but lost a leg when his airfield was bombed. Ménard had a distinguished career in the French Air Force and died in 1954. Franks & Bailey:85, 206–207.
109. Voisin:32. SHAA A129/1.
110. *Armées Françaises V/1*:Annex 1210. Davilla & Soltan:469–470, 560. SHAA A129/1.
111. Franks et al. *Casualties*:206–209,345–346. *Chronology*:41–54. Henshaw:149–167. Morrow:199. VanWyngarden, *JG I*:9. According to Morizon, 293 French aircraft were destroyed or damaged in accidents during April. UKNA Air 1/847/204/5/381–381.
112. Franks et al. *Chronicles*:54–65. UKNA Air 1/2251/209/53/1.
113. UKNA OB 1837 S1, Air 1/522/16/12/5. In May 1940 French air defence was not hampered by lack of fighters but the low intensity of operations with two sorties a day being the exception rather than the rule. Hooton. *Phoenix Triumphant*:245, 247, 255.
114. Kilduff. *Richthofen*:Appendix 1.

Chapter Five

1. For the Ypres Offensive see Edmonds *1917/ II*:32–111, 124–218, 231–363. Farndale: 184–214.*Weltkrieg XII*:425–476. *Weltkrieg XIII*:53–99. *Armée V/* 2:614–719.
2. For the air campaign see Bailey & Cony:135–173. Bülow:91–100. Christienne & Lissarrague:112–114. Henshaw:177–252. Franks et al *Casualties*:213–237,347–355 and *Chronology*:63–117. Hoeppner:114–119. Jones *IV*:109–169, 172–219, Appendices III-IX. Wise:408–440. *Nachrichtenblätter* 14–39/1917 (31 May-22 November). UKNA Air 1/768/204/4/254. Air 769/204/4/255–257. Air 770/204/4/258–259. Air 1/881/204/5/593.Air 1/2215/209/30/14–19. Air 1/2220/209/40/7–9. Air1/2221/209/40/10–11. Air 1/2229/209/41/5–8. Air 2230/209/41/9–11. Air 1/2247/209/43/6–10. MRAHM Campagne 1914–1918 Aviation.
3. Jones *IV*:142.
4. Jones *VI*:122–123, 274–275. UKNA Air 1/770/204/4/259.
5. Hoeppner:115.
6. Franks et al. *Casualties*:217–238, 348–355. *Jasta Pilots*:84–85. *Chronology*:73–120. Jones. *War in the Air IV*:141, 141 n.3. *Weltkrieg XIII*:63. On the coast the *Marinekorps* fighters (14 in July and 30 by November) were under *Kofl 4.Armee* until 9 September flying 1,216 sorties from July to November to claim16 victories for the loss of 12 aircraft with 11 casualties including four killed in action, one taken prisoner and four injured. UKNA Air 1/2398/267/23.
7. The biographies are based upon *Quarterly Army Lists:30 June 1914* & *30 September 1919*. www.rafweb.org/Biographies. Jones *VI*:275. Air 1/2230/209/41/11.
8. Webb-Bowen remained in the RAF after the war and retired as an Air Vice Marshal in 1933 before joining Imperial Airways as Staff Manager. He died in 1956.
9. Scott was a "lone wolf" minor ace but a poor pilot who decorated his office with pieces of aircraft he crashed but became commander of No 60 Squadron. When Canadian ace Captain William "Billy" Bishop joined the squadron he and Scott had much in common and the Kiwi encouraged the Canuk. See Shores et al. *Trenches*:333. Wise:405. For critical comments on his role in Bishop's VC award see Alex Revell's article in Cross & Cockade International.

10. UKNA Air 1/2215/209/30/14. Air1/2220/209/40/7. Air 1/2229/209/41/6. Air 1/2247/209/43/6–7.
11. Furse:19–46.
12. See his autobiography. He later said there was nothing of note to relate about his brigade command. Charlton. *Charlton*:237. See also Boyle:511. Wise:575 f/n.
13. Hoeppner:115–116. Kilduff. *Combat Wing*:101–2, 118.
14. Franks et al. *Chronology*:65–67. UKNA WO 157/21. Air 1/1188/204/5/2595 (entry of June 11).A captured document said the new command also included *Jasta 18* and *Jasta 28* but the latter was reportedly transferred to *6. Armee* on 26 March and returned either by 25 May or in late August. The third *Staffel* may have been *Jasta 27* under *Oberleutnant* Hermann Göring.
15. Kilduff. *Combat Wing*:107–111, 117–121. VanWyngarden, *JG I*:21. The sweeps were apparently led by the acting *Geschwader Kommodore Leutnant* Kurt-Bertram von Döring who for several days had been seeking permission to commit the unit en masse. However, he was prepared to compromise with Bufe by seeking sweeps only during the evening and allowing individual *Jasta* continuing to fly during the rest of the day. VanWyngarden, *JG I*:26–27.
16. Kilduff. *Wing*:121, 130. UKNA WO 157/24.
17. Corum. *The Luftwaffe*:21, 299 n 17. Mitcham:5.
18. Henshaw:171–188. Jones. *IV*: 114–115, 118–137, 185–186. *Weltkrieg XII*:440–441.
19. Jefford. *RAF Squadrons*: Entries for Nos 20,22 and 48 Squadrons.
20. Gould Lee:91–92. Wise:416–417. After the war Charlton described it as "stubborn stupidity" although he conceded it had some success. Charlton, *War from the Air*:50–57.
21. Franks et al. *Chronology*:73–117. Henshaw:192–250.
22. Jones *IV*:156–157. UKNA Air 1/2220/209/40/8–9. WO 157/117.
23. But the SE 5 and the Spads were both plagued by unreliable engines throughout their careers. Bruce. *Aeroplanes of the Royal Flying Corps*:561 and *British Aeroplanes*:450, *The Fokker Dr I*. Gray, *Albatros D-V*. Gray & Thetford.:52–55, 98–101. Kilduff *Combat Wing*:100. The first Fokker Triplanes were delivered to *JG I* on 28 August and Richthofen had his first victory on 1 September. The loss of two Triplanes, including Gontermann's, on 30 October and forced landings involving both Richthofens led to the fighters being withdrawn from service. Strengthened aircraft returned to the front in late December but structural failure in one of these aircraft badly injured Lothar von Richthofen on 13 March 1918.VanWyngarden, *JG I*:35, 50, 58, 62, 65, 66.
24. Franks et al. *Above the Lines*:78, 81,117, 132, 184. Henshaw:240, 241, 244, 245, 247. Shores et al. *Above the Trenches*:68–69, 90, 104, 232, 235. Wise:427 n.1, 435. UK NA Air 1/1794/204/155/1. Air 1/2386/228/11/13. Sholto Douglas was one of Freeman's pupils.
25. Henshaw:171–206. Kilduff. *Combat Wing*:147. *Weltkrieg XIII*:58. UKNA Air 1/769/204/4/255–257. Air 1/770/204/4/258–259.
26. Jones *IV*:176. UKNA Air 1/2229/209/41/9. Air1/2221/209/40/10.
27. UKNA Air 1/995/204/5/1229.
28. Franks et al. *Above the Lines*:124–125.*Jasta Pilots*:16, 46, 51, 52, 320. *Chronology*:73–116. *Weltkrieg XIII*:72.
29. Haig's diary NLS AC 3155 No117 (8 September, 29 September 1917). UKNA WO95/984 & WO95/1051.
30. Jones *IV*:129. Wise:413–414. Revell's article in Cross & Cockade International Journal.
31. Jones *IV*:129–130. Kilduff *Combat Wing*:141–142. UKNA Air 1/769/204/4/255.Air 1/2215/209/30/15.
32. Franks et al. *Chronology*:109. Henshaw:240. Jones *IV*:207–208. Kilduff *Combat Wing*:150. Wise:432–434. *JG I* airfields were major targets and a bombing raid on 20 September destroyed three *Jasta 4* fighters and damaging six with a dozen casualties among the ground crews including five dead. But attacks on 21–22 October inflicted little damage. VanWyngarden, *JG I*:55, 57.
33. Jones *IV*:115–117. Maurer *I*:337.Wise:409, 413. UKNA Air 1/768/204/4/254, Air 1/769/204/4/255–257, Air 1/770/204/4/258–259.Air 1/2220/209/40/8–9. Air 1/2229/209/41/7–8. Nos 60 and 23 Squadrons seem to have been Webb-Bowen's and Longcroft's interceptor specialists.
34. *Nachrichtenblätter 28, 34 & 36/1917* (6 September, 18 October & 1 November).
35. Büdinggen:97–98. Edmonds *1917/II*:250n.2.Henshaw:235–238. Hoeppner:128–134.
36. Edmonds *1917/II*:250. *Weltkrieg XIII*:67. *Nachrichtenblatt 31/1917* (27 September). UKNA WO95/275.

37. Jones *IV*:194. *Weltkrieg XIII*:310. UKNA WO 158/35 No 2. Haig's diary NLS AC 3155 No 118 (Entry for October 21). The daylight raids had surprising impunity to interception with only one recorded on 26 September. Rawlinson informed Haig on 21 October that his headquarters had been bombed so often he was moving. From late October *Kagohl 3* replaced *Kagohl 4* which went to Italy.

38. Henshaw:194. Hoeppner:121.; Jones *IV*:146–149. *Weltkrieg XIII*:56–58, 309. *Nachrichtenblätter 21/1917* (19 July), *26/1917* (23 August).UKNA Air 1/2247/209/43/7. *Kagohl 4*'s AEGs were augmented by single-engined Rumplers and DFWs UKNA WO 157/24. *Kagohl 1* supported the *4. Armee* reaction forces on July 31. *Nachrichtenblatt 24/1917* (August 9).

39. *Weltkrieg XIII*:310. Quote from UKNA Air 1/1188/204/5/2595. The work of the "*Infanterie-Schlachtflieger*" in supporting the reaction forces was praised in a *4. Armee* post-action report. *Nachrichtenblatt 24/1917*. *JG I* escorted *Kagohl 1* on a 15 August bombing mission and the following day covered a ground-attack mission. VanWyngarden, *JG I*:33.

40. Bean *1917*:777, 803, 822. Edmonds *1917/II*:260. Wise:435. UKNA WO 95/984, WO 95/1051, WO 157/118. Imperial War Museum Accession Number 45104. A counter-attack by *17.Infanterie Division* on 1 October was supported by "*Schlachtstaffel 24*" of *Kagohl 4*. *Nachrichtenblatt 33/1917* (11 October).

41. UKNA Air1/522/16/12/5.

42. Wise:435. UKNA WO95/1051. Haig repeated Trenchard's words and added: "In fact there is no other way of stopping them." NLS AC 3155 No 119 (2 November).

43. UKNA Air 1/61/15/9/72 Air 1/61/15/9/75. Air 1/769/204/4/255–257, Air 1/770/204/4/258–259. In June 1917 Lambe renewed his friendship with "Billy" Mitchell which began in China. Mitchell:125.

44. Hoeppner:119. UKNA Air 1/2220/209/40/9.

45. UKNA Air 1/2230/209/41/10–11.No 57 Squadron flew 198 sorties during July of which a third were reconnaissance missions. UKNA Air 1/1496/204/39/5.

46. Jones. *War in the Air IV*:129, 161,163, 166Appendix VII. Slessor:107. UKNA Air1/522/16/12/5. Air 1/769/204/4/255.

47. Jones *IV*:175–176, 182. UKNA Air 1/522/16/12/5. Air 1/769/204/4/257.

48. Yeates:37. Yeates completed a tour in 1918 having flown 248 hours in Camels during which he was twice shot down and crashed four times. Henshaw:192–250. Bailey & Cony:135–173.

49. UKNA Air 1/2230/209/41/9–11. Air1/2221/209/40/10–12.

50. Edmonds *1917/II*:138 n.2. Jones *IV*:118–119, 124–125,145, Map IV Appendix IV. Wise:419.

51. Edmonds *1917/II*:136. UKNA Air 1/918/204/5/879. Air 1/2220/209/40/8.

52. Edmonds *1917/II* :134. Bean *1917*:704. *Weltkrieg XIII*:61. Farndale:201 describes the German bombardments as "Gusts of fire and gas."

53. Jones *IV*:136–137. UKNA Air 1/918/204/5/879.

54. Jones *IV*:213–219. UKNA Air 1/918/204/5/879 (See Carthew to Game August 22, 1917).

55. Jones *IV*: 151–152, 213–219. UKNA Air 1/918/204/5/879. The brigade providing a radio link between artillery aircraft and the sound ranging system to improve the latter's effectiveness. The British exploitation of technology made their counter-battery techniques the deadliest on the Western Front.

56. Jefford. *Observers and Navigators*:52–53, 95.

57. Edmonds *1917/II*:273 n 2, 319 n. Jones *IV*: 174 n 1,202. UKNA Air 1/769/204/4/257. Air 1/918/204/5/879.

58. Hoeppner:114. *Weltkrieg XIII*:60–61. UKNA Air 1/2229/209/41/7. WO 157/22.WO 158/35 No 2.

59. Hoeppner:117–118. Neumann:427–428, 480–481. Schwarte:284. *Weltkrieg XII*:9, 9 n 2.

60. Edmonds *1917/II*:249. Jones *IV*:150–152. UKNA Air 1/2230/209/41/9. WO 157/25 (22 October). From December 1917 British aircraft also co-operated with heavy mortars.

61. Quote from Edmonds *1917/II* :170 n 1. See also Edmonds *1917/II*:169. Jones *IV*:126, 161–162. NLS Acc 3155 No 116.

62. Jones *IV*:182, 184–186. UKNA Air 1/769/204/4/256. Air 1/2229/209/41/8. Air 1/2220/209/40/9.

63. Bülow:94–95. Hoeppner:116–117. Neumann:428. UKNA Air 1/1188/204/5/2595 (2 July, 1 August, 15 August). Killed on a contact patrol during the Ypres campaign on 13 July was *Leutnant* Peter von Ustinov, uncle of film star Peter Ustinov. Ustinov:22–23.

64. Franks et al. *Casualties*:226–237, 351–355. UKNA Air 1/2230/209/41/9–10. WO 157/24 (German aviation section for week ending September 26).

65. UKNA Air 1/769/204/4/255–257, 1/770/204/4/258–259.

66. UKNA Air 1/881/204/5/593. WO 158/35 No 2.
67. Bailey & Cony: *French Air Service*:135–173. Franks et al. *Over the Front*:89. UKNA Air 1/881/204/5/593 includes a map of the French boundaries.
68. UKNA Air 1/522/16/12/5.Guynemer's death on 11 September, possibly at the hands of a DFW C.V observer, was partly due to combat fatigue, exacerbated by two forced landings due to engine failure the previous day. Guttman:63–65.
69. Personal files 14742, 15345, 15112, 14745 copies of which were kindly provided by Major Bernard Cambrelin of the Defensie Stafdepartement Intlichtingen en Veiligheid, Divisie Veiligheid. As a Major-General Crombrugge he would command the post-war Belgian air force until 1926. On 31 July the AMB had 77 aircraft and nine French Caudrons of C74 MRAHM. Aviation Aerostation Rapports Journaliers.
70. Pieters: 21, 100–101, 112–113. The King's pilot on 6 July, Count Jacques de Meeus, was shot down and killed nine days later by fighters. King Albert twice flew with No 48 Squadron RFC. Bruce. *British Aeroplanes*:134.
71. *Armées Françaises V/2*:646, 705.
72. For Malmaison see *Les Armées Françaises V/2*:911–1111. *Weltkrieg XIII*:109–124. Pedroncini:100–108.
73. Pedroncini: 41, 57.
74. *Armées Françaises V/2*:Annexes 542, 629 758. Pedroncini:59.
75. Barnett:279. Morrow:200. Pedroncini:58–59.
76. SHAT 142.056. Peuty's personal file was examined for me by Ms Laura Soyer.
77. Morrow:208–214. Façon's article in Fana de l'Aviation 348.
78. For air operations see *Armées Françaises X/1*:VI Armée. *Armées Françaises V/2*:945. Bailey & Cony:162–169. Hoeppner:122–123. *Nachrichtenblätter 33–37/1917* (October 11–November 8). SHAA A20 Dossier 2. SHAT 18N171, 19N412, 19N1124. I am again deeply indebted to Christophe Cony for details of Gérard.
79. American airmen later claimed AR (Avion de Réconnaissance) stood for "Antique Rattletrap". Davilla & Soltan:46.
80. *Armées Françaises V/2*:996, 1015. Franks et al. *Jasta Pilots*:14. *Weltkrieg XIII*:115. SHAT 19N412. 19N1124.
81. Hoeppner:123. *Weltkrieg XIII*:115 claims Stahr had only 17 squadrons including four *Kasta* with 200 aircraft, but this may refer to those closest to the battlefield. Loewenstern: Anlage 8 provides a detailed order of battle. Stahr would be the first commander of the secret Lipetsk base in Russia where German pilots were trained and new combat aircraft developed during the 1920s.
82. Fischer: 104. Neumann:444. SHAT 19N412. 19N1124.
83. SHAA A20/2. SHAT 19N412. 19N1124.
84. *Armées Françaises V/2*:1022. Bailey & Cony:162–169. Hoeppner:123. SHAT 18N171.19N412.19N1124. The after-action report SHAT 18N171 gives French aircrew losses in the second half of October included 12 killed, 2 missing, 16 wounded and 12 injured in accidents.
85. Farndale:216–217.
86. For Cambrai see Miles *1917/III*. Strutz:132–144.
87. For air operations see Hoeppner:123–124. Jones *IV*:227–259, Appendices X–XI. Wise:441–447. *Nachrichtenblätter 40–41/1917* (29 November-6 December). UKNA Air 1/2240/209/42/10–12. Air 1/2215/209/30/19–20. Air 1/678/21/13/1942.
88. Farndale:218. Henshaw. *Sky their Battlefield*:246.Jefford *Squadrons*: Nos 3, 46, 68 Squadrons. Jones *IV*:231. UKNA Air 1/2240/209/42/11.
89. Jones *IV*:Appendix IX. UKNA Air 1/2240/209/42/10. For criticism of the plans see Slessor:91.
90. Farndale:219. Miles *1917/III*:27. Jones *IV*:Appendix IX.
91. Franks et al.*Jasta Pilots*:19, 30 & *Chronology*:104,113. Hoeppner:123. Jones *IV*:231. Miles *1917/III*:36, 40, 42–43, 46. UKNA Air1/2240/209/42/10–11.
92. Henshaw:252–254. Jones *IV*:232–234. Neumann:96–100. UKNA Air 1/770/204/4/259.Air 1/2240/209/42/11.
93. *Weltkrieg XIII*:311. UKNA Air 1/770/204/4/259.
94. Franks et al. *Chronology*:118–119. Jones *IV*:245, 247–249. Quote from Miles *1917/III*:167.
95. Hoeppner:128–134. Jones *IV*: 236, 239,244–245, Appendix XI, Map 8. Miles *1917/III*:101–119. Slessor:109. Strutz: 21.

96. At the end of the first day of 72 serviceable fighters nine were missing, four had crashed and 13 were damaged, a total of 36%. See Henshaw:252–254. Jones *IV*:239 n 2. Miles *1917/III*: 90 n 1. UKNA Air1/678/21/13/1942. Air 1/2240/209/42/11.

97. Henshaw:255–256. Jones *IV*:241, 241 n 1, 245, 250. UKNA PRO Air 1/770/204/4/259. Air 1/2240/209/42/11.

98. Strutz:Anlage. UKNA Air 1/2240/209/42/11.

99. Jones *IV*:252. Miles *1917/III*:202. Strutz:Anlage.

100. Miles *1917/III*: 187,204.

101. Franks et al. *Casualties*:238, 355.Henshaw:258–259. Jones *IV*:255. UKNA Air 1/770/204/4/260. Air 1/2240/209/42/11.

102. Franks et al. *Casualties*:237–238, 355. Henshaw:252–261.

103. Franks et al. *Jasta Pilots*:81. Hoeppner:124–125. *Weltkrieg XIII*:191,Beilage 29. UKNA Air 1/2255/209/58/4 (19 September).

104. Bülow:100–102. Franks et al. *Casualties*:234–255, 354–359. Henshaw:482–484. Hoeppner:118–121. Franco-British casualties were light; the RFC lost only 16 aircraft and 16 aircrew in combat during the same period.

105. Hoeppner:123–124. Schwarte:287, 299. *Weltkrieg XIII*:309.

Chapter Six

1. *Weltkrieg XIV*:41.

2. Edmonds *1918/1*:135–160.*Weltkrieg XIV*:26–99.

3. Edmonds *1918/1*:106. *Weltkrieg* op cit.

4. For "*Michael/Mars*" see Clayton: 162–167; Edmonds *1918/1*:161–537 & *1918/2*:1–137. Herwig:402. *Armée Françaises VI/1*:268–427. *Weltkrieg XIV*:100–259; J.H.Johnson:27–43.

5. Johnson. *1918*:48–53.

6. Macdonald:257–258; 277–279.

7. Edmonds *1918/2*:481.

8. Edmonds *1918/2*:121–137, 489–490, 261 n 2. *Armées Francaise VI/1*:522. Herwig:408–409, 414. *Weltkrieg XIV*:Beilage 42. Rawlinson replaced Gough.

9. For the Battle of the Lys see *Armées Française VI/1*:429–524. Edmonds *1918/2*:138–490. Johnson.*1918*:55–63. *Weltkrieg XIV*:270–300. Also Tournès & Berthement.

10. Edmonds *1918/1*:183. Franks et al *Casualties*:256. Sulzbach:166. Pernert and his observer were shot down on 22 March and, officially, he was missing. In a rare human gesture Ludendorff issued a request for information on 23 April. Sulzbach, a gunner with *9.Infanteriedivision*, reported discovering the airmen's graves and the body was identified by Hindenburg who knew Pernert.

11. Hoeppner:147. For the text see Jones *IV*:441, Appendix 13.

12. Hoeppner:147. *Weltkrieg XIV*:41. For differences between the *Jagdgeschwader* and *Jagdgruppe* see Hauptmann Rudolf Berthold's description (VanWyngarden *JG II*:36)

13. Jones *IV*:Appendix 12.

14. Jones *IV*:Appendix 14. UKNA Air 1/675/21/13/1422. Haig's diary NLS AC 3155 No 123 (10 January). Trenchard had wanted to remain both Chief of the Air Staff and commander of the RAF in France.

15. 54 Wing also contained the Special Duty Flight. Jones *IV*:272 n2.

16. *Armée Françaises VI/1*:167–168, 168 n2, Annex 324, 363, 452. Christienne & Lissarague:123–125. Davilla & Soltan:502. Franks & Bailey:86. NLS AC 3155 No123. Trenchard and Salmond told Haig on 25 February that since Peuty's departure the Aviation Militaire Française morale had declined as it became more "defensive".

17. *Armée Françaises VI/1*: 168, Annex 416. Christienne & Lissarague:100,314. Franks & Bailey:85, 91, 94, 206. Voisin:67n2. The 13e Escadre de Bombardement was not formed until the arrival of GB 4 from Lorraine.

18. Laffin:1–99. *Quarterly Army Lists:30 June 1914* & *30 September 1919*.

19. NLS AC 3155 No 123 (22 January, 26 January, 25 February).

20. Boyle:126, 132–135, 149, 243.Laffin:1–99.

21. This and the following biographies are based upon *Quarterly Army Lists:30 June 1914* & *30 September 1919* as well as www.rafweb.org/Biographies.

22. One of Edwards' corps squadrons was under Major Trafford Leigh-Mallory.
23. Edmonds *1918/1*:155. Herwig:392–393,397. Hoeppner:147, 151–152. Macdonald:68, 80–82.
24. Shores et al *Above the Trenches*:296–297.Jones *IV*:287–290. UKNA Air 1/995/204/5/1229. Air 1/2222/209/40/14–17. Air 1/2241/209/42/13–15. WO 95/521. WO 157/26. The records show there was more enemy activity opposite 3rd Army than its neighbour. The first V Brigade combat upon returning to the Somme involved the New Zealand flight commander of No 48 Squadron Captain Keith Park, ultimately an Air Chief Marshal who distinguished himself in the defence both of England and Malta.
25. Kilduff *Combat Wing*:177. Südingen:133. VanWyngarden. *JG 1*:69. *Weltkrieg XIV*: 42, 104. Luftmacht *Teil I*:33, 35. UKNA Air 1/675/21/13/1422. Marwitz and Below had 15 balloons each while Hutier had 18. The preparations boosted morale through-out the *Luftstreitkräfte* even in *JG I*. VanWyngarden, *JG I*:65
26. Occleshaw:135. Edmonds *1918/1*:95, 95 n 3. Jones *IV*:265 n 1 noted the combat could not be identified.
27. Hoeppner:151.
28. Edmonds *1918/1*:108–109. Farndale: 260. Jones *IV*:264–269. Jefford *Squadrons* (No 25 Squadron entry). Laffin:103–104. NLS AC 3155 No 124. On 24 February Salmond briefed brigade commanders on his plans for the forthcoming offensive.
29. Franks et al. *Casualties*:359. Jones *IV*:269. UKNA Air 1/2241/209/42/15.Air 1/2222/209/40/17.
30. Jones *IV*:271, Appendix XV.
31. Edmonds *1918/1*:100–101. Jones *IV*:277–286. Neumann:446. VanWyngarden. *JG I*:66–68. UKNA Air 1/838/204/5/287. Air 1/2215/209/30/23. Air 1/2222/209/40/14–17. Air 1/2241/209/42/13–15. Air 1/2249/209/46/3
32. Edmonds *1918/1*:116 n.2, 118. UKNA Air 1/838/204/5/287.
33. Jones. *War in the Air IV*:263. UKNA Air 1/675/21/13/1422 (Appendix III)
34. For the air campaign see Bailey & Cony:201–208. Bülow:103–110. Christienne & Lissarrague:125. Franks et al. *Casualties*:255–260,360–361. & *Chronology*:148–158. Henshaw:284–307. Hoeppner:153–157. Jones *IV*:292–365. Laffin:104–114. Martel:300–302, 315–322. Mortane:376–390. Ritter:138–140. VanWyngarden. JG I: 66–71.Voisin:91–119. Wise:488–510. *Luftmacht Teil 1 & 2*. *Nachrichtenblätter 5–7/1918* (28 March-11 April). UKNA Air1/475/15/312/201. Air 1/675/21/13/1422. Air 1/838/204/5/287. Air 1/2179/209/14/36–37. Air 1/2215/209/30/23.Air 1/2222/209/40/16–17. Air1/2241/209/42/15. Air 1/2249/209/46/3. SHAA A128 Dossier 2. Many of the RAF's war diaries for April are missing.
35. Laffin:102. Maurer *I*:325–326. UKNA Air1/475/15/312/201.
36. Jones. *War in the Air IV*:354–357. Laffin. *Swifter than Eagles*: 111. UKNA Air1/475/15/312/201 Brooke-Popham, the first man in the RFC to arm his aircraft, became Controller of Aircraft Production in April and remained in the RAF after the war becoming the first commandant of both the RAF Staff College and the Imperial Defence College. He held many senior posts in the 1920s and 1930s before becoming the RAF Commander-in-Chief at Singapore in November 1940. After captivity in Japan he remained in public life following the Second World War and died in 1953.
37. UKNA Air1/475/15/312/201
38. Ibid.
39. Edmonds *1918/1*:169. Jones *IV*:320–327. UKNA Air1/475/15/312/201.For Game's comparison of Trenchard with Salmond see Laffin:120.
40. *Armées Française VI/1*:253–254, *Annex 1 Volume 1*:558–560. Voisin:68.
41. *Armées Française VI/1*:247, 253, 394. Davilla & Soltan:111. Franks et al. *Chronology*:148–158. SHAA A128/2. Some sources suggest *Jasta 56's Vizefeldwebel* Weimar, who was captured after his Albatros D.V was shot down by No 60 Squadron on 1 April was the first man to bail out of a plane in combat, but this honour is usually assigned *Vizefeldwebel* Helmut Steinbrecher of *Jasta 16* who jumped from his burning Albatros D.V near Albert on 27 June. Parachutes were used by a few German fighter pilots in 1918 but were denied Allied aircrew for a variety of obscure reasons. The German parachutes were no panacea and in about a third of cases they failed. For parachutes see Franks et al. *Chronology*:156, 196, 205–207, 214,223, 227,243,244, 254, 260, 261, 269, 273, 281 & *Jasta Pilots*:292. Morrow:239. *Nachrichtenblatt 20/18* (July 11).
42. Voisin:*La Doctrine d"Aviation Française*:100–102, 109 n1.

43. UKNA Air 1/9/15/1/26. *Grufl 2, Oberleutnant* Eberhard Milch, later the *Luftwaffe's* second-in-command, was praised by Hoeppner. *Nachrichtenblatt 8/1918* (18 April).
44. Hoeppner:156.The *4.Armee* war diary covering *Unternehmen "Georgette"* has references to air operations without mentioning the *Kofl.* Tournès & Berthement. *Le Bataille de Flandres.*
45. Bülow:104, 109. Edmonds *1918/1*:Maps 1, 12. Kilduff. *Combat Wing*:185–186 & *Richthofen*:189. Maurer *I*:325–326. VanWyngarden. *JG 1*:70–71, 78
46. Edmonds *1918/1*:500 & *1918/2*:89–90. UKNA Air 1/475/15/312/201.
47. Edmonds *1918/1*: 168–169, 472. Jones. *War in the Air IV*:320, 323–324. Laffin:103.Maurer *I*:325–326.Yeates:158. UKNA Air 1/838/204/5/287. Air 1/2179/209/14/36–37. Air 1/2222/209/40/16–17. Air 1/2241/209/42/15.
48. Edmonds *1918/1*:168–169. UKNA Air1/475/15/312/201. Air 1/675/21/13/1422. Air 1/2215/209/30/23. Air 1/2222/209/40/16–17. Air 1/2241/209/42/15. April figures based upon UKNA Air 1/9/15/1/32/1.
49. Edmonds *1918/1*:163 & 163 n 2. Jones*IV*:294.
50. UKNA Air 1/2222/209/40/16–17.
51. Davilla & Soltan:111. Martel:317. Voisin:98.
52. SHAA A128/2.UKNA Air 1/2222/209/40/16–17. Air /2249/209/46/3. Salmond informed Haig on 2 April his airmen had dropped 307 tons (312 tonnes) of bombs from 21 March to 1April. NLS AC 3155 No125.
53. Edmonds *1918/1*:419. UKNA Air1/475/15/312/201.
54. Goes. *Der Tag X*:124. Jones. *War in the Air IV*:316. The unfortunate officer run over was in *III.Armeekorps.*
55. *Weltkrieg XIV*:218, 221. *Nachrichtenblatt 6/1918* (4 April).
56. Bean *1918*: 170, 279n78, 283–284, 291. Macdonald:254.Sulzbach:154, 158–159. *Weltkrieg XIV*:174, 185, 192, 196, 207–208,210. Wise:509. Horses suffered especially during both sides' air raids because they were literally large, standing, targets.
57. Edmonds *1918/1*:259.Franks et al. *Casualties*:255–260, 360–361. *Above the Lines*:67–68. Neumann.453–455. *Nachrichtenblatt 8/1918* (April 15). Bauer later became Hitler's personal pilot. Guttman: 108.
58. Edmonds. *France and Belgium 1918/1*:245, 508. In an after-action report Lieutenant-Colonel J.Hunt, who led an ad hoc task force in 5th Army, noted: "Had the enemy's aircraft been active, enormous damage could have been done... as every road was blocked with traffic and infantry marched through the fields." UKNA WO95/521.
59. Edmonds. *France and Belgium 1918/1*:245,345.*Weltkrieg XIV*:183–184.
60. Edmonds *1918/1*:289 & *1918/2*:70 n 4. Franks et al. *Casualties*:3
61. Slessor:93.
62. Quote from Edmonds *1918/1*:1 167–168.
63. Edmonds *1918/1*:391.Henshaw:284–291. UKNA Air1/475/15/312/201. Air 1/2222/209/40/16.
64. Edmonds *1918/1*:313, 334, 347. Hoeppner:150, 155. *Luftmacht. Teil 3*:40. On 21 March balloons were a *Jasta* priority target (VanWyngarden. *JG 1*:70)
65. Edmonds *1918/1*:405. Jones *IV*:295. Macdonald:221–222. UKNA Air 1/2222/209/40/16.
66. *Weltkrieg XIV*: 149,185, 207–208, 210–211.
67. Franks et al. *Jasta War Chronology*:148–158. Maurer.*US Air Service/I*:325. VanWyngarden. *JG 1*:71, 79. American pilot Lieutenant Frank Baylies of GC 12 returned to his airfield to find it in enemy hands and barely escaped (Guttman: 95–96)
68. Bailey & Cony 201–208. Henshaw:284–307. While 42% of Hutier's fighter victories were over two-seaters in the other armies the figure was 27%.
69. Henshaw:284–307. Franks et al. *Casualties*:255–260, 360–361. *Weltkrieg XIV*: Beilage 40. *Luftmacht Teil 3*:38. UKNA Air 1/1595/204/83/28. Air 1/2386/228/9/1 NLS AC 3155 No 125. With the absence of many records for April the estimate of sorties is based upon the figures for March. It should be noted that V Brigade appears to have flown more than 1,000 sorties from 1 – 7 April. During March and April 944 aircraft were wrecked in accidents. Salmond informed Haig on 2 April that his airmen claimed 220 aircraft destroyed and 112 driven down out of control from 21 March to 1 April.

70. Jones *IV*: 371–372, Appendix XIX. *Weltkrieg XIV*:270. UKNA Air 1/471/15/312/203. Some Portuguese airmen served on the Western Front, mostly with French squadrons reflecting the long links between the two countries, although a few observers were attached to British corps squadrons supporting Portuguese divisions.

71. For the air campaign see Bailey & Cony:208–215. Bülow:118. Franks et al. *Casualties*:260–265,361–363. & *Chronology*:159–165. Henshaw:307–318. Hoeppner:157–158. Jones *IV*:366–404. Martel:322–327. Mortane:390–401.Wise:511–517. *Luftmacht Teil 3*:38–44. *Nachrichtenblätter 8–11/1918* (18 April – 9 May). SHAA A128/2.UKNA Air 1/9/15/1/32/1. Air 1/2179/209/14/37–38. Air 1/2237/209/41/28. British records are noticeably sparse.

72. Edmonds *1918/2*:164–192. Henshaw:307. UKNA Air 1/9/15/1/32/1. Air 1/2237/209/41/28. The Americans claim British ground attacks were less intense than during *"Michael/Mars"*. Maurer *I*:328.

73. Edmonds *1918/2*:193–221.Tournès & Berthement:62. *Luftmacht. Teil 3*:41–42. The only German complaint about Allied air attacks refers to *6.Armee* on 20 April *Weltkrieg XIV*:289. A *Schlasta 37* attack on enemy communications is mentioned in *Nachrichtenblatt 9/1918* (25 April).

74. Edmonds *1918/2*:254, 266, 284–287. VanWyngarden *JG II*:30–32. *Luftmacht Teil 3*.42. SHAA A128/2. UKNA Air 1/2117/207/59/1. The French maintained pressure on the Somme front dropping 38.5 tonnes of bombs by 21 April. On 12 April *4. Armee* war diary noted enemy aircraft were very active while that night *Bogohl 3* dropped 11.75 tonnes of bombs Tournès & Berthement:74, 93.

75. UKNA Air 1/2153/209/3/304. The Government proposed Trenchard replace Salmond, but Trenchard indignantly rejected this although he did write to Haig on 14 April seeking a command under him Boyle. *Trenchard*:276. NLS AC 3155 No 125.

76. Franks et al. *Casualties*:260–265, 361–363. Henshaw:307–318. *Weltkrieg XIV*:Beilage 40. UKNA Air1/476/15/312/217.

77. Franks et al. *Chronology*:159–164 & *Jasta Pilots*: 319–322, 351. Maurer *I*:328.

78. Edmonds *1918/2*: 366, 381–408, 453. Franks et al. *Above the lines*:189. Tournès & Berthement:295. VanWyngarden. *JG 1*:79.*Weltkrieg XIV*:294. *Luftmacht. Teil 3*:40, 43. On 21 April seven long range reconnaissance flights brought valuable insight for *OHL* into the strategic situation. On 25 May the British shot down *Vizefeldwebel* Karl Koller of *Jasta 76* who would become the *Luftwaffe's* last chief of staff.

79. *Nachrichtenblätter 7/1918* (April 11), *8/1918* (April 18), *14/1918* (May 30).

80. Yeates:112–115. Yeates probably based this on his own experience after being forced down on March 25 while serving with No 46 Squadron. Henshaw:291. Bolling was a visionary who was once considered as a leader for AEF aviation. Cooke:18, 23–24, 27. Sloan:199.

81. Henshaw:284–335. Sloan:49–53, 56–59, 61–63, 194–199, 211–217.

82. UKNA Air 1/2267/209/70/46.

83. The best study of this period is Herbert Johnson's *Wingless Eagle* (hereafter Johnson Eagle), which noted: "The years 1907 through 1918 were a time of failure..." For the early USAS see Johnson: *Wingless Eagle*:9,68, 116–135, 137–138, 152–156. Cooke:2–12, 21. Foulois & Glines:179, 184. Treadwell:13,20–21. Francisco "Pancho" Villa's airmen were trained by American Edwin C. "Ted" Parsons who later flew with the Escadrille Lafayette and transferred to the US Air Service in February 1918. He would have a varied post-war career before joining the US Navy's aviation arm and retiring as a rear admiral in 1954 (Guttman:115). One of those monitoring the Western Front, and a former head of the Aviation Section, was Major George O. Squier who was afraid of flying and became Pershing's Chief Signal Officer.

84. Cooke:19, 21–23. Hurley:28–29. Johnson: *Wingless Eagle*:167–168, 186.

85. For Mitchell see Hudson:4, 46–49. Hurley:2–28. Johnson: *Wingless Eagle*:136–137. Lengel: 72–73.Mitchell:27,116, 150–151, 171, 210–211.Mitchell did not actually receive his "wings" until September 1917. Mitchell was the first to propose an airborne operation but see Layman's article in Cross & Cockade.

86. Cooke:3. Johnson *Wingless Eagle*:23, 24, 41, 61, 63, 71, 118, 130, 135.

87. Cooke:80. Hudson:52–56.Hurley:33–34. Mitchell:165–166. Johnson: *Wingless Eagle*:135–137.

88. For this campaign see *Armées Française VI/2*:65–259. Clayton: 168–169. Edmonds *1918/3*:1–46, 69–72, 98. Greenwood:45–56. Johnson.*1918*:64–76.*Weltkrieg XIV*:311–392.

89. Davilla & Soltan:15–17, 137. Maurer *I*:171–195, 283–288. Early in May the 103rd Aero Squadron was attached to DAN.

90. *Armée Françaises VI/2*:Annex 186. SHAA A22 Dossier 1. Also information from Christophe Cony. Duval was promoted Général in April and his tenure as commander of the DAé was always intended to be temporary and he remained Pétain's air chief. Poli Marchetti would hold senior positions in the post-war air force.
91. Ménard and Féquant lost 100 dead and missing from 21 March – 18 May. Voisin:119. UKNA Air 1/476/15/312/217.
92. Bailey & Cony:217–219. Shores et al *Above the Trenches*:79. UKNA 1/2154/209/3/309. Air /1899/204/227/6. X Armée sent aircraft to British airfields to improve recognition. Blaxland was posted to a training squadron but returned to the front in the autumn. The other pilots were apparently merely reprimanded. Armengaud, who remained in the French air force after the war and retired in 1936 as a general, would lead the French aviation mission with the AEF. Cooke:77,121.
93. *Armées Française X*:VI Armée entry. Davilla & Soltan:15–17. SHAT 19N1124. *Luftmacht Teil 3*:47. *Schlachtgruppen A* and *B* each consisted of three *Schlasta* from *Schlachtgeschwader A* and *B* while *Schlachtgruppe C* was a new unit half of whose four *Staffeln* had supported *17.Armee* during *"Michael"*.
94. *Armées Françaises VI/2*:86. Edmonds *1918/3*:1–46, 69–72. *Luftmacht Teil 3*:47. SHAT 19N124. UKNA Air 1/675/21/13/1265. German airmen began monitoring their security preparations from 10 May and most squadrons reached their airfields only hours before the attack.
95. Franks et al. *Chronology*:169–177. *Luftmacht Teil 3*:47.SHAT 19N124.
96. For the air campaign see *Armée Françaises VI/2*:Annexes 331–331, 1128, 1171, 1172. Bailey & Cony:227–243. Bülow:120. Christienne & Lissarrague:127. Franks et al. *Casualties*:273–278, 366–367 & *Chronology*:177–186. Henshaw:331–338. Hoeppner:161. Jones *VI*:397–400. Lowenstern: 213–217. Marte:335–345. Mortane:401–426. Voisin:120–128. *Luftmacht Teil 3*:47–50. *Nachrichtenblätter 14–16 /1918* (30 May-13 June). SHAA A115 Dossier 2. SHAT 18N174 Dossier 1. SHAT 19N124. SHAT 19N1124. UKNA Air 1/675/21/13/1265.
97. UKNA Air 1/675/21/13/1265.The squadron lost two RE 8s and their crews to French fighters. Most of the squadron's losses are not confirmed in Henshaw:332. At Magneux the Germans captured 25 aircraft, 10 of them undamaged. *Nachrichtenblatt18 /1918* (27 June).
98. *Armée Françaises VI/2*:111–112, 150, Annex 331.Christienne & Lissarrague:127. Davilla & Soltan:15–17, 111, 504–507. *Luftmacht. Teil 3*:49.
99. Christienne & Lissarrague:127. Davilla & Soltan:168–169. Franks & Bailey: 225. Lamberton. *Reconnaissance and Bomber Aircraft*:82. Martel:342.Sulzbach:181. Voisin:120–128. On 31 May alone Ménard flew 223 sorties and dropped 37.75 tonnes of bombs. Vuillemin became Chief of the French Air Staff from 1938 to 1940 and has been unfairly criticized by many historians. But see Hooton *Phoenix*:164–165.
100. Franks et al. *Jasta Pilots*:321 and *Jasta* entries. VanWyngarden *JG II*:45–46
101. Bailey & Cony. *Chronology*:227–243. SHAA A128/2 (No figures for Ménard on June 4). A115/2. SHAT 18N174/1.
102. Franks et al. *Casualties*:273–278, 366–368. *Weltkrieg XIV*: Beilage 40. *Luftmacht Teil 3*:50.*Weltkrieg* shows only 60 aircraft lost by *7.Armee* between 27 May and 18 June. The French lost 97 aircraft from 27 May – 15 June. *Armée Françaises VI/2*:349.
103. VanWyngarden *JG I*:87–88, 91 & *JG II*:45.
104. For this battle see *Armées Française VI/2*:261–348. Clayton:169. Edmonds *1918/3*:172–182. Greenwood:57–62; Johnson. *1918*:77–79. *Weltkrieg XIV*:393–411.
105. *Armée Françaises VI/2*:251, 293. Jones *VI*: 401–402. Martel:345 Porch:110–111. VanWyngarden *JG I*:90. *Weltkrieg XIV*:397. UKNA Air 1/2249/209/46/5.
106. For the air campaign see Bailey & Cony:240–243. Christienne & Lissarrague:128. Franks et al. *Casualties*:278–279, 367–368 & *Chronology*:186–189. Henshaw:338–341. Hoeppner:161–162. Jones *VI*:400–405. Martel:345–346. Maurer *I*:328–330. Mortane:408–426. VanWyngarden *JG II*:50, 65.Voisin:135–139.*Luftmacht. Teil 3*:50–51. *Nachrichtenblätter16–17 /1918* (13 June – 20 June). SHAA A128/2. A115/2. SHAT 18N174/1. UKNA Air 1/2249/209/46/5.
107. *Armée Françaises VI/2*:332. Maurer *I*:328. Jones *VI*:404. SHAA A115/2. A128/2.SHAT 18N174/1. UKNA Air 1/1899/204/227/6. Air 1/1923/204/238/6. Air 1/2154/209/3/309.Air 1/2249/209/46/5. American claims the RAF carried an excessive burden are incorrect for Ménard's men actually dropped 68% of the bomb tonnage and flew about half the sorties. The French expended 60,000 rounds strafing the enemy on 11 June alone.

108. Greenwood:58.
109. Morrow:283–284. SHAA A13 Dossier 1.
110. Maurer *I*:328.
111. Gray *Fokker D.VII*.Kilduff *Combat Wing*:211–212, 220. VanWyngarden *JG I*:87, 92.
112. For the "eulogistic propaganda" surrounding the fighter see Gray & Thetford:193. Grosz. *Pfalz D XII*:8. The seven aces were Britain's Lieutenant Frederick Hunt, Americans Captain Clayton A. Bissel and Lieutenant Howard C. Knotts on the British front and Captain Charles R. D'Olive with Lieutenants Harold H. George, Murray K.Guthrie and Frank K. Hays on the Franco-American front. Bissel would command 10th Air Force in China during the Second World War to become Chennault's bête noir. In the case of 11 pilots on the British front (including two Americans) the figure includes Out of Control claims. Shores et al. *Above the Trenches*: 78–79, 97,167–168,192–193, 204, 227, 312, 329–330, 348, 355–356. Franks & Bailey: 22,35, 38–39, 43, 72–73.
113. Davilla & Soltan:505.
114. Franks et al. *Casualties*:278–279, 368 (Matz only). Morrow:298.*Weltkrieg XIV*: Beilage 40.
115. Morrow: 300. VanWyngarden *JG I*:Caption 93 & *JG II*:68,71–72.
116. *Weltkrieg XIV*:516 n.2.

Chapter Seven

1. For the "*Friedensturm*" see *Armée Françaises VI/ 2*:369–444. Edmonds *1918/3*:221–310. Greenwood:63–92. *Weltkrieg XIV*:312–465. Johnson. *1918*:79–84.
2. Greenwood:65. Porch:111.Berthelot and Gourard were under Maistre's GAC. Mitry, Mangin's X Armée and Degoutte's VI Armée were under Fayolle's GAR.
3. The Italian II Corps was supported by a French squadron BR235. Davilla & Soltan:109.
4. *Armée Françaises VI/2*:445–544 and *VII/1*:1–15. Edmonds *1918/4*:1–8.Greenwood:100–190. *Weltkrieg XIV*:466–505.
5. Edmonds *1918/3*:189–192.
6. Jones *VI*:412–413. UKNA Air 1/2249/209/46/5. Air 1/2268/209/70/195. Record books of Nos 27, 49, 98 and 107 Squadrons. IV Armée army squadrons flew 57 long range photo-reconnaissance and two night reconnaissance missions between 1 June and 15 July.
7. Patrick Façon's article in Fana de l'Aviation. SHAA A13 Dossier 1.
8. Morrow: 67, 93–94, 283, 376. SHAA A13/1.Goÿs died in 1933.
9. *Armée Françaises VI/2*:421, 454, Annex 1961. Jones *VI*:412. Bloch's men were also to radio reports of enemy air activity.
10. *Armée Françaises VI/2*:463, 475. Maurer *I*:197, 291.
11. Franks et al. *Jasta Pilots*:319–323. VanWyngarden *JG II*: 76.*Weltkrieg XIV*:544. *Luftmacht Teil 4*:53. The 7., 1. and 3. *Armees* were supported by *Bogohl 2, 5* and *1* respectively. A dozen *Jasta* were assembled for "*Hagen*" in *Jagdgruppen 3* and 6. On 14 July *JG II* received 20 Fokker D.VII allowing the Geschwader for the first time to have aircraft of only one type. VanWyngarden *JG II*: 76–77
12. *Weltkrieg XIV*:Beilage 40. SHAA A128. Dossier 2. UKNA Air 1/476/15/312/217. The last shows the British dropped 256 tonnes during the same period.
13. For the Marne air battles see *Armée Françaises VI/2*:491, Annexes 1861, 1978, 2045, 2218, 2220. Bailey & Cony: 260–264. Bülow:120–122. Christienne & Lissarague:128. Cooke:98–117. Davilla & Soltan:112, 137, 565. Franks et al *Casualties*:287–289,370–371 & *Chronology*:204–207. Henshaw:355–356. Hoeppner:162–163. Hudson:90–118. Jones *VI*:414. Martel:350–363. Maurer *I*:197–219, 291–299. Voisin:139–144. *Luftmacht Teil 4*:59–64. *Nachrichtenblätter 21–24 /1918* (18 July- 8 August). SHAA A128/2. UKNA Air 1/677/21/13/1887.
14. *Armee Françaises VI/2*:491. Bülow:121. Martel:353. Mitchell:220–222. Morrow: 284.Voisin:143–144.*Weltkrieg XIV*:417.
15. *Armée Françaises VI/2*:Annexes 2218, 2045. Edmonds *1918/3*:237. Herwig:371. Hudson:101–102. *Luftmacht Teil 4*:60. SHAA A128/2. UKNA Air 1/2249/209/46/5.IX Brigade split the front into West, Centre and East Sectors and expended 9,710 rounds of machinegun ammunition on the first day.
16. *Armée Françaises VI/2*:Annexes 2218. Bailey & Cony:262–264. Edmonds *1918/3*:234 n1. Henshaw:355–356. *Weltkrieg XIV*:Beilage 40. SHAA A128/2. UKNA Air 1/2249/209/46/5. The British lost five aircraft and another was forced to land.

17. *Armée Françaises VI/2*:Annexes 2218. Franks & Bailey:89. SHAA A128/2. During July German balloon observers controlled 2,287 shoots but had to parachute to safety on 121 occasions while 63 balloons were shot down. *Nachrichtenblatt 26 /1918* (August 22).
18. Bailey & Cony:262–264. Henshaw:356. Hudson:104. Mitchell:222. *Luftmacht Teil 3*:49. Losses were split 50:50 between the British and the French. On 16 July three German fighter pilots fell victim to self-igniting ammunition, a problem throughout the month. Franks et al. *Chronology*:206. VanWyngarden *JG II*: 77.
19. *Armée Françaises VI/2*:55, 59–62, 64–66. *Rapport du Maréchal Commandement en Chef II Partie*:33. The X Armée air commander was Chef d'Escadrons Houdeman.
20. SHAA A128/2.
21. Maurer *1*:197–219. Porch:96. SHAT 18N173 Dossier 1.
22. Bülow:122.Edmonds *1918/3*:259. Franks et al. *Chronology*:216 & *Jasta Pilots: JG II, JGr 11, Jasta 12, 13, 15, 17, 19, 48, 53, 61* entries. VanWyngarden *JG I*:102 & *JG II*: 77–78. *Luftmacht Teil 4*:62.Astonishingly in the middle of the Allied counter-offensive *JG I*'s commander since 14 July, *Oberleutnant* Hermann Göring went on four-days' leave on 26 July with Lothar von Richthofen acting as commander. Göring achieved only one victory after taking command of the *Geschwader*.VanWyngarden *JG I*:102–103.
23. Bülow:121. Edmonds *1918/3*:259. Neumann:448.
24. Edmonds *1918/3*:285–286, 289.
25. *Weltkrieg XIV*:530. SHAA A128/2. *UKNA* Air 1/476/15/312/217. The latter claimed the RAF dropped 342 tonnes and the French only 347 tonnes but figures for the latter are clearly incomplete.
26. *Nachrichtenblätter 21–22 /1918* (July 18–July 25). UKNA Air 1/1189/204/5/2595 (Text in War diary, Intelligence, Royal Flying Corps Part 3" No 172 of 11 August).
27. Bailey & Cony:264–275. Henshaw:461–462. *Weltkrieg XIV*:Beilage 40.The Americans, fighting their first major action, lost 19 aircraft in the second half of July mostly from the 1st Pursuit Group with obsolescent Nieuports but they were credited with 34 victories. The Germans show no losses for *9. Armee* which faced the largest concentration of Allied air power and their figures may be incomplete and may exclude those forced to land.
28. For this and the general advance see *Armée Françaises VII/1*:147–225. Edmonds. *1918/4*:40–178. *Weltkrieg XIV*:549–587. Johnson 86–108.
29. Edmonds *1918/4*:509–520. Johnson. *1918*:109–126.
30. Edmonds *1918/4*:9,12, 16–17,20–21,37.
31. Edmonds *1918/4*:26, 26n 1. Jones *VI*:433.
32. Edmonds *1918/4*:25.Jones *VI*:434–435. *Rapport du Maréchal Commandant*:20. X Brigade was created under Ludlow-Hewitt to support the reformed 5th Army between the Ypres and Arras fronts and included the American 17th and 148th (Fighter) Aero Squadrons. The RAF also had 219 aircraft with 5th Group as well as the Independent Force.
33. Based on Slessor:100 research into brigade war diaries and squadron records.
34. Sloan:191–232. Nicholson:507. Wise:597,649, Table 25. UKNA Air 1/925/204/5/911–912. Contemporary claims that 40% of all airmen on the Western Front were Canadian are exaggerated for some were British or US citizens. The Canadian Air Force was forming two squadrons at the end of the war. Wise:608–610. In July Salmond informed the Air Ministry he was ready to accept 28 American pilots a month but on 12 September he learned 15 American pilots would be withdrawn from RAF squadrons to join the USAS in eastern France while the 17th and 148th Aero Squadrons went to eastern France in the late autumn.
35. Franks et al. *Jasta Pilots:Jagdgruppen* entries. *Luftmacht Teil 4*:65. NLS AC 3155 No130 (entry for August 6). UKNA Air 1/9/15/1/26. *Grufln 16, 23* were with *2. Armee*, *Grufln 11, 22* with *17. Armee* and *Grufln 3, 4, 8, 12, 21* with *18.Armee*. Also within *Heeresgruppe Kronprinz Rupprecht*; 4. and 6. Armees had *Grufln 2, 7, 14, 15* and *Grufln 10, 19* respectively for *"Hagen"*. *Grufln 1, 6, 20* supported *9.Armee* while *Grufln 5, 13, 17, 18* supported 7.*Armee*. Also in *Heeresgruppe Deutscher Kronprinz* on the French front *Grufl 9* supported *3. Armee*. The *Kofl 17. Armee* was apparently *Major* Walter Stahr the former *Kofl 7.Armee* (see Chapter Five).
36. Edmonds *1918/4*:34–35, 37. Jones *VI*:433. Slessor:151. Wise:519–520, 523–525, Map 5.
37. Edmonds *1918/4*:8, 47 n4. Jones *VI*:437–440. Wise:525–530.
38. Edmonds *1918/4*:184. Jones *VI*: 464–466. Maurer *1*:331–332. UKNA Air 2/125 B.11207.

39. For the Amiens air campaign and the advance to the *Siegfriedstellung* see Bailey & Cony: 143–160. Bülow:123–124. Davilla & Soltan: 112,138, 565.Edmonds. *1918/4*:40,47, 52,83–84, 198, 237, 266, 356, 398.Franks et al.*Casualties*:295–308,373–377 & *Chronology*:219–257. Henshaw:367–413. Hoeppner:173–175. Jones *VI*:437–509. Martel:363–368. Slessor:148–199, Appendices A,B & C. Voisin:146–147. Wise: 542–561. *Luftmacht Teil 4*:64–70. *Nachrichtenblätter 25–31 /1918* (15 August-26 September). SHAA A128/2. UKNA Air 1/677/21/13/1887 (pp.57–231). Air 1/2218/209/40/1.Air 1/2176/209/14/19–20. Air 1/2224/209/40/21. Air 1/2234/209/42/21 & Air 1/2244/209/42/22. Air 1/2249/209/46/6–7.

40. Edmonds *1918/4*:83 & n.2, 84, 95, 119. Jones. *War in the Air VI*:441–442, 446–463. Slessor:Appendix B. Table 1. UKNA Air 1/677/21/13/1887 (pp.121–126, 158–159). NLS AC 3155 No130 (15 August).It is unclear who first proposed attacking the bridges but Slessor noted that from August 8–11 the RAF flew 465 sorties against them, 59% of the total bomber. From 5 August to 22 September bombers of I, III, V and IX Brigades delivered 650 tonnes of bombs but the RAF later concluded it would have been better to used massed bombers against airfields allowing dive-bomber attacks upon the bridges. Salmond later demanded recognition of these attacks in Haig's official communiqués.

41. Edmonds *1918/4*: 83–84, 95. Jones *VI*:442, 446.

42. Edmonds *1918/4*:84. Franks et al *Chronology*:220. Jones *VI*:445–446. *Weltkrieg XIV*:Beilage 40. *Weltkrieg* shows claims for 59 for the loss of three. Two German fighters were lost, with their pilots taken prisoner, and two *Jasta 79* pilots were wounded.

43. *Armées Française VII/1*:180, 184, Annex 560. Edmonds *1918/4*:84. Jones *VI*:467–468. Wise:531. *Luftmacht Teil 4*:65. UKNA Air 1/9/15/1/26. 2. *Armee* received only three squadrons by 15 August while *18.Armee* received 12, but three *Jasta* were assigned to support *2. Armee*.

44. Edmonds *1918/4*:83–84, 265–269.Franks et al. *Jasta Pilots*:Entries for *JG I, JGr 2, Jasta 4, 5, 6, 10, 11, 22, 28, 34, 37, 46 & Above the lines*:117.Jones *VI*: 443. Kilduff *Combat Wing*:224, 229–231. VanWyngarden *JG I*:109. *Luftmacht Teil 4*:68–69. UKNA Air1/9/15/1/26. Air 1/677/21/13/1887 (p.150).From 8–21 August *Schlasta* and *Jasta* of *18.Armee* expended 8 tonnes of bombs and 15,000 rounds in ground-attack missions.

45. *Armées Françaises VII/1*:157, Annexes 489, 527, 532, 535. Bailey & Cony: 143. Guttman:112.Jones *VI*:467–468. Voisin: 146. *Rapport du Maréchal*:31,33, 44. SHAA A128/2.

46. Maurer *1*:333–335.

47. *Armées Française VII/2*:27–118, 159–217, 281–310,266–309,323–339, Appendix 4.Edmonds *1918/3*:294 & *1918/5*:3–8, 14–56, 95–182. Johnson *1918*:136–145. *Weltkrieg XIV*:639–646.

48. *Armées Française VII/2*:119–132, 218–233,310–322. Edmonds *1918/4*:429–465 & *1918/5*:57–94, 185–569. Johnson *1918*:145–187. *Weltkrieg XIV*:692–703.

49. Herwig:418,424. Ludendorff resigned on 26 October and was replaced by General Wilhelm Groener.

50. For Allied losses see Franks et al.*Casualties*:302–310, 375–377 & *Bloody April... Black September*: 126–242, Appendices I, II, III , IV and VI excluding *Marine Jasta* and *Kest*. Hereafter Franks et al *April-September*. Henshaw:397–428 463–468. Jones *VI*:491. Pieters:Appendix IV. *Weltkrieg XIV*:Beilage 40 (no data for 21–23 September). The British lost 270 aircraft (including seven American) while another 107 were forced to land west of the lines. These figures exclude 5th Group and most of the Independent Force except for 16 of the latter's bombers lost supporting the St Mihiel Salient offensive. Jones's figures for missing aircraft are 235 British and 59 French.

51. Porch:82

52. *Armée Françaises VII/2*:Appendix I Table 2. Jones *Appendixes*:Appendix XXVI, XLVI.

53. Gray & Thetford:105–108. *The Fokker D.VII.*

54. Bruce. *Royal Flying Corps aeroplanes*:280–284, 548–549. *British Aeroplanes*: 138–139, 152–153, 314–315. *Fokker D.VIII. Fokker Dr I*. Davilla & Soltan:412–415, 524–525. Gray & Thetford:109–111, 191–194, 213–217. Gray *Albatros D.I-III. Albatros D.V Pfalz D.III. Siemens Schuckert D.III & D.IV.* Grosz *Pfalz D XII*. Lamberton. *Fighters*:8, 52, 68. VanWyngarden *JG I*:104, 110–111 & *JG II*:30, 40, 43, 85–86.The USAS planned to build the Bristol Fighter as the USXB-1/2 while a replacement was being developed by the British as the Bristol Badger. In July 695 Albatros fighters were with the Feldheer and by 1 August there were 169 Pfalz D.III/IIIa, 70 Albatros D.III, 100 Fokker Triplanes and some LFG Roland D.VI. By the end of August 168 Pfalz D.XII were at the front and they would equip half the *Jasta* facing the British including all of the Bavarian *JGr 8* which became *JG IV* on 3 October.

55. Franks et al *Casualties*:243–302, 356–375. Maurer*1*:337. Schwarte:287, 299. Losses include killed in action, killed in accidents, died of illness, missing and prisoners of war.
56. VanWyngarden *JG II*: 103. UKNA Air 1/9/15/1/22 (Annex I). Air 1/1189/204/5/2595 (August 8, August 21, September 23)
57. *Armée Françaises VII/1*:291–349. Edmonds *1918/4*:353–354. Johnson *1918*:126– 135. Mead:284–299. *Weltkrieg XIV*:587–610.
58. Cooke:110, 119–120, 121–123, 128–131, 133. Maurer *3*:7–8.
59. Cooke:80, 110, 127–128, 141. Maurer *1*:38, 238–240, 269,301–306.
60. Cooke:141–143. Franks et al. *Jasta Pilot*:Entries for *JG II*, *JGr Siempelkamp*, *Jasta 12, 13, 15, 19, 64, 65*. Maurer *I*:235–243, 269–273, 301–311, 365–369. VanWyngarden *JG II*:89–90.
61. Baring:294. Boyle:299–300. Davilla & Soltan:138, 566. Henshaw:407–412. Maurer *1*:37, 40, 713 & *II*:127, 713–717. Sloan:309–313, 319. US Army War College *Order of Battle*:1st US Army entry. *Rapport du Maréchal*:36. DAé arrived from 4–6 September and US source give French strength as 740 aircraft. Mitchell claimed 1,476 aircraft but estimates range from 1,238 (serviceable) to 1,481 and serviceability was poor with some American Spad squadrons reduced to half strength.
62. For the St Mihiel air campaign see Bailey & Cony:298–302. Cooke:144–159. Davilla & Soltan:112, 565. Franks et al. *Casualties*:304–305, 376 & *Chronology*:245–252. Henshaw:464–466. Hudson:119–195. Martel:368–376. Maurer *I*:38–40, 240–243, 270–273,306–311, 365–369, 383. Sloan:309–321. Treadwell:113–120. VanWyngarden *JG II*:90–97. *Nachrichtenblatt 30/1918* (September 19). SHAA A128/3. UKNA Air1/2249/209/45/8. Air 1/1997/204/273/247. USNA Microfilm M990/13 (Army Operations Reports 12–16). The first day's weather was so bad that Boenigk was still in bed when two American fighters strafed his airfield only to be driven off by JG II's two standby fighters.
63. Bailey & Cony: 298–299. Henshaw:464–466 Maurer *I*:38–39, 366 & *III*:10–11, 14. VanWyngarden *JG II*:100–105SHAA A128/3. UKNA Air 1/1997/204/273/247. Air 1/2249/209/45/8. US NA Microfilm M990/13 (Reports 12–16). The railway bombing campaign was aided by Luxembourg having one of the best train-watching organisations. This was established by a Madame Rischard, whose husband was a doctor in the Luxembourg State Railway. She was assisted by Belgian Lieutenant Baschwitz-Meau who was floated across the lines in a balloon launched from Verdun on the night of 18/19 June. Baschwitz-Meau landed safely after a two-hour flight near Grosbous more than 100 kilometres from the Allied lines. See Drake's report Paragraphs 52–55 on website mtholyoke.edu/acad and Morgan:245–248, 257–259, 275–278, 283–290.
64. Franks et al. *Jasta Pilots:JG I*. Henshaw:464–466. Maurer *I*:40. UKNA Air 1/2124/207/74/3 (Summary of air intelligence No 207 15 September). Future air commanders Major Carl Spaatz and First Lieutenant George C. Kenney flew in the campaign, Spaatz becoming the first US Air Force commander in 1947.
65. For the Argonne Offensive see *Armée Françaises VII/2*:149–158, 246–265, 339–352, Annexe 137. Edmonds *1918/5*:5–6, 9–10, 400, 462, 515, 565–566. Ferrell:43 ff. Otto:39–169. Johnson *1918*:136–139. Lengel pp.57–412. Mead:299–326,331–336.*Weltkrieg XIV*:647–651.
66. Cooke:162, 168. Maurer *I*: 247,313.
67. Cooke: 169–170. Franks et al. *Chronology*:246–257. Maurer *I*:313–316, 319. *Weltkrieg XIV*:Beilage 40.
68. Franks et al. *Jasta Pilots:JG I , JG II, JGr 1,5, 11* and *Marville, Jasta 77* and *81*. UKNA Air 1/9/15/1/22 (Annex I). Air 1/9/15/1/26.Air 1/213/207/109/1 (23 September). Air 1/2124/207/3.
69. *Armées Française X*: IVArmée entry. Cooke:163, 166. Lengel: 62–63. Savilla & Soltan:507. Sloan:351. US Army War College. *Order of Battle*:82–83. Travelling to England, Trenchard stayed with Haig and observed it was impossible to maintain independent, i.e. strategic, air operations. NLS AC 3155 No131 (24 September 1918).
70. Hudson:300. On 30 September half the 1st Pursuit Group's Spads replaced their Vickers guns with American-made Marlins. 1 Pursuit Group Records 1918 at website acepilots.com/wwi/us
71. Cooke:192–193. Sloan:353.
72. Cooke:3, 11, 110, 121, 168–169, 183. Johnson:19, 61–62, 68, 98, 132–133, 135. Milling's post war service in US Army aviation was surprisingly low key and he retired due to ill health in 1933. He held minor positions during the war, retired again and died in 1960.
73. Cooke: 2,3, 6, 21–22, 48,80,99. 110, 119, 166–167, 194–195. Johnson *Wingless Eagle*: 14, 15, 17, 77, 80, 137, 188–189. Mitchell. *Memoirs*:181–182. Sloan. *Wings of Honor*:93–95, 361. Lahm was a friend of Bullard's chief of staff Brigadier-General Stuart Heintzelman whom Mitchell had flown in

February 1918. Heintzelman's grandfather commanded a corps in the Army of the Potomac during the Civil War and was the most senior officer to make a balloon ascent. Lahm created the Air Corps Training Center and became assistant military attaché for air in Paris from 1931 but his career then petered out and he retired a few weeks before Pearl Harbor commanding an air school. He died in 1963.

74. Cooke: 197.Sloan:360–363, 370–372, 376–382.
75. For the Meuse-Argonne air campaign see Bailey & Cony:305–327. Cooke:162–201. Davilla & Soltan:138, 565. Franks et al. *Casualties*: 308–327, 377–379 & *Chronology*:257–284. Henshaw:466–472. Hudson:258–298. Martel:377–390. Maurer *I*:245–255, 275–279, 313–316, 318–319, 371–375, 385. Sloan:331–383. Treadwell:123–138. *Nachrichtenblätter 32–36/1918* (3–31 October). SHAA A128/3
76. Franks et al *April...September*:211–226. Henshaw:466–472. *Weltkrieg XIV*:Beilage 40. US NA M990/13. The Germans claimed 17 victories.
77. In August German aeronauts took to their parachutes on 181 occasions (132 balloons were lost) and in September this rose to 227, but only 63 balloons were lost. On September 15 a *Leutnant* Höfinghoff had to jump three times. *Nachrichtenblätter 31& 34 /1918* (September 26) & (October 17).
78. For fighter operations see Franks et al *Chronology*:2577—284. Henshaw:466–472. Maurer *I*:316–323. Sloan:358–359. VanWyngarden *JG II*:104–118.
79. For US bomber operations Cooke:166–167, 185. Henshaw:466–467. Maurer *I*:371–375. Sloan:167, 240, 355–356. VanWyngarden *JG II*:100–106. SHAA A128/3. UKNA Air 1/2249/209/45/8–10. USNA M990/13, M990/12, M990/14.
80. Cooke:191–192. Maurer *I*:44. Lengel: 314–315. Martel:382–383. Mitchell: 559. SHAA A128/3 (Octobre 9 1918). Only two French aircraft were lost.
81. Ferrell:123.Lengel: 71, 183–184
82. Cooke: 108.
83. Ferrell: 124. Lengel: 214, 314, 386.
84. Cooke:181, 192–193. Lengel: 163, 198, 315. 1 Pursuit Group Records 1918 at website acepilots.com/wwi/us Samples of the numerous *Schlasta* attacks may be found in Lengel: 93, 145, 200, 277, 285, 306, 341, 403.
85. Ferrell: 122–123. Maurer *I*:Appendix G. Fighter serviceability in the second half of October was from 56–64%.
86. For aerial artillery fire direction see Ferrell:62, 67, 122–123. Cooke:103,154, 156. Hudson:265. Maurer *I*:39, 248–249, 251. Maurer *III*:17. Like the Germans, the American gunners had more faith in balloons than aircraft.
87. Cooke: 177, 180–182, 189–190, 193. Ferrell:69–70. Henshaw:408. Hudson:265–268. Maurer *I*:248–249, 252–254, 278. US NA M990/12. M990/13–12.
88. *Armées Françaises VII/1*:Annex 934. *Rapport du Maréchal*:77. UKNA Air 1/475/15/312/205.
89. Information from Christophe Cony who notes that on 19 October Duval's title became Aide Major-Général, Chargé des Opérations.
90. Martel:254–255.
91. For French air operations see Christienne & Lissarague:128–132. Martel:368–390. Davilla & Soltan:112, 138, 168, 252, 565. Franks et al. *April... September*:126–242. SHAA A128/3. On October 27 Vaulgrenant was warned to prepare for a transfer to support the Lorraine offensive. *Armées Française VII/2*:333n2.
92. Edmonds *1918/4*:476 & *1918/5*:14–19. UKNA Air 1/677/21/13/1887 (216).
93. For the air campaign on the BEF's central axes see Edmonds *1918/4*:40,47, 52,83–84, 198, 237, 266, 356, 398 & *1918/5*:16–18. Franks et al.*Casualties*:308–327, 377–379; *Jasta Pilots*:319, 321,322; *Chronology*:259–284 & *April... September*:226–242. Henshaw:416–455. Jones *VI*:510–552. Wise:561–571. *Nachrichtenblätter 32–36/1918* (3–31 October). SHAA A128/2. UKNA Air 1/677/21/13/1887 (240–311). Air 1/1844/204/210/29. Air 1/2131/207/109/1. Air 1/2124/207/74/3 (No 215 23 September 1918). Air 1/2176/209/14/20–21. Air 1/2181/209/14/42. Air 1/2224/209/40/21. Air 1/2225/209/40/26–27 Air 1/2244/209/42/22–23. Air 1/2246/209/42/35. Air 1/2249/209/46/7–8.
94. Edmonds *1918/5*:391. NLS AC 3155 No132 (17 October). For Smyth-Osbourne see web site rafweb.org/Biographies which is inaccurate when it says he replaced Hogg on 1 April. Hogg was still commanding the brigade on 19 October but exactly when he departed is something of a mystery.

95. Jones *VI*:517, 525–526,536–537. Maurer *1*:330–331, 335–339. Gorrell criticised the British practice of keeping fighter squadrons at airfield alert ("stand by") before OPs. Maurer also reported a decline in enemy air operations on the British front from 27 September until the end of October due to the absence of first-class *Jasta*

96. Jones *VI*:540. UKNA Air 2/125 B.11207. 1/677/21/13/1887 (pp.80–82). The squadrons were Nos 7, 8, 10, 18, 22, 53 and 88. Radios fitted to Nos11 and 22 Bristol Fighter Squadrons in March were removed, probably for security reasons. One British document notes the radios were built in England with American microphones but an example of a Telephone Wireless Aircraft Mk II in the British Army's Royal Signals Museum in Blandford Forum, Dorset was manufactured in the United States by the General Electric Company. Aware that the Germans could intercept their signals, No 88 Squadron pilots would often address vulgar remarks to their foes. Shores et al. *Above the Trenches*: 154, Entry for Captain Charles Findlay.

97. UKNA Air 2/125 B.11207. Air 1/677/21/13/1887 (pp.80–82).

98. Edmonds *1918/5*:422. Jones *VI*: 521,549.

99. Edmonds *1918/4*:198. Neumann:448, 487. I, II, V, IX Brigade war diaries augmented by wing and squadron records for November. *Luftmacht Teil 4*:69. British bombers dropped only 119 tonnes during the day. A "*Schlachtstaffel 12*" of *Bogohl 4* also struck roads and road junctions.

100. Henshaw:397–455, Appendix II. Jones *VI*:530, 544–547 & *Appendices*:Appendix XXX. Laffin:137.The DH9a was so superior it could fly unescorted missions and only nine were brought down from 1 September to 11 November compared with 137 DH 9s, but at the war's end Salmond had only four DH 9a squadrons.

101. Jones *VI*:550–551. Maurer *1*:335–336. I, II, and V Brigade war diaries. IX Brigade fighters ceased to be used as fighter-bombers from the end of August.

102. Edmonds *1918/4*:220. Jones *VI*:469, 477n1. Wise:542–546, 554. Brigade war diaries. No detailed records of No 73 Squadron survive but in good visibility tank losses to artillery fire reportedly declined.

103. Jones *VI*:474–475.

104. Jones *VI*:525. Maurer *1*:332–333, 335–336.

105. Jones *VI*:516–517, 520–521. Maurer *1*:335–336. Smythies was a former Royal Engineer and had once been an instructor at the Electrical School before joining the RFC in 1915.

106. Edmonds *1918/5*:186, 200, 213. Maurer *1*:333.Wise:553. On 7 October Salmond informed Haig that if the enemy collapsed and the Cavalry Corps advanced he would support it with 300 aircraft. NLS AC 3155 No132 (7 October 1918). For the vulnerability of horses to air attack see Slessor:95.

107. Edmonds *1918/4*:314 & *1918/5*:217.UKNA Air 1/9/15/1/22 (Annex I). Air 1/9/15/1/26.

108. Jones *VI*:480. Neumann:453–456.

109. Edmonds*1918/4*:258, 264–265, 286. & *1918/5*:12–13. Laffin:139. Maurer*1*:335–336. During the autumn the Allies eroded the enemy kite balloon force which was still so important to German gunners and the *Drachen* rarely rose more than 600 metres.

110. Jones *VI*:516, 519, 536. UKNA Air 2/125 B.11207. In September the RAF directed fire ("shoots") on 1,484 pre-selected targets, another 78 on long-range targets and engaged 2,575 targets detected by the flash of their guns and sent 74,201 zone calls.

111. Jones *VI*:516, 519.UKNA Air 1/2268/209/70/200. Record books of Nos10, 13, 15, 21, 42, 35, 59 and 82 Squadrons. For detailed instructions to III Brigade's No 13 Squadron supporting XVII Corps see Jones *VI*: 514–516. During October more than 23,000 photographs were taken by Salmond's men Laffin:140, 142.

112. Edmonds *1918/5*:299, 426, 491, 577. Jones *VI*:492. Nicholson:397, 435. UKNA Air 1/2268/209/70/200.

113. Edmonds *1918/3*:202. Record books of Nos 10, 13, 15, 21, 42, 35, 59 and 82 Squadrons. In 22–31 August the REs of No 59 Squadron supporting 3rd Army flew 50 supply sorties, representing nearly 21% of squadron activity, while the Armstrong Whitworths of No 35 Squadron supporting 5th Army flew 27 re-supply sorties representing 25.5% of its operations. Nos 35 and 59 Squadron record books, UKNA Air 1/1782/204/150/17–18. Air 1/1400/204/27/21.

114. *Armées Française X*:VI Armée entry. Jones *VI*:531–532. Pieters:86–87. Sloan: 266–268. Treadwell:104–108. Vrancken:258, 260. UKNA Air 1/2232/209/41/21. Copy of Crombrugge's personal file, 11904, kindly provided by Major Bernard Cambrelin. The Belgians were still operating

15 Farmans for photo-reconnaissance and bombing and French squadrons augmented their forces. The NBG was envisaged as having 12 (later 8) squadrons, divided evenly between the Navy's night and Marine day units, the former with Caproni 450 and the latter with Liberty-powered DH-4s. Only the Marine "C" or 7th Squadron saw combat but 23 sailors and 40 Marines volunteered to fly with Lambe's squadrons. One of the group's staff officers, Ensign David Judd, had previously flown with SPA 3. Guttman:90. Nearly 70 US Navy and Marine Corps personnel served with Allied squadrons, all but five with the RAF and usually in bombing squadrons. Lieutenant David S.Ingalls became the Navy's only air ace (six victories) with No 213 Squadron and during the Second World War was a rear Admiral. Franks & Bailey, Front pp.47–48, Sloan pp.280–281.

115. Franks et al:236, 263 & *Jasta Pilots*:319, 321–322. Gray & Thetford:xxxiv. Nowarra:14. UKNA Air1/213/207/109/1. Air 1/2124/207/74/3(No 215 23 September 1918).

116. For the Flanders air campaign see Bailey & Cony:307–327. Franks et al. *Jasta Pilots*:29, 44. *Chronology*:261–284. *April... September*:232–242. Henshaw:423–455. Jones *VI*:531–541. Pieters:16–19, 113–116, Appendices IV, XII & XIII. Treadwell:106–108. Vrancken:256–261, 265–283. *Nachrichtenblätter 32–36/1918* (October 3–31). SHAA A128 Dossier 3.UKNA Air 1/2232/209/41/21–22 & Air 1/2237/209/41/34.

117. Edmonds *1918/5*:90–91. Jones *VI*:534. Sloan:272. Vrancken:266–267. British involvement included Lambe's No 218 Squadron with DH 9s and Webb-Bowen's No 82 Squadron with Armstrong Whitworths.

118. Hooton:17–24.

119. For post-war developments see Budiansky: 125–200.

Epilogue

1. For the problems encountered by the French in 1940 see Cain:137–141. Cain is the best source in English on the development of French air power between the wars.

2. The Tactical School radicals preached the strategic bombing mantra in lectures.

3. For the origins of BCR see Cain:28, 30, 42, 87. Its failures became glaringly obvious during the 1935 manoeuvres. For the He 177 and British aircraft Hooton: 156–157.

4. Hooton: 99–100.

BIBLIOGRAPHY

Books

Aders, Gebhard. *History of the German Night Fighter Force 1917–1945.* London: Jane's Publishing Company, 1979.

The Allied Armies under Marshal Foch in the Franco-Belgian Theater of Operations. Volume 2–Report of the Military Board of Supply. Washington DC: Government Printing Office, 1925.

d'Ané, Roman (editor). *Dictionnaire de Biographie Française Volume XII.* Paris: Libraire Letouzer et Ané, 1970.

Bailey, Frank W. & Christophe Cony. *The French Air Service War Chronology 1914–1918: Day-to-day claims and losses by French fighter, bomber and two-seat pilots on the Western Front.* London: Grub Street, 2002.

Baring, Maurice. *Flying Corps Headquarters 1914–1918.* London, Buchan & Enright. 1985.

Barnett, Correlli. *The Swordbearers: Studies in supreme command in the First World War.* London: Penguin Books, 1966.

Bean, C.E.W. *Official History of Australia in the War of 1914–1918: Volume IV. The A.I.F. in France 1917.* Sydney: Angus & Robertson Ltd, 1933.

—— *Official History of Australia in the War of 1914–1918: Volume V. The A.I.F. in France 1918.* Sydney: Angus & Robertson Ltd, 1937.

Bond, Brian and Nigel Cave. *Haig: A reappraisal 70 years on.* Barnsley: Pen & Sword Books, 1999.

Boyle, Andrew. *Trenchard: Man of vision.* London: Collins, 1962.

Bruce, J.M. *The aeroplanes of the Royal Flying Corps (Military Wing).* London, Putnam, 1982.

—— *British Aeroplanes 1914–1918.* London: Putnam, 1957.

———— *The Fokker D.VIII (Profile 67)*. Leatherhead: Profile Publications, 1966.

————*The Fokker Dr I (Profile 55)*. Leatherhead: Profile Publications , 1965.

Budiansky, Stephen. *Air Power*. New York: Viking, 2003

Büdinggen, Oberstleutnant. *Entwicklung und Einsatz der deutschen Flakwaffe und des Luftschutzes im Weltkrieg*. Berlin: E. S. Mittler & Sohn,1938.

Bülow, Himer Freiherr von. *Geschichte der Luftwaffe*. Frankfurt-am-Main: Verlag, Moritz Diesterweg, 1934.

Cain, Anthony Christopher. *The Forgotten Air Force: French air doctrine in the 1930s*. Washington: Smithsonian Institution Press, 2002.

Castex, Jean, Louis Laspalles and José Barès. *Général Barès: Créateur et inspirateur de l'Aviation*. Paris: Nouvelles Editions Latines, 1994.

Chambre, René. *Dans l'Enfer du Ciel*. Paris: Editions Baudinière, 1933.

Charlton, Air Commodore L.E.O. *War from the Air: Past, Present, Future*. London: Thomas Nelson & Sons Ltd, 1935.

Charlton, L.E.O. *Charlton*. London: Faber and Faber Ltd, 1931.

Christienne, Général Charles. *L'aviation Française 1890–1918. Un certain âge d'or*. Paris: Groupe Éditions Atlas, 1988.

Christienne, Charles and Pierre Lissarrague (Translated Frances Kianka). *A History of French Military Aviation*. Washington DC: Smithsonian Institution Press, 1986.

Clayton, Anthony. *Paths of Glory. The French Army 1914–1918*. London: Cassell Military Paperbacks, 2003.

Cooke, James J. *The US Air Service in the Great War 1917–1919*. Westport: Praeger, 1996.

Corum, James S. *The Luftwaffe: Creating the Operational Air War*. Lawrence: University of Kansas Press, 1997.

Corum, James S. and Muller, Richard R. *The Luftwaffe's Way of War: German Air Force doctrine 1911–1945*. Baltimore/Charleston:

The Nautical & Aviation Publishing Company of America, 1998.

Cuneo, John. *The Air Weapon 1914–1916*. Harrisburg, PA: Military Service Publishing Co, 1947.

—— *Winged Mars*. Harrisburg, PA: The Military Service Publishing Company, 1942.

Davilla, Dr James J. and Arthur M. Soltan. *French Aircraft of the First World War*. Stratford, Connecticut: Flying Machines Press, 1997.

Duffy, Christopher. *Through German Eyes: The British and the Somme 1916*. Weidenfeld & Nicolson, London, 2006.

Edmonds, Brigadier-General Sir James E. *Military Operations in France and Belgium 1916, Volume I*. London: Macmillan and Co Ltd, 1932.

—— *Military Operations in France and Belgium 1917 Volume II*. London: His Majesty's Stationery Office, 1948.

—— *Military Operations in France and Belgium, 1918 Volume I*. London: Macmillan and Co Ltd, 1935.

—— *Military Operations in France and Belgium, 1918 Volume II*. London: Macmillan and Co Ltd, 1937.

—— *Military Operations in France and Belgium, 1918 Volume III*. London: Macmillan and Co Ltd, 1939.

—— *Military Operations in France and Belgium, 1918 Volume IV*. London: His Majesty's Stationery Office, 1947.

Étévé, Albert. *La Victoire des Cocardes: L'Aviation françaises avant et pendant la première guerre mondiale*. Paris: Robert Laffont, 1970.

Falls, Captain Cyril. *History of the Great War: Military Operations in France and Belgium 1917 Volume 1*. London: Macmillan and Co Ltd, 1940.

Farndale, General Sir Martin. *History of the Royal Regiment of Artillery: Western Front 1914–1918*. London: The Royal Artillery Institution, 1986.

Ferrell, Robert H. *America's Deadliest Battle: Meuse-Argonne 1918*. Lawrence: University of Kansas Press, 2007.

Fischer, William Edward Junior. *The Development of Military Night Aviation to 1919*. Alabama: Air University Press, Maxwell Air Force Base, 1998.

Foulois, Benjamin D. and C. V. Glines. *From the Wright Brothers to the Astronauts*. New York: McGraw-Hill, 1968.

Franks, Norman. *Sharks Among Minnows: Germany's first fighter pilots and the Fokker Eindecker period. July 1915 to September 1916*. London: Grub Street Publishing, 2002.

Franks, Norman, Frank Bailey and Rick Duiven. *Casualties of the German Air Service 1914–1920*. London: Grub Street, 1999.

——— *The Jasta Pilots: Detailed listings and histories August 1916–November 1918*. London: Grub Street, 1996.

——— *The Jasta War Chronology. A complete listing of claims and losses August 1916–November 1918*. London: Grub Street, 1998.

Franks, Norman L. R. and Frank W. Bailey. *Over the Front; A complete record of the fighter aces and units of the United States and French Air Services*. London: Grub Street, 1992.

Franks, Norman L. R., Frank W. Bailey and Russell Guest. *Above the lines. A complete record of the Fighter aces of the German Air Service, Naval Air Service and Flanders Marine Corps 1914–1918*. London: Grub Street, 1996.

Franks, Norman L. R., Russell Guest and Frank W. Bailey. *Bloody April. Black September*. London: Grub Street, 1995.

Fredette, Raymond H. *The Sky on Fire: The First Battle of Britain 1917–1918*. New York: Harcourt, Brace, Jovanovich, 1966.

Furse, Anthony. *Wilfred Freeman*. Staplehurst: Spellmount Ltd, 2000.

Goes, Gustav. *Chemin des Dames*. Hamburg: Hanseatische Verlagsanstalt Hamburg, 1938.

——— *Der Tag X: Die grosse Schlacht in Frankreich 21 März-5.April 1918*. Berlin: Verlag Tradition Wilhelm Kolk, 1933.

Gray, Peter. *The Albatros D V (Profile 9)*. Leatherhead: Profile Publications, 1965.

———— *The Albatros D.I-III(Profile 127)*. Leatherhead: Profile Publications, 1966.

———— *Fokker D.VII, The.* (*Profile 25*). Leatherhead: Profile Publications, 1965.

———— *The Pfalz D.III* (*Profile 43*). Leatherhead: Profile Publications, 1965.

———— *The Siemens Schuckert D.III & D.IV* (*Profile 86*). Leatherhead: Profile Publications, 1966.

Gray, Peter and Owen Thetford. *German Aircraft of the First World War*. London: Putnam & Company Ltd, 1962.

Greenwood, Paul. *The Second Battle of the Marne 1918*. Shrewsbury: Airlife Publishing, 1998.

Grosz, Peter M. *Halberstadt CL II*. Berkhamstead: Windsock Data File # 27, Albatros Publications, 1999.

———— *The Roland C II*. Leatherhead: Profile Publications, 1967.

———— *The Pfalz D XII*. (*Profile 199*). Leatherhead: Profile Publications, 1967.

Guttman, John. *Groupe de Combat 12 'Les Cigognes'*. Oxford: Osprey Publishing, 2004.

Haddow, G.W. and Peter Grosz. *The German Giants*. London: Putnam, 1962.

Hart, Peter. *Somme Success. The Royal Flying Corps and the Battle of the Somme 1916*. Barnsley: Pen & Sword Books Ltd, 2001.

Henniker, Colonel A.M. *Transportation on the Western Front*. London: His Majesty's Stationery Office, 1937.

Henshaw, Trevor. *The Sky Their Battlefield: Air fighting and the complete list of Allied air casualties from enemy action in the First War*. London: Grub Street, 1995.

Herwig, Professor Holger H. *The First World War: Germany and Austria-Hungary 1914–1918*. London: Arnold Publishing, 1997.

Hoeppner, General Ernst von. *Deutschlands Krieg in der Luft*. Leipzig: K. F. Koehler Verlag, 1921.

Hooton, E. R. *Eagle in Flames. The Fall of the Luftwaffe.* London: Arms & Armour Press, 1999.

———— *Phoenix Triumphant. The rise and rise of the Luftwaffe.* London: Arms & Armour Press, 1994.

Horne, Alistair. *The Price of Glory.* Harmondsworth: Penguin Books, 1964.

Hudson, James J. *Hostile Skies: A combat history of the American Air Service in World War I.* Syracuse, NY: Syracuse University Press, 1968.

Hurley, Alfred F. *Billy Mitchell. Crusader for Air Power.* Bloomington: Indiana University Press, 1975.

Imrie, Alex. *Pictorial History of the German Army Air Service 1914–1918.* London: Ian Allan, 1971.

Jefford, Wing Commander C. G. *RAF Squadrons: A comprehensive record of the movement and equipment of all RAF squadrons and their antecedents since 1912.* Shrewsbury: Airlife Publishing Ltd, 1988.

———— *Observers and Navigators and other non-pilot aircrew in the RFC, RNAS and RAF.* Shrewsbury: Airlife Publishing Ltd, 2001.

Johnson, Herbert A. *Wingless Eagle. U.S. Army Aviation through World War I.* Chapel Hill: The University of North Carolina Press, 2001.

Johnson, J. H. *1918 The Unexpected Victory.* London: Arms and Armour Press, 1997

Jones, H. A. *The War in the Air Volume II.* Oxford: Clarendon Press, 1928.

———— *The War in the Air Volume III.* Oxford: Clarendon Press, 1931.

———— *The War in the Air Volume IV.* Oxford: Clarendon Press, 1934.

———— *The War in the Air Volume V.* Oxford: Clarendon Press, 1935.

———— *The War in the Air Volume VI.* Oxford: Clarendon Press, 1937.

———— *The War in the Air. Appendices.* Oxford: Clarendon Press, 1937.

Kilduff, Peter. *Germany's First Air Force 1914–1918.* London: Arms & Armour Press, 1991.

———— *The Red Baron Combat Wing: Jagdgeschwader Richthofen in Battle.* London: Arms & Armour Press, 1997.

———— *Richthofen: Beyond the legend of the Red Baron.* London: Brockhampton Press, 1999.

Laffin, John: *Swifter than Eagles.* Edinburgh: William Blackwood & Sons Ltd, 1964.

Lamberton, W. M. *Fighter Aircraft of the 1914–1918 War.* Letchworth: Harleyford Publications Ltd, 1960.

———— *Reconnaissance & Bomber Aircraft of the 1914–1918 War.* Letchworth: Harleyford Publications, 1962.

Lee, Arthur Gould. *No Parachute: The exploits of a fighter pilot in the First World War.* London. Jarrolds Publishers, 1968.

———— *Open Cockpit; A pilot in the Royal Flying Corps.* London: Jarrolds 1969.

Lengel, Edward G. *To Conquer Hell: The Battle of Meuse-Argonne 1918.* London: Aurum Press, 2008.

Lewis, Cecil. *Sagittarius Rising.* New York: Harcourt, Brace and Co, 1936.

Loewenstern, Baron Elard von. *Deutsche Tat im Weltkrieg 1914–1918 Band 81: Der Frontflieger.* Berlin: Verlag Bernard & Graefe, 1937.

Macdonald, Lyn. *To the Last Man: Spring 1918.* London: Penguin Books, 1998.

Martel, René. *L'aviation Française de Bombardement. Des origines au 11 Novembre 1918.* Paris: Paul Hartmann diteur, 1939.

Maurer Maurer (editor). *The US Air Service in World War I Volume I.* Washington DC: The Office of Air Force History', Headquarters USAF, 1978.

———— *The US Air Service in World War I Volume IV.* Washington DC: The Office of Air Force History', Headquarters USAF, 1979.

Mead, Gary. *The Doughboys: America and the First World War.* London: Allen Lane, The Penguin Press, 2000.

Middlebrook, Martin. *The First Day on the Somme.1 July 1916*. London: Penguin Books,1971.

Miles, Captain Wilfred. *Military Operations in France and Belgium. 1916 Volume II*. London: Macmillan and Co, 1938.

———— *Military Operations in France and Belgium 1917 Volume III*. London: His Majesty's Stationery Office,1948.

Ministère de la Guerre. *Les Armées Françaises dans la Grande Guerre Tome IV Volume 1*. Paris: Imprimerie Nationale, 1926.

———— *Les Armées Françaises dans la Grande Guerre Tome IV Volume 2*. Paris: Imprimerie Nationale, 1933.

———— *Les Armées Françaises dans la Grande Guerre Tome IV Volume 3*. Paris: Imprimerie Nationale, 1936.

———— *Les Armées Françaises dans la Grande Guerre Tome V Volume 1*. Paris: Imprimerie Nationale, 1931.

———— *Les Armées Françaises dans la Grande Guerre Tome V Volume 2*. Paris: Imprimerie Nationale, 1937.

———— *Les Armées Françaises dans la Grande Guerre Tome VI Volume 1*. Paris: Imprimerie Nationale, 1931.

———— *Les Armées Françaises dans la Grande Guerre Tome VI Volume 2*. Paris: Imprimerie Nationale, 1934.

———— *Les Armées Françaises dans la Grande Guerre Tome VII Volume 1*. Paris: Imprimerie Nationale, 1923.

———— *Les Armées Françaises dans la Grande Guerre Tome VII Volume 2*. Paris: Imprimerie Nationale, 1938.

———— *Les Armées Françaises dans la Grande Guerre Tome X Volume 1*. Paris: Imprimerie Nationale, 1923.

Mitcham, Samuel W. Jr. *Men of the Luftwaffe*. Novato: Presidio Press, 1988.

Mitchell, Brigadier-General William. *Memoirs of World War I: From Start to Finish of our Greatest War*. Westport, Connecticut: Greenward Press Publishers, 1975.

Morgan, Janet. *The Secrets of Rue St Roch: Hope and Heroism Behind Enemy Lines in the First World War.* London; Penguin Books, 2005 (Alan Lane, 2004).

Morizon, Alain. *L'Aviation en 1917.* Paris: Service Historique de l'Armée de l'Air, 1967.

Morris, Alan. *Bloody April.* London: Jarrolds Publishers, 1967.

——— *First of the Many: The story of the Independent Force, RAF.* London: Jarrolds Publishers, 1968.

Morrow, John H. *The Great War in the Air.* Washington DC: Smithsonian Institution Press, 1993.

Mortane, Jacques. *Histoire de la Guerre Aérienne 1914–1918.* Paris: L'Edition Francaise Illustrée, 1921.

——— *Special Missions of the Air.* London: The Aeroplane & General Publishing Co Ltd, 1919.

Neumann, Major Georg Paul. *Die deutschen Luftstreitkräfte im Weltkrieg.* Berlin: E. S. Mittler & Sohn, 1920.

Nicholson, Colonel G.W.L. *Canadian Expeditionary Force 1914–1919. The Official History of the Canadian Army in the First World War.* Ottawa: Queen's Printer and Controller of Stationery, 1962.

Nowarra, Heinz J. *Marine Aircraft of the 1914–1918 War.* Letchworth: Harleyford Publications Ltd, 1966.

Occleshaw, Michael. *Armour Against Fate.* London: Columbus Books, 1989.

Otto, Ernst. *Sternenbanner gegen Schwarz-weiss-rot.* Berlin: Verlag Tradition Wilhelm Kolk, 1930.

Pedroncini, Guy. *Pétain: Général en Chef.* Paris: Presses Universitaires de France, 1974.

Pieters, Walter M. *Above Flanders' Fields.* London: Grub Street, 1998.

Porch, Douglas. *The French Secret Services: From the Dreyfus Affair to the Gulf War.* London: Macmillan General Books, 1996.

Prior, Robin and Trevor Wilson. *Passchendaele: the untold story.* London: Yale University Press, 1996.

Pujo, Leon. *Le Général Pujo et la Naissance de l'Aviation Françaises*. Paris: Service Historique de l'Armée de l'Air, 1986.

Quarterly Army List: 30 June 1914. London: His Majesty's Stationary Office, 1914.

Quarterly Army List: 30 September 1919. London: His Majesty's Stationary Office, 1919.

Reichsarchiv. *Schlachten des Weltkrieges XV. Die Tragödie von Verdun 1916. Teil:*

Die Zermürbungsschlacht. Berlin, 1929.

Reichskriegsministerium. *Der Weltkrieg 1914–1918. Die militärischen Operationen zu Lande, Band X*. Berlin: E. S. Mittler und Sohn, 1936.

——— *Der Weltkrieg 1914–1918. Die militärischen Operationen zu Lande, Band XI*. Berlin: E. S. Mittler und Sohn, 1938.

——— *Der Weltkrieg 1914–1918. Die militärischen Operationen zu Lande, Band XII*. Berlin: E. S. Mittler und Sohn, 1939.

——— *Der Weltkrieg 1914–1918. Die militärischen Operationen zu Lande, Band XIII*. Berlin: E. S. Mittler und Sohn, 1942.

——— *Der Weltkrieg 1914–1918. Die militärischen Operationen zu Lande, Band XIV*. Berlin: E. S. Mittler und Sohn, 1944.

Ritter, Hauptmann Hans. *Der Luftkrieg*. Berlin: Verlag von K. F. Koehler, 1926.

Robinson, Douglas. *The Zeppelin in Combat*. London: G.T.Foulis,1961.

Schwarte, Generalleutnant M. *Die Militärischen Lehren des Grossen Kriegs*. Berlin: E. S. Mittler & Sohn, 1920.

Shores, Christopher, Norman Franks & Russell Guest. *Above the Trenches. A complete record of the fighter aces and units of the British Empire air forces 1915–1920*. London: Grub Street, 1990.

——— *Above the Trenches. Supplement*. London: Grub Street, 1996.

Slessor, Wing Commander J. C. *Air Power and Armies*. London: Oxford University Press, 1936.

Sloan, James J. Jr. *Wings of Honor; American airmen in World War I.* Atglen, PA: Schiffer Military/Aviation History, 1994.

Smith, Peter. *Dive Bomber! An Illustrated History.* Annapolis: Naval Institute Press, 1982.

—— *Dive Bombers in Action.* London: Blandford Press, 1988.

—— *Stuka Squadron. Stukagruppe 77 – the Luftwaffe's fire brigade.* Wellingborough, Patrick Stephens Limited, 1990.

Stosch, Oberleutnant Albrecht von. *Schlachten des Weltkrieges Band 20: Somme Nord I. Teil - Die Brennpunkte der Schlacht im Juli 1916.* Oldenburg: Druck und Verlag von Gerhard Stalling, 1927.

Strutz, Hauptmann Dr Georg. *Schlachten des Weltkrieges Nr 31: Die Tankschlacht bei Cambrai.* Oldenburg: Verlag Gerhard Stalling, 1929.

Südingen, Oberstleutnant. *Entwicklung und Einsatz der deutschen Flakwaffe und des Luftschutzes im Weltkrieg Kriegswissenschaftlichten Abteilung der Luftwaffe: Kriegsgeschichtliche Einzelschriften der Luftwaffe Erster Band.* Berlin: Ernst Siegfried Mittler & Sohn, 1938.

Sulzbach, Herbert. *With the German Guns.* London: Leo Cooper Ltd, 1973.

Tournès, Colonel René & Capitaine Henry Berthenet. *Le Bataille de Flandres d'après le journal de marche et les ordres de la IVe Armée allemande Avril 9–30, 1918.* Paris: Charles Lavauzelle, 1925.

Treadwell, Terry C. *America's First Air War.* Shrewsbury: Airlife Publishing Ltd, 2000.

Tredrey, F. D. *Pioneer Pilot: The Great Smith-Barry.* London: Peter Davies, 1976.

Tuchman, Barbara W. *August 1914.* London: Papermac, 1989.

Ustinov, Peter. *Dear me.* Harmondsworth, England: Penguin Books Ltd, Harmondsworth, England 1979.

Van Wyngarden, Greg. *Early German Aces of World War 1.* Oxford: Osprey Publishing, Oxford, 2006.

Voisin, Général André. *La Doctrine de l'Aviation Française de Combat au Cours de la Guerre.* Paris: Éditions Berger-Levrault, 1932.

Vrancken, Ludo. *De Geschiedenis van de Belgische Militaire Vliegerij 1900--1918*. Brussels: Centre d'Histoire Militaire/Centrum voor Militaire Geschiedenis, Musée Royal de l'Armée/Koninklijk Legermuseum, 1999.

War College, US Army. *Order of Battle of the United States Land Forces in the World War. American Expeditionary Forces*. Washington DC, Government Printing Office, 1937.

Wise, S.F. *Canadian Airmen and the First World War*. Toronto: University of Toronto Press, 1980.

Winter, Denis. *The First of the Few: Fighter pilots in the First World War*. London: Allen Lane, 1982.

——— *Haig's Command*. New York: Viking Penguin, 1991.

Yeates, V. M. *Winged Victory*. St Albans: Mayflower Publishing Ltd, 1975.

No author. *Rapport du Maréchal Commandant en Chef les Armées françaises du Nord et du Nord*

Articles

Bissy, J. de Lannoy de, *Les Photographies aériennes et leur étude au pointe de vue militaire*, Revue Militaire Française, Tome 12 (April–June 1924) 257–277

Braybrook, Roy, *Fighters in the RAF. Part I-Biplane era. The flight from reality*, Air Enthusiast, September 1971.

Layman, Richard D., *The Mitchell Paratroop Plan-Feasible or Fantastic*, Cross & Cockade International, Vol 17 No 1.

Façon, Patrick, *Marie Charles Duval et le Breguet XIV artisans méconnus de la victoire de 1918*. Fana de l'Aviation No 348 (Novembre 1998).

Nilsson, Thomas, *The Caproni in French Service and a history of the re-formed Groupe de Bombardement B2*, Cross & Cockade International, Vol 35 No 3.

Paquet, Commandant, *Le 2e bureau en campagne*, Revue Militaire Française No 22 (1923) 83–102, No 23(1924) 181–201.

Pesques-Courbier, Simone, *Les Bombardements Aeriens des Usines Sidèrurgiques de l'Est en 1914–1918*, Service Historique de l'Air, Recueil d'Articles et Études 1979–1981, Paris, 1985.

Revell, Alex, *The Bishop Affair*, Cross & Cockade International Journal, Vol 32 No 1.

Rohrbach, A., *Leistungen der R-Flugzeuge bei Kriegsflügen*, Zeitschrift für Flugtechnik und Motorluftschifffahrt, No 5, 1921.

Williams, Adrian J., *The RFC/RAF Engine Repair Shops*, Cockade International, Vol 17 No 4.

Wright, Peter, *Aerial Photo Coding Part 4*, Cross & Cockade International Journal, winter 2001.

Unknown, *He taught the world to fly*, RAF Flying Review, Vol XVIII No 6.

Unknown, *Die deutschen Flieger in den letzten Angriffsschlachten*, Luftmacht, 1935.

Primary Sources Consulted

Belgium

Defensie Stafdepartement Intlichtingen en Veiligheid, Divisie Veiligheid

Personal file 11904. Roland van Crombrugge.

Personal file 14742. Ernst Isserentant.

Personal file 15345. Paul Hiernaux .

Personal file 15112. Robert Desmet.

Personal file 14745. Jules Jaumotte.

Musée Royal de l'Armée et d'Histoire Militaire (MRAHH)

Campagne 1914–1918 Aviation Aerostation Rapports Journaliers. Boite 13–14.

United Kingdom

National Archives (UKNA)

Air 1/9/15/1/22. Reichsarchiv Answers to Air Ministry Questions 15 January 1922.

Air 1/9/15/1/26. Information from the German *Reichsarchiv* on the distribution of German Aeroplanes on the Western Front.

Air 1/9/15/1/27. Information from German Reichsarchiv on German Army Aviation Commander's Reports on Somme.

Air 1/9/15/1/32/1. Consolidated statement of work in the field January–November 1918.

Air 1/21/13/1777. The Battle of Arras (Preparatory Period) November 1916–April 1917.

Air 1/61/15/9/72. RNAS Dunkerque Command Bombing statistics, particulars of bombing attacks.

Air 1/61/15/9/75. Bombing Raids Statistics.

Air 1/163/15/361/1. Short History of I Flight.

Air 1/245/209/30/13. 9 Wing War Diary May 1917.

Air 1/471/15/312/203. British and Belgian Air Force comparison of strengths.

Air 1/475/15/312/189. Parachute flares and beacons.

Air 1/475/15/312/201. General Salmond's letters to General Trenchard re operations during the German Offensive 21–27 March 1918.

Air 1/475/15/312/205. Major J. P. C. Sewell's Report on French corps aviation.

Air 1/475/15/312/212. Programme of development June 1918–June 1919.

Air 1/476/15/312/215. Statistics on bombing.

Air 1/476/15/312/217. Comparisons of British and French results.

Air1/522/16/12/5. Air Policy.

Air 1/675/21/13/1265. The German attack on the 27th May 1918.

Air 1/675/21/13/1422. Air operations during German offensive on Western Front March 1918.

Air 1/676/21/13/1849. Air Historical Branch record of the Arras campaign.

Air 1/677/21/13/1887. J. C. Nerney, Air Historical Branch manuscript history. *The Western Front-Air Operations, May-November 1918.*

Air 1/678/21/13/1942. Battle of Cambrai (Air Historical Branch account) 20 November – 7 December 1917.

Air 1/762/204/4/165. Summaries of brigade & wing operations July 1916.

Air 1/765/204/4/244–248. Summaries of brigade & wing operations August-December 1916.

Air 1/767/204/4/249–260. Summaries of brigade & wing operations January-December 1917.

Air 1/838/204/5/287. Daily summaries of RFC work and operations in France December 1917–March 26, 1918.

Air 1/847/204/5/381–381.Casualty reports for the RFC April 1917.

Air 1/881/204/5/593. French operations orders for I Armée July 1– November 1, 1917.

Air 1/881/204/5/594. Operations Orders by Major-General Trenchard October 1–November 27 1916.

Air 1/881/204/5/599. French resumés of operations to RFC Headquarters July 2–October 31, 1917.

Air 1/881/204/5/600. French resumés of operations to RFC Headquarters April 12–June 30 1917.

Air 1/918/204/5/879. Correspondence re co-operation of aircraft with artillery January to November 1917.

Air 1/920/204/5/884. (RFC) Brigade/wing commanders' conferences.

Air 1/925/204/5/911. American Flying Corps in France.

Air 1/925/205/5/912. American squadrons with the RAF.

Air 1/995/204/5/1229. Return of numbers of Allied and Hostile Aeroplanes September 23 1915–March 10, 1918.

Air 1/996/204/5/1232. Correspondence and instructions re wireless interception Part I October 13 1916 to April 29, 1917.

Air 1/996/204/5/1233. Correspondence and instructions re wireless interception scheme Part II April 15 1917– March 5 1918.

Air 1/997/204/5/1241. Organisation and General Principles of the French Flying Corps.

Air 1/1189/204/5/2595. War diary, Intelligence, Royal Flying Corps.

Air 1/1283/204/11/11. Report by Commandant du Peuty to RFC headquarters 25 May 1916.

Air 1/1283/204/11/14. Reports of April 16, 1916 by Captain R. A. Cooper on a visit to the French army at Verdun March 12–19, 1916.

Air 1/1303/204/11/169. Report by Commandant du Peuty on air operations over Verdun sent to RFC Headquarters and forwarded to London on 15 May 1916.

Air 1/1367/204/22/24. No 10 Squadron record book.

Air 1/1389/204/25/43. No 27 Squadron record book.

Air 1/1389/204/25/44. Bombing Raids and Patrol Reports 9 August 1916 to 2 April 1918.

Air 1/1400/204/27/21. No 59 Squadron record book.

Air 1/1441/204/35/8. No 8 Naval Squadron record book.

Air 1/1443/204/36/2 & 3. I Brigade war diaries January & February 1918.

Air 1/1496/204/39/5. No 57 Squadron record book.

Air1/1513/204/88/38. Special Missions: Pigeon dropping etc III Brigade March 1916–April 1918.

Air 1/1513/204/58/39. III Brigade correspondence on aerial defence.

Air 1/1548/204/78/2 & 1. 15 Wing summary of work July-August 1916.

Air 1/1557/204/80/1 & 2. 14 Wing summaries of work 1916.

Air 1/1558/204/80/6–8. 14 Wing war diaries August, October, November 1916.

Air 1/1577/204/80/96. Principles of Organisation Paragraph II and Reports from Verdun April 4, 1916, and further reports (to RFC Headquarters) from Verdun.

Air 1/1587/204/82/61. Captured documents and prisoners' statement June-July 1917.

Air 1/1587/204/82/63. IV Brigade correspondence re hostile aircraft.

Air 1/1595/204/83/28. V Brigade work summary April 1918.

Air 1/1596/204/83/38. V Brigade work summaries August-October 1918.

Air 1/1626/204/90/4. No 13 Squadron record book.

Air 1/1732/204/130/4. No 101 Squadron record book.

Air 1/1780/204/150/11.No 59 Squadron record book.

Air 1/1782/204/150/17–18. No 35 Squadron record book.

Air 1/1794/204/155/1. No 84 Squadron war diary.

Air 1/1844/204/210/29. X Brigade work summaries August- November 1918.

Air 1/1899/204/227/6. Correspondence and reports of accidental bombing and shooting up of Allied personnel April 2–July 20 1918.

Air 1/1914/204/230/1. Procedure for night flying August 1918.

Air 1/1914/204/230/3. Patrol reports No 151 Squadron.

Air 1/1914/204/230/4. Combats in the air No 151 Squadron.

Air 1/1914/204/230/5. 54 Wing monthly return of bombs April-November 1918.

Air 1/1914/204/230/7. 54 Wing summary of work from June 1 1918.

Air 1/1923/204/238/6. No 49 Squadron record book.

Air 1/1977/204/273/63. American operations file.

Air 1/1997/204/273/245.Landing of agents over lines at night.

Air 1/1997/204/273/247. Co-operation Attack on St Mihiel Salient by American 1st Army.

Air 1/2117/207/59/1. RAF daily summary of operations in foreign theatres March 21–May 31 1918.

Air 1/2124/207/74/3. Summaries of Air Intelligence May 1–November 9 1918.

Air 1/2131/207/109/1. Maps showing the distribution of the German air force September 23 1918.

Air 1/2153/209/3/304. Naval squadrons at Dunkirk.

Air 1/2153/209/3/307. Arrangements for night bombing squadrons.

Air 1/2154/209/3/309. French military aeronautics.

Air 1/2166/209/11/9. 1 Wing war diary July 1915.

Air 1/2166/209/11/12. 1 Wing war diary October-December 1915.

Air 1/2176/209/14/19–21.I Brigade war diaries August-October 1918.

Air 1/2177/209/14/24–27.I Brigade war diaries March-June 1917.

Air 1/2179/209/14/36–38.I Brigade war diaries March-May 1918.

Air 1/2181/209/14/42.I Brigade war diary November 1918.

Air 1/2198/209/1–5. 41 Wing war diaries October 1917–February 1918.

Air 1/2215/209/30/3–8. 9 Wing war diary July-December 1916.

Air 1/2215/209/30/11–20. 9 Wing war diaries March- December 1917.

Air 1/2215/209/30/23. 9 Wing war diary March 1918.

Air 1/2215/219/30/2–7. 9 Wing war diaries June-November 1916.

Air 1/2215/209/30/8–13. 9 Wing war diaries December 1916–May 1917.

Air 1/2215/209/30/23. 9 Wing war diary March 1918.

Air1/2218/209/40/1.V Brigade war diary August 1918.

Air 1/2219/209/40/4–7.V Brigade war diaries March-June 1917.

Air 1/2220/209/40/7–11.V Brigade war diaries June-November 1917.

Air 1/2222/209/40/14–17. V Brigade war diaries January-April 1918.

Air 1/2223/209/40/20.V Brigade war diary July 1918.

Air 1/2224/209/40/21.V Brigade war diary September 1918.

Air 1/2224/209/40/22–24. V Brigade war diaries September-November 1916.

Air 1/2225/209/40/26–27. V Brigade war diary war diaries October-November 1918.

Air 1/2229/209/41/5–11 .II Brigade war diaries May-November 1917.

Air 1/2232/209/41/20–22. II Brigade war diaries August-October 1918.

Air 1/2237/209/41/28. II Brigade war diaries April 1918.

Air 1/2237/209/41/34. II Brigade war diary November 1918.

Air 1/2238/209/42/3–12. III Brigade war diaries March-December 1917.

Air 1/2241/209/42/13–15. III war diaries January-March 1918.

Air 1/2244/209/42/22–23. III Brigade war diaries September-October 1918.

Air 1/2246/209/42/35. III Brigade war diary November 1918.

Air 1/2247/209/43/6–10. IV Brigade war diaries June-November 1917.

Air 1/2247/209/43/11–12. IV Brigade war diary April-September 1916.

Air 1/2248/209/43/15. V Brigade war diaries October-November 1916.

Air 1/2249/209/45/1–10. III Brigade war diaries February-November 1918.

Air 1/2249/209/46/3–8.IX Brigade war diaries January-October 1918.

Air 1/2251/209/53/1.French Air Service losses. 19 November 1917.

Air 1/2255/209/58/4.RFC Intelligence War Dairies.

Air 1/2267/209/70/46. Formation of American Air Service September 1917–November 1918.

Air 1/2268/209/70/190. Co-operation between artillery and aircraft.

Air 1/2399/280/1. The use of aircraft in connection with espionage.

Air 1/2267/209/70/35. Copies of correspondence re bombing of hospitals by the enemy May-June 1918.

Air 1/2268/209/70/190. Co-operation between artillery and aircraft.

Air 1/2268/209/70/195. Étude sur les indices d'attaque ayant précédé l'offensive allemande du 15 Juillet 1918 sur le front de Champagne by Chef de Bataillon Boucher.

Air 1/2268/209/70/200. Intelligence reports, GHQ BEF.

Air 1/2386/228/9/1. RAF Staff College Andover notes.

Air 1/2386/228/11/13. An account by RAF Staff College students of war experiences by Squadron Leader W.S. Douglas.

Air 1/2393/230/2. Autobiography Air Vice Marshal Sir John Higgins.

Air 1/2398/267/23. History of the Marine Chasing Group April 15 1916–April 30 1918.

Air 2/17/207/58/2. Enemy night flying map of June 7, 1918.

Air 2/125/B.11207. Resume of W/T work in progress in RAF BEF November 1918.

WO 95/275. 2nd Army war diaries January-October 1917.

WO 95/483. No 44 AA section war diary.

WO 95/521. 5th Army war diaries January-March 1918.

WO 95/984. I Anzac war diaries October-December 1917.

WO 95/1051. Canadian Corps war diaries October-November 1917.

WO 157/21.GHQ Summary of Information June 1917.

WO 157/22. GHQ Summary of Information July 1917.

WO 157/24. GHQ Summary of Information September 1917.

WO 157/25. GHQ Summary of Information October 1917.

WO 157/26. GHQ Summary of Information November 1917.

WO 157/117. 2nd Army Summary of Intelligence August 1917.

WO 157/118. 2nd Army Summary of Intelligence September 1917.

WO 158/34. Summary of Operations Royal Flying Corps February 10–November 17, 1916.

WO 158/35. No 1 Summary of operations, Royal Flying Corps April 8–September 30 1917.

WO 158/35 No 2. Summary of operations by Royal Flying Corps April 8–September 30 1917.

WO 158/328. 4th Army summary of operations.

National Library of Scotland (NLS),

Earl Haig's diaries (AC 3155)

No 106 (May-June 1916), No 108 (September 1916), No 112 (April 1917), No 113 (May 1917), No 116 (August 1917), No 117 (September 1917), No 118 (October 1917), No 119 (November 1917), No 123 (January-February 1918), No 124 (March 1918), No 125 (April 1–15 1918), No 128 (June 1918), No130 (August 1918), No 131 (September 1918), No 132 (October 1918).

Earl Haig's papers (AC 3155)

No 192, No347.

Imperial War Museum (IWM)

Accession Number 45104. *OHL* list of destroyed enemy aircraft.

France

Service Historique de l'Armée de l'Air (SHAA)

A13 Dossier 1. Notes de service et circulaire reçu ou addressées par le Grand Quartier Général Janvier-Juin 1918.

A20 Dossier 1 & Dossier 2. Organisation et administration des unités. Organisation de l'aviation des corps d'armées et des corps de cavalerie & aéronautique des armées.

A22Dossier 1. Division Aériennes et groupement.

A108 Dossier 2. Opération et functionment de l'Aéronautique GAN, GAC, DAé, I, II, III, V, VI, VII, VIII, X Armées et X CA.

A109. Ordres de Bataille.

A115 Dossier 2. Télegrammes d'opérations aériennes 15 Mai au 26 Mai et 4 Juin au 1 Juillet 1918.

A124 Dossier 1 & Dossier 2. Télegrammes de reconnaissances aériennes 12 Février au 15 Mars 1916 & 15 Mars au 11 Avril 1916.

A126. Resumé journaliers des opérations aériennes 30 Juin au 31 Decembre 1916.

A128 Dossier 2. Resumés journaliers des opérations aériennes par les armées Février 14–Août 31 1918.

A128 Dossier 3. Resumés journaliers des opérations aériennes par les armées Septembre 1–Novembre 11 1918.

A129 Dossier 1. Resumés journaliers des opérations aeriennes établis par région par le GQG 2 Janvier-31 Décembre 1917.

A130 Dossier 1. Resumés d'operations et comptes rendus du GAR 9 Avril-7 Mai 1917.

A 166/2. Activitiés d'aviation de bombardement des groupes d'armées 16 Octobre 1917–31 Octobre 1918.

A187. Relations avec Italie.

Service Historique de l'Armée de Terre (SHAT)

18N171 Dossier 3. Comptes rendus des grandes unités et groupements de Groupes d'Armées du Nord Novembre 1916–April 1918.

18N173 Dossier 1. Compte rendu bi-mensuel d'operations Aériennes.

18N174 Dossier 1. Comptes rendues recus des armées Février 1918–Janvier 1919.

18N412. Resumés d'opérations aériennnes de Groupe des Armées de Reserve.

19N124. Campagne contre l'Allemande Campagne contre l'Allemagne. VI Armée Aéronautique Juin 13 1918.

19N488. Comptes rendus journaliers de Commandant de l'Aéronautique de II Armée Février 1915–Juillet 1918.

19N489 Dossier 2. Campagne contre l'Allemagne II Armée Aéronautique.

19N1124. Opérations de l'aéronautique de la VIe Armée. Report Juin 13 1918.

26N42 Dossier 4. Journal de Marche VI Armée 1 Juillet–30 Septembre 1916. 142.056. Personal file of Paul Ferdinand du Peuty.

United States of America

US National Archives (USNA)
Microfilms
M990/13. Army operations reports 1–58.
M990/12. Army Group operations reports 1–16.
M990/14. 1st Day Bombardment Group war diary.

Web sites
frontflieger.de (Frontflieger-die Soldaten der Deutschen Fliegertruppe 1914–1918)
Rafweb.org/Biographies (Biographies of RAF and RFC commanders)
mtholyoke.edu/acad/intrel/ww1.htm. (Lieutenant-Colonel R. J. Drake, 'History of Intelligence (B), British Expeditionary Force, France from January 1917 to April 1919')
aupress.maxwell.af.mil/Books
acepilots.com/wwi/us. 1 Pursuit Group Records 1918

INDEX

Air Forces

Escadres de Bombardement 200
1er Brigade d'Aviation 61, 230
2eme Brigade d'Aviation 61, 230, 233
Groupement Bloch 230
Groupement Chabert 82, 220, 222
Groupement de Chasse et Reconnaissance 121, 128
Groupement de Combat du GAR 153
Groupement de Combat de la Somme (Brocard) 120
Groupement Féquant 61, 64, 200, 220
Groupement Laurens 82 224, 236
Groupement Ménard 61, 64, 200, 220
Groupement Villomé 82, 220, 230
1er Escadre de Combat 60, 200, 233
2eme Escadre de Combat 61, 200
11e Escadre 82, 83, 257
12e Escadre 82, 222-223
13e Escadre 82, 224
14e Escadres 82, 257
GB 1 44, 82, 83, 157, 230
GB 2 44, 82, 83, 220
GB 3 82, 120, 156
GB 4 82
GB 5 44, 82
GB 6 82
GB 7 82
GB 8 82, 236
GB 9 82
GB 10 82, 236
GB 18 (Gruppo Bombardemento 18) 83
GB 51 82
GC 11 39, 50, 61, 153-154, 184, 231
GC 12 120, 123, 153, 208, 232, 236, 250
GC 13 54, 61, 123, 184, 200
GC 14 54, 153, 208
GC 15 54, 61, 157, 223
GC 16 224, 236
GC 17 61
GC 18 61
GC 19 61
GC 20 222
GC 21 220, 222, 231, 250
GC 22 231, 250
GC 23 265
Groupe Brocard
Groupe de Combat de Cachy VI e Armée
BR 214 256
C 4 46
C 11 45
C 46 153
F 35 155
MF 22 46
MF 25 44
MF 33 46

German (*Fliegertruppen/Luftstreitkräfte*)

FFA 4 35
FFA 6 29
FFA 40 79
Jasta 1 61, 105, 156
Jasta 2 61, 105, 107, 111, 113, 115
Jasta 3 61, 140
Jasta 4 137, 140, 143
Jasta 5 191-192
Jasta 6 226
Jasta 7 50
Jasta 8 166
Jasta 9 152
Jasta 11 70, 115, 132, 136, 139, 145, 158, 214, 225
Jasta 12 141, 226
Jasta 14 50
Jasta 18 166
Jasta 19 226, 231
Jasta 23 55
Jasta 24 55
Jasta 27 166, 171
Jasta 28 166, 174
Jasta 29 174
Jasta 33 140
Jasta 36 174, 192
Jasta 61 244
Jasta 73 87
Kampf-Einsitzer Staffeln B(ertincourt) 102
KEK Nord/Abwehrkommando Nord (AKN) 35, 100, 102
KEK Sivry 40-41
KEK Süd (AKS) 35, 100, 102
KEK Vaux 102
Riesenfliegerabteilung 500 241
Schusta 7 147
Schusta 9 177
Schusta 22-28 78
Schusta 30 217

Italian (*Regia Aeronautica*) 272
Grupo 18 220

PERSONNEL INDEX